# Wiley 11th Hour Guide for 2017 Level III CFA Exam

Thousands of candidates from more than 100 countries have relied on these Study Guides to pass the CFA® Exam. Covering every Learning Outcome Statement (LOS) on the exam, these review materials are an invaluable tool for anyone who wants a deep-dive review of all the concepts, formulas, and topics required to pass.

Wiley study materials are produced by expert CFA Charterholders, CFA Institute members, and investment professionals from around the globe. For more information, contact us at info@efficientlearning.com.

# Wiley 11th Hour Guide for 2017 Level III CFA Exam

WILEY

Published by John Wiley & Sons, Inc., Hoboken, New Jersey.
Published simultaneously in Canada.



For general information on our other products and services or for technical support, please contact our Customer Care Department within the United States at (800) 762-2974, outside the United States at (317) 572-3993 or fax (317) 572-4002.

Wiley publishes in a variety of print and electronic formats and by print-on-demand. Some material included with standard print versions of this book may not be included in e-books or in print-on-demand. If this book refers to media such as a CD or DVD that is not included in the version you purchased, you may download this material at http://booksupport.wiley.com. For more information about Wiley products, visit www.wiley.com.



ISBN 978-1-119-33093-6; 978-1-119-34828-3 (epub); 978-1-119-33107-0 (epdf)

# Contents


Foreword VII

**Ethical and Professional Standards**

Study Session 1: Code of Ethics and Standards of Professional Conduct 1

Study Session 2: Ethical and Professional Standards in Practice 57

**Behavioral Finance**

Study Session 3: Behavioral Finance 69

**Private Wealth Management**

Study Session 4: Private Wealth Management (1) 91

Study Session 5: Private Wealth Management (2) 113

**Institutional Investors**

Study Session 6: Portfolio Management for Institutional Investors 137

**Capital Market Expectations**

Study Session 7: Applications of Economic Analysis to Portfolio Management 155

**Asset Allocation**

Study Session 8: Asset Allocation and Related Decisions in Portfolio Management (1) 179

Study Session 9: Asset Allocation and Related Decisions in Portfolio Management (2) 195

**Fixed Income**

Study Session 10: Fixed-Income Portfolio Management (1) 215

Study Session 11: Fixed-Income Portfolio Management (2) 241

**Equity Portfolio Management**

Study Session 12: Equity Portfolio Management 259

**Alternative Investments**

Study Session 13: Alternative Investments for Portfolio Mangement 281

**Risk Management**

Study Session 14: Risk Management 307

**Risk Management Application of Derivatives**

Study Session 15: Risk Management Applications of Derivatives 315

**Portfolio Trading, Monitoring, and Rebalancing**

Study Session 16: Trading, Monitoring, and Rebalancing 333

**Performance Evaluation**

Study Session 17: Performance Evaluation 343

**Global Investment Performance Standards**

Study Session 18: Global Investment Performance Standards 351

## Foreword

Wiley 11th Hour Guide for 2017 Level III CFA Exam is a concise and easy-to-understand review book that is meant to supplement your review for the CFA Level III exam. It becomes extremely difficult to go through the entire curriculum in the last few weeks leading up to the exam, so we have condensed the material for you. You must remember, though, that this book is not meant to be a primary study tool for the exam. It is designed to help you review the material in an efficient and effective manner so that you can be confident on exam day.

## About the Author

Wiley's Study Guides are written by a team of highly qualified CFA charterholders and leading CFA instructors from around the globe. Our team of CFA experts work collaboratively to produce the best study materials for CFA candidates available today.

Wiley's expert team of contributing authors and instructors is led by Content Director Basit Shajani, CFA. Basit founded online education start-up Élan Guides in 2009 to help address CFA candidates' need for better study materials. As lead writer, lecturer, and curriculum developer, Basit's unique ability to break down complex topics helped the company grow organically to be a leading global provider of CFA Exam prep materials. In January 2014, Élan Guides was acquired by John Wiley & Sons, Inc., where Basit continues his work as Director of CFA Content. Basit graduated magna cum laude from the Wharton School of Business at the University of Pennsylvania with majors in finance and legal studies. He went on to obtain his CFA charter in 2006, passing all three levels on the first attempt. Prior to Élan Guides, Basit ran his own private wealth management business. He is a past president of the Pakistani CFA Society.

There are many more expert CFA charterholders who contribute to the creation of Wiley materials. We are thankful for their invaluable expertise and diligent work. To learn more about Wiley's team of subject matter experts, please visit: www.efficientlearning.com/cfa/why-wiley/

# Study Session 1: Code of Ethics and Standards of Professional Conduct

# CODE OF ETHICS AND STANDARDS OF PROFESSIONAL CONDUCT

Cross-Reference to CFA Institute Assigned Reading #1

The Code of Ethics consists of high-level objectives that are expected of all CFA candidates and charterholders. Be sure that you know the six components of the Code of Ethics and how the Professional Conduct Program (PCP) operates, including investigations into alleged violations of the Code of Ethics and Standards of Professional Conduct.

## CFA Institute Professional Conduct Program

All CFA Institute members and candidates enrolled in the CFA Program are required to comply with the Code and Standards. The CFA Institute Board of Governors maintains oversight and responsibility for the Professional Conduct Program (PCP), which, in conjunction with the Disciplinary Review Committee (DRC), is responsible for enforcement of the Code and Standards. The DRC is a volunteer committee of CFA charterholders who serve on panels to review conduct and partner with Professional Conduct staff to establish and review professional conduct policies. The CFA Institute Bylaws and Rules of Procedure for Professional Conduct (Rules of Procedure) form the basic structure for enforcing the Code and Standards. The Professional Conduct division is also responsible for enforcing testing policies of other CFA Institute education programs as well as the professional conduct of Certificate in Investment Performance Measurement (CIPM) certificates.

Professional Conduct inquiries come from a number of sources.

- Members and candidates must self-disclose on the annual Professional Conduct Statement all matters that question their professional conduct, such as involvement in civil litigation or a criminal investigation or being the subject of a written complaint.
- Written complaints received by Professional Conduct staff can bring about an investigation.
- CFA Institute staff may become aware of questionable conduct by a member or candidate through the media, regulatory notices, or another public source.
- Candidate conduct is monitored by proctors who complete reports on candidates suspected to have violated testing rules on exam day.
- CFA Institute may also conduct analyses of scores and exam materials after the exam, as well as monitor online and social media to detect disclosure of confidential exam information.

When an inquiry is initiated, the Professional Conduct staff conducts an investigation that may include:

- Requesting a written explanation from the member or candidate.
- Interviewing the member or candidate, complaining parties, and third parties.
- Collecting documents and records relevant to the investigation.

Upon reviewing the material obtained during the investigation, the Professional Conduct staff may:

- Take no disciplinary sanction.
- Issue a cautionary letter.
- Continue proceedings to discipline the member or candidate.

If the Professional Conduct staff believes a violation of the Code and Standards or testing policies has occurred, the member or candidate has the opportunity to reject or accept any charges and the proposed sanctions. If the member or candidate does not accept the charges and proposed sanction, the matter is referred to a panel composed of DRC members. Panels review materials and presentations from Professional Conduct staff and from the member or candidate. The panel's task is to determine whether a violation of the Code and Standards or testing policies occurred and, if so, what sanction should be imposed.

Sanctions imposed by CFA Institute may have significant consequences; they include public censure, suspension of membership and use of the CFA designation, and revocation of the CFA charter. Candidates enrolled in the CFA Program who have violated the Code and Standards or testing policies may be suspended or prohibited from further participation in the CFA Program. CFA Institute does not impose fines on those who have violated the Standards.

### Adoption of the Code and Standards

The Code and Standards apply to individual members of CFA Institute and candidates in the CFA Program. CFA Institute does encourage firms to adopt the Code and Standards, however, as part of their code of ethics. Those who claim compliance should fully understand the requirements of each of the principles of the Code and Standards.

Once a party—nonmember or firm—ensures its code of ethics meets the principles of the Code and Standards, that party should make the following statement whenever claiming compliance:

"[Insert name of party] claims compliance with the CFA Institute Code of Ethics and Standards of Professional Conduct. This claim has not been verified by CFA Institute."

CFA Institute welcomes public acknowledgment, when appropriate, that firms are complying with the CFA Institute Code of Ethics and Standards of Professional Conduct and encourages firms to notify it of the adoption plans.

## CFA INSTITUTE CODE OF ETHICS AND STANDARDS OF PROFESSIONAL CONDUCT

### The Code of Ethics

Members of CFA Institute (including CFA charterholders) and candidates for the CFA designation ("Members and Candidates") must:

- Act with integrity, competence, diligence, and respect and in an ethical manner with the public, clients, prospective clients, employers, employees, colleagues in the investment profession, and other participants in the global capital markets.
- Place the integrity of the investment profession and the interests of clients above their own personal interests.
- Use reasonable care and exercise independent professional judgment when conducting investment analysis, making investment recommendations, taking investment actions, and engaging in other professional activities.
- Practice and encourage others to practice in a professional and ethical manner that will reflect credit on themselves and the profession.
- Promote the integrity and viability of the global capital markets for the ultimate benefit of society.
- Maintain and improve their professional competence and strive to maintain and improve the competence of other investment professionals.

### Standards of Professional Conduct

I. Professionalism
   A. Knowledge of the Law
   B. Independence and Objectivity
   C. Misrepresentation
   D. Misconduct

II. Integrity of Capital Markets
   A. Material Nonpublic Information
   B. Market Manipulation

III. Duties to Clients
   A. Loyalty, Prudence and Care
   B. Fair Dealing
   C. Suitability
   D. Performance Presentation
   E. Preservation of Confidentiality

IV. Duties to Employers
   A. Loyalty
   B. Additional Compensation Arrangements
   C. Responsibilities of Supervisors

V. Investment Analysis, Recommendations and Actions
   A. Diligence and Reasonable Basis
   B. Communication with Clients and Prospective Clients
   C. Record Retention

VI. Conflicts of Interest
   A. Disclosure of Conflicts
   B. Priority of Transactions
   C. Referral Fees

VII. Responsibilities as a CFA Institute Member or CFA Candidate
   A. Conduct as members and candidates in the CFA program
   B. Reference to CFA Institute, the CFA Designation, and the CFA Program

The Code of Ethics and the Standards of Practice apply to *all* candidates in the CFA program and members of CFA Institute. All examples and other extracts from the Standards of Practice Handbook that are included in this Reading are reprinted with permission of CFA Institute.

# GUIDANCE FOR STANDARDS I-VII

Cross-Reference to CFA Institute Assigned Reading #2

The seven Standards of Professional Conduct contain detailed rules of minimum behavior that are required of all CFA candidates and charterholders. As in previous levels, you are responsible for knowing all seven Standards and the subsections of each one. In total, there are 22 subsections that you must master. While you do not need to know the standard letter and number, you will have to know under which major heading each of the subsections appears.

## Standard I(A): Knowledge of the Law

### The Standard

Members and candidates must understand and comply with all applicable laws, rules, and regulations (including the CFA Institute Code of Ethics and Standards of Professional Conduct) of any government, regulatory organization, licensing agency, or professional association governing their professional activities. In the event of conflict, members and candidates must comply with the more strict law, rule, or regulation. Members and candidates must not knowingly participate or assist in and must dissociate from any violation of such laws, rules, or regulations.

### Guidance

- Members and candidates must understand the applicable laws and regulations of the countries and jurisdictions where they engage in professional activities.
- On the basis of their reasonable and good faith understanding, members and candidates must comply with the laws and regulations that directly govern their professional activities and resulting outcomes and that protect the interests of the clients.
- When questions arise, members and candidates should know their firm's policies and procedures for accessing compliance guidance.
- During times of changing regulations, members and candidates must remain vigilant in maintaining their knowledge of the requirements for their professional activities.

### Relationship between the Code and Standards and Applicable Law

- When applicable law and the Code and Standards require different conduct, members and candidates must follow the stricter of the applicable law or the Code and Standards.
    - "Applicable law" is the law that governs the member's or candidate's conduct. Which law applies will depend on the particular facts and circumstances of each case.
    - The "more strict" law or regulation is the law or regulation that imposes greater restrictions on the action of the member or candidate, or calls for the member or candidate to exert a greater degree of action that protects the interests of investors.

ET

### Global Application of the Code and Standards

Members and candidates who practice in multiple jurisdictions may be subject to varied securities laws and regulations. The following chart provides illustrations involving a member who may be subject to the securities laws and regulations of three different types of countries:

NS: country with no securities laws or regulations

LS: country with *less* strict securities laws and regulations than the Code and Standards

MS: country with *more* strict securities laws and regulations than the Code and Standards

| Applicable Law | Duties | Explanation |
|---|---|---|
| Member resides in NS country, does business in LS country; LS law applies. | Member must adhere to the Code and Standards. | Because applicable law is less strict than the Code and Standards, the member must adhere to the Code and Standards. |
| Member resides in NS country, does business in MS country; MS law applies. | Member must adhere to the law of MS country. | Because applicable law is stricter than the Code and Standards, member must adhere to the more strict applicable law. |
| Member resides in LS country, does business in NS country; LS law applies. | Member must adhere to the Code and Standards. | Because applicable law is less strict than the Code and Standards, member must adhere to the Code and Standards. |
| Member resides in LS country, does business in MS country; MS law applies. | Member must adhere to the law of MS country. | Because applicable law is stricter than the Code and Standards, member must adhere to the more strict applicable law. |
| Member resides in LS country, does business in NS country; LS law applies, but it states that law of locality where business is conducted governs. | Member must adhere to the Code and Standards. | Because applicable law states that the law of the locality where the business is conducted governs and there is no local law, the member must adhere to the Code and Standards. |
| Member resides in LS country, does business in MS country; LS law applies, but it states that law of locality where business is conducted governs. | Member must adhere to the law of MS country. | Because applicable law of the locality where the business is conducted governs and local law is stricter than the Code and Standards, member must adhere to the more strict applicable law. |
| Member resides in MS country, does business in LS country; MS law applies. | Member must adhere to the law of MS country. | Because applicable law is stricter than the Code and Standards, member must adhere to the more strict applicable law. |

*(Table continued on next page...)*

| Applicable Law | Duties | Explanation |
|---|---|---|
| Member resides in MS country, does business in LS country; MS law applies, but it states that law of locality where business is conducted governs. | Member must adhere to the Code and Standards. | Because applicable law states that the law of the locality where the business is conducted governs and local law is less strict than the Code and Standards, member must adhere to the Code and Standards. |
| Member resides in MS country, does business in LS country with a client who is a citizen of LS country; MS law applies, but it states that the law of the client's home country governs. | Member must adhere to the Code and Standards. | Because applicable law states that the law of the client's home country governs (which is less strict than the Code and Standards), member must adhere to the Code and Standards. |
| Member resides in MS country, does business in LS country with a client who is a citizen of MS country; MS law applies, but it states that the law of the client's home country governs. | Member must adhere to the law of MS country. | Because applicable law states that the law of the client's home country governs and the law of the client's home country is stricter than the Code and Standards, the member must adhere to the more strict applicable law. |

**Participation in or Association with Violations by Others**

- Members and candidates are responsible for violations in which they *knowingly* participate or assist. Standard I(A) applies when members and candidates know or should know that their conduct may contribute to a violation of applicable laws, rules, or regulations or the Code and Standards.
- If a member or candidate has reasonable grounds to believe that imminent or ongoing client or employer activities are illegal or unethical, the member or candidate must dissociate, or separate, from the activity.
- In extreme cases, dissociation may require a member or candidate to leave his or her employment.
- Members and candidates may take the following steps before dissociating from ethical violations of others when direct discussions with the person or persons committing the violation are unsuccessful.
    - Attempt to stop the behavior by bringing it to the attention of the employer through a supervisor or the firm's compliance department.
    - If this attempt is unsuccessful, then members and candidates have a responsibility to step away and dissociate from the activity. Inaction combined with continuing association with those involved in illegal or unethical conduct may be construed as participation or assistance in the illegal or unethical conduct.
- CFA Institute strongly encourages members and candidates to report potential violations of the Code and Standards committed by fellow members and candidates, although a failure to report is less likely to be construed as a violation than a failure to dissociate from unethical conduct.

### Investment Products and Applicable Laws

- Members and candidates involved in creating or maintaining investment services or investment products or packages of securities and/or derivatives should be mindful of where these products or packages will be sold as well as their places of origination.
- They should understand the applicable laws and regulations of the countries or regions of origination and expected sale, and should make reasonable efforts to review whether associated firms that are distributing products or services developed by their employing firms also abide by the laws and regulations of the countries and regions of distribution.
- Finally, they should undertake the necessary due diligence when transacting cross-border business to understand the multiple applicable laws and regulations in order to protect the reputation of their firms and themselves.

## Recommended Procedures for Compliance

### Members and Candidates

Suggested methods by which members and candidates can acquire and maintain understanding of applicable laws, rules, and regulations include the following:

- Stay informed: Members and candidates should establish or encourage their employers to establish a procedure by which employees are regularly informed about changes in applicable laws, rules, regulations, and case law.
- Review procedures: Members and candidates should review, or encourage their employers to review, the firm's written compliance procedures on a regular basis to ensure that the procedures reflect current law and provide adequate guidance to employees about what is permissible conduct under the law and/or the Code and Standards.
- Maintain current files: Members and candidates should maintain or encourage their employers to maintain readily accessible current reference copies of applicable statutes, rules, regulations, and important cases.

### Distribution Area Laws

- Members and candidates should make reasonable efforts to understand the applicable laws—both country and regional—for the countries and regions where their investment products are developed and are most likely to be distributed to clients.

### Legal Counsel

- When in doubt about the appropriate action to undertake, it is recommended that a member or candidate seek the advice of compliance personnel or legal counsel concerning legal requirements.
- If a potential violation is being committed by a fellow employee, it may also be prudent for the member or candidate to seek the advice of the firm's compliance department or legal counsel.

### Dissociation

- When dissociating from an activity that violates the Code and Standards, members and candidates should document the violation and urge their firms to attempt to persuade the perpetrator(s) to cease such conduct. Note that in order to dissociate from the conduct, a member or candidate may have to resign his or her employment.

**Firms**

Members and candidates should encourage their firms to consider the following policies and procedures to support the principles of Standard I(A):

- Develop and/or adopt a code of ethics.
- Provide information on applicable laws.
- Establish procedures for reporting violations.

## Standard I(B) Independence and Objectivity

**The Standard**

Members and candidates must use reasonable care and judgment to achieve and maintain independence and objectivity in their professional activities. Members and candidates must not offer, solicit, or accept any gift, benefit, compensation, or consideration that reasonably could be expected to compromise their own or another's independence and objectivity.

**Guidance**

- Members and candidates should endeavor to avoid situations that could cause or be perceived to cause a loss of independence or objectivity in recommending investments or taking investment action.
- Modest gifts and entertainment are acceptable, but special care must be taken by members and candidates to resist subtle and not-so-subtle pressures to act in conflict with the interests of their clients. Best practice dictates that members and candidates reject any offer of gift or entertainment that could be expected to threaten their independence and objectivity.
- Receiving a gift, benefit, or consideration from a *client* can be distinguished from gifts given by entities seeking to influence a member or candidate to the detriment of other clients.
- When possible, prior to accepting "bonuses" or gifts from clients, members and candidates should disclose to their employers such benefits offered by clients. If notification is not possible prior to acceptance, members and candidates must disclose to their employer benefits previously accepted from clients.
- Members and candidates are personally responsible for maintaining independence and objectivity when preparing research reports, making investment recommendations, and taking investment action on behalf of clients. Recommendations must convey the member's or candidate's true opinions, free of bias from internal or external pressures, and be stated in clear and unambiguous language.
- When seeking corporate financial support for conventions, seminars, or even weekly society luncheons, the members or candidates responsible for the activities should evaluate both the actual effect of such solicitations on their independence and whether their objectivity might be perceived to be compromised in the eyes of their clients.

**Investment-Banking Relationships**

- Some sell-side firms may exert pressure on their analysts to issue favorable research reports on current or prospective investment banking clients. Members and candidates must not succumb to such pressures.
- Allowing analysts to work with investment bankers is appropriate only when the conflicts are adequately and effectively managed and disclosed. Firm managers have a responsibility to provide an environment in which analysts are neither coerced nor enticed into issuing research that does not reflect their true opinions. Firms should require public disclosure of actual conflicts of interest to investors.

- Any "firewalls" between the investment banking and research functions must be managed to minimize conflicts of interest. Key elements of enhanced firewalls include:
  - Separate reporting structures for personnel on the research side and personnel on the investment banking side.
  - Compensation arrangements that minimize pressures on research analysts and reward objectivity and accuracy. Ideally, compensation should be tied to the quality of the research and not the operating performance of the investment bank.

**Public Companies**

- Analysts may be pressured to issue favorable reports and recommendations by the companies they follow. In making an investment recommendation, the analyst is responsible for anticipating, interpreting, and assessing a company's prospects and stock price performance in a factual manner.
- Due diligence in financial research and analysis involves gathering information from a wide variety of sources, including public disclosure documents (such as proxy statements, annual reports, and other regulatory filings) and also company management and investor-relations personnel, suppliers, customers, competitors, and other relevant sources. Research analysts may justifiably fear that companies will limit their ability to conduct thorough research by denying analysts who have "negative" views direct access to company managers and/or barring them from conference calls and other communication venues. This concern may make it difficult for them to conduct the comprehensive research needed to make objective recommendations.

**Buy-Side Clients**

- Portfolio managers may have significant positions in the security of a company under review. A rating downgrade may adversely affect the portfolio's performance, particularly in the short term, because the sensitivity of stock prices to ratings changes has increased in recent years. A downgrade may also affect the manager's compensation, which is usually tied to portfolio performance. Moreover, portfolio performance is subject to media and public scrutiny, which may affect the manager's professional reputation. Consequently, some portfolio managers implicitly or explicitly support sell-side ratings inflation.
- Portfolio managers have a responsibility to respect and foster the intellectual honesty of sell-side research. Therefore, it is improper for portfolio managers to threaten or engage in retaliatory practices, such as reporting sell-side analysts to the covered company in order to instigate negative corporate reactions.

**Fund Manager and Custodial Relationships**

- Research analysts are not the only people who must be concerned with maintaining their independence. Members and candidates who are responsible for hiring and retaining outside managers and third-party custodians should not accepts gifts, entertainment, or travel funding that may be perceived as impairing their decisions.

**Credit Rating Agency Opinions**

- Members and candidates employed at rating agencies should ensure that procedures and processes at the agencies prevent undue influences from a sponsoring company during the analysis. Members and candidates should abide by their agencies' and the industry's standards of conduct regarding the analytical process and the distribution of their reports.

- When using information provided by credit rating agencies, members and candidates should be mindful of the potential conflicts of interest. And because of the potential conflicts, members and candidates may need to independently validate the rating granted.

**Issuer-Paid Research**

- Some companies hire analysts to produce research reports in case of lack of coverage from sell-side research, or to increase the company's visibility in financial markets.
- Analysts must engage in thorough, independent, and unbiased analysis and must fully disclose potential conflicts, including the nature of their compensation. It should also be clearly mentioned in the report that the research has been paid for by the subject company. At a minimum, research should include a thorough analysis of the company's financial statements based on publicly disclosed information, benchmarking within a peer group, and industry analysis.
- Analysts must try to limit the type of compensation they accept for conducting research. This compensation can be direct, such as payment based on the conclusions of the report or more indirect, such as stock warrants or other equity instruments that could increase in value based on positive coverage in the report. In those instances, analysts would have an incentive to avoid negative information or conclusions that would diminish their potential compensation.
- Best practice is for analysts to accept only a flat fee for their work prior to writing the report, without regard to their conclusions or the report's recommendations.

**Travel Funding**

- The benefits related to accepting paid travel extend beyond the cost savings to the member or candidate and his firm, such as the chance to talk exclusively with the executives of a company or learning more about the investment options provided by an investment organization. Acceptance also comes with potential concerns; for example, members and candidates may be influenced by these discussions when flying on a corporate or chartered jet, or attending sponsored conferences where many expenses, including airfare and lodging, are covered.
- To avoid the appearance of compromising their independence and objectivity, best practice dictates that analysts always use commercial transportation at their expense or at the expense of their firm rather than accept paid travel arrangements from an outside company.
- In case of unavailability of commercial travel, they may accept modestly arranged travel to participate in appropriate information gathering events, such as a property tour.

**Performance Measurement and Attribution**

- Members and candidates working within a firm's investment performance measurement department may also be presented with situations that challenge their independence and objectivity. As performance analysts, their analyses may reveal instances where managers may appear to have strayed from their mandate. Additionally, the performance analyst may receive requests to alter the construction of composite indices owing to negative results for a selected account or fund. Members or candidates must not allow internal or external influences to affect their independence and objectivity as they faithfully complete their performance calculation and analysis-related responsibilities.

**Influence during the Manager Selection/Procurement Process**

- When serving in a hiring capacity, members and candidates should not solicit gifts, contributions, or other compensation that may affect their independence and objectivity. Solicitations do not have to benefit members and candidates personally to conflict with Standard I(B). Requesting contributions to a favorite charity or political organization may also be perceived as an attempt to influence the decision-making process. Additionally, members and candidates serving in a hiring capacity should refuse gifts, donations, and other offered compensation that may be perceived to influence their decision-making process.
- When working to earn a new investment allocation, members and candidates should not offer gifts, contributions, or other compensation to influence the decision of the hiring representative. The offering of these items with the intent to impair the independence and objectivity of another person would not comply with Standard I(B). Such prohibited actions may include offering donations to a charitable organization or political candidate referred by the hiring representative.

**Recommended Procedures for Compliance**

Members and candidates should adhere to the following practices and should encourage their firms to establish procedures to avoid violations of Standard I(B):

- Protect the integrity of opinions: Members, candidates, and their firms should establish policies stating that every research report concerning the securities of a corporate client should reflect the unbiased opinion of the analyst.
- Create a restricted list: If the firm is unwilling to permit dissemination of adverse opinions about a corporate client, members and candidates should encourage the firm to remove the controversial company from the research universe and put it on a restricted list so that the firm disseminates only factual information about the company and not the analyst's recommendation.
- Restrict special cost arrangements: When attending meetings at an issuer's headquarters, members and candidates should pay for commercial transportation and hotel charges. No corporate issuer should reimburse members or candidates for air transportation. Members and candidates should encourage issuers to limit the use of corporate aircraft to situations in which commercial transportation is not available or in which efficient movement could not otherwise be arranged.
- Limit gifts: Members and candidates must limit the acceptance of gratuities and/or gifts to token items. Standard I(B) does not preclude customary, ordinary business-related entertainment as long as its purpose is not to influence or reward members or candidates. Firms should consider a strict value limit for acceptable gifts that is based on the local or regional customs and should address whether the limit is per gift or an aggregate annual value.
- Restrict investments: Members and candidates should encourage their investment firms to develop formal polices related to employee purchases of equity or equity-related IPOs. Firms should require prior approval for employee participation in IPOs, with prompt disclosure of investment actions taken following the offering. Strict limits should be imposed on investment personnel acquiring securities in private placements. Note that a restriction is not a complete prohibition.
- Review procedures: Members and candidates should encourage their firms to implement effective supervisory and review procedures to ensure that analysts and portfolio managers comply with policies relating to their personal investment activities.

- Independence policy: Members, candidates, and their firms should establish a formal written policy on the independence and objectivity of research and implement reporting structures and review procedures to ensure that research analysts do not report to and are not supervised or controlled by any department of the firm that could compromise the independence of the analyst.
- Appointed officer: Firms should appoint a senior officer with oversight responsibilities for compliance with the firm's code of ethics and all regulations concerning its business.

## Standard I(C) Misrepresentation

### The Standard

Members and candidates must not knowingly make any misrepresentations relating to investment analysis, recommendations, actions, or other professional activities.

### Guidance

- A misrepresentation is any untrue statement or omission of a fact or any statement that is otherwise false or misleading.
- A member or candidate must not knowingly omit or misrepresent information or give a false impression of a firm, organization, or security in the member's or candidate's oral representations, advertising (whether in the press or through brochures), electronic communications, or written materials (whether publicly disseminated or not).
    - In this context, "knowingly" means that the member or candidate either knows or should have known that the misrepresentation was being made or that omitted information could alter the investment decision-making process.
- Members and candidates who use webpages should regularly monitor materials posted on these sites to ensure that they contain current information. Members and candidates should also ensure that all reasonable precautions have been taken to protect the site's integrity and security and that the site does not misrepresent any information and does provide full disclosure.
- Members and candidates should not guarantee clients any specific return on volatile investments. Most investments contain some element of risk that makes their return inherently unpredictable. For such investments, guaranteeing either a particular rate of return or a guaranteed preservation of investment capital (e.g., "I can guarantee that you will earn 8% on equities this year" or "I can guarantee that you will not lose money on this investment") is misleading to investors.
- Note that Standard I(C) does not prohibit members and candidates from providing clients with information on investment products that have guarantees built into the structure of the products themselves or for which an institution has agreed to cover any losses.

### Impact on Investment Practice

- Members and candidates must not misrepresent any aspect of their practice, including (but not limited to) their qualifications or credentials, the qualifications or services provided by their firm, their performance record and the record of their firm, and the characteristics of an investment.

- Members and candidates should exercise care and diligence when incorporating third-party information. Misrepresentations resulting from the use of the credit ratings, research, testimonials, or marketing materials of outside parties become the responsibility of the investment professional when it affects that professional's business practices.
- Members and candidates must disclose their intended use of external managers and must not represent those managers' investment practices as their own.

**Performance Reporting**

- Members and candidates should not misrepresent the success of their performance record by presenting benchmarks that are not comparable to their strategies. The benchmark's results should be reported on a basis comparable to that of the fund's or client's results.
- Note that Standard I(C) does not require that a benchmark always be provided in order to comply. Some investment strategies may not lend themselves to displaying an appropriate benchmark because of the complexity or diversity of the investments included.
- Members and candidates should discuss with clients on a continuous basis the appropriate benchmark to be used for performance evaluations and related fee calculations.
- Members and candidates should take reasonable steps to provide accurate and reliable security pricing information to clients on a consistent basis. Changing pricing providers should not be based solely on the justification that the new provider reports a higher current value of a security.

**Social Media**

- When communicating through social media channels, members and candidates should provide only the same information they are allowed to distribute to clients and potential clients through other traditional forms of communication.
- Along with understanding and following existing and newly developing rules and regulations regarding the allowed use of social media, members and candidates should also ensure that all communications in this format adhere to the requirements of the Code and Standards.
- The perceived anonymity granted through these platforms may entice individuals to misrepresent their qualifications or abilities or those of their employer. Actions undertaken through social media that knowingly misrepresent investment recommendations or professional activities are considered a violation of Standard I(C).

**Omissions**

- Members and candidates should not knowingly omit inputs used in any models and processes they use to scan for new investment opportunities, to develop investment vehicles, and to produce investment recommendations and ratings as resulting outcomes may provide misleading information. Further, members and candidates should not present outcomes from their models as facts because they only represent expected results.
- Members and candidates should encourage their firms to develop strict policies for composite development to prevent cherry picking—situations in which selected accounts are presented as representative of the firm's abilities. The omission of any accounts appropriate for the defined composite may misrepresent to clients the success of the manager's implementation of its strategy.

**Plagiarism**

- Plagiarism refers to the practice of copying, or using in substantially the same form, materials prepared by others without acknowledging the source of the material or identifying the author and publisher of the material. Plagiarism includes:
  - Taking a research report or study performed by another firm or person, changing the names, and releasing the material as one's own original analysis.
  - Using excerpts from articles or reports prepared by others either verbatim or with only slight changes in wording without acknowledgment.
  - Citing specific quotations supposedly attributable to "leading analysts" and "investment experts" without specific reference.
  - Presenting statistical estimates of forecasts prepared by others with the source identified but without qualifying statements or caveats that may have been used.
  - Using charts and graphs without stating their sources.
  - Copying proprietary computerized spreadsheets or algorithms without seeking the cooperation or authorization of their creators.
- In the case of distributing third-party, outsourced research, members and candidates can use and distribute these reports as long as they do not represent themselves as the author of the report. They may add value to clients by sifting through research and repackaging it for them, but should disclose that the research being presented to clients comes from an outside source.
- The standard also applies to plagiarism in oral communications, such as through group meetings; visits with associates, clients, and customers; use of audio/video media (which is rapidly increasing); and telecommunications, such as through electronic data transfer and the outright copying of electronic media. One of the most egregious practices in violation of this standard is the preparation of research reports based on multiple sources of information without acknowledging the sources. Such information would include, for example, ideas, statistical compilations, and forecasts combined to give the appearance of original work.

**Work Completed for Employer**

- Members and candidates may use research conducted by other analysts within their firm. Any research reports prepared by the analysts are the property of the firm and may be issued by it even if the original analysts are no longer with the firm.
- Therefore, members and candidates are allowed to use the research conducted by analysts who were previously employed at their firms. However, they cannot reissue a previously released report solely under their own name.

**Recommended Procedures for Compliance**

Factual presentations: Firms should provide guidance for employees who make written or oral presentations to clients or potential clients by providing a written list of the firm's available services and a description of the firm's qualifications. Firms can also help prevent misrepresentation by specifically designating which employees are authorized to speak on behalf of the firm.

Qualification summary: In order to ensure accurate presentations to clients, the member or candidate should prepare a summary of her own qualifications and experience, as well as a list of the services she is capable of performing.

Verify outside information: When providing information to clients from third parties, members and candidates should ensure the accuracy of the marketing and distribution materials that pertain to the third party's capabilities, services, and products. This is because inaccurate information can damage their individual and their firm's reputations as well as the integrity of the capital markets.

Maintain webpages: If they publish a webpage, members and candidates should regularly monitor materials posted to the site to ensure the site maintains current information.

Plagiarism policy: To avoid plagiarism in preparing research reports or conclusions of analysis, members and candidates should take the following steps:

- *Maintain copies:* Keep copies of all research reports, articles containing research ideas, material with new statistical methodology, and other materials that were relied on in preparing the research report.
- *Attribute quotations:* Attribute to their sources any direct quotations, including projections, tables, statistics, model/product ideas, and new methodologies prepared by persons other than recognized financial and statistical reporting services or similar sources.
- *Attribute summaries:* Attribute to their sources paraphrases or summaries of material prepared by others.

## Standard I(D) Misconduct

**The Standard**

Members and candidates must not engage in any professional conduct involving dishonesty, fraud, or deceit, or commit any act that reflects adversely on their professional reputation, integrity, or competence.

**Guidance**

- While Standard I(A) addresses the obligation of members and candidates to comply with applicable law that governs their professional activities, Standard I(D) addresses *all* conduct that reflects poorly on the professional integrity, good reputation, or competence of members and candidates. Any act that involves lying, cheating, stealing, or other dishonest conduct is a violation of this standard if the offense reflects adversely on a member's or candidate's professional activities.
- Conduct that damages trustworthiness or competence may include behavior that, although not illegal, nevertheless negatively affects a member's or candidate's ability to perform his or her responsibilities. For example:
    - Abusing alcohol during business hours might constitute a violation of this standard because it could have a detrimental effect on the member's or candidate's ability to fulfill his or her professional responsibilities.
    - Personal bankruptcy may not reflect on the integrity or trustworthiness of the person declaring bankruptcy, but if the circumstances of the bankruptcy involve fraudulent or deceitful business conduct, the bankruptcy may be a violation of this standard.
- In some cases, the absence of appropriate conduct or the lack of sufficient effort may be a violation of Standard I(D). The integrity of the investment profession is built on trust. A member or candidate—whether an investment banker, rating or research analyst, or portfolio manager—is expected to conduct the necessary due diligence to properly understand the nature and risks of an investment before making an investment recommendation. By not taking these steps and, instead, relying on someone else in the process to perform them, members or candidates may violate the

trust their clients have placed in them. This loss of trust may have a significant impact on the reputation of the member or candidate and the operations of the financial market as a whole.

- Note that Standard I(D) or any other standard should not be used to settle personal, political, or other disputes unrelated to professional ethics.

**Recommended Procedures for Compliance**

Members and candidates should encourage their firms to adopt the following policies and procedures to support the principles of Standard I(D):

- Code of ethics: Develop and/or adopt a code of ethics to which every employee must subscribe, and make clear that any personal behavior that reflects poorly on the individual involved, the institution as a whole, or the investment industry will not be tolerated.
- List of violations: Disseminate to all employees a list of potential violations and associated disciplinary sanctions, up to and including dismissal from the firm.
- Employee references: Check references of potential employees to ensure that they are of good character and not ineligible to work in the investment industry because of past infractions of the law.

## Standard II(A) Material Nonpublic Information

**The Standard**

Members and candidates who possess material nonpublic information that could affect the value of an investment must not act or cause others to act on the information.

**Guidance**

- Standard II(A) is related to information that is material and is nonpublic. Such information must not be used for direct buying and selling of individual securities or bonds, nor to influence investment actions related to derivatives, mutual funds, or other alternative investments.

**Material Information**

Information is "material" if its disclosure would likely have an impact on the price of a security, or if reasonable investors would want to know the information before making an investment decision. Material information may include, but is not limited to, information relating to the following:

- Earnings.
- Mergers, acquisitions, tender offers, or joint ventures.
- Changes in assets.
- Innovative products, processes, or discoveries.
- New licenses, patents, registered trademarks, or regulatory approval/rejection of a product.
- Developments regarding customers or suppliers (e.g., the acquisition or loss of a contract).
- Changes in management.
- Change in auditor notification or the fact that the issuer may no longer rely on an auditor's report or qualified opinion.

- Events regarding the issuer's securities (e.g., defaults on senior securities, calls of securities for redemption, repurchase plans, stock splits, changes in dividends, changes to the rights of security holders, public or private sales of additional securities, and changes in credit ratings).
- Bankruptcies.
- Significant legal disputes.
- Government reports of economic trends (employment, housing starts, currency information, etc.).
- Orders for large trades before they are executed.
- New or changing equity or debt ratings issued by a third party (e.g., sell-side recommendations and credit ratings).
- To determine if information is material, members and candidates should consider the source of information and the information's likely effect on the relevant stock price.
    - The less reliable a source, such as a rumor, the less likely the information provided would be considered material.
    - The more ambiguous the effect on price, the less material the information becomes.
    - If it is unclear whether the information will affect the price of a security and to what extent, information may not be considered material.

**Nonpublic Information**

- Information is "nonpublic" until it has been disseminated or is available to the marketplace in general (as opposed to a select group of investors). "Disseminated" can be defined as "made known."
    - For example, a company report of profits that is posted on the Internet and distributed widely through a press release or accompanied by a filing has been effectively disseminated to the marketplace.
- Members and candidates must be particularly aware of information that is selectively disclosed by corporations to a small group of investors, analysts, or other market participants. Information that is made available to analysts remains nonpublic until it is disseminated to investors in general.
- Analysts should also be alert to the possibility that they are selectively receiving material nonpublic information when a company provides them with guidance or interpretation of such publicly available information as financial statements or regulatory filings.
- A member or candidate may use insider information provided legitimately by the source company for the specific purpose of conducting due diligence according to the business agreement between the parties for such activities as mergers, loan underwriting, credit ratings, and offering engagements. However, the use of insider information provided by the source company for other purposes, especially to trade or entice others to trade the securities of the firm, conflicts with this standard.

**Mosaic Theory**

- A financial analyst may use significant conclusions derived from the analysis of public information and nonmaterial nonpublic information as the basis for investment recommendations and decisions. Under the "mosaic theory," financial analysts are free to act on this collection, or mosaic, of information without risking violation, even when the conclusion they reach would have been material inside information had the company communicated the same.
- Investment professionals should note, however, that although analysts are free to use mosaic information in their research reports, they should save and document all their research [see Standard V(C)].

**Social Media**

- Members and candidates participating in online discussion forums/groups with membership limitations should verify that material information obtained from these sources can also be accessed from a source that would be considered available to the public (e.g., company filings, webpages, and press releases).
- Members and candidates may use social media platforms to communicate with clients or investors without conflicting with this standard.
- Members and candidates, as required by Standard I(A), should also complete all appropriate regulatory filings related to information distributed through social media platforms.

**Using Industry Experts**

- The increased demand for insights for understanding the complexities of some industries has led to an expansion of engagement with outside experts. Members and candidates may provide compensation to individuals for their insights without violating this standard.
- However, members and candidates are ultimately responsible for ensuring that they are not requesting or acting on confidential information received from external experts, which is in violation of security regulations and laws or duties to others.

**Investment Research Reports**

- It might often be the case that reports prepared by well-known analysts may have an effect on the market and thus may be considered material information. Theoretically, such a report might have to be made public before it was distributed to clients. However, since the analyst is not a company insider, and presumably prepared the report based on publicly available information, the report does not need to be made public just because its conclusions are material. Investors who want to use that report can become clients of the analyst.

**Recommended Procedures for Compliance**

Achieve public dissemination: If a member or candidate determines that some nonpublic information is material, she should encourage the issuer to make the information public. If public dissemination is not possible, she must communicate the information only to the designated supervisory and compliance personnel in her firm and must not take investment action on the basis of the information.

Adopt compliance procedures: Members and candidates should encourage their firms to adopt compliance procedures to prevent the misuse of material nonpublic information. Particularly important is improving compliance in areas such as review of employee and proprietary trading, documentation of firm procedures, and the supervision of interdepartmental communications in multi-service firms.

Adopt disclosure procedures: Members and candidates should encourage their firms to develop and follow disclosure policies designed to ensure that information is disseminated in the marketplace in an equitable manner. An issuing company should not discriminate among analysts in the provision of information or blackball particular analysts who have given negative reports on the company in the past.

Issue press releases: Companies should consider issuing press releases prior to analyst meetings and conference calls and scripting those meetings and calls to decrease the chance that further information will be disclosed.

Firewall elements: An information barrier commonly referred to as a "firewall" is the most widely used approach to prevent communication of material nonpublic information within firms. The minimum elements of such a system include, but are not limited to, the following:

- Substantial control of relevant interdepartmental communications, preferably through a clearance area within the firm in either the compliance or legal department;
- Review of employee trading through the maintenance of "watch," "restricted," and "rumor" lists;
- Documentation of the procedures designed to limit the flow of information between departments and of the enforcement actions taken pursuant to those procedures;
- Heightened review or restriction of proprietary trading while a firm is in possession of material nonpublic information.

Appropriate interdepartmental communications: Based on the size of the firm, procedures concerning interdepartmental communication, the review of trading activity, and the investigation of possible violations should be compiled and formalized.

Physical separation of departments: As a practical matter, to the extent possible, firms should consider the physical separation of departments and files to prevent the communication of sensitive information.

Prevention of personnel overlap: There should be no overlap of personnel between the investment banking and corporate finance areas of a brokerage firm and the sales and research departments or between a bank's commercial lending department and its trust and research departments. For a firewall to be effective in a multi-service firm, an employee can be allowed to be on only one side of the wall at any given time.

A reporting system: The least a firm should do to protect itself from liability is have an information barrier in place. It should authorize people to review and approve communications between departments. A single supervisor or compliance officer should have the specific authority and responsibility of deciding whether or not information is material and whether it is sufficiently public to be used as the basis for investment decisions.

Personal trading limitations: Firms should also consider restrictions or prohibitions on personal trading by employees and should carefully monitor both proprietary trading and personal trading by employees. Further, they should require employees to make periodic reports (to the extent that such reporting is not already required by securities laws) of their own transactions and transactions made for the benefit of family members.

Securities should be placed on a restricted list when a firm has or may have material nonpublic information. Further, the watch list (seen only by compliance personnel) should be shown to only the few people responsible for compliance to monitor transactions in specified securities. The use of a watch list in combination with a restricted list has become a common means of ensuring an effective procedure.

Record maintenance: Multi-service firms should maintain written records of communications among various departments. Firms should place a high priority on training and should consider instituting comprehensive training programs, to enable employees to make informed decisions.

Proprietary trading procedures: Procedures concerning the restriction or review of a firm's proprietary trading while it possesses material nonpublic information will necessarily depend on the types of proprietary trading in which a firm may engage. For example, when a firm acts as a market maker, a prohibition on proprietary trading may be counterproductive to the goals of maintaining the confidentiality of information and market liquidity. However, in case of risk-arbitrage trading, a firm should suspend arbitrage activity when a security is placed on the watch list.

Communication to all employees: Written compliance policies and guidelines should be circulated to all employees of a firm. Further, they must be given sufficient training to either be able to make an informed decision or to realize that they need to consult a compliance officer before engaging in questionable transactions.

## Standard II(B) Market Manipulation

### The Standard

Members and candidates must not engage in practices that distort prices or artificially inflate trading volume with the intent to mislead market participants.

### Guidance

- Members and candidates must uphold market integrity by prohibiting market manipulation. Market manipulation includes practices that distort security prices or trading volume with the intent to deceive people or entities that rely on information in the market.
- Market manipulation includes (1) the dissemination of false or misleading information and (2) transactions that deceive or would be likely to mislead market participants by distorting the price-setting mechanism of financial instruments.

### Information-Based Manipulation

- Information-based manipulation includes, but is not limited to, spreading false rumors to induce trading by others.
    - For example, members and candidates must refrain from "pumping up" the price of an investment by issuing misleading positive information or overly optimistic projections of a security's worth only to later "dump" the investment (i.e., sell it) once the price, fueled by the misleading information's effect on other market participants, reaches an artificially high level.

### Transaction-Based Manipulation

- Transaction-based manipulation involves instances where a member or candidate knew or should have known that his or her actions could affect the pricing of a security. This type of manipulation includes, but is not limited to, the following:
    - Transactions that artificially affect prices or volume to give the impression of activity or price movement in a financial instrument, which represent a diversion from the expectations of a fair and efficient market.
    - Securing a controlling, dominant position in a financial instrument to exploit and manipulate the price of a related derivative and/or the underlying asset.

Note that Standard II(B) is not intended to preclude transactions undertaken on legitimate trading strategies based on perceived market inefficiencies. The *intent* of the action is critical to determining whether it is a violation of this standard.

## Standard III(A) Loyalty, Prudence, and Care

### The Standard

Members and candidates have a duty of loyalty to their clients and must act with reasonable care and exercise prudent judgment. Members and candidates must act for the benefit of their clients and place their clients' interests before their employer's or their own interests.

### Guidance

- Standard III(A) clarifies that client interests are paramount. A member's or candidate's responsibility to a client includes a duty of loyalty and a duty to exercise reasonable care. Investment actions must be carried out for the sole benefit of the client and in a manner the member or candidate believes, given the known facts and circumstances, to be in the best interest of the client. Members and candidates must exercise the same level of prudence, judgment, and care that they would apply in the management and disposition of their own interests in similar circumstances.
- Prudence requires caution and discretion. The exercise of prudence by investment professionals requires that they act with the care, skill, and diligence that a reasonable person acting in a like capacity and familiar with such matters would use. In the context of managing a client's portfolio, prudence requires following the investment parameters set forth by the client and balancing risk and return. Acting with care requires members and candidates to act in a prudent and judicious manner in avoiding harm to clients.
- Standard III(A), however, is not a substitute for a member's or candidate's legal or regulatory obligations. As stated in Standard I(A), members and candidates must abide by the most strict requirements imposed on them by regulators or the Code and Standards, including any legally imposed fiduciary duty.
- Members and candidates must also be aware of whether they have "custody" or effective control of client assets. If so, a heightened level of responsibility arises. Members and candidates are considered to have custody if they have any direct or indirect access to client funds. Members and candidates must manage any pool of assets in their control in accordance with the terms of the governing documents (such as trust documents and investment management agreements), which are the primary determinant of the manager's powers and duties.

### Understanding the Application of Loyalty, Prudence, and Care

- Standard III(A) establishes a minimum benchmark for the duties of loyalty, prudence, and care that are required of all members and candidates regardless of whether a legal fiduciary duty applies. Although fiduciary duty often encompasses the principles of loyalty, prudence, and care, Standard III(A) does not render all members and candidates fiduciaries. The responsibilities of members and candidates for fulfilling their obligations under this standard depend greatly on the nature of their professional responsibilities and the relationships they have with clients.
- There is a large variety of professional relationships that members and candidates have with their clients. Standard III(A) requires them to fulfill the obligations outlined explicitly or implicitly in the client agreements to the best of their abilities and with loyalty, prudence, and care. Whether a member or candidate is structuring a new securitization transaction, completing a credit rating analysis, or leading a public company, he or she must work with prudence and care in delivering the agreed-on services.

### Identifying the Actual Investment Client

- The first step for members and candidates in fulfilling their duty of loyalty to clients is to determine the identity of the "client" to whom the duty of loyalty is owed. In the context of an investment manager managing the personal assets of an individual, the client is easily identified. When the manager is responsible for the portfolios of pension plans or trusts, however, the client is not the person or entity who hires the manager but, rather, the beneficiaries of the plan or trust. The duty of loyalty is owed to the ultimate beneficiaries.
- Members and candidates managing a fund to an index or an expected mandate owe the duty of loyalty, prudence, and care to invest in a manner consistent with the stated mandate. The decisions of a fund's manager, although benefiting all fund investors, do not have to be based on an individual investor's requirements and risk profile. Client loyalty and care for those investing in the fund are the responsibility of members and candidates who have an advisory relationship with those individuals.

### Developing the Client's Portfolio

- Professional investment managers should ensure that the client's objectives and expectations for the performance of the account are realistic and suitable to the client's circumstances and that the risks involved are appropriate. In most circumstances, recommended investment strategies should relate to the long-term objectives and circumstances of the client.
- When members and candidates cannot avoid potential conflicts between their firm and clients' interests, they must provide clear and factual disclosures of the circumstances to the clients.
- Members and candidates must follow any guidelines set by their clients for the management of their assets.
- Investment decisions must be judged in the context of the total portfolio rather than by individual investments within the portfolio. The member's or candidate's duty is satisfied with respect to a particular investment if the individual has thoroughly considered the investment's place in the overall portfolio, the risk of loss and opportunity for gains, tax implications, and the diversification, liquidity, cash flow, and overall return requirements of the assets or the portion of the assets for which the manager is responsible.

### Soft Commission Policies

- An investment manager often has discretion over the selection of brokers executing transactions. Conflicts may arise when an investment manager uses client brokerage to purchase research services, a practice commonly called "soft dollars" or "soft commissions." A member or candidate who pays a higher brokerage commission than he or she would normally pay to allow for the purchase of goods or services, without corresponding benefit to the client, violates the duty of loyalty to the client.
- From time to time, a client will direct a manager to use the client's brokerage to purchase goods or services for the client, a practice that is commonly called "directed brokerage." Because brokerage commission is an asset of the client and is used to benefit that client, not the manager, such a practice does not violate any duty of loyalty. However, a member or candidate is obligated to seek "best price" and "best execution" and be assured by the client that the goods or services purchased from the brokerage will benefit the account beneficiaries. In addition, the member or candidate should disclose to the client that the client may not be getting best execution from the directed brokerage.
    - "Best execution" refers to a trading process that seeks to maximize the value of the client's portfolio within the client's stated investment objectives and constraints.

ET

### Proxy Voting Policies

- Part of a member's or candidate's duty of loyalty includes voting proxies in an informed and responsible manner. Proxies have economic value to a client, and members and candidates must ensure that they properly safeguard and maximize this value.
- An investment manager who fails to vote, casts a vote without considering the impact of the question, or votes blindly with management on non-routine governance issues (e.g., a change in company capitalization) may violate this standard. Voting of proxies is an integral part of the management of investments.
- A cost-benefit analysis may show that voting all proxies may not benefit the client, so voting proxies may not be necessary in all instances.
- Members and candidates should disclose to clients their proxy voting policies.

### Recommended Procedures for Compliance

### Regular Account Information

Members and candidates with control of client assets should:

- Submit to each client, at least quarterly, an itemized statement showing the funds and securities in the custody or possession of the member or candidate plus all debits, credits, and transactions that occurred during the period.
- Disclose to the client where the assets are to be maintained, as well as where or when they are moved.
- Separate the client's assets from any other party's assets, including the member's or candidate's own assets.

### Client Approval

- If a member or candidate is uncertain about the appropriate course of action with respect to a client, the member or candidate should consider what he or she would expect or demand if the member or candidate were the client.
- If in doubt, a member or candidate should disclose the questionable matter in writing to the client and obtain client approval.

### Firm Policies

Members and candidates should address and encourage their firms to address the following topics when drafting the statements or manuals containing their policies and procedures regarding responsibilities to clients:

- ***Follow all applicable rules and laws:*** Members and candidates must follow all legal requirements and applicable provisions of the Code and Standards.
- ***Establish the investment objectives of the client:*** Make a reasonable inquiry into a client's investment experience, risk and return objectives, and financial constraints prior to making investment recommendations or taking investment actions.
- ***Consider all the information when taking actions:*** When taking investment actions, members and candidates must consider the appropriateness and suitability of the investment relative to (1) the client's needs and circumstances, (2) the investment's basic characteristics, and (3) the basic characteristics of the total portfolio.
- ***Diversify:*** Members and candidates should diversify investments to reduce the risk of loss, unless diversification is not consistent with plan guidelines or is contrary to the account objectives.

- *Carry out regular reviews:* Members and candidates should establish regular review schedules to ensure that the investments held in the account adhere to the terms of the governing documents.
- *Deal fairly with all clients with respect to investment actions:* Members and candidates must not favor some clients over others and should establish policies for allocating trades and disseminating investment recommendations.
- *Disclose conflicts of interest:* Members and candidates must disclose all actual and potential conflicts of interest so that clients can evaluate those conflicts.
- *Disclose compensation arrangements:* Members and candidates should make their clients aware of all forms of manager compensation.
- *Vote proxies:* In most cases, members and candidates should determine who is authorized to vote shares and vote proxies in the best interests of the clients and ultimate beneficiaries.
- *Maintain confidentiality:* Members and candidates must preserve the confidentiality of client information.
- *Seek best execution:* Unless directed by the client as ultimate beneficiary, members and candidates must seek best execution for their clients. (Best execution is defined in the preceding text.)
- *Place client interests first:* Members and candidates must serve the best interests of clients.

## Standard III(B) Fair Dealing

**The Standard**

Members and candidates must deal fairly and objectively with all clients when providing investment analysis, making investment recommendations, taking investment action, or engaging in other professional activities.

**Guidance**

- Standard III(B) requires members and candidates to treat all clients fairly when disseminating investment recommendations or making material changes to prior investment recommendations, or when taking investment action with regard to general purchases, new issues, or secondary offerings.
- The term "fairly" implies that the member or candidate must take care not to discriminate against any clients when disseminating investment recommendations or taking investment action. Standard III(B) does not state "equally" because members and candidates could not possibly reach all clients at exactly the same time. Further, each client has unique needs, investment criteria, and investment objectives, so not all investment opportunities are suitable for all clients.
- Members and candidates may provide more personal, specialized, or in-depth service to clients who are willing to pay for premium services through higher management fees or higher levels of brokerage. Members and candidates may differentiate their services to clients, but different levels of service must not disadvantage or negatively affect clients. In addition, the different service levels should be disclosed to clients and prospective clients and should be available to everyone (i.e., different service levels should not be offered selectively).

**Investment Recommendations**

- An investment recommendation is any opinion expressed by a member or candidate in regard to purchasing, selling, or holding a given security or other investment. The opinion may be disseminated to customers or clients through an initial detailed research report, through a brief update report, by addition to or deletion from a list of recommended securities, or simply by oral communication. A recommendation that is distributed to anyone outside the organization is considered a communication for general distribution under Standard III(B).
- Each member or candidate is obligated to ensure that information is disseminated in such a manner that all clients have a fair opportunity to act on every recommendation. Members and candidates should encourage their firms to design an equitable system to prevent selective or discriminatory disclosure and should inform clients about what kind of communications they will receive.
- The duty to clients imposed by Standard III(B) may be more critical when members or candidates change their recommendations than when they make initial recommendations. Material changes in a member's or candidate's prior investment recommendations because of subsequent research should be communicated to all current clients; particular care should be taken that the information reaches those clients who the member or candidate knows have acted on or been affected by the earlier advice.
- Clients who do not know that the member or candidate has changed a recommendation and who, therefore, place orders contrary to a current recommendation should be advised of the changed recommendation before the order is accepted.

**Investment Action**

- Members or candidates must treat all clients fairly in light of their investment objectives and circumstances. For example, when making investments in new offerings or in secondary financings, members and candidates should distribute the issues to all customers for whom the investments are appropriate in a manner consistent with the policies of the firm for allocating blocks of stock. If the issue is oversubscribed, then the issue should be prorated to all subscribers. If the issue is oversubscribed, members and candidates should forgo any sales to themselves or their immediate families in order to free up additional shares for clients.
    - If the investment professional's family-member accounts are managed similarly to the accounts of other clients of the firm, however, the family-member accounts should not be excluded from buying such shares.
- Members and candidates must make every effort to treat all individual and institutional clients in a fair and impartial manner.
- Members and candidates should disclose to clients and prospective clients the documented allocation procedures they or their firms have in place and how the procedures would affect the client or prospect. The disclosure should be clear and complete so that the client can make an informed investment decision. Even when complete disclosure is made, however, members and candidates must put client interests ahead of their own. A member's or candidate's duty of fairness and loyalty to clients can never be overridden by client consent to patently unfair allocation procedures.
- Treating clients fairly also means that members and candidates should not take advantage of their position in the industry to the detriment of clients. For instance, in the context of IPOs, members and candidates must make bona fide public distributions of "hot issue" securities (defined as securities of a public offering that are trading at

a premium in the secondary market whenever such trading commences because of the great demand for the securities). Members and candidates are prohibited from withholding such securities for their own benefit and must not use such securities as a reward or incentive to gain benefit.

## Recommended Procedures for Compliance

### Develop Firm Policies

- A member or candidate should recommend appropriate procedures to management if none are in place.
- A member or candidate should make management aware of possible violations of fair-dealing practices within the firm when they come to the attention of the member or candidate.
- Although a member or candidate need not communicate a recommendation to all customers, the selection process by which customers receive information should be based on suitability and known interest, not on any preferred or favored status.

A common practice to assure fair dealing is to communicate recommendations simultaneously within the firm and to customers. Members and candidates should consider the following points when establishing fair-dealing compliance procedures:

- Limit the number of people involved.
- Shorten the time frame between decision and dissemination.
- Publish guidelines for pre-dissemination behavior.
- Simultaneous dissemination.
- Maintain a list of clients and their holdings.
- Develop and document trade allocation procedures that ensure:
    - Fairness to advisory clients, both in priority of execution of orders and in the allocation of the price obtained in execution of block orders or trades.
    - Timeliness and efficiency in the execution of orders.
    - Accuracy of the member's or candidate's records as to trade orders and client account positions.

With these principles in mind, members and candidates should develop or encourage their firm to develop written allocation procedures, with particular attention to procedures for block trades and new issues. Procedures to consider are as follows:

- Requiring orders and modifications or cancellations of orders to be documented and time stamped.
- Processing and executing orders on a first-in, first-out basis with consideration of bundling orders for efficiency as appropriate for the asset class or the security.
- Developing a policy to address such issues as calculating execution prices and "partial fills" when trades are grouped, or in a block, for efficiency.
- Giving all client accounts participating in a block trade the same execution price and charging the same commission.
- When the full amount of the block order is not executed, allocating partially executed orders among the participating client accounts pro rata on the basis of order size while not going below an established minimum lot size for some securities (e.g., bonds).
- When allocating trades for new issues, obtaining advance indications of interest, allocating securities by client (rather than portfolio manager), and providing a method for calculating allocations.

**Disclose Trade Allocation Procedures**

- Members and candidates should disclose to clients and prospective clients how they select accounts to participate in an order and how they determine the amount of securities each account will buy or sell. Trade allocation procedures must be fair and equitable, and disclosure of inequitable allocation methods does not relieve the member or candidate of this obligation.

**Establish Systematic Account Review**

- Member and candidate supervisors should review each account on a regular basis to ensure that no client or customer is being given preferential treatment and that the investment actions taken for each account are suitable for each account's objectives.
- Because investments should be based on individual needs and circumstances, an investment manager may have good reasons for placing a given security or other investment in one account while selling it from another account and should fully document the reasons behind both sides of the transaction.
- Members and candidates should encourage firms to establish review procedures, however, to detect whether trading in one account is being used to benefit a favored client.

**Disclose Levels of Service**

- Members and candidates should disclose to all clients whether the organization offers different levels of service to clients for the same fee or different fees.
- Different levels of service should not be offered to clients selectively.

## Standard III(C) Suitability

**The Standard**

1. When Members and candidates are in an **advisory relationship with a client**, they must:
    a. Make a reasonable inquiry into a client's or prospective client's investment experience, risk and return objectives, and financial constraints prior to making any investment recommendation or taking investment action and must reassess and update this information regularly.
    b. Determine that an investment is suitable to the client's financial situation and consistent with the client's written objectives, mandates, and constraints before making an investment recommendation or taking investment action.
    c. Judge the suitability of investments in the context of the client's total portfolio.
2. When members and candidates are **responsible for managing a portfolio to a specific mandate, strategy, or style**, they must make only investment recommendations or take only investment actions that are consistent with the stated objectives and constraints of the portfolio. In other words, there is no need for an investment policy statement when managing to a specific mandate.

**Guidance**

- Standard III(C) requires that members and candidates who are in an investment advisory relationship with clients consider carefully the needs, circumstances, and objectives of the clients when determining the appropriateness and suitability of a given investment or course of investment action.

- In judging the suitability of a potential investment, the member or candidate should review many aspects of the client's knowledge, experience related to investing, and financial situation. These aspects include, but are not limited to, the risk profile of the investment as compared with the constraints of the client, the impact of the investment on the diversity of the portfolio, and whether the client has the means or net worth to assume the associated risk. The investment professional's determination of suitability should reflect only the investment recommendations or actions that a prudent person would be willing to undertake. Not every investment opportunity will be suitable for every portfolio, regardless of the potential return being offered.
- The responsibilities of members and candidates to gather information and make a suitability analysis prior to making a recommendation or taking investment action fall on those members and candidates who provide investment advice in the course of an advisory relationship with a client. Other members and candidates who are simply executing specific instructions for retail clients when buying or selling securities, may not have the opportunity to judge the suitability of a particular investment for the ultimate client.

**Developing an Investment Policy When an Advisory Relationship Exists**

- When an advisory relationship exists, members and candidates must gather client information at the inception of the relationship. Such information includes the client's financial circumstances, personal data (such as age and occupation) that are relevant to investment decisions, attitudes toward risk, and objectives in investing. This information should be incorporated into a written investment policy statement (IPS) that addresses the client's risk tolerance, return requirements, and all investment constraints (including time horizon, liquidity needs, tax concerns, legal and regulatory factors, and unique circumstances).
- The IPS also should identify and describe the roles and responsibilities of the parties to the advisory relationship and investment process, as well as schedules for review and evaluation of the IPS.
- After formulating long-term capital market expectations, members and candidates can assist in developing an appropriate strategic asset allocation and investment program for the client, whether these are presented in separate documents or incorporated in the IPS or in appendices to the IPS.

**Understanding the Client's Risk Profile**

- The investment professional must consider the possibilities of rapidly changing investment environments and their likely impact on a client's holdings, both individual securities and the collective portfolio.
- The risk of many investment strategies can and should be analyzed and quantified in advance.
- Members and candidates should pay careful attention to the leverage inherent in many synthetic investment vehicles or products when considering them for use in a client's investment program.

**Updating an Investment Policy**

- Updating the IPS should be repeated at least annually and also prior to material changes to any specific investment recommendations or decisions on behalf of the client.
  - For an individual client, important changes might include the number of dependents, personal tax status, health, liquidity needs, risk tolerance, amount of wealth beyond that represented in the portfolio, and extent to which compensation and other income provide for current income needs.
  - For an institutional client, such changes might relate to the magnitude of unfunded liabilities in a pension fund, the withdrawal privileges in an employee savings plan, or the distribution requirements of a charitable foundation.
- If clients withhold information about their financial portfolios, the suitability analysis conducted by members and candidates cannot be expected to be complete; it must be based on the information provided.

**The Need for Diversification**

- The unique characteristics (or risks) of an individual investment may become partially or entirely neutralized when it is combined with other individual investments within a portfolio. Therefore, a reasonable amount of diversification is thus the norm for many portfolios.
- An investment with high relative risk on its own may be a suitable investment in the context of the entire portfolio or when the client's stated objectives contemplate speculative or risky investments.
- Members and candidates can be responsible for assessing the suitability of an investment only on the basis of the information and criteria actually provided by the client.

**Addressing Unsolicited Trading Requests**

- If an unsolicited request is expected to have only a minimum impact on the entire portfolio because the size of the requested trade is small or the trade would result in a limited change to the portfolio's risk profile, the member or candidate should focus on educating the investor on how the request deviates from the current policy statement, and then she may follow her firm's policies regarding the necessary client approval for executing unsuitable trades. At a minimum, the client should acknowledge the discussion and accept the conditions that make the recommendation unsuitable.
- If an unsolicited request is expected to have a material impact on the portfolio, the member or candidate should use this opportunity to update the investment policy statement. Doing so would allow the client to fully understand the potential effect of the requested trade on his or her current goals or risk levels.
- If the client declines to modify her policy statements while insisting an unsolicited trade be made, the member or candidate will need to evaluate the effectiveness of her services to the client. The options available to the members or candidates will depend on the services provided by their employer. Some firms may allow for the trade to be executed in a new unmanaged account. If alternative options are not available, members and candidates ultimately will need to determine whether they should continue the advisory arrangement with the client.

**Managing to an Index or Mandate**

Some members and candidates do not manage money for individuals but are responsible for managing a fund to an index or an expected mandate. The responsibility of these members and candidates is to invest in a manner consistent with the stated mandate but without having to prepare the IPS for the client.

**Recommended Procedures for Compliance**

**Investment Policy Statement**

In formulating an investment policy for the client, the member or candidate should take the following into consideration:

- *Client identification*—(1) type and nature of client, (2) the existence of separate beneficiaries, and (3) approximate portion of total client assets that the member or candidate is managing.
- *Investor objectives*—(1) return objectives (income, growth in principal, maintenance of purchasing power) and (2) risk tolerance (suitability, stability of values).
- *Investor constraints*—(1) liquidity needs, (2) expected cash flows (patterns of additions and/or withdrawals), (3) investable funds (assets and liabilities or other commitments), (4) time horizon, (5) tax considerations, (6) regulatory and legal circumstances, (7) investor preferences, prohibitions, circumstances, and unique needs, and (8) proxy voting responsibilities and guidance.
- *Performance measurement benchmarks.*

**Regular Updates**

- The investor's objectives and constraints should be maintained and reviewed periodically to reflect any changes in the client's circumstances.

**Suitability Test Policies**

- With the increase in regulatory required suitability tests, members and candidates should encourage their firms to develop related policies and procedures. The test procedures should require the investment professional to look beyond the potential return of the investment and include the following:
    - An analysis of the impact on the portfolio's diversification.
    - A comparison of the investment risks with the client's assessed risk tolerance.
    - The fit of the investment with the required investment strategy.

## Standard III(D) Performance Presentation

**The Standard**

When communicating investment performance information, members and candidates must make reasonable efforts to ensure that it is fair, accurate, and complete.

**Guidance**

- Members and candidates must provide credible performance information to clients and prospective clients and to avoid misstating performance or misleading clients and prospective clients about the investment performance of members or candidates or their firms.
- Standard III(D) covers any practice that would lead to misrepresentation of a member's or candidate's performance record, whether the practice involves performance presentation or performance measurement.

ET

- Members and candidates should not state or imply that clients will obtain or benefit from a rate of return that was generated in the past.
- Research analysts promoting the success or accuracy of their recommendations must ensure that their claims are fair, accurate, and complete.
- If the presentation is brief, the member or candidate must make available to clients and prospects, on request, the detailed information supporting that communication. Best practice dictates that brief presentations include a reference to the limited nature of the information provided.

**Recommended Procedures for Compliance**

**Apply the GIPS Standards**

- Compliance with the GIPS standards is the best method to meet their obligations under Standard III(D).

**Compliance without Applying GIPS Standards**

Members and candidates can also meet their obligations under Standard III(D) by:

- Considering the knowledge and sophistication of the audience to whom a performance presentation is addressed.
- Presenting the performance of the weighted composite of similar portfolios rather than using a single representative account.
- Including terminated accounts as part of performance history with a clear indication of when the accounts were terminated.
- Including disclosures that fully explain the performance results being reported (for example, stating, when appropriate, that results are simulated when model results are used, clearly indicating when the performance record is that of a prior entity, or disclosing whether the performance is gross of fees, net of fees, or after tax).
- Maintaining the data and records used to calculate the performance being presented.

## Standard III(E) Preservation of Confidentiality

**The Standard**

Members and candidates must keep information about current, former, and prospective clients confidential unless:

1. The information concerns illegal activities on the part of the client;
2. Disclosure is required by law; or
3. The client or prospective client permits disclosure of the information.

**Guidance**

- Members and candidates must preserve the confidentiality of information communicated to them by their clients, prospective clients, and former clients. This standard is applicable when (1) the member or candidate receives information because of his or her special ability to conduct a portion of the client's business or personal affairs and (2) the member or candidate receives information that arises from or is relevant to that portion of the client's business that is the subject of the special or confidential relationship.
- If disclosure of the information is required by law or the information concerns illegal activities by the client, however, the member or candidate may have an obligation to report the activities to the appropriate authorities.

**Status of Client**

- This standard protects the confidentiality of client information even if the person or entity is no longer a client of the member or candidate. Therefore, members and candidates must continue to maintain the confidentiality of client records even after the client relationship has ended.
- If a client or former client expressly authorizes the member or candidate to disclose information, however, the member or candidate may follow the terms of the authorization and provide the information.

**Compliance with Laws**

- As a general matter, members and candidates must comply with applicable law. If applicable law requires disclosure of client information in certain circumstances, members and candidates must comply with the law. Similarly, if applicable law requires members and candidates to maintain confidentiality, even if the information concerns illegal activities on the part of the client, members and candidates must not disclose such information.
- When in doubt, members and candidates should consult with their employer's compliance personnel or legal counsel before disclosing confidential information about clients.

**Electronic Information and Security**

- Standard III(E) does not require members or candidates to become experts in information security technology, but they should have a thorough understanding of the policies of their employer.
- Members and candidates should encourage their firm to conduct regular periodic training on confidentiality procedures for all firm personnel, including portfolio associates, receptionists, and other non-investment staff who have routine direct contact with clients and their records.

**Professional Conduct Investigations by CFA Institute**

- The requirements of Standard III(E) are not intended to prevent members and candidates from cooperating with an investigation by the CFA Institute Professional Conduct Program (PCP). When permissible under applicable law, members and candidates shall consider the PCP an extension of themselves when requested to provide information about a client in support of a PCP investigation into their own conduct.

**Recommended Procedures for Compliance**

The simplest, most conservative, and most effective way to comply with Standard III(E) is to avoid disclosing any information received from a client except to authorized fellow employees who are also working for the client. In some instances, however, a member or candidate may want to disclose information received from clients that is outside the scope of the confidential relationship and does not involve illegal activities. Before making such a disclosure, a member or candidate should ask the following:

- In what context was the information disclosed? If disclosed in a discussion of work being performed for the client, is the information relevant to the work?
- Is the information background material that, if disclosed, will enable the member or candidate to improve service to the client?

**Communicating with Clients**

- Members and candidates should make reasonable efforts to ensure that firm-supported communication methods and compliance procedures follow practices designed for preventing accidental distribution of confidential information.
- Members and candidates should be diligent in discussing with clients the appropriate methods for providing confidential information. It is important to convey to clients that not all firm-sponsored resources may be appropriate for such communications.

## Standard IV(A) Loyalty

**The Standard**

In matters related to their employment, members and candidates must act for the benefit of their employer and not deprive their employer of the advantage of their skills and abilities, divulge confidential information, or otherwise cause harm to their employer.

**Guidance**

- Members and candidates should protect the interests of their firm by refraining from any conduct that would injure the firm, deprive it of profit, or deprive it of the member's or candidate's skills and ability.
- Members and candidates must always place the interests of clients above the interests of their employer but should also consider the effects of their conduct on the sustainability and integrity of the employer firm.
- In matters related to their employment, members and candidates must comply with the policies and procedures established by their employers that govern the employer-employee relationship—to the extent that such policies and procedures do not conflict with applicable laws, rules, or regulations or the Code and Standards.
- The standard does not require members and candidates to subordinate important personal and family obligations to their work.

**Employer Responsibilities**

- Employers must recognize the duties and responsibilities that they owe to their employees if they expect to have content and productive employees.
- Members and candidates are encouraged to provide their employer with a copy of the Code and Standards.
- Employers are not obligated to adhere to the Code and Standards. In expecting to retain competent employees who are members and candidates, however, they should not develop conflicting policies and procedures.

**Independent Practice**

- Members and candidates must abstain from independent competitive activity that could conflict with the interests of their employer.
- Members and candidates who plan to engage in independent practice for compensation must notify their employer and describe the types of services they will render to prospective independent clients, the expected duration of the services, and the compensation for the services.
- Members and candidates should not render services until they receive consent from their employer to all of the terms of the arrangement.
    - "Practice" means any service that the employer currently makes available for remuneration.
    - "Undertaking independent practice" means engaging in competitive business, as opposed to making preparations to begin such practice.

**Leaving an Employer**

- When members and candidates are planning to leave their current employer, they must continue to act in the employer's best interest. They must not engage in any activities that would conflict with this duty until their resignation becomes effective.
- Activities that might constitute a violation, especially in combination, include the following:
    - Misappropriation of trade secrets.
    - Misuse of confidential information.
    - Solicitation of the employer's clients prior to cessation of employment.
    - Self-dealing (appropriating for one's own property a business opportunity or information belonging to one's employer).
    - Misappropriation of clients or client lists.
- A departing employee is generally free to make arrangements or preparations to go into a competitive business before terminating the relationship with his or her employer as long as such preparations do not breach the employee's duty of loyalty.
- A member or candidate who is contemplating seeking other employment must not contact existing clients or potential clients prior to leaving his or her employer for purposes of soliciting their business for the new employer. Once notice is provided to the employer of the intent to resign, the member or candidate must follow the employer's policies and procedures related to notifying clients of his or her planned departure. In addition, the member or candidate must not take records or files to a new employer without the written permission of the previous employer.
- Once an employee has left the firm, the skills and experience that an employee obtained while employed are not "confidential" or "privileged" information. Similarly, simple knowledge of the names and existence of former clients is generally not confidential information unless deemed such by an agreement or by law.
- Standard IV(A) does not prohibit experience or knowledge gained at one employer from being used at another employer. Firm records or work performed on behalf of the firm that is stored in paper copy or electronically for the member's or candidate's convenience while employed, however, should be erased or returned to the employer unless the firm gives permission to keep those records after employment ends.
- The standard does not prohibit former employees from contacting clients of their previous firm as long as the contact information does not come from the records of the former employer or violate an applicable "non-compete agreement." Members and candidates are free to use public information after departing to contact former clients without violating Standard IV(A) as long as there is no specific agreement not to do so.

**Use of Social Media**

- Members and candidates should understand and abide by all applicable firm policies and regulations as to the acceptable use of social media platforms to interact with clients and prospective clients.
- Specific accounts and user profiles of members and candidates may be created for solely professional reasons, including firm-approved accounts for client engagements. Such firm-approved business-related accounts would be considered part of the firm's assets, thus requiring members and candidates to transfer or delete the accounts as directed by their firm's policies and procedures.
- Best practice for members and candidates is to maintain separate accounts for their personal and professional social media activities. Members and candidates should discuss with their employers how profiles should be treated when a single account includes personal connections and also is used to conduct aspects of their professional activities.

### Whistleblowing

Sometimes, circumstances may arise (e.g., when an employer is engaged in illegal or unethical activity) in which members and candidates must act contrary to their employer's interests in order to comply with their duties to the market and clients. In such instances, activities that would normally violate a member's or candidate's duty to his or her employer (such as contradicting employer instructions, violating certain policies and procedures, or preserving a record by copying employer records) may be justified. However, such action would be permitted only if the intent is clearly aimed at protecting clients or the integrity of the market, not for personal gain.

### Nature of Employment

- Members and candidates must determine whether they are employees or independent contractors in order to determine the applicability of Standard IV(A). This issue will be decided largely by the degree of control exercised by the employing entity over the member or candidate. Factors determining control include whether the member's or candidate's hours, work location, and other parameters of the job are set; whether facilities are provided to the member or candidate; whether the member's or candidate's expenses are reimbursed; whether the member or candidate seeks work from other employers; and the number of clients or employers the member or candidate works for.
- A member's or candidate's duties within an independent contractor relationship are governed by the oral or written agreement between the member and the client. Members and candidates should take care to define clearly the scope of their responsibilities and the expectations of each client within the context of each relationship. Once a member or candidate establishes a relationship with a client, the member or candidate has a duty to abide by the terms of the agreement.

## Recommended Procedures for Compliance

### Competition Policy

- A member or candidate must understand any restrictions placed by the employer on offering similar services outside the firm while employed by the firm.
- If a member's or candidate's employer elects to have its employees sign a non-compete agreement as part of the employment agreement, the member or candidate should ensure that the details are clear and fully explained prior to signing the agreement.

### Termination Policy

- Members and candidates should clearly understand the termination policies of their employer. Termination policies should:
    - Establish clear procedures regarding the resignation process, including addressing how the termination will be disclosed to clients and staff and whether updates posted through social media platforms will be allowed.
    - Outline the procedures for transferring ongoing research and account management responsibilities.
    - Address agreements that allow departing employees to remove specific client-related information upon resignation.

**Incident-Reporting Procedures**

- Members and candidates should be aware of their firm's policies related to whistleblowing and encourage their firm to adopt industry best practices in this area.

**Employee Classification**

- Members and candidates should understand their status within their employer firm.

## Standard IV(B) Additional Compensation Arrangements

**The Standard**

Members and candidates must not accept gifts, benefits, compensation, or consideration that competes with or might reasonably be expected to create a conflict of interest with their employer's interest unless they obtain written consent from all parties involved.

**Guidance**

- Members and candidates must obtain permission from their employer before accepting compensation or other benefits from third parties for the services rendered to the employer or for any services that might create a conflict with their employer's interest.
  - Compensation and benefits include direct compensation by the client and any indirect compensation or other benefits received from third parties.
  - "Written consent" includes any form of communication that can be documented (for example, communication via e-mail that can be retrieved and documented).

**Recommended Procedures for Compliance**

- Members and candidates should make an immediate written report to their supervisor and compliance officer specifying any compensation they propose to receive for services in addition to the compensation or benefits received from their employer.
- The details of the report should be confirmed by the party offering the additional compensation, including performance incentives offered by clients.
- This written report should state the terms of any agreement under which a member or candidate will receive additional compensation; "terms" include the nature of the compensation, the approximate amount of compensation, and the duration of the agreement.

## Standard IV(C) Responsibilities of Supervisors

**The Standard**

Members and candidates must make reasonable efforts to ensure that anyone subject to their supervision or authority complies with applicable laws, rules, regulations, and the Code and Standards.

**Guidance**

- Members and candidates must promote actions by all employees under their supervision and authority to comply with applicable laws, rules, regulations, firm policies, and the Code and Standards.
- A member's or candidate's responsibilities under Standard IV(C) include instructing those subordinates to whom supervision is delegated about methods to promote compliance, including preventing and detecting violations of laws, rules, regulations, firm policies, and the Code and Standards.

- At a minimum, Standard IV(C) requires that members and candidates with supervisory responsibility make reasonable efforts to prevent and detect violations by ensuring the establishment of effective compliance systems. However, an effective compliance system goes beyond enacting a code of ethics, establishing policies and procedures to achieve compliance with the code and applicable law, and reviewing employee actions to determine whether they are following the rules.
- To be effective supervisors, members and candidates should implement education and training programs on a recurring or regular basis for employees under their supervision. Further, establishing incentives—monetary or otherwise—for employees not only to meet business goals but also to reward ethical behavior offers supervisors another way to assist employees in complying with their legal and ethical obligations.
- A member or candidate with supervisory responsibility should bring an inadequate compliance system to the attention of the firm's senior managers and recommend corrective action. If the member or candidate clearly cannot discharge supervisory responsibilities because of the absence of a compliance system or because of an inadequate compliance system, the member or candidate should decline in writing to accept supervisory responsibility until the firm adopts reasonable procedures to allow adequate exercise of supervisory responsibility.

**System for Supervision**

- Members and candidates with supervisory responsibility must understand what constitutes an adequate compliance system for their firms and make reasonable efforts to see that appropriate compliance procedures are established, documented, communicated to covered personnel, and followed.
    - "Adequate" procedures are those designed to meet industry standards, regulatory requirements, the requirements of the Code and Standards, and the circumstances of the firm.
    - To be effective, compliance procedures must be in place prior to the occurrence of a violation of the law or the Code and Standards.
- Once a supervisor learns that an employee has violated or may have violated the law or the Code and Standards, the supervisor must promptly initiate an assessment to determine the extent of the wrongdoing. Relying on an employee's statements about the extent of the violation or assurances that the wrongdoing will not reoccur is not enough. Reporting the misconduct up the chain of command and warning the employee to cease the activity are also not enough. Pending the outcome of the investigation, a supervisor should take steps to ensure that the violation will not be repeated, such as placing limits on the employee's activities or increasing the monitoring of the employee's activities.

**Supervision Includes Detection**

- Members and candidates with supervisory responsibility must also make reasonable efforts to detect violations of laws, rules, regulations, firm policies, and the Code and Standards. If a member or candidate has adopted reasonable procedures and taken steps to institute an effective compliance program, then the member or candidate may not be in violation of Standard IV(C) if he or she does not detect violations that occur despite these efforts. The fact that violations do occur may indicate, however, that the compliance procedures are inadequate.
- In addition, in some cases, merely enacting such procedures may not be sufficient to fulfill the duty required by Standard IV(C). A member or candidate may be in violation of Standard IV(C) if he or she knows or should know that the procedures designed to promote compliance, including detecting and preventing violations, are not being followed.

## Recommended Procedures for Compliance

### Codes of Ethics or Compliance Procedures

- Members and candidates are encouraged to recommend that their employers adopt a code of ethics, and put in place specific policies and procedures needed to ensure compliance with the codes and with securities laws and regulations
- Members and candidates should encourage their employers to provide their codes of ethics to clients.

### Adequate Compliance Procedures

Adequate compliance procedures should:

- Be contained in a clearly written and accessible manual that is tailored to the firm's operations.
- Be drafted so that the procedures are easy to understand.
- Designate a compliance officer whose authority and responsibility are clearly defined and who has the necessary resources and authority to implement the firm's compliance procedures.
- Describe the hierarchy of supervision and assign duties among supervisors.
- Implement a system of checks and balances.
- Outline the scope of the procedures.
- Outline procedures to document the monitoring and testing of compliance procedures.
- Outline permissible conduct.
- Delineate procedures for reporting violations and sanctions.

Once a compliance program is in place, a supervisor should:

- Disseminate the contents of the program to appropriate personnel.
- Periodically update procedures to ensure that the measures are adequate under the law.
- Continually educate personnel regarding the compliance procedures.
- Issue periodic reminders of the procedures to appropriate personnel.
- Incorporate a professional conduct evaluation as part of an employee's performance review.
- Review the actions of employees to ensure compliance and identify violators.
- Take the necessary steps to enforce the procedures once a violation has occurred.

Once a violation is discovered, a supervisor should:

- Respond promptly.
- Conduct a thorough investigation of the activities to determine the scope of the wrongdoing.
- Increase supervision or place appropriate limitations on the wrongdoer pending the outcome of the investigation.
- Review procedures for potential changes necessary to prevent future violations from occurring.

### Implementation of Compliance Education and Training

- Regular ethics and compliance training, in conjunction with the adoption of a code of ethics, is critical to investment firms seeking to establish a strong culture of integrity and to provide an environment in which employees routinely engage in ethical conduct in compliance with the law.

**Establish an Appropriate Incentive Structure**

- Supervisors and firms must look closely at their incentive structure to determine whether the structure encourages profits and returns at the expense of ethically appropriate conduct. Only when compensation and incentives are firmly tied to client interests and *how* outcomes are achieved, rather than *how much* is generated for the firm, will employees work to achieve a culture of integrity.

## Standard V(A) Diligence and Reasonable Basis

**The Standard**

Members and candidates must:

1. Exercise diligence, independence, and thoroughness in analyzing investments, making investment recommendations, and taking investment actions.
2. Have a reasonable and adequate basis, supported by appropriate research and investigation, for any investment analysis, recommendation, or action.

**Guidance**

- The requirements for issuing conclusions based on research will vary in relation to the member's or candidate's role in the investment decision-making process, but the member or candidate must make reasonable efforts to cover all pertinent issues when arriving at a recommendation.
- Members and candidates enhance transparency by providing or offering to provide supporting information to clients when recommending a purchase or sale or when changing a recommendation.

**Defining Diligence and Reasonable Basis**

- As with determining the suitability of an investment for the client, the necessary level of research and analysis will differ with the product, security, or service being offered. The following list provides some, but definitely not all, examples of attributes to consider while forming the basis for a recommendation:
    - Global, regional, and country macroeconomic conditions.
    - A company's operating and financial history.
    - The industry's and sector's current conditions and the stage of the business cycle.
    - A mutual fund's fee structure and management history.
    - The output and potential limitations of quantitative models.
    - The quality of the assets included in a securitization.
    - The appropriateness of selected peer-group comparisons.
- The steps taken in developing a diligent and reasonable recommendation should minimize unexpected downside events.

**Using Secondary or Third-Party Research**

- If members and candidates rely on secondary or third-party research, they must make reasonable and diligent efforts to determine whether such research is sound.
    - Secondary research is defined as research conducted by someone else in the member's or candidate's firm.
    - Third-party research is research conducted by entities outside the member's or candidate's firm, such as a brokerage firm, bank, or research firm.

- Members and candidates should make reasonable inquiries into the source and accuracy of all data used in completing their investment analysis and recommendations.
- Criteria that a member or candidate can use in forming an opinion on whether research is sound include the following:
    - Assumptions used.
    - Rigor of the analysis performed.
    - Date/timeliness of the research.
    - Evaluation of the objectivity and independence of the recommendations.
- A member or candidate may rely on others in his or her firm to determine whether secondary or third-party research is sound and use the information in good faith unless the member or candidate has reason to question its validity or the processes and procedures used by those responsible for the research.
- A member or candidate should verify that the firm has a policy about the timely and consistent review of approved research providers to ensure that the quality of the research continues to meet the necessary standards. If such a policy is not in place at the firm, the member or candidate should encourage the development and adoption of a formal review practice.

**Using Quantitatively Oriented Research**

- Members and candidates must have an understanding of the parameters used in models and quantitative research that are incorporated into their investment recommendations. Although they are not required to become experts in every technical aspect of the models, they must understand the assumptions and limitations inherent in any model and how the results were used in the decision-making process.
- Members and candidates should make reasonable efforts to test the output of investment models and other pre-programmed analytical tools they use. Such validation should occur before incorporating the process into their methods, models, or analyses.
- Although not every model can test for every factor or outcome, members and candidates should ensure that their analyses incorporate a broad range of assumptions sufficient to capture the underlying characteristics of investments. The omission from the analysis of potentially negative outcomes or of levels of risk outside the norm may misrepresent the true economic value of an investment. The possible scenarios for analysis should include factors that are likely to have a substantial influence on the investment value and may include extremely positive and negative scenarios.

**Developing Quantitatively Oriented Techniques**

- Members and candidates involved in the development and oversight of quantitatively oriented models, methods, and algorithms must understand the technical aspects of the products they provide to clients. A thorough testing of the model and resulting analysis should be completed prior to product distribution.
- In reviewing the computer models or the resulting output, members and candidates need to pay particular attention to the assumptions used in the analysis and the rigor of the analysis to ensure that the model incorporates a wide range of possible input expectations, including negative market events.

**Selecting External Advisers and Sub-Advisers**

- Members and candidates must review managers as diligently as they review individual funds and securities.
- Members and candidates who are directly involved with the use of external advisers need to ensure that their firms have standardized criteria for reviewing these selected external advisers and managers. Such criteria would include, but would not be limited to, the following:
  - Reviewing the adviser's established code of ethics,
  - Understanding the adviser's compliance and internal control procedures,
  - Assessing the quality of the published return information, and
  - Reviewing the adviser's investment process and adherence to its stated strategy.

**Group Research and Decision Making**

In some instances, a member or candidate will not agree with the view of the group. If, however, the member or candidate believes that the consensus opinion has a reasonable and adequate basis and is independent and objective, the member or candidate need not decline to be identified with the report. If the member or candidate is confident in the process, the member or candidate does not need to dissociate from the report even if it does not reflect his or her opinion.

**Recommended Procedures for Compliance**

Members and candidates should encourage their firms to consider the following policies and procedures to support the principles of Standard V(A):

- Establish a policy requiring that research reports, credit ratings, and investment recommendations have a basis that can be substantiated as reasonable and adequate.
- Develop detailed, written guidance for analysts (research, investment, or credit), supervisory analysts, and review committees that establishes the due diligence procedures for judging whether a particular recommendation has a reasonable and adequate basis.
- Develop measurable criteria for assessing the quality of research, the reasonableness and adequacy of the basis for any recommendation or rating, and the accuracy of recommendations over time.
- Develop detailed, written guidance that establishes minimum levels of scenario testing of all computer-based models used in developing, rating, and evaluating financial instruments.
- Develop measurable criteria for assessing outside providers, including the quality of information being provided, the reasonableness and adequacy of the provider's collection practices, and the accuracy of the information over time.
  - Adopt a standardized set of criteria for evaluating the adequacy of external advisers.

## Standard V(B) Communication with Clients and Prospective Clients

**The Standard**

Members and candidates must:

1. Disclose to clients and prospective clients the basic format and general principles of the investment processes they use to analyze investments, select securities, and construct portfolios, and must promptly disclose any changes that might materially affect those processes.

2. Disclose to clients and prospective clients significant limitations and risks associated with the investment process.
3. Use reasonable judgment in identifying which factors are important to their investment analyses, recommendations, or actions, and include those factors in communications with clients and prospective clients.
4. Distinguish between fact and opinion in the presentation of investment analyses and recommendations.

**Guidance**

- Members and candidates should communicate in a recommendation the factors that were instrumental in making the investment recommendation. A critical part of this requirement is to distinguish clearly between opinions and facts.
- Follow-up communication of significant changes in the risk characteristics of a security or asset strategy is required.
- Providing regular updates to any changes in the risk characteristics is recommended.

**Informing Clients of the Investment Process**

- Members and candidates must adequately describe to clients and prospective clients the manner in which they conduct the investment decision-making process. Such disclosure should address factors that have positive and negative influences on the recommendations, including significant risks and limitations of the investment process used.
- The member or candidate must keep clients and other interested parties informed on an ongoing basis about changes to the investment process, especially newly identified significant risks and limitations.
- Members and candidates should inform the clients about the specialization or diversification expertise provided by the external adviser(s).

**Different Forms of Communication**

- Members and candidates using any social media service to communicate business information must be diligent in their efforts to avoid unintended problems because these services may not be available to all clients. When providing information to clients through new technologies, members and candidates should take reasonable steps to ensure that such delivery would treat all clients fairly and, if necessary, be considered publicly disseminated.
- If recommendations are contained in capsule form (such as a recommended stock list), members and candidates should notify clients that additional information and analyses are available from the producer of the report.

**Identifying Risks and Limitations**

- Members and candidates must outline to clients and prospective clients significant risks and limitations of the analysis contained in their investment products or recommendations.
- The appropriateness of risk disclosure should be assessed on the basis of what was known at the time the investment action was taken (often called an *ex ante* basis). Members and candidates must disclose significant risks known to them at the time of the disclosure.
- Members and candidates cannot be expected to disclose risks they are unaware of at the time recommendations or investment actions are made.
- Having no knowledge of a risk or limitation that subsequently triggers a loss may reveal a deficiency in the diligence and reasonable basis of the research of the member or candidate but may not reveal a breach of Standard V(B).

ET

### Report Presentation

- A report writer who has done adequate investigation may emphasize certain areas, touch briefly on others, and omit certain aspects deemed unimportant.
- Investment advice based on quantitative research and analysis must be supported by readily available reference material and should be applied in a manner consistent with previously applied methodology. If changes in methodology are made, they should be highlighted.

### Distinction between Facts and Opinions in Reports

- Violations often occur when reports fail to separate the past from the future by not indicating that earnings estimates, changes in the outlook for dividends, or future market price information are **opinions** subject to future circumstances.
- In the case of complex quantitative analyses, members and candidates must clearly separate fact from statistical conjecture and should identify the known limitations of an analysis.
- Members and candidates should explicitly discuss with clients and prospective clients the assumptions used in the investment models and processes to generate the analysis. Caution should be used in promoting the perceived accuracy of any model or process to clients because the ultimate output is merely an estimate of future results and not a certainty.

### Recommended Procedures for Compliance

- Members and candidates should encourage their firms to have a rigorous methodology for reviewing research that is created for publication and dissemination to clients.
- To assist in the after-the-fact review of a report, the member or candidate must maintain records indicating the nature of the research and should, if asked, be able to supply additional information to the client (or any user of the report) covering factors not included in the report.

## Standard V(C) Record Retention

### The Standard

Members and candidates must develop and maintain appropriate records to support their investment analyses, recommendations, actions, and other investment-related communications with clients and prospective clients.

### Guidance

- Members and candidates must retain records that substantiate the scope of their research and reasons for their actions or conclusions. The retention requirement applies to decisions to buy or sell a security as well as reviews undertaken that do not lead to a change in position.
- Records may be maintained either in hard copy or electronic form.

### New Media Records

- Members and candidates should understand that although employers and local regulators are developing digital media retention policies, these policies may lag behind the advent of new communication channels. Such lag places greater responsibility on the individual for ensuring that all relevant information is retained. Examples of non-print media formats that should be retained include, but are not limited to e-mails, text messages, blog posts, and Twitter posts.

### Records Are Property of the Firm

- As a general matter, records created as part of a member's or candidate's professional activity on behalf of his or her employer are the property of the firm.
- When a member or candidate leaves a firm to seek other employment, the member or candidate cannot take the property of the firm, including original forms or copies of supporting records of the member's or candidate's work, to the new employer without the express consent of the previous employer.
- The member or candidate cannot use historical recommendations or research reports created at the previous firm because the supporting documentation is unavailable.
- For future use, the member or candidate must re-create the supporting records at the new firm with information gathered through public sources or directly from the covered company and not from memory or sources obtained at the previous employer.

### Local Requirements

- Local regulators and firms may also implement policies detailing the applicable time frame for retaining research and client communication records. Fulfilling such regulatory and firm requirements satisfies the requirements of Standard V(C).
- In the absence of regulatory guidance or firm policies, CFA Institute recommends maintaining records for at least seven years. If there is regulatory guidance, then the member or candidate must follow this guidance, even if the minimum number of years is less than seven.

### Recommended Procedures for Compliance

The responsibility to maintain records that support investment action generally falls with the firm rather than individuals. Members and candidates must, however, archive research notes and other documents, either electronically or in hard copy, that support their current investment-related communications.

## Standard VI(A) Disclosure of Conflicts

### The Standard

Members and candidates must make full and fair disclosure of all matters that could reasonably be expected to impair their independence and objectivity or interfere with respective duties to their clients, prospective clients, and employer. Members and candidates must ensure that such disclosures are prominent, are delivered in plain language, and communicate the relevant information effectively.

### Guidance

- Best practice is to avoid actual conflicts or the appearance of conflicts of interest when possible. Conflicts of interest often arise in the investment profession.
- When conflicts cannot be reasonably avoided, clear and complete disclosure of their existence is necessary.
- In making and updating disclosures of conflicts of interest, members and candidates should err on the side of caution to ensure that conflicts are effectively communicated.

**Disclosure of Conflicts to Employers**

- When reporting conflicts of interest to employers, members and candidates must give their employers enough information to assess the impact of the conflict.
- Members and candidates must take reasonable steps to avoid conflicts and, if they occur inadvertently, must report them promptly so that the employer and the member or candidate can resolve them as quickly and effectively as possible.
- Any potential conflict situation that could prevent clear judgment about or full commitment to the execution of a member's or candidate's duties to the employer should be reported to the member's or candidate's employer and promptly resolved.

**Disclosure to Clients**

- The most obvious conflicts of interest, which should always be disclosed, are relationships between an issuer and the member, the candidate, or his or her firm (such as a directorship or consultancy by a member; investment banking, underwriting, and financial relationships; broker/dealer market-making activities; and material beneficial ownership of stock).
- Disclosures should be made to clients regarding fee arrangements, sub-advisory agreements, or other situations involving nonstandard fee structures. Equally important is the disclosure of arrangements in which the firm benefits directly from investment recommendations. An obvious conflict of interest is the rebate of a portion of the service fee some classes of mutual funds charge to investors.

**Cross-Departmental Conflicts**

- Other circumstances can give rise to actual or potential conflicts of interest. For instance:
    - A sell-side analyst working for a broker/dealer may be encouraged, not only by members of her or his own firm but by corporate issuers themselves, to write research reports about particular companies.
    - A buy-side analyst is likely to be faced with similar conflicts as banks exercise their underwriting and security-dealing powers.
    - The marketing division may ask an analyst to recommend the stock of a certain company in order to obtain business from that company.
- Members, candidates, and their firms should attempt to resolve situations presenting potential conflicts of interest or disclose them in accordance with the principles set forth in Standard VI(A).

**Conflicts with Stock Ownership**

- The most prevalent conflict requiring disclosure under Standard VI(A) is a member's or candidate's ownership of stock in companies that he or she recommends to clients or that clients hold. Clearly, the easiest method for preventing a conflict is to prohibit members and candidates from owning any such securities, but this approach is overly burdensome and discriminates against members and candidates. Therefore:
    - Sell-side members and candidates should disclose any materially beneficial ownership interest in a security or other investment that the member or candidate is recommending.
    - Buy-side members and candidates should disclose their procedures for reporting requirements for personal transactions.

**Conflicts as a Director**

- Service as a director poses three basic conflicts of interest.
    - A conflict may exist between the duties owed to clients and the duties owed to shareholders of the company.
    - Investment personnel who serve as directors may receive the securities or options to purchase securities of the company as compensation for serving on the board, which could raise questions about trading actions that might increase the value of those securities.
    - Board service creates the opportunity to receive material nonpublic information involving the company.
- When members or candidates providing investment services also serve as directors, they should be isolated from those making investment decisions by the use of firewalls or similar restrictions.

**Recommended Procedures for Compliance**

- Members or candidates should disclose special compensation arrangements with the employer that might conflict with client interests, such as bonuses based on short-term performance criteria, commissions, incentive fees, performance fees, and referral fees.
- Members' and candidates' firms are encouraged to include information on compensation packages in firms' promotional literature.

## Standard VI(B) Priority of Transactions

**The Standard**

Investment transactions for clients and employers must have priority over investment transactions in which a member or candidate is the beneficial owner.

**Guidance**

- This standard is designed to prevent any potential conflict of interest or the appearance of a conflict of interest with respect to personal transactions.
- Client interests have priority. Client transactions must take precedence over transactions made on behalf of the member's or candidate's firm or personal transactions.

**Avoiding Potential Conflicts**

- Although conflicts of interest exist, nothing is inherently unethical about individual managers, advisers, or mutual fund employees making money from personal investments as long as (1) the client is not disadvantaged by the trade, (2) the investment professional does not benefit personally from trades undertaken for clients, and (3) the investment professional complies with applicable regulatory requirements.
- Some situations occur in which a member or candidate may need to enter a personal transaction that runs counter to current recommendations or what the portfolio manager is doing for client portfolios such as personal financial hardship. In these situations, the same three criteria given in the preceding paragraph should be applied in the transaction so as to not violate Standard VI(B).

### Personal Trading Secondary to Trading for Clients

- The objective of the standard is to prevent personal transactions from adversely affecting the interests of clients or employers. A member or candidate having the same investment positions or being co-invested with clients does not always create a conflict.
- Personal investment positions or transactions of members or candidates or their firm should never, however, adversely affect client investments.

### Standards for Nonpublic Information

- Standard VI(B) covers the activities of members and candidates who have knowledge of pending transactions that may be made on behalf of their clients or employers, who have access to nonpublic information during the normal preparation of research recommendations, or who take investment actions.
- Members and candidates are prohibited from conveying nonpublic information to any person whose relationship to the member or candidate makes the member or candidate a beneficial owner of the person's securities.
- Members and candidates must not convey this information to any other person if the nonpublic information can be deemed material.

### Impact on All Accounts with Beneficial Ownership

- Members or candidates may undertake transactions in accounts for which they are a beneficial owner only after their clients and employers have had adequate opportunity to act on a recommendation.
- Personal transactions include those made for the member's or candidate's own account, for family (including spouse, children, and other immediate family members) accounts, and for accounts in which the member or candidate has a direct or indirect pecuniary interest, such as a trust or retirement account.
- Family accounts that are client accounts should be treated like any other firm account and should neither be given special treatment nor be disadvantaged because of the family relationship. If a member or candidate has a beneficial ownership in the account, however, the member or candidate may be subject to preclearance or reporting requirements of the employer or applicable law.

### Recommended Procedures for Compliance

- Members and candidates should urge their firms to establish such policies and procedures.
- The specific provisions of each firm's standards will vary, but all firms should adopt certain basic procedures to address the conflict areas created by personal investing. These procedures include the following:
    - Limited participation in equity IPOs.
    - Restrictions on private placements.
    - Establish blackout/restricted periods.
    - Reporting requirements, including:
        - Disclosure of holdings in which the employee has a beneficial interest.
        - Providing duplicate confirmations of transactions.
        - Preclearance procedures.
- Disclosure of policies to investors.

## Standard VI(C) Referral Fees

### The Standard

Members and candidates must disclose to their employer, clients, and prospective clients, as appropriate, any compensation, consideration, or benefit received from or paid to others for the recommendation of products or services.

### Guidance

- Members and candidates must inform their employer, clients, and prospective clients of any benefit received for referrals of customers and clients.
- Members and candidates must disclose when they pay a fee or provide compensation to others who have referred prospective clients to the member or candidate.
- Appropriate disclosure means that members and candidates must advise the client or prospective client, before entry into any formal agreement for services, of any benefit given or received for the recommendation of any services provided by the member or candidate. In addition, the member or candidate must disclose the nature of the consideration or benefit.

### Recommended Procedures for Compliance

- Members and candidates should encourage their employers to develop procedures related to referral fees. The firm may completely restrict such fees. If the firm does not adopt a strict prohibition of such fees, the procedures should indicate the appropriate steps for requesting approval.
- Employers should have investment professionals provide to the clients notification of approved referral fee programs and provide the employer regular (at least quarterly) updates on the amount and nature of compensation received.

## Standard VII(A) Conduct as Participants in CFA Institute Programs

### The Standard

Members and candidates must not engage in any conduct that compromises the reputation or integrity of CFA Institute or the CFA designation or the integrity, validity, or security of CFA Institute programs.

### Guidance

- Standard VII(A) prohibits any conduct that undermines the public's confidence that the CFA charter represents a level of achievement based on merit and ethical conduct.
- Conduct covered includes but is not limited to:
  - Giving or receiving assistance (cheating) on any CFA Institute examinations,
  - Violating the rules, regulations, and testing policies of CFA Institute programs,
  - Providing confidential program or exam information to candidates or the public,
  - Disregarding or attempting to circumvent security measures established for any CFA Institute examinations,
  - Improperly using an association with CFA Institute to further personal or professional goals, and
  - Misrepresenting information on the Professional Conduct Statement or in the CFA Institute Continuing Education Program.

**Confidential Program Information**

- Examples of information that cannot be disclosed by candidates sitting for an exam include but are not limited to:
  - Specific details of questions appearing on the exam and
  - Broad topical areas and formulas tested or not tested on the exam.
- All aspects of the exam, including questions, broad topical areas, and formulas, tested or not tested, are considered confidential until such time as CFA Institute elects to release them publicly.

**Additional CFA Program Restrictions**

- Violating any of the testing policies, such as the calculator policy, personal belongings policy, or the Candidate Pledge, constitutes a violation of Standard VII(A).
- Examples of information that cannot be shared by members involved in developing, administering, or grading the exams include but are not limited to:
  - Questions appearing on the exam or under consideration.
  - Deliberation related to the exam process.
  - Information related to the scoring of questions.

**Expressing an Opinion**

- Standard VII(A) does *not* cover expressing opinions regarding CFA Institute, the CFA Program, or other CFA Institute programs.
- However, when expressing a personal opinion, a candidate is prohibited from disclosing content-specific information, including any actual exam question and the information as to subject matter covered or not covered in the exam.

## Standard VII(B) Reference to CFA Institute, the CFA Designation, and the CFA Program

**The Standard**

When referring to CFA Institute, CFA Institute membership, the CFA designation, or candidacy in the CFA Program, members and candidates must not misrepresent or exaggerate the meaning or implications of membership in CFA Institute, holding the CFA designation, or candidacy in the CFA Program.

**Guidance**

- Standard VII(B) is intended to prevent promotional efforts that make promises or guarantees that are tied to the CFA designation. Individuals may refer to their CFA designation, CFA Institute membership, or candidacy in the CFA Program but must not exaggerate the meaning or implications of membership in CFA Institute, holding the CFA designation, or candidacy in the CFA Program.
- Standard VII(B) is not intended to prohibit factual statements related to the positive benefit of earning the CFA designation. However, statements referring to CFA Institute, the CFA designation, or the CFA Program that overstate the competency of an individual or imply, either directly or indirectly, that superior performance can be expected from someone with the CFA designation are not allowed under the standard.
- Statements that highlight or emphasize the commitment of CFA Institute members, CFA charterholders, and CFA candidates to ethical and professional conduct or mention the thoroughness and rigor of the CFA Program are appropriate.
- Members and candidates may make claims about the relative merits of CFA Institute, the CFA Program, or the Code and Standards as long as those statements are implicitly or explicitly stated as the opinion of the speaker.

- Standard VII(B) applies to any form of communication, including but not limited to communications made in electronic or written form (such as on firm letterhead, business cards, professional biographies, directory listings, printed advertising, firm brochures, or personal resumes), and oral statements made to the public, clients, or prospects.

**CFA Institute Membership**

The term "CFA Institute member" refers to "regular" and "affiliate" members of CFA Institute who have met the membership requirements as defined in the CFA Institute Bylaws. Once accepted as a CFA Institute member, the member must satisfy the following requirements to maintain his or her status:

- Remit annually to CFA Institute a completed Professional Conduct Statement, which renews the commitment to abide by the requirements of the Code and Standards and the CFA Institute Professional Conduct Program.
- Pay applicable CFA Institute membership dues on an annual basis.

If a CFA Institute member fails to meet any of these requirements, the individual is no longer considered an active member. Until membership is reactivated, individuals must not present themselves to others as active members. They may state, however, that they were CFA Institute members in the past or refer to the years when their membership was active.

**Using the CFA Designation**

- Those who have earned the right to use the Chartered Financial Analyst designation may use the trademarks or registered marks "Chartered Financial Analyst" or "CFA" and are encouraged to do so but only in a manner that does not misrepresent or exaggerate the meaning or implications of the designation.
- The use of the designation may be accompanied by an accurate explanation of the requirements that have been met to earn the right to use the designation.
- "CFA charterholders" are those individuals who have earned the right to use the CFA designation granted by CFA Institute. These people have satisfied certain requirements, including completion of the CFA Program and required years of acceptable work experience. Once granted the right to use the designation, individuals must also satisfy the CFA Institute membership requirements (see above) to maintain their right to use the designation.
- If a CFA charterholder fails to meet any of the membership requirements, he or she forfeits the right to use the CFA designation. Until membership is reactivated, individuals must not present themselves to others as CFA charterholders. They may state, however, that they were charterholders in the past.
- Given the growing popularity of social media, where individuals may anonymously express their opinions, pseudonyms or online profile names created to hide a member's identity should not be tagged with the CFA designation.

**Referring to Candidacy in the CFA Program**

- Candidates in the CFA Program may refer to their participation in the CFA Program, but such references must clearly state that an individual is a *candidate* in the CFA Program and must not imply that the candidate has achieved any type of partial designation. A person is a candidate in the CFA Program if:
    - The person's application for registration in the CFA Program has been accepted by CFA Institute, as evidenced by issuance of a notice of acceptance, and the person is enrolled to sit for a specified examination; or
    - The registered person has sat for a specified examination but exam results have not yet been received.

- If an individual is registered for the CFA Program but declines to sit for an exam or otherwise does not meet the definition of a candidate as described in the CFA Institute Bylaws, then that individual is no longer considered an active candidate. Once the person is enrolled to sit for a future examination, his or her CFA candidacy resumes.
- CFA candidates must never state or imply that they have a partial designation as a result of passing one or more levels, or cite an expected completion date of any level of the CFA Program. Final award of the charter is subject to meeting the CFA Program requirements and approval by the CFA Institute Board of Governors.
- If a candidate passes each level of the exam in consecutive years and wants to state that he or she did so, that is not a violation of Standard VII(B) because it is a statement of fact. If the candidate then goes on to claim or imply superior ability by obtaining the designation in only three years, however, he or she is in violation of Standard VII(B).

**Proper and Improper References to the CFA Designation**

| Proper References | Improper References |
|---|---|
| "Completion of the CFA Program has enhanced my portfolio management skills." | "CFA charterholders achieve better performance results." |
| "John Smith passed all three CFA examinations in three consecutive years." | "John Smith is among the elite, having passed all three CFA examinations in three consecutive attempts." |
| "The CFA designation is globally recognized and attests to a charterholder's success in a rigorous and comprehensive study program in the field of investment management and research analysis." | "As a CFA charterholder, I am the most qualified to manage client investments." |
| "The credibility that the CFA designation affords and the skills the CFA Program cultivates are key assets for my future career development." | "As a CFA charterholder, Jane White provides the best value in trade execution." |
| "I enrolled in the CFA Program to obtain the highest set of credentials in the global investment management industry." | "Enrolling as a candidate in the CFA Program ensures one of becoming better at valuing debt securities." |
| "I passed Level I of the CFA exam." | "CFA, Level II" |
| "I am a 2010 Level III candidate in the CFA Program." | "CFA, Expected 2011" |
| "I passed all three levels of the CFA Program and will be eligible for the CFA charter upon completion of the required work experience." | "Level III CFA Candidate" |
| "As a CFA charterholder, I am committed to the highest ethical standards." | "CFA, Expected 2011"<br>"John Smith, Charter Pending" |

**Proper Usage of the CFA Marks**

- Upon obtaining the CFA charter from CFA Institute, charterholders are given the right to use the CFA marks, including Chartered Financial Analyst®, CFA®, and the CFA logo (a certification mark).
- The Chartered Financial Analyst and CFA marks must always be used either after a charterholder's name or as adjectives (never as nouns) in written documents or oral conversations. For example, to refer to oneself as "a CFA" or "a Chartered Financial Analyst" is improper.
- Members and candidates must not use a pseudonym or fictitious phrase meant to hide their identity in conjunction with the CFA designation. CFA Institute can verify only that a specific individual has earned the designation according to the name that is maintained in the membership database.
- The CFA logo certification mark is used by charterholders as a distinctive visual symbol of the CFA designation that can be easily recognized by employers, colleagues, and clients. As a certification mark, it must be used only to directly refer to an individual charterholder or group of charterholders.

**Correct and Incorrect Use of the Chartered Financial Analyst and CFA Marks**

| Correct | Incorrect | Principle |
|---|---|---|
| He is one of two CFA charterholders in the company. | He is one of two CFAs in the company. | The CFA and Chartered Financial Analyst designations must always be used as adjectives, never as nouns or common names. |
| He earned the right to use the Chartered Financial Analyst designation. | He is a Chartered Financial Analyst. | |
| Jane Smith, CFA | Jane Smith, C.F.A.<br>John Doe, cfa<br><br>John, a CFA-type portfolio manager. | No periods.<br><br>Always capitalize the letters<br><br>"CFA." |
| John Jones, CFA | The focus is on Chartered Financial Analysis.<br><br>CFA-equivalent program.<br>Swiss-CFA. | Do not alter the designation to create new words or phrases. |
| John Jones, Chartered Financial Analyst | Jones Chartered Financial Analysts, Inc. | The designation must not be used as part of the name of a firm. |
| Jane Smith, CFA<br>John Doe, Chartered Financial Analyst | Jane Smith, **CFA**<br>John Doe, **Chartered Financial Analyst** | The CFA designation should not be given more prominence (e.g., larger or bold font) than the charterholder's name. |

*(Table continued on next page...)*

ET

| Correct | Incorrect | Principle |
|---|---|---|
| Level I candidate in the CFA Program. | Chartered Financial Analyst (CFA), September 2011. | Candidates in the CFA Program must not cite the expected date of exam completion and award of charter. |
| Passed Level I of the CFA examination in 2010. | CFA Level I. CFA degree expected in 2011. | No designation exists for someone who has passed Level I, Level II, or Level III of the exam. The CFA designation should not be referred to as a degree. |
| I have passed all three levels of the CFA Program and may be eligible for the CFA charter upon completion of the required work experience. | CFA (Passed Finalist)<br>CFA Charter Pending<br>Pending CFA<br>Charterholder | A candidate who has passed Level III but has not yet received his or her charter cannot use the CFA or Chartered Financial Analyst designation. |
| CFA Charter, 2009, CFA Institute (optional: Charlottesville, Virginia, USA) | CFA Charter, 2009, CFA Society of the UK | In citing the designation in a resume, a charterholder should use the date that he or she received the designation and should cite CFA Institute as the conferring body. |
| John Smith, CFA | Crazy Bear CFA (Online social media user name) | Charterholders should not attach the CFA designation to anonymous or fictitious names meant to conceal their identity. |

# Study Session 2: Ethical and Professional Standards in Practice

## APPLICATION OF THE CODE AND STANDARDS
### Cross-Reference to CFA Institute Assigned Reading #3

There are two case studies at Level III, "The Consultant" and "Pearl Investment Management." In the first case, the consultant in question, Mark Vernley, CFA, a petroleum engineer, has been accused of having a conflict of interest resulting from his personal portfolio's holdings. In the second case, Peter Sherman has just completed his MBA and joins Pearl Investment Management as an account manager. Pearl is an investment firm specializing in equities. The case tracks Sherman's progress at Pearl up to the point when he eventually becomes a Level II candidate in the CFA Program.

You will not be tested in these two specific cases, so there is no need to memorize them. However, we highlight some of the main ethical findings and compliance procedures for three notable Standards of Professional Conduct.

Mark Vernley has maintained compliance with the Code and Standards; however, he has been accused of a conflict of interest. Specifically, he owns $50,000 of shares in Highridge Oil Pipeline. He recently wrote a proposal for Highridge that included a plan that has been approved by a regulatory agency. One of Highridge's competitors complained to the regulator about a conflict of interest stemming from Vernley's personal holdings. However, the regulator rejected the competitor's complaint. Vernley is upset about the perception of a conflict of interest and the reputational damage it could inflict.

Vernley has two possible courses of action with respect to conflicts of interest, either real or perceived:

1. Avoid the conflict of interest. Instead of owning shares in Highridge, Vernley could do any of the following:
   - Sell his Highridge stock and other energy-related stocks. The case mentions that this is an extreme action, especially as a divestiture could trigger tax consequences.
   - Place the Highridge shares in a "blind trust" whereby investment decisions would be made by an independent portfolio manager so that Vernley would not know the exact direction and magnitude of future Highridge stock transactions.
   - Invest in a mutual fund (or exchange-traded fund) that specializes in the energy sector.
2. Disclose the conflict, prominently and in plain English, allowing Vernley's clients to determine the materiality of a real or perceived conflict of interest.

An adequate compliance statement might read like this: "All employees must disclose at least on a quarterly basis all security transactions for their own personal accounts and those accounts in which they maintain a beneficial ownership."

> Trade allocation is discussed in Standard III(B), Fair Dealing. However, this is the first time that we learn how to properly correct managers' errors related to client accounts. Expect to be tested on this one particular point. It is very important.

There are multiple violations at Pearl Investment Management, and the most notable is the misallocation of initial public offering (IPO) shares in two clients' accounts.

Assume that the firm has two clients: Client A and Client B. Client A's account is suitable for IPO shares, but Client B's account is not suitable for the same stock. The firm mistakenly allocates the IPO shares to Client B's account. After the passage of time, the error is discovered.

Here are the steps necessary to correct the error:

1. The trades are reallocated at the IPO price, not the price prevailing when the error is detected. So, Client A receives the shares at the IPO price and Client B receives the cash that was used originally to purchase the shares.
2. Because Client B should not have purchased the IPO shares in the first place, Client B should also be credited with short-term interest related to the cash holding. In the case study, interest from Client A's account (who received the shares) was used to cover for the error. This is unethical. Instead, the firm itself should have paid the short-term interest to Client B's account.

An adequate compliance procedure might read like this: "When trade allocation errors are discovered, clients' portfolios will be restored with no loss of value to the client. The firm will cover the loss of short-term credit interest to accounts for which trades have been reversed."

Finally, Standard IV(C) is noteworthy. Specifically, watch for supervisors who fail to supervise because their firm's employee handbook contains a compliance manual that is monitored by a compliance department. Even in the presence of a compliance department, a supervisor must supervise his or her subordinates to ensure that the compliance procedures are adequate and are being followed.

# ASSET MANAGER CODE OF PROFESSIONAL CONDUCT

Cross-Reference to CFA Institute Assigned Reading #4

This reading is the third part of Ethics and Professional Standards at Level III (the two others being the Code and Standards and case studies). As this reading is specific to Level III, it is highly likely to be tested as a separate item set. The Asset Manager Code of Professional Conduct (AM Code) applies to investment firms that actually manage money. Spend time mastering the AM Code as it could be one of the easiest item sets in the afternoon session. Many of the components of the AM Code have been adopted from the Standards of Professional Conduct that individual CFA charterholders and candidates must adhere to, so you will be familiar with a lot of details already.

Unlike GIPS, don't worry about the difference between required and recommended standards because AM Code is intentionally broadly written to make it easy for firms of all sizes to adapt it. On the exam, expect the questions to read: "Is the action consistent with both the required and recommended standards?"

The AM Code is a firm-wide set of voluntary professional standards that are aimed at investment firms around the world who manage money for clients. Adoption of the AM Code allows investors and potential clients to find managers who are ethically sound.

As ethical leadership begins at the top of any company, it is recommended that AM Code be adopted by senior management and the board of directors.

There are four main points to consider before discussing the main standards:

1. There is no partial claim of compliance. If the firm does not follow all parts of the AM Code, then the firm cannot claim partial compliance.
2. A compliant firm must use an exactly worded statement consisting of two sentences whenever it claims compliance: "[Insert name of firm] claims compliance with the CFA Institute Asset Manager Code of Professional Conduct. This claim has not been verified by CFA Institute."
3. Firms must notify CFA Institute that they are claiming compliance. This is done for information purposes only.
4. Like the GIPS standards, CFA Institute does not enforce the quality control of a firm's claim of compliance with the AM Code. CFA Institute does not verify the manager's claim of compliance.

## GENERAL PRINCIPLES OF CONDUCT

The Asset Manager Code of Professional Conduct mandates the following with respect to a firm's clients:

1. Act in a professional and ethical manner at all times.
2. Act for the benefit of clients.
3. Act with independence and objectivity.
4. Act with skill, competence, and diligence.
5. Communicate with clients in a timely and accurate manner.
6. Uphold the applicable rules governing capital markets.

## ASSET MANAGER CODE OF PROFESSIONAL CONDUCT

### Loyalty to Clients

Managers must:

1. Place client interests ahead of their own interests.

   The interests of the client are paramount over all other interests. Firms should develop and implement policies and procedures to detect and prevent abuses including all aspects of the Manager-client relationship (e.g., investment selection, transactions, monitoring, and custody). The firm's compensation arrangement should align the financial interests of clients and Managers to eliminate incentives that could result in conflicts of interest.
2. Preserve the confidentiality of information communicated by clients within the scope of the Manager-client relationship.

   Managers should draft a privacy policy that addresses the collection, retention, protection, and dissemination of confidential client information. The policy should be written with specific mention of anti-money-laundering procedures and implemented to prevent the firm from being implicated in criminal activity. The duty to maintain confidentiality does not imply that the Manager should not report suspected illegal activities to authorities.
3. Refuse to participate in any business relationship or accept any gift that could reasonably be expected to affect their independence, objectivity, or loyalty to clients.

   Managers must establish policies and procedures for accepting and reporting gifts, including entertainment. Firms should create specific limits for accepting gifts and prohibit the acceptance of any cash gifts. Managers may maintain multiple business relationships with a client as long as they manage and disclose any potential conflicts of interest.

> Be sure to note the prohibition against the acceptance of cash gifts. This is more stringent than the main Code and Standards of Professional Conduct.

### Investment Process and Actions

Managers must:

1. Use reasonable care and prudent judgment when managing client assets.

   Managers must exhibit the same level of care, skill, and diligence that a trained professional acting in the same capacity would use in managing the client's assets. Prudence requires managing assets that balances risk and return while acting in a prudent and judicious manner in avoiding harm to clients.
2. Not engage in practices designed to distort prices or artificially inflate trading volume.

   Market manipulation is illegal, erodes investor confidence, and disrupts efficient functioning of financial markets. Managers should refrain from practices that distort market prices and/or trading volumes to give an illusion of activity. Information-based manipulation including spreading false rumors with the intent to motivate trading by others in such a way that benefits the firm or its clients is also prohibited by this standard.
3. Deal fairly and objectively with all clients when providing investment information, making investment recommendations, or taking investment action.

   Preferential treatment should not be granted to certain clients at the expense of others. Violation of this standard would include communicating recommendations to favored clients to the detriment of other clients or allocating over-subscribed offerings at the exclusion of some clients. Firms are not prohibited from offering varied levels of

> Sidecar investments are not explained in the official curriculum. On the exam, it would be in the context of private equity. Specifically, a sidecar allows the general partner (GP) to raise more money beyond what is committed by the limited partners (LPs) without having to undertake a formal fundraising round. Considering who will participate in the sidecar, the GP must choose fairly from the LPs (who would be considered clients).

service, but the qualification for such services must be disclosed and made available to all. Secondary investment opportunities such as "side-letter," "sidecar," or "tag-along" deals with certain clients is permissible as long as they are fairly allocated among those clients that meet the suitability criteria.

4. Have a reasonable and adequate basis for investment decisions.

   Investment action should only be taken after the Manager has conducted thorough research and established a reasonable basis for a decision. Managers may employ third-party research as long as they perform appropriate due diligence to ensure that the source is reliable and has a reasonable basis for its conclusions. Managers should thoroughly understand complex strategies and communicate these in a way that their clients can understand.

5. When managing a portfolio or pooled fund according to a specific mandate, strategy, or style:
   a. Take only investment actions that are consistent with the stated objectives and constraints of that portfolio or fund.

      Managers should not deviate from their specified mandate or strategies, especially in the case of pooled funds for which the Managers do not know the specific financial situation of each client in the fund. Clients must be able to evaluate the suitability of the investment funds or strategies for themselves and trust that Managers will not diverge from the stated or agreed-on mandates or strategies.
   b. Provide adequate disclosures and information so investors can consider whether any proposed changes in the investment style or strategy meet their investment needs.

      Managers must disclose to clients when a change in style is proposed, proposing enough time for clients to react to the change. If a client then wishes to redeem his shares, the Manager should not penalize him for doing so and ought to waive any redemption charges, if any.

6. When managing separate accounts and before providing investment advice or taking investment action on behalf of the client:
   a. Evaluate and understand the client's investment objectives, tolerance for risk, time horizon, liquidity needs, financial constraints, any unique circumstances (including tax considerations, legal or regulatory constraints, etc.) and any other relevant information that would affect investment policy.
   b. Determine that an investment is suitable to a client's financial situation.Managers must make an effort to understand the client's investment requirements and develop an investment policy statement (IPS) prior to taking any investment actions for clients. Managers should review the IPS with the client at least annually or when changes necessitate the need and discuss risk tolerances (both the ability and willingness of the client to bear risk), return objectives, time horizon, liquidity requirements, liabilities, tax considerations, and any legal, regulatory, or other unique circumstances. The IPS should be used to assess the suitability of investment opportunities in the context of the investor's entire portfolio.

## Trading

Managers must:

1. Not act or cause others to act on material nonpublic information that could affect the value of a publicly traded investment.

   Managers must adopt compliance procedures that prohibit trading on material nonpublic information. When in possession of nonpublic information, Managers must take appropriate steps to keep such information confidential. This provision is not meant to prevent Managers from using the mosaic theory to draw conclusions—that is, combine pieces of material public information with pieces of immaterial nonpublic information to draw actionable conclusions.

2. Give priority to investments made on behalf of the client over those that benefit the Manager's interests.

   Managers must not trade ahead of clients or take advantage of information or recommendations before clients have had a chance to act first. Arrangements are permissible in pooled funds where Managers put their own capital at risk alongside that of their clients so long as clients are not disadvantaged. Managers should develop reporting procedures that require employees to disclose personal holding, provide trade confirmations for personal investment transactions, and submit preclearance requests prior to making personal trades.
3. Use commissions generated from client trades to pay for only investment-related products or services that directly assist the Manager in its investment decision-making process, and not in the management of the firm.

   Managers should use client brokerage for the client's benefit, including "soft dollars," and disclose methods or policies followed when such brokerage is used. Soft dollars must only be used to benefit clients by aiding the Manager in making investment decisions on their behalf.
4. Maximize client portfolio value by seeking best execution for all client transactions.

   Managers have the obligation to seek best execution (lowest cost/highest value) for all trades made on behalf of clients. Some clients may request that the Manager place trades through a specific broker to obtain research from that broker, known as "client-directed" brokerage. In such cases, the client must be informed that he might not be getting the best execution and the client is required to provide written acknowledgment to the Manager that best execution might not be achieved.
5. Establish policies to ensure fair and equitable trade allocation among client accounts.

   When taking investment actions, Managers must treat clients fairly. This includes access to oversubscribed issues and IPOs, which must be allocated fairly (pro rata in round-lots) among interested clients for whom such investments are suitable. Managers should disclose written allocation procedures on how initial public offerings and private placements will be handled.

### Risk Management, Compliance, and Support

Managers must:

1. Develop and maintain policies and procedures to ensure that their activities comply with the provisions of this Code and all applicable legal and regulatory requirements.

   Firms should document applicable laws, rules, and regulations in a written compliance manual to ensure that Managers meet their legal requirements when managing client assets. Firms should also develop or adopt a written code of ethics and disseminate written procedures for reporting violations.
2. Appoint a compliance officer responsible for administering the policies and procedures and for investigating complaints regarding the conduct of the Manager or its personnel.

   The Manager should designate a competent compliance officer and establish a clear chain of command for reporting, investigating, and enforcing compliance issues. Managers may designate an existing employee or hire a separate individual who is independent from the investment personnel and reports directly to the CEO or board of directors.

3. Ensure that portfolio information provided to clients by the Manager is accurate and complete and arrange for independent third-party confirmation or review of such information. Managers should undertake independent third-party verification of information through regular audits. Not only does such verification improve client trust, it can help Managers recognize and prevent potential problems.
4. Maintain records for an appropriate period of time in an easily accessible format.

   Managers must maintain records that support their investment recommendations and actions on behalf of clients. Managers should also maintain records that substantiate their compliance with the Code, related policies and procedures, and any violations that occur. Records may be maintained either in hard copy or electronic form, but must be easily accessible by clients. Managers must determine the appropriate minimum time frame for keeping records. **In the absence of regulatory or firm policies**, this period must be a minimum of seven years.

This standard is exactly the same as the Code and Standards of Professional Conduct. Be careful on the exam; this can be tricky. Note that if other requirements apply, then those will apply, even if they state a shorter period of time than seven years. Use seven years ONLY when there is no local regulatory or company-specific guidance.

5. Employ qualified staff and sufficient human and technological resources to thoroughly investigate, analyze, implement, and monitor investment decisions and actions.

   Managers must ensure that client assets are invested, administered, and protected by a qualified and honest staff. Managers must employ adequate resources to effectively analyze and implement investment strategies. Managers must have adequate resources to monitor such portfolio holdings and strategies. This provision is not meant to prohibit outsourcing where appropriate.
6. Establish a business-continuity plan to address disaster recovery or periodic disruptions of the financial markets.

   A basic business-continuity plan should consider:
   - Data maintenance (backup), preferably off-site, for all required client information.
   - Systems for analyzing, trading, and monitoring investments if primary systems fail.
   - Communication protocols with critical vendors and suppliers.
   - Employee communication protocols and coverage of critical operations.
   - Client communication protocols in the event of extended outages.
   - Periodic testing of contingency plans should be conducted on a firm-wide basis.
7. Establish a **firm-wide** risk management process that identifies, measures, and manages the risk position of the Manager and its investments, including the sources, nature, and degree of risk exposure.

   Managers face market risk, credit risk, liquidity risk, counterparty risk, concentration risk, and various types of operational risk. These risks should be analyzed as part of a comprehensive risk management process for portfolios, investment strategies, and the firm. Managers should perform stress tests, scenario tests, and backtests as part of developing risk models that comprehensively capture the full range of their actual and contingent risk exposures. The goal of such models is to determine how various changes in market and investment conditions could affect investments and be explained to clients.

## Performance and Valuation

Managers must:

1. Present performance information that is fair, accurate, relevant, timely, and complete. Managers must not misrepresent the performance of individual portfolios or of their firm.

Managers must not misrepresent their track record, especially by using historical performance that they did not personally achieve or by selectively picking periods of superior performance. Managers must clearly identify hypothetical or modeled results. Managers should provide as much additional information as is feasible to clarify performance results.

2. Use fair-market prices to value client holdings and apply, in good faith, methods to determine the fair value of any securities for which no independent, third-party market quotation is readily available.

   Pooled funds with independent members on the board of directors should give such members the responsibility to review end of period valuations. If pooled funds have no independent members, they should delegate the valuation review to an independent third party. Managers should use widely accepted valuation methods, consistently applied, to value portfolio holdings.

### Disclosures

Managers must:

1. Communicate with clients on an ongoing and timely basis. Managers must select appropriate methods of communicating with clients so that they can evaluate their financial status.
2. Ensure that disclosures are truthful, accurate, complete, and understandable and are presented in a format that communicates the information effectively. Managers must ensure that they do not misrepresent information in any way. Managers must make disclosures in plain language that effectively communicate with clients and prospects. Managers must determine the manner, frequency, and circumstances of disclosures.
3. Include any material facts when making disclosures or providing information to clients regarding themselves, their personnel, investments, or the investment process.

   Managers must provide full and complete information, defined as information that reasonable investors would want to know when making the investment decision or choosing whether to continue using the Manager.
4. Disclose the following:
   a. Conflicts of interests generated by any relationships with brokers or other entities, other client accounts, fee structures, or other matters.

      Managers should avoid all conflicts, if possible. Where they cannot be avoided, Managers must disclose conflicts in enough detail so that clients can make reasonable judgments about the Manager's objectivity.
   b. Regulatory or disciplinary action taken against the Manager or its personnel related to professional conduct.

      Managers must disclose situations in which firm personnel have been disciplined for violating standards related to integrity, ethics, or competence.
   c. The investment process, including information regarding lock-up periods, strategies, risk factors, and use of derivatives and leverage.

      Managers must disclose how investment decisions are made and implemented, including identification and discussion of the relevant risk factors.
   d. Management fees and other investment costs charged to investors, including what costs are included in the fees and the methodologies for determining fees and costs.

      Return information provided to clients should include both before and after-fee returns, as well as any unusual expenses. Managers must clearly explain, in plain language, the methodology of determining all costs charged to investors and when they apply. All fees charged to clients should be listed retrospectively and broken down in a meaningful way (commissions, management fee, incentive fee, and so forth) so that clients can determine how much, and for what, they have actually been charged. Prospective clients should be provided with an estimate of the fees they would be expected to incur.

e. The amount of any soft or bundled commissions, the goods and/or services received in return, and how those goods and/or services benefit the client.

   Client commissions used in soft dollar arrangements must be disclosed. Disclosures must describe the amount of commissions spent, the products or services received, and how the client benefited.

f. The performance of clients' investments on a regular and timely basis.

   Managers must provide regular, ongoing performance reporting. Such reporting should occur at least quarterly and, when possible, within 30 days after the end of the quarter.

g. Valuation methods used to make investment decisions and value client holdings.

   Managers should disclose the valuation methods used to determine account balances by asset class (market close, internal models, third-party valuations, and so forth). Such disclosures should be specific and communicated in a way that clients can understand.

h. Shareholder voting policies.

   Managers who exercise voting authority must exercise it in an informed and responsible manner for the benefit of the client. Managers must disclose such policies and procedures to clients. Proxy voting policies should specify guidelines for instituting regular review for material issues, methods of reviewing them, guidance about additional actions required when votes are against management, and a system to delegate share-voting responsibilities. Clients should be able to obtain information from the Manager about how their shares were voted.

i. Trade allocation policies.

   Managers must disclose how trades are allocated and the priority a client can expect to receive in the allocation process. Managers must disclose any changes in this trading policy.

j. Results of the review or audit of the fund or account.

   Managers must disclose audit results to clients if the fund or account has been subject to an audit.

k. Significant personnel or organizational changes that have occurred at the Manager level.

   Managers should make clients aware of any significant managerial changes in a timely manner. These might include staff changes or merger and acquisition activities of the Manager.

l. Risk management processes.

   Managers must disclose their risk management processes, any material changes, and specific risk information to each client. Relevant risk metrics at the individual product/portfolio level should also be provided.

# STUDY SESSION 3: BEHAVIORAL FINANCE

BF

# THE BEHAVIORAL FINANCE PERSPECTIVE
Cross-Reference to CFA Institute Assigned Reading #5

## Traditional Finance Perspective

### Utility-Maximizing Decision Making

*Utility* describes satisfaction from consuming a good or service. Because no direct measurement of satisfaction can be made, economists usually consider the satisfaction of one choice against other choices.

*Utility theory* recognizes choices people make as a rational judgment between *expected* levels of satisfaction.

BF

Rational judgment involves the ability to:

1. Assign a probability to potential outcomes.
2. Use Bayesian inference to update outcome probabilities based on new information (i.e., conditioned probabilities).
3. Decide a course of action expected to maximize utility (i.e., rational decision making).

Rational decision making involves adhering to the premises (i.e., axioms) of utility theory:

- *Completeness.* There are well-defined preferences over the set of all known choices (i.e., between A and B, A and C, and B and C) and an ability to choose between them.
- *Transitivity.* There is internal consistency of decisions (i.e., if prefer A to B, and B to C, then will prefer A to C).
- *Independence.* Preference order persists with addition of a lesser choice to two existing choices; allows additivity of utility (i.e., given completeness and transitivity, still prefer A to B if C is added in the same amount to both).
- *Continuity.* An unbroken utility curve describes equal utility derived from different combinations of two goods.

IMPORTANT: Different people will have different utilities and assign different probabilities for each potential outcome, so they are unlikely to all reach the same asset price conclusion.

Rational economic man (REM) will then determine the highest utility curve (i.e., furthest from the origin) within a budget constraint.

This gives rise to the idea that security prices contain all available information; that is, each price represents the present value sum of expected future outcomes.

BF

### Risk Aversion

*Risk aversion* describes a rational decision maker's reluctance to equate probability-weighted expected utility $E(U_x)$ with a *known* utility $U_x$.

A utility *risk premium* must be offered to a risk-averse investor, with $E(U_x) - U_x$ sufficient to offset the aversion. Other risk preferences:

> IMPORTANT: Don't confuse marginal utility curves (i.e., representing utility for one good) with indifference curves (i.e., representing trade-off preference of one good for another good). However, the diminishing utility of each good gives shape to the curve representing indifference between the two.

- Risk neutral: $E(U_x) - U_x = 0$ (i.e., indifference between the expected value and the actual value)
- Risk seeking: $E(U_x) - U_x > 0$ (i.e., prefers to invest in uncertain alternatives; likes gambling)

### Diminishing Marginal Utility

*Marginal utility* is the additional utility from each additional unit of consumption.

*Diminishing marginal utility* describes how consuming more and more of the same thing yields less and less additional satisfaction in a *concave* marginal utility curve.

Risk-averse investors exhibit diminishing marginal utility for increases in wealth. Risk-neutral investors have straight-line utility curves, whereas risk-seeking investors have convex (bowl-shaped) curves.

## Behavioral Finance Perspectives

> IMPORTANT: If investors are not completely rational, then markets are not always efficient as envisioned in neoclassical economics.

*Behavioral finance* recognizes that psychological variables distort rational decision-making processes assumed for neoclassical economics (i.e., traditional finance).

### Prospect Theory

*Prospect theory* relaxes the traditional risk-aversion assumption and makes assumptions consistent with *expected* utility theory.

Prospect theory assigns value (i.e., utility) to *changes* in wealth rather than *levels* of wealth, and replaces probability with decision weights. The value function is concave for gains implying risk aversion, and convex for losses implying risk seeking. Decision weights are less than probabilities.

The concave value function in the *domain of gains* recognizes the risk-averse preference for a smaller certain gain to a slightly larger potential gain. The convex value function in the *domain of losses* recognizes the risk-seeking preference for a slightly larger potential loss to a certain loss.

Prospect theory identifies two phases:

1. Framing/editing: Decision maker decides on heuristics and uses them to rank alternatives:
   - Framing—presenting the choice or options
   - Editing—narrowing options based on constraints and identifying appropriate options for further study

2. Evaluation/choice: Decision maker forms expected value for each choice as the sum of probability-weighted values for expected outcomes.

Editing simplifies the choice by reformulating and organizing available options using two sets of operations:

1. Operations for each prospect separately:
    - Codification—Perceive outcomes as gains and losses relative to a reference point rather than final states of wealth.
    - Combination—Sum probabilities associated with identical gains or losses.
    - Segregation—Separate the probability of an event not happening from the probability of it happening.
2. Operations applied to two or more prospects:
    - Cancellation—Common outcomes between choices are discarded; the remainder are compared.
    - Simplification—Round the probability for each outcome.
    - Detection of dominance—Discard less likely outcomes without further examination.

IMPORTANT: Using these heuristics can result in inconsistent choices depending on how the alternative prospects are framed.



IMPORTANT: Prospect theory hypothesizes that people are loss averse rather than risk averse; that is, they will have different attitudes toward risk depending on their reference point (a gain or a loss).

## Neuro-Economics

*Neuro-economics* seeks to describe behavioral decision making in terms of neural events (i.e., blood flow and chemical levels in different parts of the brain). Traditional finance makes simplifying assumptions about the effects of these events.

Scientists have found that dopamine levels rise in expectation of reward as well as receipt of a reward, whereas failed expectations result in low serotonin levels that create impulsiveness, irritability, anxiety, and depression.

Euphoric effects of high dopamine levels could explain overconfidence and risk-taking behavior. Depressive effects of low serotonin levels could explain fear of loss, failure to make needed changes, and use of high-risk, low-probability strategies to escape losses.

The amygdala (part of the inner brain) may be responsible for market panics rather than rational responses to falling prices.

Traditional economists dispute whether neuro-economic theories adequately describe economic reality.

Traditional finance focuses on how decisions *should be* made; behavioral finance focuses on how decisions *are* made.

## Cognitive Limitations

Even with computers, people suffer from intellectual, informational, computational, and financial limitations, which they attempt to circumvent:

- *Bounded rationality*. Acting rationally within bounds around decision making:
    - *Parameters*—Deciding how much will be done to aggregate relevant information and reach decisions.
    - *Heuristics*—Rules of thumb to make analysis less burdensome.

- *Satisficing* (satisfy + suffice). Finding adequate rather than optimal solutions:
  - *Adequate solution*—Resolves the situation while meeting the needs of the decision maker.
  - *Optimal solution*—Maximizes utility available from a decision.

Satisficing often occurs as the result of time and cost limitations.

IMPORTANT: Bounded rationality applies to a decision maker who acts rationally, but within a bounded set of goals.

BF

- Means-end analysis: Move toward the goal in stages rather than looking for alternative methods.
- Divide and conquer: Break the problem into subproblems and create solutions for subproblems rather than solving the holistic problem.
- Focus on the situation without regard for the surrounding economic and political environment; limiting alternatives makes this easier.

### Summary of Effects

IMPORTANT: People are *risk averse* when there is a moderate to high probability of gains with a low probability of losses, but are *risk seeking* when there is a high probability of losses versus a low probability of gains.

- Underweight moderate- and high-probability outcomes (i.e., moderate gains or losses); overweight low-probability outcomes (i.e., extreme gains or losses).
- Risk seeking (i.e., convex value function) below a wealth reference point; risk averse (i.e., concave value function) above a wealth reference point.
- The value function is steeper for losses than for gains (i.e., avoiding loss is more important than achieving gains).

## Portfolio Construction

### Traditional Perspective

The traditional perspective assumes that professional managers can determine from mean-variance efficient portfolios the single portfolio most suitable based on investment objectives, risk tolerance obtained via a questionnaire, and an investor's constraints or other circumstances.

Behavioral models suggest investors and managers do not have perfect information or react perfectly to that information.

No behavioral model has gained acceptance sufficient to replace the traditional perspective.

### Consumption and Savings

People classify wealth into current income, currently owned assets, and the present value of future income; replaces life cycle approach, which says people spend and save money to achieve a short-term and long-term spending and saving plan.

IMPORTANT: Investors will undersave for future income based on full consumption of current income and much if not all of their current assets.

- Mental accounting: Although wealth is fungible, people look at it as coming from different sources.
- Framing: People use the source of the wealth as a basis for decisions about how to spend or save; current income has high marginal propensity to consume, while any income saved becomes current assets or future income.
- Self-control: Long-term sources are unavailable for current spending.

## Asset Pricing

In traditional finance, present value involves a discount factor that includes real required return (assumed to be equal across investors), objectively determined risk premiums, and an inflation premium.

*Behavioral stochastic discount factor–based (SDF-based)* asset pricing models include an additional premium for sentiment in required return.

- Bullish: Overestimate expected growth; underestimate volatility with great confidence. Sentiment risk decreases required return.
- Bearish: Underestimate expected growth; overestimate volatility with little confidence. Sentiment risk increases required return.

> IMPORTANT: Positive sentiment is a negative risk premium.



The standard deviation of analyst forecasts serves as a sentiment risk measure; widely dispersed forecasts indicate lower analyst enthusiasm about expected security performance.

Value stocks have greater dispersion of analyst earnings estimates. To compensate the sentiment risk, expected earnings are valued using higher required return. Lower valuation results in lower price-earnings (P/E) ratios.

Sophisticated investors can systematically exploit systematic investor sentiment errors but cannot systematically exploit random errors.

## Portfolio Theory

Traditional approaches use mean-variance analysis and consider covariance in establishing an optimal diversified portfolio on the efficient frontier.

*Behavioral portfolio theory (BPT)* acknowledges five differences in risk aversion in the domain of gains versus risk seeking in the domain of losses:

1. Given equal priority, upside goals receive more funding than minimizing potential losses.
2. Strategic asset allocation depends on the goal assigned to the funding layer; allocation for higher goals includes riskier assets.
3. Lower risk tolerance in the domain of gains results in a greater number of securities there; concavity of utility curve indicates faster satiation of specific security.
4. A perceived information advantage for a security results in overallocation to that security.
5. Loss aversion creates a need for greater cash balances to meet funding needs without liquidating loss positions, and may result in a greater number of potential losing positions.

> IMPORTANT: A BPT portfolio uses bonds (insurance policy) to fund critical goals in the domain of gains, and uses risky securities (lottery ticket) to fund aspirational goals in the domain of losses.

## Adaptive Markets

The *adaptive markets hypothesis (AMH)* holds that market participants must adapt to competition for scarce resources to survive. The AMH updates the *efficient market hypothesis (EMH)* for bounded rationality, satisficing, and evolutionary principles.

Biases toward continuing previously successful behavior rather than adapting as competition shifts are explained by use of heuristics (i.e., rules of thumb) learned to become successful.

Implications:

- The most important goal is survival.
- Market participants must adapt or die.
- Changes in the competitive market and risk preferences cause risk premiums to change over time.
- Successfully exploiting pricing anomalies can yield excess return.
- Any strategy will have periods of higher return and lower return.

# INDIVIDUAL BEHAVIORAL BIASES

Cross-Reference to CFA Institute Assigned Reading #6

## Categories of Behavioral Bias

The major categories of individual behavioral bias are:

- Behavioral finance micro (BFMI): Individual investor (i.e., biases):
  - *Cognitive errors* (conscious)—Faulty analysis process resulting from memory, information processing, or statistical errors (e.g., using rules of thumb).
  - *Emotional biases* (unconscious)—Faulty reasoning resulting from feelings and impulses.
- Behavioral finance macro (BFMA): Market behavior (e.g., anomalies)

IMPORTANT: Investors can identify the sources of and therefore overcome cognitive errors more easily than emotional biases.

BF

Cognitive errors involve faulty reasoning; emotional biases result from pleasure seeking or pain avoidance.

Emotions include perceptions, beliefs, or feelings that arise spontaneously as a mental state without conscious effort. Emotions may be real or imagined, and individuals experiencing them may only be able to work around them rather than control them.

In some cases, market participants make cognitive errors that justify their emotional biases.

## Cognitive Errors

Cognitive errors occur when investors fail to gather appropriate information, consider it carefully, and update probabilities.

### Belief Persistence Biases

A *belief persistence bias* involves cognitive errors that reject contradictory new information:

- Selective exposure: Notice only information of interest.
- Selective perception: Ignore or modify contradictory information.
- Selective retention: Remember and consider only confirming information.

*Conservatism bias* results when financial market participants (FMPs) overweight initial observations or information and then fail to adequately update perceptions when new information arises.

This bias is related to the amount of effort involved in information acquisition, data processing, and updating existing projections (i.e., cognitive costs).

FMPs should consider new information and react decisively when a new conclusion arises.

*Confirmation bias* results when people only notice belief-confirming information, or disregard or fail to properly weight contradictory information.

FMPs may ignore negative information once they have decided, or may develop screening criteria that bolster positive information about the investment. In the process, good investments may be screened out.

Concentrated positions often result, especially if the investor's own company is involved.

FMPs should attempt to overcome confirmation bias by actively seeking opinions contradictory to their own. Investment ideas should be confirmed via third-party research before confirming the opinion via purchases.

*Representativeness bias* involves classifying new information based on meaning derived from past information, even if it doesn't fit:



- *Base-rate neglect* ignores the probability that new information matches existing information used for classification.
- *Sample-size neglect* uses isolated cases or small sample sizes to represent the general case.

FMPs may continue to apply existing methods of using information in classifying investment opportunities, or make investments based on small bits of information. Investors will fire their investment manager when supposed results don't occur, or sell a security when they cannot properly classify new information.

FMPs can avoid representativeness bias by proper asset allocation, making changes only when adequate information to support a change has developed, and using longer-term performance data.

To avoid representativeness bias, investors should ask whether an investment belongs to group A or is statistically more likely to belong to group B.

*Illusion of control bias* occurs when people believe they have more control or influence than they actually have.

Suffering from illusion of control bias leads to overconcentration in portfolio positions and frequent trading that increases costs and drives down returns compared to buy-and-hold strategies.

Detection of illusion of control bias requires understanding the complexity of capital markets with little prospect for control. Success depends on systematic factors (e.g., economic growth, market sentiment, etc.) rather than any investor skill.

FMPs should seek contrary opinions. Investors can remind themselves of their own fallibility by keeping transaction records, including the rationale for any trade.

*Hindsight bias* involves remembering only information that reinforces existing beliefs. This stems from a viewpoint that results in the past were inevitable rather than risky at the time. In part, this follows from filling in memory gaps with preferential information.

Suffering from hindsight bias leads to a false sense of confidence, and can lead investors to believe money manager performance should have been better than it was.

FMPs should keep transaction records, including the rationale for any trade. They should remind themselves that managers should invest according to their strategy and that this will result in ups and downs over time. Educating investors and measuring managers against benchmarks can help toward this end.

### Information-Processing Biases

This category of cognitive biases results from irrational information use.

*Anchoring and adjustment bias* involves people developing an initial estimate (the anchor) and subsequently adjusting that estimate up or down.

Consequences of this bias are that people weight the anchor too heavily and then make insufficient adjustments that bias the final estimate regardless of the new information's importance.

Overcoming this bias involves discovery of whether the investor is sticking to the original anchor for legitimate reasons.

Investors should be advised that past prices contain little information about the future expectations for their investments.

*Mental accounting bias* occurs when people treat money differently depending on its source or expected use. Although money is inherently fungible (i.e., each currency unit is interchangeable with other units), people segregate these pools of funds from other uses, with some pools believed more important to protect than others.

IMPORTANT: Investors may engage in offsetting positions (i.e., buying and selling the same security) as well as concentrated positions that move together with high correlation.

Consequences of mental accounting bias include failing to consider correlation of returns among various pools. This can result in inefficient diversification. People also use income from investments rather than reinvesting it, thus eroding principal.

Effective education about the drawbacks of engaging in this behavior can help overcome mental accounting bias. Combining all their assets can surprise investors about how much they have and what they can accomplish by allocating across all the pools. Using total return rather than pool-focused returns will also help them understand how wealth can grow while maintaining moderate income withdrawals.

*Framing bias* occurs when people decide differently based on how the decision maker views the risks and returns of the choice as well as how the choice is formulated. This involves risk seeking in the domain of losses versus risk aversion in the domain of gains.

*Narrow framing* results when people decide a subset of the big picture such as return potential without due consideration of the risks.

Consequences of framing bias include identifying the same opportunity differently depending on whether it is stated in the domain of losses (e.g., probability of not achieving goal is 25%) or is the complementary statement in the domain of gains (e.g., probability of achieving goal is 75%).

Investors may also choose suboptimal investments depending on how they are framed, even with properly identified risk tolerances.

IMPORTANT: Investors should always focus on expected risks and returns rather than past performance.

Excessive trading may also occur with short-term price fluctuations.

Investors should try to be neutral when analyzing investments (i.e., without loss or gain framing). This bias can be mitigated by determining whether a riskier investment was selected in the domain of losses rather than the domain of gains.

*Availability bias* uses shortcuts (i.e., heuristics) to investment outcomes based on how readily information comes to mind.



- Retrievability: The first thing to be recalled is considered the most likely.
- Categorization: Searches take place within perceived relevant sets of information.
- Narrow range of experience: More weight is attached to experiential observation.
- Resonance: People project their preferences onto others, and believe there is a higher probability of believing/liking what they do.

Consequences include being overly swayed by advertising, or restricting investments to familiar categories (e.g., domestic equities). Failure to diversify may result from retrievability and categorization, and will tend to cause inadequate diversification. Improper asset allocation can result from investments or companies that don't resonate.

Detection should focus on determining whether the investment selection results from what FMPs have heard recently or what they like, or whether it results from a disciplined approach—that is, a long-term focus, a proper strategic asset allocation, and thorough research and analysis of investment options.

Investors can also keep in mind the ultimate outcome of asset bubbles when other investors are caught up in a new bubble.

IMPORTANT: The *disposition effect* describes how people will dispose of winners quickly, which limits upside potential, but will hold losing positions in hopes of avoiding losses on a position, which increases position risk.

## Emotional Biases

Fewer *emotional biases* have been identified, but they are harder to control for than cognitive errors because people are often invested in their feelings more than in cognitive processes. Individuals will often become defensive when faced with their own emotional biases.

### Loss Aversion Bias

*Loss aversion* results from the declining marginal utility of wealth. People strongly prefer avoiding losses to scoring gains, and people will incur additional risk to avoid losses.

IMPORTANT: The *house-money effect* describes investors with gains—especially unexpected gains—in an investment as believing that money to be different from other money, and engaging in more risk-seeking behavior with it.

FMPs suffering from loss aversion bias may also trade excessively when selling winners, which results in higher costs and lower returns.

Loss aversion bias combines with framing bias to attract those in loss positions to attempt recoupment.

*Myopic loss aversion* is a special case in which people tend to use bonds for long-term funding (rather than a properly diversified portfolio) in the domain of gains, and use equities with an outsized risk profile for short-term gains in the domain of losses. Over time, this results in unjustifiably high equity risk premiums.

IMPORTANT: A long-term investor will be more likely to accept portfolio risk than a short-term investor, so investments should be reviewed regularly but infrequently.

Loss aversion bias can be mitigated by a disciplined approach; it is impossible to completely eliminate the pain of an investment loss.



### Overconfidence Bias

*Overconfidence bias* results when people overestimate their analytical abilities and judgment, as well as the usefulness of information they possess. Although showing aspects of both cognitive and emotional biases, it is included as an emotional bias because it is difficult to get people to revise self-perceptions:

- *Prediction overconfidence.* Assigning unrealistically narrow confidence intervals to predictions, resulting in poorly diversified portfolios.
- *Certainty overconfidence.* Assigning unrealistically high probabilities to outcomes for which the investor is responsible, often resulting in excessive trading when investments fail to meet return predictions.

Overconfidence becomes intensified when combined with *self-attribution bias*, which is related to investor self-esteem:

- Self-enhancing—claiming responsibility for success
- Self-protecting—denial of responsibility of failure

FMPs with overconfidence bias:

- Underestimate risks and returns.
- Hold concentrated portfolio positions.
- Engage in excessive trading.
- Underperform the market.

To detect and mitigate overconfidence, traders should review trading records, understand the reasons for winners and losers, and calculate portfolio performance over at least a two-year period. This process disciplines the FMP against too much risk and excessive trading.

### Self-Control Bias

*Self-control bias* results when people fail to act in their long-term interests and instead succumb to short-term satisfaction. This outcome may result from *hyperbolic discounting* in which people prefer smaller payoffs now to larger future payoffs.

Self-control bias can result in undersaving for the future. FMPs then attempt to make up the shortfall by accepting too much portfolio risk, which puts the asset base in jeopardy.

When combined with mental accounting, FMPs will overallocate to bonds for income. This further stretches the portfolios' ability to meet long-term goals due to lack of reinvested earnings as well as lack of capital appreciation. Risk-seeking FMPs are likely to invest in risky equity securities to make up the difference.

FMPs should integrate a written personal budget and investment plan.

## Status Quo Bias

> IMPORTANT: FMPs with concentrated holdings in company stock should examine how they would fare if a simultaneous force reduction and falling share price occurred.

BF

*Status quo bias* occurs when people prefer to do nothing rather than make a change (i.e., they maintain the status quo). While regret-aversion bias and endowment bias involve a reason not to change (although it may be emotional rather than rational), status quo bias requires no conscious decision. Try not to confuse the status quo bias (do nothing) with conservatism (slow to update new information).

FMPs with status quo bias—especially when paired with regret-aversion bias and endowment bias—will maintain inappropriate risk profiles and fail to explore outcome-improving alternatives.

Detection and mitigation involve educating FMPs on risk-reducing and return-enhancing diversification.

## Endowment Bias

*Endowment bias* occurs when FMPs value an asset in their possession more than if they were to buy it. This contrasts with rational economic man (REM), who would purchase a good for the same price at which he sells it.

> IMPORTANT: Emotional attachment that threatens financial goals must be moderated rather than accepted and worked around. Advisors should learn emotional intelligence to deal with such issues.

The "endowment" of special importance to a security or an investment may result from inheritance from a loved one or simply from making the effort to buy it. On occasion, people cite disloyalty as the reason for not wishing to sell at an appropriate price.

FMPs suffering from endowment bias will continue to maintain an inadvisable asset allocation, refusing to diversify and preferring not to make changes (i.e., elements of status quo bias).

Detection and mitigation of endowment bias might include asking investors what they would invest in if they received the same amount of cash rather than the investment. It may be appropriate to ask the former owner's intention for the investment.

It may be appropriate to ease into a new investment before cashing out the endowed investment and risking investor disaffection.

## Regret-Aversion Bias

*Regret-aversion bias* occurs when people avoid making decisions for fear they will be unsuccessful. While similar to status quo bias, regret aversion differs in that there is a reason (i.e., regret) they prefer not to decide rather than simply a lack of initiative as with status quo bias.

> IMPORTANT: Fear of regret may cause herding action, where people sell or purchase securities with the market to avoid regretting a decision that runs counter to prevailing opinion.

Regret aversion can cause FMPs to hold losing positions for fear they might rebound after the sale, or to exit and remain out of a market in which they just lost money when the prudent action would be to remain invested:

- Errors of commission—actions people take
- Errors of omission—actions people could have taken but did not

Consequences involve underperforming portfolios of low-risk securities and failing to reach investment goals. Well-known or popular companies are chosen rather than those equally likely to succeed.

FMPs can detect and mitigate the effects of regret-aversion bias by understanding diversification benefits. Advisors should illustrate how everyone makes mistakes and why bubbles can be as bad as downturns.

### Asset Allocation and Investment Policy

Behavioral portfolio theory employs goals-based investing in which an optimized portfolio considers each goal separately as a layer of the composite asset structure. Risk management for the portfolio considers the probability and likelihood of losses.

IMPORTANT: Where traditional theory suggests people are risk averse, behavioral portfolio theory suggests they are loss averse.



This approach helps investors understand the appropriate level of risk for their goals, as well as satisfying loss aversion preferences.

In this approach, the base of the investments pyramid assigns low-risk investments to the client's obligations and needs. Moderate-risk investments fund priorities and desires, while higher-risk or speculative investments fund aspirational goals.

IMPORTANT: A behavioral portfolio may not be efficient from a mean-variance optimization standpoint because each layer has been optimized separately, but will be easily understood and followed by investors.

#### Behaviorally Modified Asset Allocation

Rational portfolio allocation involves selecting from efficient portfolios that optimize risk and return identified via questionnaire and goal setting.

*Behaviorally modified asset allocation* distinguishes between cognitive biases and emotional biases to determine which preferences can be modified and which must be followed, and establishes a portfolio based on a modified asset allocation the investor will follow.

IMPORTANT: Moderating a bias involves recognizing the bias and attempting to either eliminate or reduce the impact of the bias.

Two considerations determine whether an advisor should adapt to or moderate client biases:

1. Level of wealth: Greater wealth compared with needs allows greater adaptation because only high-impact events jeopardize the client's standard of living (i.e., standard of living risk [SLR]).
2. Type of behavioral bias:
   - Moderate cognitive biases with a high SLR.
   - Adapt to emotional biases with a low SLR.

As much as +/–10% adaptation will be required for the high-SLR emotional bias situations, while low-SLR cognitive bias adjustments will be closer to +/–2%.

IMPORTANT: A blended recommendation of moderating and adapting becomes appropriate when clients exhibit low-SLR emotional bias situations or high-SLR cognitive bias situations.

# BEHAVIORAL FINANCE AND INVESTMENT PROCESSES
Cross-Reference to CFA Institute Assigned Reading #7

## Classification by Investor Type

### Uses and Limitations

Investor types are a heuristic that is useful for establishing the type and degree of behavioral adjustments that should be made in client interactions and portfolio construction.

Limitations include:

BF

- Investors don't approach different aspects of their lives with equal confidence or care.
- Bottom-up approaches in which the advisor tests for all potential biases may be too time-consuming for some advisors.
- Quantitative measures work better to moderate cognitive biases (i.e., middle of the active–passive scale).
- The same individual may exhibit both cognitive errors and emotional biases.
- The same individual may exhibit multiple investor-type characteristics.
- Aging results in behavioral changes.
- Individuals act irrationally and unpredictably.

IMPORTANT: All categorization schemes exhibit the limitation that investor changes may invalidate advisor-selected types.

## Behavioral Advisor–Client Relations

### Successful Relationship Characteristics

IMPORTANT: A behavioral finance approach helps clients and advisors build stronger bonds, which are important in maintaining a long-term relationship.

- Advisor understands client goals, constraints, and behavioral characteristics, and integrates these into the investment policy statement (IPS).
- Advisor has a consistent, systematic approach with the client.
- Advisor effectively communicates progress toward goals.
- Advisor and client both benefit.

### Limitations of Risk Questionnaires

Risk tolerance appears to change with question framing.

IMPORTANT: Risk tolerance questionnaires may fail to properly assess emotional biases.

Questionnaires supply information for only broad risk tolerance parameters; other assessment tools are helpful.

Risk tolerance is a cognitive process for institutional investors but an emotional process for individual investors.

## Behavioral Portfolio Construction

Behavioral biases influence how investors use securities in constructing portfolios.

### Inertia and Default

Even with no transaction charges, most investors decide not to change an asset allocation (i.e., status quo bias).

Some plans now offer target date funds that become more conservative as investors approach retirement. However, such plans may be unable to adapt to individual situations.

### Naive Diversification and Framing

*Naive diversification* describes asset allocation that exhibits cognitive errors resulting from framing or using simple heuristics (i.e., rules of thumb).



For example, with simple heuristics investors may allocate equally to a stock and a balanced fund (i.e., $1/n$ diversification), although the balanced fund also includes equities.

With framing different funds as different choices (rather than asset classes to choose from), the same investor may allocate equally across many funds where equity funds predominate and equally across many funds in another case where bond funds predominate, resulting in dramatically different allocations to equities and to bonds in the two cases.

### Company Stock Investment

Plan participants overallocate funds to shares of their company's stock. This could be due to financial incentives, but it also occurs in the absence of incentives. Other explanations:

- Employees have familiarity with the company and overconfidence in its stock.
- Employees expect that future returns will be like those in the past.
- Framing and status quo effects: Employees look at the company's matching contributions of stock as investment advice and allocate more of their own money to company stock.
- Loyalty effects: Employees believe they are helping the company.

### Overconfidence

Overconfidence results in excessive trading, as investors believe they have superior outlooks on the market or security.

Overconfident investors have not only higher trading costs, but higher opportunity costs for sold assets (i.e., *disposition effect*).

### Home Bias

Although information costs can result in investor preference for their own country's assets, other explanations include status quo, availability, confirmation, endowment, and illusion of control biases.

### Mental Accounting

Traditional asset allocation considers the entirety of the investor's assets in an allocation designed to optimize return for the expressed risk tolerance, taking into consideration the asset class covariances.

Behavioral asset allocation considers each goal as a separate layer of a pyramid, with an asset allocation appropriate for the risk tolerance associated to each goal. Low-risk investments fund obligations and needs on the pyramid bottom (i.e., most important), moderate-risk investments fund priorities and desires, and higher-risk and speculative investments fund aspirational goals at the top of the pyramid.



## Analyst Forecasts

### Biases in Research

> IMPORTANT: Look for the term "however" to indicate a potential contrary data point or opinion, and the term "moreover" to indicate a potential confirming data point or opinion.

Too much structured information can lead to *representativeness bias* in which available data matches analyst expectations. Adequate data is important to successful forecasts, but may exceed what is necessary.

A *story* explains evidence with a fitting scenario. Analysts who use a story to fit extraneous evidence and then reach a conclusion may be showing representativeness bias.

Analysts who reach a conclusion and then accept or seek only supporting evidence engage in *confirmation bias*. Research should include contrary opinions.

In the *conjunction fallacy*, analysts use probabilities additively rather than in conjunction as a method of supporting their conclusions.

Analysts engage in the *gambler's fallacy* when they overweight probability of mean reversion, and the *hot hand fallacy* when they overweight the probability of continued similar returns rather than some reversion.

Studies suggest that analysts estimate the values of growth companies using too little risk and estimate the values of value companies using too much risk. The continued trajectory of each may be representativeness bias combined with confirmation bias.

Analysts can guard against anchoring and adjustment bias by carefully evaluating previous forecasts, but constructing a base scenario for a new forecast that uses the current environment. Systematically collecting and evaluating information, including contrary data or opinion, can help avoid emotional biases as well as cognitive biases.

> IMPORTANT: Analysts should gather all relevant information before reaching a conclusion, and ensure that information is assessed relative to the current environment.

Assigning probabilities can help avoid assuming absolutely likely or totally unlikely scenarios. Updating scenarios using a Bayesian conditioning process will speed the process and maintain structure, while enforcing review of previous work to assess its validity.

### Biases in Management-Supplied Information

*Anchoring and adjustment bias* describes the process of putting undue weight on a starting value (i.e., the anchor) and adjusting the forecast for new data based on the starting value rather than a new objective value. The management of an analysis target that frames the business as successful can create an anchor position for the analyst against which further results and achievements merely provide an adjustment.

*Overconfidence bias* and *illusion of control bias* may influence company management's optimism. *Self-attribution bias* to attract management incentives may create an expression of responsibility for success, and work together with other biases to underestimate the probability of failure.

IMPORTANT: Analysts guard against management influence by maintaining a systematic approach.

Pro forma and other reframing situations usually result in better outcomes than actual results. Analysts should view these reframing situations for possible anchoring concerns.

## Biases in Forecasting



Analysts are subject to behavioral biases, and in some cases their expertise and an *illusion of knowledge bias* combine to create *overconfidence bias*. The illusion of knowledge bias may arise from having a great deal of data, although adding more information doesn't increase forecast accuracy. Instead, it can simply increase confidence.

*Representativeness* bias occurs when available data matches the forecast. *Availability bias* involves giving more weight to readily available information. These two biases reinforce each other and provide a basis for overconfidence.

The *illusion of control bias* can make people believe there is less forecast risk, even though having more and representative information will not remove forecast risk. Using complex models can reinforce the illusion of control bias, although more complex models may be less robust (i.e., have lower forecasting accuracy) outside the narrow range of the forecast.

Confidence increases still further with *self-attribution bias*—that is, analysts believing they cause success and only others are responsible for failure. Skewed forecasts (i.e., nonsymmetrical confidence intervals) and misdirected performance incentives may be signs of self-attribution bias.

Analysts can be especially overconfident when holding a contrarian viewpoint.

*Hindsight bias* further feeds the *illusion of control bias* and *overconfidence bias* by allowing analysts to misremember actual situations or remember only positive outcomes (i.e., selective recall) in further ego enhancement.

Including additional data that cannot be analyzed in the same way as other data may increase overconfidence via the *illusion of knowledge bias*, but will add little accuracy. Ensuring a large enough sample size using comparable data will reduce inaccuracy and unjustified confidence.

Analysts can avoid or compensate for overconfidence via accurate, timely, and well-structured feedback (i.e., based on analytical review of the base assumptions versus actual results).

Peer and supervisor review help to properly attribute success and failure. Rewards for accuracy are also important.

IMPORTANT: Including at least one valid counterargument will better calibrate confidence.

Analyst conclusions should be as straightforward and specific as possible to avoid *hindsight bias*. If the forecast can be objectively reviewed via the data, assumptions, and model, the analyst has less opportunity to impose a subjective viewpoint attributing success.

### Investment Committee Decision Biases

Applying many sets of skills to a research report or asset allocation decision can result in superior outcomes. Individual biases, however, can creep into committee decisions. *Social proof bias* results when analysts accept the judgment of others rather than using it as another decision point.

People often support a leader's position, regardless of whether it results in success, or moderate their own positions to better fit with the committee consensus.

BF

IMPORTANT: Diverse viewpoints can be protected if the chairperson obtains opinions in advance of the committee meeting.

Feedback for past committee decisions is slow and inaccurate. Good work becomes more likely when:

- Diverse member cultures, experiences, and skills are present (i.e., less prone to *social proof bias*).
- The committee's environment encourages dissent.
- Members have adhered to an agenda.
- They have reached a clear decision.

### Market Behavioral Biases

The *efficient market hypothesis (EMH)* describes markets in which participants cannot earn excess returns after fees and expenses (i.e., small excess returns before fees and expenses may be obtainable).

IMPORTANT: Publishing an anomaly will typically cause arbitrage that removes the anomaly.

A market *anomaly* describes persistent excess returns with predictable direction. However, persistent excess returns may also indicate shortcomings in the underlying asset pricing model:

- Rational behavior not captured by the model (e.g., investor response to taxes)
- Reward for excess risk not perceived for the model

#### Momentum Effects

*Momentum* describes correlation between past and future price behavior when it should be random. Upward momentum lasts for about two years; return to trend takes between two and five years.

*Herding* behavior involves trading on the same side of a trade as other investors to capture private information, or acting as other investors do when their own private information would tell them otherwise. Herding reflects cognitive dissonance or regret avoidance when designed to reassure and comfort investors.

*Anchoring* on the purchase price and a belief that risk has increased (although an increase in fundamental values may also be indicated) explain willingness to sell. *Availability bias* (i.e., recency effect) causes investors to believe a trend should continue because it has continued.

*Hindsight bias* causes investors to believe they should have known a trend would continue, and may buy into a heavily appreciated security simply to avoid regret at not owning it. This creates a *trend-chasing effect*.

Reversion to the mean may take longer than the original trend, as those who purchased the security want to avoid regret (*disposition effect* of loss aversion) and hold on to it with the hope it will go back up (*gambler's fallacy*).

IMPORTANT: Market trending patterns result from emotional biases and belief in mean reversion.

## Bubbles and Crashes

*Asset bubbles* occur when an asset class price index trades more than two standard deviations above or below the long-term trend. Traditional finance theory indicates that bubbles should not occur more than 5% of the time, but occur 10% of the time for some asset classes in some markets.

*Crashes* involve a price collapse of 30% or more over several months.

IMPORTANT: It is not a behavioral bias if rational investors hold a position during an asset bubble if they are unsure of when the market will break.



During bubbles, investors may exhibit the following biases:

- Overconfidence: An investor rejects contradictory information, underestimates risks, overtrades, and fails to diversify.
- Self-attribution bias: Even if an FMP sells positions too soon, profits lead to self-attribution.
- Confirmation bias: Selling for a gain tends to confirm decisions for an original purchase and reinforce self-attribution bias.
- Hindsight bias: An investor misremembers justifications for an investment to better attribute personal success.

*Noise trading* involves trading on irrelevant information rather than new relevant information. Part of the overconfidence bias results from an *illusion of knowledge bias* created through market noise (i.e., unjustified price increases, high trading volume, etc.).

*Anchoring* occurs when FMPs fail to sufficiently update beliefs and instead engage in self-attribution bias to rationalize losses and flawed decisions as someone else's fault and any continued gains as personal success.

The *disposition effect* encourages FMPs to hold on to losing positions.

## Value and Growth

*Value stocks* include companies with low P/E ratios, low ratios of price to cash flow (P/CF), low ratios of price to dividends (P/D), and high ratios of equity book value to market value (BV/MV). Growth stocks are the opposite.

Value stocks have outperformed growth stocks; small-cap stocks have outperformed large-cap stocks.

Fama and French believe book-market ratios and size effects could be rational given expectation of greater risk exposure, less ability to weather economic downtrends, and so on.

IMPORTANT: Writing put options can reflect the additional return required to compensate investors for excess risk perceived in nongrowth equities.

Other studies recognize mispricing:

- Halo effect: Good growth record may overshadow pricing risk.
- Overconfidence: Growth rates are predicted with more confidence than is justified.
- Home bias: Attraction of a stock is influenced by personal experience.

# Study Session 4: Private Wealth Management (1)

PWM

# MANAGING INDIVIDUAL INVESTOR PORTFOLIOS
Cross-Reference to CFA Institute Assigned Reading #8

## Investment Policy Statement

### Return Calculation

When you read through the exam question relating to the investment policy statement (IPS) for the individual investor, you will see that there are two possible investment goals for the portfolio:

1. The investor wishes to **maintain the real value of the portfolio**. For calculation purposes, this means that the present value (PV) of the asset base is equal to the future value (FV) of the asset base. In this situation, you will *not* be given an investment horizon (N).

   The required real after-tax rate of return is simply:

   | Annual after-tax withdrawal from the portfolio / Asset base |
   |---|

   The asset base excludes the value of the family home.

   To convert the after-tax withdrawal to a pre-tax withdrawal:

   | Pre-tax withdrawal = After-tax withdrawal / (1 – Tax rate on withdrawals) |
   |---|

   | Nominal pre-tax return = Real pre-tax return + Inflation rate |
   |---|

   | Nominal after-tax return = Real after-tax return + Inflation rate |
   |---|

2. The investor wishes to **grow the portfolio**. For calculation purposes, this means that the present value (PV) of the asset base is equal to the future value (FV) of the asset base. In this situation, you *will* be given an investment horizon (N).

   To find the required rate of return, you will need to populate the time value of money (TMV) worksheet:

   **PV:** The present value of the asset base entered with a minus sign
   **FV:** The projected future value that the investor would like to have, entered with a positive sign
   **N:** Investment horizon
   **PMT:** If the investor is saving, enter using a minus sign; if the investor is withdrawing from the portfolio, use a plus sign in front of the payment.

   **Compute for I / Y**
   The **PMT** is given in either pre-tax or after-tax terms. Convert the after-tax PMT to a pre-tax PMT using the same calculation (as earlier) where the investor wishes to maintain the real value of the portfolio. If **FV** is expressed in real terms, then add the given inflation rate to the computed I/Y.

PWM

### Ability to Take Risk

You will most likely be asked to categorize an investor as having above- or below-average ability to take risk based on facts presented to you in the question. Generally, the more flexibility that a client has, the greater the ability to take risk.

| Above-Average Ability | Below-Average Ability |
|---|---|
| Long time horizon. | Typically, investment advisors don't tend to see clients with short time horizons. |
| Client is in good health. | Client is in poor health. |
| Client lives in a country with free health care, or employer provides health insurance during retirement. | Client lives in a country without free health care, or the employer does not provide health insurance during retirement. |
| No financial dependents (children or parents). | Financial dependents (children or parents). |
| Large asset base compared with financial needs. | Small asset base compared with financial needs. |
| Other income source during retirement. | No other income source during retirement. |
| Ability to return to work after retirement. | No ability or intention to return to work after retirement. |
| Is debt-free. | Has debts. |
| Owns family home. | Does not own family home. |

PWM

### Willingness to Take Risk

You will most likely be asked to categorize an investor as having above- or below-average willingness to take risk based on facts presented to you in the question. Willingness is based the psychological profile of the investor.

| Above-Average Willingness | Below-Average Willingness |
|---|---|
| Stated preference for being comfortable with market volatility. | Stated preference for being in control of investments. |
| Asset base consists of high-risk equities. | Asset base consists of low-duration bonds or cash. |
| Client is self-employed or an entrepreneur. | Client is a salaried employee. |
| Client is not influenced by previous investment experience. | Unpleasant previous investment experience prevents client from making a similar investment. |
| Wants to retire earlier in life. | Wants to retire later in life. |

### Risk Tolerance

Risk tolerance is the combination of ability to take risk and willingness to take risk. When ability and willingness accord with each other, then the tolerance will reflect this. For example, a client with below-average ability and below-average willingness will have below-average tolerance.

If ability and willingness are not in accord with each other, it is more difficult to determine the overall tolerance. An acceptable answer might be that you would average out the above-average willingness with the below-average willingness.



### Time Horizon Constraint

There are two parts to time horizon:

1. **Length:** Most investors will have a long-term horizon, as the portfolio will be used to fund living expenses from retirement until the client's death.
2. **Stage:** This refers to a period when the client is expected to have significant changes in income or expenses. A client who is currently working can have a two-stage time horizon, consisting of the first period lasting to the retirement date and the second stage lasting from retirement until death. For a client who is already retired, this would be considered a single-stage time horizon.

### Liquidity Constraint

There are three major reasons why an investor needs to hold cash:

1. **Ongoing needs** are the difference between living expenses and income. If expenses exceed income, then the investor will need to have the difference in cash to make up the difference. For an investor whose expenses and income balance out, there is no need for cash. An investor who is saving with income in excess of expenses has no ongoing need for cash.
2. **One-time expenditures within one year** could include the need to pay off debts, such as a mortgage or credit cards. Ignore any one-time expenditures beyond one year.

3. **Emergencies:** There is no predetermined amount that a client needs to hold for emergencies. However, a client may specify an amount to be held aside as cash.

### Tax Constraint

Watch for:

1. Tax rate on withdrawals from the portfolio
2. Difference between tax rates on dividends, interest income, and capital gains
3. Holdings of low-basis stock

### Legal and Regulatory

If nothing is explicitly stated within the case, the CFA Institute Code and Standards of Professional Conduct apply, specifically Standard III (A) Clients: Loyalty, Prudence, and Care. Watch for clients who are corporate insiders and own shares in their company's stock. They will be subject to restricted periods in trading their shares.

### Unique

This constraint consists of any client-imposed restrictions, such as the desire to avoid owning shares in companies that distill alcohol, manufacture tobacco, and have reputations for polluting. The client may also wish to direct trades to a preferred broker, known as client-directed brokerage.



### Psychological Profiling

In some cases, you might need to identify an investor as having one of four investor personality types.

### Four Investor Personality Types

| | Decisions Based on Thinking | Decisions Based on Feeling |
|---|---|---|
| | **Methodical** | **Cautious** |
| More risk averse | • Relies on hard facts<br>• Follows analysts or conducts own research on trading strategies<br>• Not emotionally attached to investments because of reliance on analysis and databases | • Disciplined and conservative<br>• Strong need for security from current or past experiences<br>• Preference for low-volatility investments (principal protection)<br>• Dislikes losing small amounts<br>• Overanalyzes and misses opportunities<br>• Portfolio low turnover |
| | **Individualist** | **Spontaneous** |
| Less risk averse | • Self-assured and hardworking<br>• Considers information from various sources<br>• Takes action by him- or herself<br>• Believes that work and unique insights will be rewarded with long-term investment success | • Always adjusting portfolio holdings following the market or second-guessing self<br>• Doubtful of investment advice<br>• Highest portfolio turnover<br>• Most investors have below-average returns<br>• Quick to make decisions<br>• More concerned about missing a trend than with portfolio risk |

PWM

### Strategic Asset Allocation

You might be presented with a choice of three to five strategic portfolios, one of which will best satisfy the client's overall investment policy statement. To determine which portfolio is best, follow the four-step process of elimination:

1. **Return:** Eliminate portfolios that fail to meet the client's return objective. You might have to convert a pre-tax nominal return to an after-tax real return, so be sure that you know this formula:

$$\text{After-tax real return} = \text{Pre-tax nominal return} \times (1 - \text{Tax rate}) - \text{Inflation rate}$$

2. **Risk:** Eliminate portfolios that fail to meet the client's quantifiable risk objective. Shortfall risk is expressed as the expected return minus two standard deviations. Roy's safety-first criterion is another risk measure, which is the expected return minus the lowest acceptable return divided by the expected standard deviation; portfolios with the highest safety-first criteria are preferred.
3. **Constraints:** Eliminate portfolios that fail to meet the investor's constraints. The most quantifiable constraint is the cash holding. Eliminate portfolios that do not contain enough cash to satisfy the liquidity constraint. Be careful not to consider portfolios that contain too much cash.

4. **After eliminating based on 1 through 3, select the portfolio with the highest risk-adjusted performance.** The most common measure is the Sharpe ratio. But do this step only in the case of a tie. Do not choose the portfolio with the highest Sharpe ratio without having first eliminated portfolios based on return, risk, and constraints.

### Monte Carlo Simulation

For a client who is subject to uncertain income, expenses, and tax rates, Monte Carlo simulation might be more appropriate than a deterministic approach in which each variable is held constant. There are four key points to consider with Monte Carlo simulation:

1. Inputs should be based on forward-looking expectations, not purely historical results.
2. Asset class return expectations should be replaced with expected investment return, which is the asset class return minus investment fees.
3. Monte Carlo simulation assumes path dependency, which is important when a client is withdrawing money from the portfolio during a capital market decline.
4. Clients can estimate their expected portfolio values at any point in time, which can be helpful for a client who is concerned about longevity risk (outliving assets).

# GLOBAL TAXES AND PRIVATE WEALTH MANAGEMENT
Cross-Reference to CFA Institute Assigned Reading #9

## Tax Types

Major tax revenue sources are:

- Income:
  - Ordinary income—Salaries
  - Investment income (also known as capital income)—Interest, dividends, realized and unrealized capital gains
- Consumption:
  - Sales—Collected in one step, usually at the point of sale
  - Value added—Collected at various production stages but passed on to the ultimate consumer
- Wealth:
  - Accumulated—Taxes on real estate and other property
  - Transfers—Intergenerational and other transfers (e.g., gifts) of accumulated property

## Taxes on Income

### Common Elements

PWM

Most countries have a *progressive tax structure* (i.e., increasingly higher-percentage tax rates) applied against ordinary income bands.

| Regime | Ordinary Income | Interest Income | Dividends | Capital Gains |
|---|---|---|---|---|
| Common progressive | Progressive | Some favorable or exempt | Some favorable or exempt | Some favorable or exempt |
| Heavy interest | Progressive | Ordinary rates | Some favorable or exempt | Some favorable or exempt |
| Heavy dividend | Progressive | Some favorable or exempt | Ordinary rates | Some favorable or exempt |
| Heavy capital gain | Progressive | Some favorable or exempt | Some favorable or exempt | Ordinary rates |
| Light capital gain | Progressive | Ordinary rates | Ordinary rates | Some favorable or exempt |
| Flat and light | Flat | Some favorable or exempt | Some favorable or exempt | Some favorable or exempt |
| Flat and heavy | Flat | Some favorable or exempt | Ordinary rates | Ordinary rates |

In general, "heavy" refers to ordinary income tax rates applicable to one or more categories; "light" refers to favorable or exempt taxation on one or more categories.

*Common progressive* is most common. *Light capital gain* is second most common. *Heavy capital gain* is least common.

## After-Tax Returns and Accumulations

*Accrual taxes* are imposed annually as opposed to *deferred taxes*, which are imposed after some time.

### Accrual Taxes

A *future value* factor applied to a starting amount of capital results in the terminal value at the end of $n$ accumulation periods given return $r$ and tax rate $t$. The subscript $i$ represents a scenario for interest income or preferred equity income, which most countries tax on an accrual basis.

The future value factor for a currency unit given return on an investment periodically taxed is:

$$FV_i = [1 + r(1 - t_i)]^n$$

*Tax drag* describes the effect of the tax on final accumulation. Additional tax drag is the difference between nominal and effective tax rates.

For an accrual tax:

- Nominal tax rate is less than effective tax rate.
- The difference between nominal and effective tax rate grows as interest rate increases.
- The difference between nominal and effective tax rate grows as time horizon increases.
- The effect of higher interest rate and longer accumulation is multiplicative.

PWM

### Deferred Taxation

The future value factor when deferring taxes until the end of an investment horizon is:

$$\begin{aligned} FV_g &= (1+r)^n - [(1+r)^n - 1]t_g \\ &= (1+r)^n(1 - t_g) + t_g \end{aligned}$$

> IMPORTANT: The value of deferral over a long horizon can more than offset a higher tax rate compared to a lower accrual tax rate.

Assuming the same nominal tax rate, deferring taxes increases investment return over the horizon. The advantage of deferral grows as return and time horizon increase.

Some jurisdictions offer lower deferred tax rates for gains earned over long horizons (i.e., one year or greater as with long-term capital gains) to encourage longer-term investing.

### Deferred Capital Gain

*Capital gain* indicates the difference between market value and cost basis (i.e., purchase price). Newly invested capital has no embedded gain, but a security with market value greater than its cost basis will have an embedded capital gain. In some cases, the embedded gain is transferred from another taxpayer. A lower cost basis increases embedded gain. For $B$ equal to basis as a percentage of the market value, the future value factor is:

$$\begin{aligned} FV_{gb} &= (1+r)^n(1 + t_g) + t_g - (1 + B)t_g \\ &= (1+r)^n(1 - t_g) + t_gB \end{aligned}$$

The $t_gB$ term adds back the nontaxable basis. If basis equals market value (as with a new purchase), then $B$ equals 1 and the equation here is the same as in the deferred taxation section.

### Wealth Taxes

A *wealth tax* is levied periodically against a capital base at a lower rate than income- or gains-based taxes.

$$FV_w = [(1+r)(1+t_w)]^n$$

IMPORTANT: Wealth taxes are like returns-based and gains-based taxes in that increasing investment horizon results in tax consuming a greater share of growth (i.e, increases tax drag).

Wealth taxes are different from returns-based and gains-based taxes:

- For $r > t$, decreased proportion of investment growth is taxed.
- For $r = t$, all of investment growth is taxed.
- For $0 < r < t$, increased proportion of investment growth is taxed.
- For $r < 0$, tax reduces principal (i.e., not just growth).

### Blended Tax Environment

Pre-tax portfolio return $r$ is a function of the component returns (i.e., dividends, interest, realized capital gain) in percentage proportion $p$. The deferred (i.e., unrealized) gain is not considered here. After-tax portfolio realized return $r^*$ is:

IMPORTANT: As less of the total return results from realized capital gain, more will result from unrealized capital gain.

PWM

$$r^* = r(1 - p_d t_d - p_i t_i - p_g t_g)$$

*Effective tax rate* describes actual tax as a proportion of taxable income. Assuming the same tax rate applies to realized and deferred gains:

IMPORTANT: The proportion of gain, $p_g$, subject to immediate tax does not include unrealized gain.

$$T^* = \frac{t_g(1 - p_i - p_d - p_g)}{(1 - p_i t_i - p_d t_d - p_g t_g)}$$

The after-tax future value for each currency unit with both realized and unrealized gains is:

IMPORTANT: This formula can replace all future versions, assuming the variables are known. It considers taxes against the realized and unrealized portions of blended return.

$$FV_{after-tax} = (1+r^*)^n(1-T^*) + T^* - (1-B)t_g$$

### Accrual Equivalent Return

*Accrual equivalent after-tax return* describes the annual return $r_{AE}$ at which a portfolio with value $V_0$ would grow to result in the same future value $V_t$as the pre-tax return after all taxes have been levied.

$$r_{AE} = \sqrt[n]{\frac{V_t}{V_0}} - 1$$

The *tax drag* is accrual equivalent after-tax return less actual return for the portfolio.

MPORTANT: Accrual equivalent return will always be less than annual taxable return, but approaches annual taxable return as the time horizon increases. The convergence is faster as the proportion of unrealized return increases.

Accrual equivalent returns are useful for standardizing results of different portfolio strategies for comparison.

### Accrual Equivalent Tax Rates

An accrual equivalent tax rate, $T_{AE}$, equates after-tax return to the accrual equivalent return:

$$T_{AE} = 1 - \frac{r_{AE}}{r}$$

Increasing the proportion of tax-advantaged investments in the portfolio and minimizing ordinary income results in the lowest $T_{AE}$.

Accrual equivalent tax rates can be used to:

- Illustrate the tax benefits of increasing holding periods.
- Judge the tax efficiency of asset classes or portfolio strategies.
- Understand the impact of tax law changes, investor circumstances, or changes in behavior (e.g., gifting).

PWM

IMPORTANT: This future value calculation is the same as that for zero-basis capital gains recognized only at the end of an investment horizon.

## Tax-Advantaged Accounts

### Tax-Deferred Accounts (TDAs)

*Tax-deferred accounts (TDAs)* involve contributions from untaxed ordinary income (i.e., tax-deductible contributions) and tax-free growth during the holding period. Withdrawals are usually taxed at the account owner's current ordinary income rate at the time of withdrawal.

$$FV_{TDA} = (1+r)^n(1-t)$$

### Tax-Exempt Accounts

*Tax-exempt accounts (TEAs)* involve after-tax contributions that grow tax free through the investment horizon and remain untaxed when withdrawn; that is, they have no future tax liabilities.

$$FV_{TEA} = (1+r)^n$$

IMPORTANT: Assuming $t_0 = t_t$, TDAs and TEAs offer no substantial after-tax difference.

When considering the impact of taxes prior to the initial contribution:

$$FV_{TEA} = (1-t)(1+r)^n$$

### After-Tax Asset Allocation

After-tax return advantages are:

- TEAs: Lower beginning tax rate (i.e., at initial contribution)
- TDAs: Lower ending tax rate (i.e., at withdrawal)

## Taxes and Investment Risk

An investor's share of investment risk on a taxed return is $\sigma(1 - t)$ where $\sigma$ is pre-tax risk.

## Maximizing After-Tax Wealth

Investors may have multiple types of accounts due to contribution limits for TEAs and TDAs. *Tax alpha* concerns the value created from properly using asset and account types that maximize an investor's after-tax wealth.

### Asset Location

The *asset location decision* involves choices among taxable, TDA, and TEA accounts (where available) based on the tax profile of assets but allocated across each to optimize risk/return decisions.

- Tax-advantaged: Higher-taxed asset types
- Taxable: Lower-taxed asset types

Offsetting short positions in the taxable account can be used to offset overallocation to the highly taxed asset in the tax-advantaged account.

Active management or options-overlay strategies may not lend themselves to deferred-tax portfolios; that is, trading and active management have to earn higher pre-tax alpha than passive management.



Asset allocation should be appropriate not only to asset class, but to holding period. Choice of asset location cannot overcome investment strategies that generate negative alpha or extreme tax inefficiency.

### Tax-Loss Harvesting

Tax-loss harvesting involves offsetting gains in one security by realizing losses in other securities. Selling a security at a loss and reinvesting in another lower-value security essentially resets the potential gain (i.e., deferral).

Unrealized tax losses at death of the owner will generally not be transferable. The asset basis is often stepped up to market value at death, and the embedded loss is not transferred.

> IMPORTANT: These strategies become more important as the tax rate on capital gains increases.

If part of a position with different entry prices must be sold, it often makes sense to sell the highest-basis portion of the assets first and defer taxes on the lowest-basis portion. This is called highest in, first out (HIFO).

Such strategies may not be useful where tax rates are lower now than they will be in the future. Higher future tax rates would suggest that gains be taken now (i.e., under the lower tax rate environment).

### Holding Period Management

> IMPORTANT: Compare accrual equivalent returns across diverse tax structures.

Short-term trading may not offer the same active management advantages when a lower tax is available on long-term gains.

## After-Tax Mean Variance Optimization (MVO)

The same asset held in different types of accounts (i.e., taxable, TDA, TEA) is a different asset for mean variance optimization (MVO) because it results in different after-tax holding period returns.

After-tax accrual equivalent returns and after-tax standard deviations can be substituted in the optimization process.

The optimization model should constrain allocations as required to avoid overallocating to the TDA/TEA types of accounts.

# ESTATE PLANNING IN A GLOBAL CONTEXT
Cross-Reference to CFA Institute Assigned Reading #10

## Basic Estate Planning Concepts

### Estates, Wills, and Probate

*Estate* describes all the assets a person owns or controls. *Estate planning* describes the process of transferring assets during life and at death.

A *will* specifies the rights others have over the *testator's* property at death. *Probate* is the legal process that establishes the validity of a will.

*Intestacy* is the state of dying without a will; the court decides disposition of assets based on local law.

Property may be passed by joint ownership, living trusts, retirement plans, and other structures that avoid the expense, public nature, and contestability of the probate process.

Assets transferred to an *irrevocable trust* are not considered part of an estate because the grantor of assets funding the trust no longer owns or controls them.

### Structures of Civil Law, Common Law, Shari'a Law

*Civil law* countries apply abstract principles established by law to cases. Civil law is the most widely used system.

*Common law* countries use court cases to establish abstract principles. Common law primarily derives from the British system and includes U.S. courts.

Courts following the law of Islam (i.e., *Shari'a*) are like civil law systems regarding estate planning. Shari'a law can usually be followed in non-Islamic countries by using a will, except where the instructions conflict with local law.

A *trust*, unique to common law, allows the *settlor* to entrust assets to management by a *trustee*. France, Germany, and other civil law countries do not recognize trusts.

### Spouses and Other Heirs

*Forced heirship rules* limit an owner's discretion regarding the share of property transferred to children and spouses.

*Clawback* provisions allow heirs to gain back their rightful share of property disposed during the owner's lifetime to avoid forced heirship.

Spouses also have marital property rights in most jurisdictions:

- Separate property regimes (civil law): Individual may own property and dispose of it subject to remaining spouse's other rights; may have choice of separate or community property rights.

- Community property regimes: Indivisible 50% interest in income earned during marriage:
  - Gifts and inheritances received outside of marriage remain separate property.
  - 50% of decedent's assets transfer directly to spouse; remainder transfers via provisions of the will.

### Tax Considerations

Where wealth-based taxes are levied annually, transfer taxes are levied only during gifting or inheritance:

- Inter vivos transfers (i.e., lifetime gratuitous transfers):
  - Without intent of anything in exchange
  - Taxed against transferor's estate
- Inheritance (i.e., testamentary gratuitous transfers):
  - Received from decedent (at death)
  - Taxed against recipient

There may be an untaxed allowance on both inter vivos and testamentary transfers.

Transfers to spouses are tax exempt in most jurisdictions.

Tax status depends on:

- Location of asset (i.e., domestic or foreign)
- Donor's residence or domicile
- Recipient's residence
- Type of asset (e.g., movable versus immovable)

PWM

## Core and Excess Capital

IMPORTANT: Excess capital can be safely transferred to beneficiaries without causing failure to meet lifestyle needs.

*Core capital* describes assets designated for maintaining a given lifestyle, funding additional desired spending goals, and providing an emergency reserve for unexpected spending requirements.

*Excess capital* is assets greater than liabilities and the emergency reserve (i.e., excess of assets above core capital).

The present value of spending needs can be calculated as:

- Nominal spending needs discounted at a nominal discount rate, or
- Real spending needs discounted at a real discount rate (i.e., without inflation)

Core capital requirement can be calculated as:

- The present value of spending needs through life expectancy, or
- Each expected future cash flow multiplied by the joint survival probability

### Survival Probability Approach

Joint survival probability for a couple is:

$$p(survival_J) = p(survival_H) + p(survival_W) - p(survival_H) \times p(survival_W)$$

Based on joint survival probability, present value of joint spending needs is:

$$PV(spending_J) = \sum_{t=1}^{N} \frac{p(survival_J) \times (spending_J)}{(1+r)^t}$$

IMPORTANT: A more conservative approach assumes both spouses live through the longest expectancy for either life.

The survival probability approach discounts each period's spending needs by the real risk-free rate because they are nonsystematic (i.e., unrelated to market-based risk inherent in the assets). However, they can be hedged using life insurance.

IMPORTANT: Do *not* discount expected spending with the required return on a portfolio of assets used to fund them.

The emergency reserve incorporated into liabilities considers the shortfall risk of funding assets. A two-year emergency reserve is designed to satisfy anxiety about market cycles and is usually sufficient for planning.

### Monte Carlo Approach

The Monte Carlo approach examines many paths, with outcomes based on random values within ranges for each variable (i.e., portfolio return, mortality, emergency experiences, tax changes, etc.). Combining the many potential outcomes gives a feeling of the portfolio's risk as a funding portfolio.



## Transferring Excess Capital

Inter vivos gifting bypasses the estate tax on a bequest at death. Local jurisdictions have implemented gift and donation taxes to minimize the revenue loss from inter vivos gifting.

### Tax-Free Gifting

*Relative value* describes the relative benefit of an inter vivos gift to the value of a bequest at death. In this scenario, the relative value of the tax-free gift equals return on investments purchased with a gift $r_g$ less tax on the gift's return $t_{ig}$, divided by return on estate investments $r_e$ less tax on the estate investment return $t_{ie}$ and tax on the estate bequest $T_e$.

$$RV_{tax-freeGift} = \frac{FV_{Gift}}{FV_{Bequest}} = \frac{[1 + r_g(1 - t_{ig})]^n}{[1 + r_e(1 - t_{ie})]^n (1 - T_e)}$$

### Gifts Taxable to the Recipient

For a gift taxable to the recipient:

$$RV_{taxable\ Gift} = \frac{FV_{Gift}}{FV_{Bequest}} = \frac{[1 + r_g(1 - t_{ig})]^n (1 - T_g)}{[1 + r_e(1 - t_{ie})]^n (1 - T_e)}$$

IMPORTANT: Taxable gifts can still be efficient if the tax rate on gifts to the recipient (numerator) is less than the estate tax rate (denominator).

It is also tax efficient to gift assets with higher expected returns to the second generation and keep lower-expected-return assets with the first generation to be passed at death.

In some jurisdictions the authorities may confiscate a gift if the recipient is unable to liquidate the investment to satisfy the gift tax.

### Gifts Taxable to the Donor

Cross-border gifts could result in tax against proceeds given and received.

The value of the gift increases if it is taxable to donor's estate rather than to recipient. Assuming $r_g = r_e$ and $t_{ig} = t_{ie}$:

$$RV_{donor\,Taxable\,Gift} = \frac{FV_{gift}}{FV_{bequest}} = \frac{[1+r_g(1-t_{ig})]^n(1-T_g+T_gT_e)}{[1+r_e(1-t_{ie})]^n(1-T_e)}$$

$T_gT_e$ represents the tax benefit to the recipient of reducing the estate with the gift rather than paying estate tax on the gift.

The value of the gift multiplied by the tax benefit of reducing the estate could be considered a credit for making the gift.

PWM

### Generation Skipping

Gifting assets to the third generation avoids tax on first- and second-generation bequests. The value of skipping the first and second generations relative to making the two bequests depends on the first-generation estate tax rate:

$$RV_{generation\ Skipping\ Gift} = \frac{1}{(1-T_e)}$$

Some jurisdictions levy a generation-skipping transfer tax to recover the amount that would have been lost as tax revenue.

### Spousal Exemptions

Spouses in most jurisdictions may make unlimited gifts or bequests to the other spouse without tax, or bequests taxable only above some threshold.

Because there are exclusions for each spouse, it may be efficient to gift the excludable amount to a third party so as not to lose the exclusion from the taxable estate.

> IMPORTANT: Discounts for lack of liquidity are not additive with discounts for minority interest; the combination of the two will tend to be less than their sum.

### Valuation Discounts

*Valuation discounts* for lack of liquidity and minority interest may be applied to privately held family businesses. Assets subject to valuation discounts will have lower transfer taxes than comparable assets not subject to such discounts.

Assets may be placed in a *family limited partnership (FLP)* to create valuation discounts for transfer purposes. Even cash and marketable securities placed in an FLP may be eligible, although the assigned discount will be less than for privately held companies.

FLPs are also used to accumulate family member shares to reduce commission costs and gain access to investments requiring a threshold investment.

### Deemed Disposition

Bequests in some jurisdictions may result in tax only on the amount over basis, much like a capital gains tax. This *deemed disposition* of the asset treats the bequest as if it were a sale.

### Charitable Gifts

*Charitable gratuitous transfers* involve gifts to charities and result in tax advantages:

- Very few jurisdictions levy a tax against gifts to charitable organizations.
- Most jurisdictions provide a tax deduction for such gifts.
- Charities may be exempt from tax on investment gains.

For planned charitable giving, gifting early makes more sense than a bequest at death:

$$RV_{charitable\ Gift} = \frac{FV_{charitable\ Gift}}{FV_{bequest}} = \frac{(1+r_g)^n + T_{oi}\left[1+r_e(1-t_{ie})\right]^n(1-T_e)}{\left[1+r_e(1-t_{ie})\right]^n(1-T_e)}$$



In the numerator:

- First term: No tax on investment returns associated with the gift amount
- Second term: Tax deduction against ordinary income ($T_{oi}$) for amount of gift

Donor can:

- Increase amount of gift with same effect on estate, or
- Use less estate capital to achieve a charitable goal.

## Estate Planning Structures

### Trusts

In a *trust*, a *settlor* (i.e., *grantor*) transfers assets to a *trustee*, who manages the assets for beneficiaries. Beneficiaries have beneficial ownership of trust assets.

- Revocable trust: Owner retains right to assets and may revoke trust relationship:
  - Reports and pays taxes on investment returns.
  - Claims against the settlor may be satisfied using trust assets.
- Irrevocable trust: Owner forfeits right to assets and may not revoke trust relationship:
  - Trustee reports and pays taxes (if any).
  - Claims against the settlor cannot be satisfied from trust assets.

Trust distributions to beneficiaries:

- Fixed: Certain amounts and times as specified in the trust document.
- Discretionary: Trustee makes payments to beneficiaries with discretion uncontrolled by the trust document or the grantor.

Trusts are legal relationships in common law and may not be recognized by civil law jurisdictions, although many do. The irrevocable trust offers the most asset protection for the settlor while the discretionary trust offers the most asset protection for the beneficiaries.

### Foundations

A foundation is set up to promote education, philanthropy, and so on. A public foundation is set up by public entities (e.g., corporations); a private foundation is set up by an individual or a family and has its own board.

A foundation is a legal person set up in civil law.

### Life Insurance

Life insurance can be a useful tool in jurisdictions where trusts are not recognized (i.e., civil law jurisdictions) or where tax outcomes are uncertain:

- Death benefits are not taxed.
- There are minimal or no reporting requirements.
- Premiums are not includable in estates or as gifts taxable to beneficiaries.
- Cash values may accumulate inside the policy value without tax.
- Loans against or withdrawals from cash value may be made by the owner without tax consequences.
- Policy passes directly to beneficiaries (i.e., avoids probate).
- Creditors cannot attach premiums in settlement of claims.



IMPORTANT: Jurisdictions require a minimum risk before allowing the benefits listed.

Life insurance is valuable in:

- Providing liquidity to pay taxes on bequests (if any).
- Funding trusts in the case of minors, spendthrifts, or disabled persons.

## Cross-Border Planning

### Residence and Source of Income

- *Source jurisdiction* countries (i.e., also known as territorial tax systems):
  - Tax income earned within their borders.
  - Tax noncitizen residents, but not nonresident citizens.
- *Residence jurisdiction* countries tax residents' worldwide income.

The United States taxes its citizens (regardless of residence) and noncitizen residents on worldwide income.

The United Kingdom taxes residents living abroad (resident nondomiciliaries or RNDs) only on income remitted in the United Kingdom. UK RNDs may locate in residence jurisdiction countries where they are not taxed on earnings.

### Tax on Wealth and Wealth Transfers

The United States levies taxes on:

- Worldwide wealth transfers of citizens and residents.
- Estate transfers of U.S. assets held by noncitizens and nonresidents:
    - Real estate
    - Movable property
    - Financial assets

Generally, the principles are:

- Source jurisdiction: Tax transfers of assets within a country.
- Residence jurisdiction: Tax all assets transferred by resident.

Disputes among jurisdictions are handled by treaty or other agreement.

### Exit Taxes

Countries may impose an *exit tax* in an attempt to reduce taxes lost when high net worth individuals (HNWIs) renounce citizenship and expatriate to another country. The exit tax will often create a deemed disposition for assets leaving the country, which then creates a tax on the gain over basis.

Expatriated citizens may also owe tax on income earned during a "shadow period" after renunciation.



### Double Taxation

Conflicts may lead to taxation for the same income or assets across multiple jurisdictions:

- Residence-source conflict (most common): A resident of a residence jurisdiction country earns income in a source jurisdiction country.
- Source-source conflict: Two source jurisdiction countries disagree about where the money was earned.
- Residence-residence conflict: Two residence jurisdiction countries disagree about the residence of an income earner.

The residence jurisdiction country in a source-residence conflict will generally be expected to provide relief from taxation for its resident:

- Credit: Residence jurisdiction country provides a tax credit for taxes paid in the source jurisdiction country; tax is limited to maximum of residence country or source country.
- Exemption: Residence jurisdiction country exempts foreign source income from taxation; tax is limited to source country tax.
- Deduction: Residence jurisdiction country allows deduction for tax paid in the source jurisdiction country; this results in highest tax.

$$
\begin{aligned}
T_{deduction\,Method} &= T_R + T_S(1 - T_R) \\
&= T_R + T_S - T_R T_S
\end{aligned}
$$

The Organization for Economic Cooperation and Development (OECD) Model Treaty specifies source-residence conflict resolution:

- Credit or exemption methods are endorsed.
- Interest/dividend income are sourced in the paying entity's country (withheld in source country).
- Capital gains on movable property and financial assets are taxed in seller's residence country.
- Capital gains on immovable property are taxed in asset's source country.

Double tax treaty (DTT) residence-residence conflict resolution considers:

- Permanent home
- Center of vital interests
- Habitual dwelling
- Citizenship

DTTs typically do not resolve source-source conflicts.

### Transparency and Avoidance

Financial advisors should attempt to legally minimize client taxes:

- Avoidance (legal minimization) conforms to the law.
- Evasion is misrepresenting or misreporting relevant information to circumvent tax obligations.



Jurisdictions with banking secrecy laws are not appropriate for helping clients evade tax. They are appropriate only for avoiding public scrutiny of transactions.

Most banks have become qualified intermediaries (QIs) to provide beneficial ownership information on U.S. securities while avoiding disclosure for non-U.S. clients.

The European Union Savings Directive requires EU members (except Austria, Belgium, and Luxembourg) to exchange information with one another. The three excluded members apply tax at the source and provide that information to the client's country of residence.

# Study Session 5: Private Wealth Management (2)

PWM

# SINGLE-ASSET POSITIONS
Cross-Reference to CFA Institute Assigned Reading #11

## The Concentration Problem

*Concentrated single-asset positions* are those positions in which a client has 25% of assets. These positions are often made up of highly appreciated real estate, private companies, or public stock presenting liquidity and tax issues.

Highly concentrated public stock positions may result from:

- Incentive awards to executives
- Private company going public via an initial public offering (IPO)
- Buy-and-hold investment strategy

Going from a position in private company shares to public company shares may have tax-favored aspects and may solve the liquidity problem, but may not solve the problem of low basis (and high tax liability).

Real estate faces property-specific concentration problems.

### Investment Risks

Concentrated positions may not earn fair risk-adjusted returns due to nonsystematic risk.

- Systematic risk: The capital asset pricing model (CAPM) identifies equity market risk, but other models include:
  - Business cycle risk
  - Inflation risk
  - Other macroeconomic factors
- Nonsystematic risk (i.e., company-specific risk): Exposure to events that affect the company but not the industry or market:
  - Business environment
  - Operations
  - Reputation

IMPORTANT: A diversified portfolio has a much lower chance of suffering large losses.

*Property-specific risks* are the nonsystematic component of real property—that is, risks that affect the property but not the general real estate market:

- Environmental liability
- Credit risk of replacing investment-grade tenants with lower-quality tenants

## Managing Concentrated Positions

### Objectives for Concentrated Positions

Typical financial objectives and considerations include:

- Risk reduction: Obtain diversification; owners tend to overestimate value and underestimate volatility.
- Monetization: Generate liquidity to satisfy cash flow needs and diversification objectives.
- Optimization (i.e., tax efficiency):
    - Minimize immediate tax consequences of monetization.
    - Defer tax recognition.

Other objectives and considerations are:

- Concentrated stock positions:
    - Maintain control of voting shares.
    - Retain upside potential while increasing current income.
- Privately owned businesses:
    - Maintain overall control.
    - Business phase not optimal for sale (e.g., just entering growth phase, new product under development, etc.).
    - Desire to cede control to loyal management team.
    - Pass control to next generation.
- Investment real estate:
    - Maintain operating control for property used in another business.
    - Benefit from price appreciation of recent purchase or value-added development.
    - Pass control to next generation.



### Liquidity and Tax Considerations

Concentrated positions are generally illiquid, except for public stock. Public stock may be illiquid if:

- The position represents a large percentage of float.
- Applicable securities laws restrict liquidity (e.g., insider rules).

Privately held companies and real estate may suffer from:

- Lack of a public market for ownership shares.
- Different classes of buyers calculating different ownership values.

If sellable, the appreciated asset may trigger substantial taxable gains.

## Legal and Other Constraints

Legal, regulatory, and company-specific constraints are often country specific, but generally result in restrictions on:

- Amount and timing of share sales:
    - Blackout periods (i.e., period around earnings and other announcements when insiders cannot sell)
    - Lockup periods (i.e., period after IPO when shareholders cannot sell)
- Avoidance of insider trading
- Compliance with notice, disclosure, and reporting requirements

Margin rules determine how much equity an investor must maintain relative to the portfolio value:

- Rules-based: Substantial margin required for additional investment in same security
- Risk-based: Completely marginable if portfolio insurance (i.e., protective put)

Off-balance-sheet debt such as a *prepaid variable forward* (i.e., collar plus a loan) is not considered a sale for tax purposes but also is not subject to margin requirements.

Short sales to lock in a position may be construed as constructive sales if the owner offers own shares for the short.

Liquidity should be considered because any hedge will be subject to adjustment as market conditions change.

PWM

It is difficult to hedge a recent IPO, because the stock has no trading history (i.e., dealer wants to avoid sharp spikes).

## Psychological Considerations

Advisors need to consider cognitive and emotional biases to determine the best approach:

- Emotional biases (difficult to overcome and may need to be worked around):
    - Status quo bias:
        - General bias against change
        - Husband/wife saying never to sell
        - Duty to pass to heirs
        - Coworkers looking down on selling
        - Loyalty/gratitude to employer
    - Overconfidence and familiarity
    - Extrapolation of past returns
    - Endowment effects—Demanding higher selling price than client would pay to purchase shares
- Cognitive biases (may be easier to overcome if pointed out):
    - Confirmation bias—Information that confirms beliefs
    - Conservatism bias—Unwillingness to update for new information
    - Availability heuristic—Probabilities influenced by ability to recall
    - Anchoring and adjustment—Adjustments from an original viewpoint rather than fresh viewpoint
    - Illusion of control—Overestimating personal control

### Goal-Based Planning Considerations

Rather than managing the total portfolio as an integrated tool for obtaining multiple goals, financial planning often works with investors' behaviors by segregating assets into risk buckets:

> IMPORTANT: Personal and market risk are combined in a core portfolio or primary capital described elsewhere. Aspirational risk is described elsewhere as appropriate for surplus capital.

- Personal risk: Prevention of poverty (i.e., emergency funds); low-volatility investments (e.g., Treasuries)
- Market risk: Maintaining current lifestyle; average risk-adjusted returns
- Aspirational risk: Enhancing lifestyle; above-average or speculative returns

When deciding to sell a concentrated position, clients should consider whether the assets will be needed to maintain the current lifestyle or prevent poverty.

### Asset Location and Wealth Transfers

The type of tax on asset earnings often relates to the asset class of the security, which may be altered by the account type. *Asset location* refers to whether the funds are in a taxable or a tax-deferred/tax-exempt account.

Planning before appreciation allows simple strategies such as gifts to family members or trusts, and *estate freeze strategies* (i.e., transferring future appreciation to heirs to minimize estate and gift taxes).

PWM

Estate freeze strategies involve passing assets through closely held family corporations that avoid constructive transfer that triggers a tax event. Classic family-owned corporations may have two classes of stock: the voting preferred shares held by the current generation and a junior common equity class with no voting privileges. The low-value common stock is passed with little current tax consequence.

> IMPORTANT: The interaction of lack of liquidity and lack of marketability discounts is less than the sum of the two.

Postappreciation strategies include gifting highly concentrated positions to a *family limited partnership (FLP)*. The current generation becomes the general partner and retains control over underlying assets. The limited partnership interest available to heirs reduces the value of the underlying assets by a lack of liquidity discount and a lack of marketability discount.

The asset owner can also make charitable contributions of the appreciated assets that allow them to bypass taxes on all the gain.

### Five-Step Process

A consistent method of delivering services to each client will help assure that objectives are met:

1. Identify objectives and constraints—elements of the investment policy statement (IPS).
2. Identify tools and strategies to satisfy objectives and meet client needs.
3. Compare tax advantages and disadvantages.
4. Compare nontax advantages and disadvantages.
5. Formulate and document an optimal strategy.

## Managing Risk in Concentrated Positions

### Tax Considerations

Different tools can result in different tax outcomes, although the diversification outcome is the same. Advisors can add value by optimizing the outcome within the realm of after-tax results.

### Non-Tax Considerations

Hedging instruments and other tools have various advantages and drawbacks other than tax outcome:

- Price discovery: Over-the-counter (OTC) instruments transpire via a dealer whereas exchange-traded instruments have active price discovery in an open market.
- Fee transparency: Exchange-traded instruments have transparent fees and expenses whereas OTC pricing masks these.
- Flexible terms: OTC derivatives have more flexible terms and may be completely customizable; exchange-traded securities are less flexible and may not be customized.
- Position offset: Exchange-traded derivatives may be offset by taking an exactly opposite position with the same maturity; OTC derivatives are more difficult to find offsetting positions for.
- Counterparty credit risk:
    - Exchange-traded securities are often marked to market, and the counterparty will have less credit risk than in an OTC-traded derivative that is not marked to market.
    - Investors incur less risk working with intermediaries on an exchange versus counterparties in an OTC transaction.
- Minimum size: Exchange-traded derivatives have lower minimums than OTC derivatives.



## Concentrated Public Shares

*Monetization* involves converting the concentrated positions in publicly traded equity to cash by hedging the position (i.e., removing both the upside and downside) and then borrowing against the hedged position. This results in:

- A hedged, essentially riskless position
- Money market return on the value of the long position
- High loan-to-value (LTV) ratio against the long position

In addition:

- Income generated by the hedged position offsets borrowing costs.
- Borrowed proceeds can be reinvested in a diversified portfolio.

Removing risk from the position can be accomplished by:

1. Short sale against the box (least expensive): Selling short using the same position held long as collateral; may not be allowed in some jurisdictions.
2. Total return equity swap: Owner exchanges returns from concentrated position for fixed or floating payments.

3. Forward sale contract or single-stock futures contract: short forward contract against the asset.
4. Options (i.e., forward conversion): Synthetic short forward position (i.e., long put and short call).

Tax considerations:

- Are potential losses available for offset against current income, or are they added to the basis of the concentrated position?
- Are carrying costs deductible or added to the basis of the hedge?
- Does a contract requiring physical settlement ultimately result in short- or long-term gain?
- Is any gain from the hedge taxed at short- or long-term gains rates?
- Does the hedge affect tax on income and dividends from the underlying? (No tax impact is preferred.)

Investors may also buy *puts* to protect against downside risk while participating in upside potential and deferring capital gains tax. Reduce costs by:

- Lowering the exercise price (i.e., investor self-insures for price loss between at- and out-of-the-money)
- Purchasing shorter-maturity puts
- Purchasing at-the-money puts and selling out-of-the-money puts (put spread)
- Using knock-out puts (which expire when the stock price reaches a certain level)



*Zero-premium collars* accomplish the same goals as the put strategies (i.e., protect, participate at least to some extent, and defer tax) at a lower cost:

- Buy a put that is at- or just out-of-the-money, and simultaneously sell a call at a price high enough for the premium income to offset the put price.
- If the share price remains above the put price and below the call price, both puts and calls expire worthless.
- The call buyer will exercise if the share price goes above the call price.
- The client may exercise if the share price goes below the put price.

IMPORTANT: A margin loan against the collared position can then be used to purchase diversifying assets.

Clients can increase their upside potential by selling a higher-priced call and:

- Lowering the put price (self-insured against greater downside risk)
- Using a put spread (self-insured below the short put)
- Financing part of the put price out-of-pocket

IMPORTANT: A prepaid variable forward (PVF) may also be cash settled at maturity with a new PVF taken out as required to finance amounts above the call strike price.

A *prepaid variable forward (PVF)* combines the hedge and margin loan in the same instrument to obtain the same result as the zero-premium or zero-cost collar. The number of shares delivered at maturity varies with the share price at maturity:

- Less than put price: All shares are delivered and put strike price is received.
- Between put and call price: Investor delivers put strike price worth of shares.
- Above call price: Investor delivers put strike price worth of shares and pays price difference between market price and call strike price.

A *mismatch in character* occurs when the derivative used to hedge the underlying concentrated position has a different tax treatment (e.g., options received as compensation are taxed as ordinary income whereas options purchased may ultimately be taxed at capital gains tax rates).

> IMPORTANT: In some jurisdictions, the loss created on a mismatched strategy may not be offset against the ordinary income from options received as compensation.

A *yield enhancement strategy*, such as writing covered calls, allows the investor greater income on the underlying concentrated position but does not reduce risk on the underlying:

- Investor sells calls at a strike price and earns premium income.
- This is attractive if investor believes shares will trade in a range.
- Investor retains downside risk.
- This prepares the investor for an eventual sale at a predetermined liquidation value.

A tax-optimized equity strategy combines investment and tax management; there are two types:

- Index-tracking separately managed portfolio:
    - Tracks benchmark but outperforms it from an investment and tax perspective.
    - Offers opportunistic capital loss harvesting and gain deferral to offset periodic concentrated portfolio liquidations.
- Completeness portfolio: Tracks index given concentrated portfolio characteristics and new investments, with less emphasis on concentrated portfolio liquidations.

An *exchange fund* allows several investors with concentrated positions to contribute those positions for a share of a now more diversified exchange fund. The cost basis of each investor's shares in the exchange fund is the same as that investor's basis in the concentrated position; there is no taxable event to trigger a capital gain.

> IMPORTANT: In a cross hedge, using puts will likely be more important for downside protection, because the hedging instrument will not capture the nonsystematic risk of the concentrated position.



A *cross hedge* (i.e., hedging instrument against a similar underlying) may be appropriate in jurisdictions where proper derivatives for hedging are unavailable or where laws or costs preclude direct hedging.

## Concentrated Private Shares

Additional concerns regarding concentrated positions in private equity include:

- Asset rich but cash poor; that is, net worth is tied up primarily in the firm.
- Liquidity may be limited due to company restrictions on sales outside the firm.
- Owners' shares are often highly appreciated; selling triggers large tax liability.
- Dilution or loss of control occurs at sale.

### Strategic Buyers

*Strategic buyers* are often other firms in the industry that view acquisition of other middle market companies as a low-risk way of gaining market share and earnings growth, especially in a slow-growth market.

> IMPORTANT: Strategic buyers will often pay top dollar for such an acquisition.

### Financial Buyers

*Financial buyers* raise funds from institutional investors and acquire companies to be managed under the umbrella of a *private equity fund*. Financial buyers usually cannot accrue financial and operational synergies the way strategic buyers can, and will not pay as much to acquire the company.

IMPORTANT: In leveraged recapitalization, the owner owes tax on the portion withdrawn as cash but defers the gain on shares remaining in the recapitalized firm.

### Recapitalization

In *leveraged recapitalization*, owners transfer stock for cash and retain only a minority interest in the recapitalized firm. The private equity firm pays for its purchased equity via debt through senior and mezzanine (i.e., subordinated) lenders.

After a few years, the private equity firm holding majority interest may take the recapitalized company to an initial public offering, sale to a strategic or financial buyer, or another recapitalization. At that stage, the former owner may be substantially cashed out and may or may not continue to run the company.

### Management Buyout (MBO)

In a *management buyout (MBO)*, key employees or executives borrow money to purchase the owner's shares. Financing may be difficult to obtain for MBOs because the employees often don't perform as expected when they have the additional burdens of management.



Owners must then take only a partial withdrawal of capital with a promissory note for the remainder, with the final amount contingent on company performance.

Based on financing dynamics and potential effects of a failed MBO, owners should consider this strategy only if a third-party buyer isn't available and the management offer meets or exceeds what a third party would pay.

### Divestiture of Noncore Assets

*Noncore assets* do not directly bear on the growth or success of the business. Owners may liquidate noncore assets while continuing to run the core business, and reinvest proceeds from the divestiture in a more diversified asset pool.

In some cases, assets may play a role in potential growth of the core business but have a higher use for other purposes. These assets may also be repurposed to unlock value, even by selling to a competitor with a different use in mind.

### Sale or Gifting to Family

For the same reasons management may have trouble seeking financing in an MBO, family may have trouble assembling financing to purchase the business assets. The owner may carry a substantial portion of the agreed price in a promissory note.

Gifting strategies provide a viable alternative provided the owner has substantial assets outside the concentrated position with which to meet lifestyle and other needs.

### Personal Line of Credit Secured by Company Shares

IMPORTANT: Exercising the put triggers a taxable event for the owner.

In this strategy, the owner takes a personal loan from the company with the value of shares backing the loan amount. A put travels with the loan amount, which allows the owner to sell shares back to the company in an amount sufficient to extinguish the loan.

While the loan is outstanding, the owner retains control of the company, avoids a taxable sale event, and can use the proceeds of the loan to diversify.

### Initial Public Offering

Initial public offerings (IPOs) offer a method of exchanging ownership in a private company for publicly traded shares. Going public, however, exposes the owner to greater scrutiny. While removing some of the liquidity constraints of private company equity, it leaves the owner with a concentrated public equity position.

### Employee Share Ownership Plan Exchanges

*Employee share ownership plan (ESOP) exchange* is another staged exit strategy in which the company buys the owner's shares for distribution to employees. In a leveraged ESOP exchange, the company borrows money to purchase owner shares. This takes place over time, optimizing the tax burden on the owner as shares are purchased.

U.S. tax rules permit deferral of the gain only on Subchapter C shares purchased by an ESOP (i.e., not Subchapter S shares). The deferral on gain, along with continued control and stepped-up basis to heirs, makes this strategy compelling.



## Investment Real Estate

Alternatives to outright sale of investment property include:

- Mortgage the property:
    - Set the LTV ratio at the point where the net rental income equals the mortgage finance cost.
    - There are no tax consequences.
    - Use the proceeds from the new loan to diversify.
    - Nonrecourse loans are a put back to the lender for the mortgage amount.
- Donor-advised funds:
    - Contribute property now for charitable deduction.
    - Endowment purchases diversified portfolio or manages property.
    - Tax-free growth within charity, no recapture of depreciation, no capital gains tax due.
    - Advise funds until disbursements begin.
- Sale and leaseback: Owner sells to another party at market terms and leases back at market terms.
    - Owner retains use of facility.
    - Sale frees up owner's capital for diversifying portfolio, redeploying into core business, and so on.
    - Sale triggers taxable gain for tax purposes.
    - Rental payments on lease are completely deductible.

# RISK MANAGEMENT FOR INDIVIDUALS
Cross-Reference to CFA Institute Assigned Reading #12

## Human Capital and Financial Capital

The two primary components of an individual's wealth are:

1. ***Financial capital:*** Includes all tangible assets such as cash in bank accounts, stocks, bonds, and the family home.
2. ***Human capital:*** The present value of future expected labor income. Human capital is its own asset class and has its own return and risk characteristics. Young people have a lot of human capital compared with financial capital. At retirement, human capital is equal to zero.

Three key assumptions in the calculation of human capital are:

1. ***Mortality rates***, which are based on actuarial assumptions on the probability of survival at a given age.
2. ***Risk-free rate***, which is the same for everybody.
3. ***Income volatility adjustment***, which is a subjective amount added to the risk-free rate. People with riskier occupations with higher income volatility will have a higher overall discount rate. Higher discount rates are associated with lower human capital, all else equal.



The income volatility risk associated with human capital can be diversified by appropriate financial capital. For example, an executive in the oil and gas industry has high income volatility, so human capital will be equity-like. To diversify, the executive will need less risky bonds as financial capital. By contrast, tenured professors' human capital is bond-like, so they will need more higher-risk equities in their financial capital.

A family's need for financial products changes over seven stages of financial life.

**Seven Financial Stages of Life**

| Stage Name | Description and Age Range | Key Characteristics | Financial Advisor Can Help With ... |
|---|---|---|---|
| Education phase | Investing in knowledge through formal education or skill development | • Financially dependent on parents<br>• Very little financial capital<br>• Almost no focus on savings or risk management | Those with dependents might need life insurance |
| Early career | Has completed education and enters workforce (age 18 to 20s or early 30s) | • Gets married, has children, buys home<br>• High family and housing expenses may not allow for retirement savings | Life insurance can supplement lack of sufficient financial and human capital |
| Career development | Specific skill development within a given field (age 35 to 50) | • Accumulation for children's college education<br>• Large purchases such as vacation home, travel | Retirement saving |
| Peak accumulation | Moving toward maximum earnings and greatest opportunity for wealth accumulation (age 51 to 60) | • Retirement planning and travel<br>• High career risk as high-paying job might not be replaced | Reducing investment risk<br><br>Developing retirement income strategies |
| Preretirement | A few years before planned retirement age | • Income often at career highs | Decrease investment risk<br><br>Tax planning for retirement distributions |
| Early retirement (first 10 years) | Period of comfortable income and enough assets to cover living expenses | • Using savings for enjoyment<br>• Most active period of retirement<br>• Less likely to suffer from cognitive or mobility impairments | Still a need for asset growth, as this phase could last 20 years |
| Late retirement | Unknown duration | • Physical activity declines<br>• Cognitive or physical problems may deplete savings<br>• May be need for long-term health care | Annuities to reduce or eliminate longevity risk |

PWM

Human capital can be added to a family's tangible, marketable financial assets and liabilities to derive the ***economic (holistic) balance sheet***.

### Economic (Holistic) Balance Sheet

| Assets | | Liabilities | |
|---|---|---|---|
| Financial capital | | Debt | |
| Liquid assets | $275,000 | Credit card debt | $15,000 |
| Investment assets | $1,265,000 | Car loan | $35,000 |
| Personal property | $2,150,000 | Home mortgage | $685,000 |
| Subtotal | $3,690,000 | Home equity loan | $60,000 |
| | | Subtotal | $795,000 |
| Human capital | $1,800,000 | Lifetime consumption needs | $3,500,000 |
| Pension value | $250,000 | Bequests | $300,000 |
| **Total Assets** | **$5,740,000** | **Total Liabilities** | **$4,595,000** |
| | | **New Wealth** | **$1,145,000** |

The holistic balance sheet also includes the ***present value of vested pensions*** as an intangible asset. Intangible liabilities include ***lifetime consumption needs*** and ***bequests*** (both are covered in more detail in the reading on estate planning). These items are shaded in gray on the holistic balance sheet.

PWM

The family's ***net wealth*** is $1,145,000, which is the difference between economic assets and economic liabilities. This is not to be confused with ***net worth***, which is the difference between financial assets and financial liabilities, which is equal to $2,895,000.

There are three items to consider when determining the appropriate discount rate to use for vested employer pensions:

1. Plan's financial health, such as its funded status: We would use a lower discount rate for income from plans with a fund surplus than for plans with a fund deficit.
2. Credit quality of the sponsoring company: If the company has issued long-term bonds, the yield can serve as a proxy for the discount rate.
3. Additional credit support: In some countries, the government offers a guarantee in case a local defined-benefit pension plan becomes insolvent.

### Premature Death Risk (Mortality Risk)

Life insurance can be used to protect against premature death (mortality) risk. There are two types of life insurance:

1. ***Temporary life insurance*** is insurance for a certain period of time specified at purchase, known as a term. If the individual survives for the entire term, say 20 years, then the policy will terminate unless it automatically renews. Premiums can either remain fixed (or level) or increase over the term as the mortality risk increases. *There is no cash value for term life insurance.*

2. ***Permanent insurance*** provides lifetime coverage, assuming the premiums are paid over the entire period. Policy premiums are fixed, and there is generally a cash value associated with the policy. There are two basic types of permanent insurance: whole life and universal life. Whole life insurance remains in force for the entire life of the insured. Universal life insurance has more flexibility than whole life insurance to vary the face amount of insurance, pay higher or lower premiums, and invest the cash value.

Both types of insurance are deemed ***noncancelable***; the policy lapses only at the end of the term (for temporary insurance) or upon death (for permanent insurance), provided that the premiums have been paid.

Here are some more general terms mainly related to permanent insurance that you need to be familiar with:

- *Participating/nonparticipating:* Participating allows for the cash value to grow at a higher rate than the guaranteed value based on the profits of the insurance company. Fixed growth values are known as nonparticipating.
- *Nonforfeiture clause:* A policyholder has the option to receive a portion of benefits if premium payments are missed and the policy lapses. There are three options: cash surrender option, where the cash value is paid; paid-up option, where the cash value is used to purchase a single-premium whole life policy; and extended term option, where the cash value is used to purchase a term life policy, usually with the same face value as the previous policy.
- *Riders:* Riders provide protection beyond the basic policy or other modification to a basic policy provision. One example is accidental death or dismemberment (AD&D), which increases the payout if or when the insured dies or is dismembered by an accident. Other common riders include accelerated death benefit, where those who are terminally ill can receive the death benefits while still alive; guaranteed insurability, which allows the policyholder to buy more insurance later at predefined periods; and waiver of premium, where future premiums are waived if the insured becomes disabled.
- *Viatical settlement:* A viatical settlement allows the policyholder to sell the policy to a third party. After buying the policy, the third party is responsible for paying premiums and will receive the death benefit when the insured dies.

PWM

The basic elements of a life insurance policy include:

- *Term and type of insurance:* For example, 30-year temporary life policy.
- *Amount of benefits:* For example, $250,000.
- *Limitations under which death benefit could be withheld:* These could include suicide of the insured within two years after purchasing the policy, or material misrepresentations made by the insured during the application process.
- *Contestability period:* The period when the insurance company can investigate and deny claims.
- *Premium schedule:* Specifying the amount and frequency of premiums to be paid to the insurance company.
- *Riders:* Modifications to basic coverage (see previous points).

There are four parties involved in every life insurance policy, which are also considered basic elements:

1. ***Insured:*** The person whose death triggers the death benefit payment.
2. ***Policy owner:*** Owns the policy and is responsible for paying premiums. In most policies, the insured and the policy owner are the same person. When the insured is not the policy owner, the owner must have an insurable interest in the life of the insured. Examples of insurable interests include an ex-spouse purchasing insurance on the other ex-spouse following a divorce to cover future spousal or child-support payments or a company purchasing insurance on a key executive.
3. ***Beneficiary (or beneficiaries):*** Receives the death benefit, either as a lump sum (more common) or as an annuity (less common).
4. ***Insurer:*** The insurance company that writes the policy and pays the death benefits to the beneficiary when the insured dies.

Note that the insurance company will require the owner to have a reason for taking out the policy (i.e., *insurable interest*) other than to gamble on the insured's death.

There are three main considerations in pricing a life insurance policy:

1. ***Mortality expectations:*** Probability that the insured will die during the term of the policy. Actuaries rely on historical data and future mortality expectations based on age, gender, and other significant medical conditions, such as smoking/nonsmoking. During the underwriting process, actuaries make adjustments to the mortality tables to recognize other factors such as family disease history, risky hobbies, and so forth. All else held equal, men live shorter lives than women, and, given the same age, a man is expected to pay more for life insurance.
2. ***Discount rate (or interest factor):*** Represents the insurance company's assumed rate of return on its investment portfolio.
3. ***Loading:*** Life insurance company expenses and profits, if any, discussed later.

PWM

Mortality expectations and the discount rate are used to calculate the ***net premium*** that is paid to the life insurance company. The ***gross premium*** equals the net premium plus a load representing the two types of costs to the life insurance company:

1. ***Underwriting costs:*** Sales commission to the agent who sold the commission plus the cost of a physical exam, if required.
2. ***Ongoing expenses:*** Overhead and administration expenses, monitoring the policy, and verifying death claims. Renewal commissions are paid to the selling agent for the first years of the policy as an incentive to provide advice to the policyholder and to discourage the policy owner from terminating the policy.

The load may also include a profit based on the type of life insurance company:

- ***Stock companies*** are owned by shareholders and have a profit motive, so they add a projected profit to the load.
- ***Mutual companies*** are owned by the policyholders themselves, so there is no profit motive, although the gross premium is typically higher than the net premium plus expenses. If mortality outcomes and investment returns are more favorable than expected, the policyholders receive a nontaxable return of their premiums equal to the difference between the gross premium and net premium plus expenses.

Policyholders have a choice when deciding the term to purchase. Annual renewable (one-year) policies for a new insured at a particular age have lower annual premiums than longer-term policies, such as 20 years, which must average out the higher mortality charges in later years. Insurance companies offer loss leaders (i.e., low initial rates) on annually renewable insurance, with policyholders switching to other companies at the end of the short term. However, illness or an accident could cause the renewed policy to be much more expensive.

Whole life policies offer level premiums and the prospect of accumulation of cash value within the policy. The cash value can be withdrawn when the policy endows (matures) or when the policy is terminated by the policyholder. The cash value can also be borrowed as a loan while keeping the life insurance component of the policy in force, but the loan remains a liability that must be subtracted from any death benefit paid. Cash values increase slowly in the early years of the whole life policy as the insurance company makes up for its underwriting expenses. The insurance company is required by regulators to maintain a policy reserve, which is a liability for the company, in the amount of the cash value to be paid out to the insureds if they have not died by the time it is due to be paid.

*Payment of premiums to the insurance company to assume mortality risks results in lower lifetime wealth.*

The premium and the face value of the whole life policy remain constant, and the cash value increases, but the insurance value decreases over time. This tends to follow the typical pattern of requiring less life insurance as a person gets older and the need to protect human capital diminishes. Remember, human capital tends to fall toward zero as an individual reaches retirement.



When thinking about the cost of life insurance, there is more to consider than just choosing the policy with the lowest premium. There are many variables at play, and it is not easy for potential consumers to compare the cost of life insurance policies. However, there are two methods used to compare the prices of whole life insurance policies:

1. The ***net payment cost index*** assumes that the insured person will die at the end of a specified period, such as 20 years.
2. The ***surrender cost index*** assumes that the policy will be surrendered at the end of the period and that the policyholder will receive the projected cash value.

### Disability Income Insurance

Disability income insurance is designed to reduce earnings risk caused by the insured becoming less than fully employed as a result of injury or disability. Disabilities tend to be for short periods of time rather than for life.

There are three definitions of full disability that address inability to perform the duties of:

1. One's regular occupation
2. Any occupation for which one is suited by education and experience
3. Any occupation

Using the first definition, a surgeon who loses the use of his or her dominant hand is deemed to be disabled. Using the second definition, a surgeon able to perform the duties of a general practitioner would not be deemed disabled. Using the third definition, even if the surgeon could not practice as a doctor but could teach at a medical school (or hold any other occupation), the individual would not be deemed disabled. For professionals with highly specialized skills, insurance contracts that include the first definition provide the most inclusive coverage, though they will have more expensive premiums.

As an extension to the definition of fully disabled, partial disability means that although the insureds cannot perform all of the duties of their profession, they can remain employed at a lower income. Residual disability means that the insured can perform all professional duties but cannot earn as much money after the disability.

Premiums tend to be fixed, are based on the age of the insured, and are underwritten on the health and occupation of the insured. Coverage is through individual policies and through many employers. Disabled individuals will receive a percentage of the difference between their pre- and post-injury income, usually 60% to 80%, because other pre-injury expenses will be lower (such as commuting to work) and to reduce the likelihood of fraudulent claims.

Additional contract terms include:

*Benefit period:* How long the payments will be made, typically until retirement. Usually, a minimum number of years of benefits is specified, such as five years, to encourage those close to retirement to maintain their policies.



*Elimination period (waiting period):* The number of days that the insured must be disabled before payments begin. The typical elimination period in the United States is 90 days. The shorter the elimination period, the higher the premium.

*Rehabilitation clause:* Provides benefits for physical therapy to get the insured back to work as quickly as possible.

*Waiver of premium:* The policy owner may suspend premiums during a disability period, and premiums paid during the elimination period are returned.

*Option to purchase additional insurance rider:* The policy owner may increase coverage without further proof of insurability.

*Cost of living rider:* Benefits will be increased by an accepted cost of living index or some specified percentage each year.

*Noncancelable and guaranteed renewable:* The insurance company must renew the policy annually provided premiums are paid, and there will be no changes to the premium or promised disability benefits, even if employment income declines.

*Noncancelable:* The insurance company must renew the policy annually provided that premiums are paid, but premiums can be increased for the entire underwriting class although not for one particular individual. This is less expensive than a guaranteed renewable policy, but insurance companies with historical losses are expected to raise their premiums.

### Homeowner's Insurance

A homeowner's policy can be specified as:

- *All risks:* All risks are included except those specified as being excluded.
- *Named risks:* Only risks specifically listed are covered by the policy.

The claims can be settled in one of two ways:

1. ***Replacement cost:*** The benefit pays the amount required to repair or replace an item with a new item of similar quality based on today's prices.
2. ***Actual cash value:*** The benefit equals replacement cost less depreciation.

Clearly, the replacement cost policy will have higher premiums than the actual cash value policy.

A key part of the insurance policy is the *deductible*, which is the amount that the policyholder must pay before any money is paid by the insurance company. Insurance companies price their policies to encourage the use of a higher deductible. A higher deductible means a lower insurance premium. Consider two policy alternatives:

- *Alternative 1:* Policy with a $500 deductible with annual premium of $3,000.
- *Alternative 2:* Policy with a $1,000 deductible with an annual premium of $2,900.

The lower deductible costs $100 more in annual premium. The purchaser needs to think whether the additional $100 of premium is worth the $500 difference between deductibles. A higher deductible means that the policyholder retains more risk but increases expected wealth over time by paying lower premiums to the insurance company.

In addition to homeowner's insurance to cover the cost of casualty losses, some mortgage lenders require homeowners to have life insurance sufficient to repay the mortgage should the borrower die. As the mortgage balance declines over time, an insurance policy can be purchased with a declining face value and premiums. By contrast, insurance companies want the house to be insured for its full value (less the value of the land, which cannot be lost or destroyed) so that it will receive larger premiums. If a house is underinsured, say less than 80% of its replacement cost, any losses are reimbursed at a lower rate.



Homeowners' liability is also addressed within the insurance policy to cover visitors injured in an accident in the home, but excludes professional and business liability, which may be covered separately.

### Automobile Insurance

Automobile and other vehicle insurance rates are based on the value of vehicle and underwritten on the primary driver's age and driving record.

There are two types of coverage:

1. ***Collision insurance*** covers damage from an accident.
2. ***Comprehensive insurance*** covers damage from other causes, such as fire, hail, glass breakage, and theft.

The insurance amount is up to the replacement cost of the automobile with the same make and model in the same condition. If the cost to repair the automobile is greater than its actual cash value, the insurer will most often pay only the cash value. Liability, including injury and property damage, is also included in the policy. Like a homeowner's policy, the automobile policyholder also retains risk through the use of a deductible. Personal watercraft (boats) and trailers might require a separate insurance policy or an endorsement, which is coverage added to an existing policy.

### Health/Medical Insurance

In the United States, there are three kinds of health insurance:

1. *Indemnity plan:* Allows the insured to go to any medical service provider, but the insured must pay a specified percentage of "reasonable and customary" fees.
2. *Preferred provider organization (PPO):* Allows the insured to go to a network of physicians who charge lower prices to individuals within the plan than to individuals who obtain health care on their own.
3. *Health maintenance organization (HMO):* Allows office visits at no or low cost to encourage individuals to seek treatment for minor medical issues before they become serious.

Comprehensive major medical insurance covers most health care expenses, including physician's fees, surgical fees, hospitalization, lab fees, X-rays, and other "reasonable and customary" diagnostic and treatment expenses.

Other key terms and features that could affect the premium of health insurance include:

- *Deductible:* The amount that the insured pays before the insurance company pays any benefit.
- *Coinsurance:* The percentage of any expense that the insurance company will pay, typically 80%.
- *Copayments:* Fixed payments that the insured must make for a particular service, such as $250 per doctor office visit.
- *Maximum out-of-pocket expense (stop-loss limit):* Individual and family maximum amount of expenses incurred beyond which the insurance company will pay 100%.
- *Maximum yearly and lifetime benefits:* Maximum amounts that the insurance company will pay within the respective time periods.
- *Preexisting conditions:* Health conditions that the insured had when applying for insurance that the policy may or may not cover.
- *Preadmission certificate:* An approval from the insurance company before a scheduled (nonemergency) hospital visit or treatment.

### Liability Insurance

The liability coverage in the homeowner's and automobile policy may be inadequate to cover a significant accident. In this case, a separate *personal umbrella liability* insurance policy can be purchased. Consider a situation where an automobile policy provides $300,000 of liability coverage but the insured driver causes $650,000 worth of damage. The umbrella policy would pay the additional $350,000 beyond the automobile policy coverage. Such umbrella policies are relatively inexpensive.

Other forms of insurance include title insurance, which ensures that the ownership of property and real estate is not in doubt. Pseudo-insurance contracts (also known as service contracts) are sold when purchasing an automobile, home appliance, or other costly product to avoid repair costs. They are offered at the time of purchase, so sellers can charge a high rate because buyers have limited opportunity to compare insurance prices. Such contracts often include a deductible.

## Annuities

Annuities are designed to protect against longevity risk. In other words, individuals will live for an unknown number of years after retirement and need to even out their spending over an uncertain time frame. Private annuities can be purchased from insurance companies. Life insurance provides financial protection for beneficiaries if policyholders die too young, whereas annuities protect people financially who live longer than expected.

Similar to life insurance, there are four parties to an annuity:

1. *Annuitant:* The annuitant is the person who receives the benefits while alive.
2. *Contract owner:* In most cases, the annuitant owns the contract. However, an employer can purchase an annuity for a retiring employee.
3. *Beneficiary (or beneficiaries):* Beneficiaries receive benefits when the annuitant dies provided that the annuity is purchased with a "period certain," which is a minimum guaranteed payment period.
4. *Insurer:* The insurer is the insurance company that is licensed to sell the annuity.

There are five annuity types, depending on whether the annuity is paid out immediately (single-premium immediate annuity or SPIA) or is deferred, and whether the underlying investments in the annuity are more bond-like (fixed) or equity-like (variable).

1. *Immediate fixed annuity:* This is the most common type of annuity, in which the annuitant trades a single lump sum of money at retirement in exchange for a regular promised payment for as long as the annuitant is alive. Payments are expressed as a percentage of the initial payment, which is also known as the *income yield*. So, if an insurance company quotes a 6% income yield, then in exchange for every $100,000 in lump-sum premium, the annuitant will receive $6,000 per year.

   Women live longer than men on average, so women will receive lower income yields. Payments increase with age because of the higher likelihood of death. Annuity pricing also depends on prevailing market yields on bonds because insurance companies tend to invest conservatively. When current yields on bonds are lower than historical bond yields, annuity payments will be low compared with historical averages. If life expectancy is rising at the same time, then payouts will be even lower.
2. *Immediate variable annuity:* The annuitant trades a single lump sum of money today in exchange for a promised income benefit for as long as the annuitant is alive. The income benefit varies over time, depending on the investment performance of the portfolio's underlying assets. During up markets, the payment will go up. During down markets, the payment will go down. The annuitant can purchase an income floor that provides protection during down markets. Without the floor, it is possible that payments could stop if the underlying asset values fall to zero.
3. *Deferred fixed annuity:* The annuitant pays premiums on an ongoing basis prior to retirement and receives an annuity payout at some future date. At any time prior to retirement, the investor can cash out the accumulated funds, which may be subject to a surrender charge. At retirement, the annuitant can either cash out or annuitize the accumulated funds with a periodic fixed payment, with most investors choosing to annuitize.
4. *Deferred variable annuity:* The annuitant pays a premium on an ongoing basis prior to retirement and receives an annuity payout at some future date. The annuitant can choose from a menu of investment options, similar to the purchase of mutual funds. However, the annuity is purchased through a salesperson who is licensed to sell

insurance products. Compared with mutual funds, deferred variable annuities can be more expensive and have limited investment options.

Deferred variable annuities can include a death benefit to a beneficiary. In exchange for a fee, the insurance company will pay the entire amount used to purchase the annuity when the annuitant dies, and the value of the contract is less than the initial investment. The annuitant can surrender the contract prior to retirement in exchange for a surrender charge. At retirement, the annuitant can simply start taking a variable income based on investment performance, add a contract rider, or annuitize the contract by converting it to an immediate payout annuity. Few investors actually annuitize a deferred variable annuity.

Without a rider, there is no guaranteed income stream for life, as the underlying investments could fall in value until they are worthless. Then the annuity payments would stop, possibly while the annuitant is still alive. A guaranteed minimum withdrawal benefit for life rider can be added to construct a guaranteed income stream for life. In up markets, the initial investment may not be depleted, and any remaining value will be paid to the beneficiary. If the investment value is depleted because of poor investment performance, the insurance company will continue to pay the minimum benefit until the annuitant's death.

5. ***Advanced life deferred annuity (ALDA):*** An ALDA is a hybrid of deferred fixed annuity and immediate fixed annuity and is known as pure longevity insurance. In exchange for an immediate lump-sum payment, ALDA payments begin later in life well after retirement, typically when the annuitant turns 80 or 85. The premiums will be much lower than an immediate payment annuity. There are three reasons for the lower premium: (1) the insurance company can earn a return on the initial lump sum before making the first payment; (2) life expectancy of a person who is 80 years old is much lower than a person aged 65 at a normal retirement age; and (3) the annuitant may die before payments are made.



When selecting between fixed and variable annuities, there are a number of important considerations:

1. ***Volatility of the benefit amount:*** Investors who have a high risk tolerance might be better suited to a variable annuity, while those who need assurance of benefit payouts are better suited to a fixed annuity.
2. ***Flexibility:*** Immediate fixed annuities are irrevocable and cannot be undone. Variable annuities are tied to the investment performance of a subaccount, which can allow for withdrawals by the annuitant.
3. ***Future market expectations:*** If the investor believes that the markets are going to perform better in the future, a variable annuity is a better choice than a fixed annuity. A fixed annuity locks the investor into a portfolio of bond-like assets subject to interest rate risk. An investor in a fixed annuity who expects that interest rates will increase may defer purchasing the annuity until after rates increase. However, there is a risk that life expectancy will be longer in the future, resulting in lower payouts.
4. ***Fees:*** Variable annuities tend to have higher fees than fixed annuities. Immediate fixed annuities are easier to compare with each other, an important feature when comparing annuity payouts among insurance companies.
5. ***Inflation concerns:*** Fixed annuities are nominal payouts and do not change with inflation. However, a rider can be added to a fixed annuity to increase benefits in line with inflation. Some variable annuities automatically allow for payments to increase or decrease with inflation.

There are five payout methods:

1. ***Life annuity:*** Payments are made until the death of the annuitant.
2. ***Period-certain annuity:*** Payments are made for a specific number of periods, regardless of the life span of the annuitant.
3. ***Life annuity with period certain:*** Payments are made for the entire life of the annuitant or for a minimum number of years (most common is 10 years) even if the annuitant dies. If the annuitant dies within the minimum number of years, payments continue to the beneficiary for the remainder of the period certain.
4. ***Life annuity with refund:*** A life annuity with refund guarantees that the annuitant or beneficiary receives payments equal to the total amount paid into the contract, which equals the initial investment less fees.
5. ***Joint life annuity:*** Payments continue for two or more annuitants, such as a husband-wife couple, as long as either one of them is alive. Payments stop when the surviving annuitant dies.

Individuals can self-insure longevity risk either by making periodic withdrawals from their own investment portfolios or by annuitizing through a life insurance company. In an annuity, each payment is a combination of interest, principal (premium), and mortality credits. Mortality credits are benefits that surviving members of the annuity pool receive from those who have passed away. Self-insurers do not receive mortality credits, only the interest and principal. However, they face longevity risk.

Annuitants pay a higher price for insurance in exchange for the mitigation and possible elimination of longevity risk. In other words, in exchange for lower shortfall risk (lower risk of running out of money during one's lifetime), the investor has less wealth because of annuity premiums. This trade-off is similar to an efficient frontier for a risky portfolio.

PWM

The international shift away from defined benefit (DB) pension plans has caused a shift toward annuities. At the individual level, there are five factors that would likely ***increase demand*** for any annuity:

1. Longer-than-average life expectancy
2. Greater preference for lifetime income
3. Less concern for leaving money to heirs
4. More conservative investing preferences
5. Lower guaranteed income from other sources (such as pensions)

These five factors would be associated with low wealth and low shortfall risk. The decision to retain risk or buy insurance is determined by a household's risk tolerance. At the same level of wealth, a more risk-tolerant household will prefer to retain more risk, either through higher insurance deductibles or by simply not buying insurance. A risk-averse household would have lower deductibles and would purchase more insurance. For all households, insurance products that have a higher load (expenses) will encourage a household to retain more risk. Finally, as the variability of income increases, the need for life insurance decreases because the present value of future earnings (human capital) will be lower with a higher discount rate.

 

The following table shows the appropriateness of the four risk management techniques, depending on the severity of loss and the frequency of loss.

| Loss Characteristics | High Frequency | Low Frequency |
|---|---|---|
| High severity | Risk avoidance | Risk transfer |
| Low severity | Risk reduction | Risk retention |

Volume 2, Level III CFA Program Curriculum 2017

An investment advisor will often be asked how much life insurance is enough. There are two techniques:

1. The ***human life value method*** estimates the present value of earnings that must be replaced.
2. The ***needs analysis method*** estimates the financial needs of the dependents.

# Study Session 6: Portfolio Management for Institutional Investors

INST

# MANAGING INSTITUTIONAL INVESTOR PORTFOLIOS

Cross-Reference to CFA Institute Assigned Reading #13

## Pension Funds

### Plan Types

| | Defined Contribution (DC) | Defined Benefit (DB) |
|---|---|---|
| Sponsor obligation | Contribution or match | Employee retirement benefit |
| Investment risk | Participant | Plan sponsor |
| Asset ownership | Participant (after vesting) | Plan sponsor |
| Early termination risk | Retain vested benefits | May lose benefits |
| Portability | Easily portable to new company 401(k) | May not be portable to 401(k) |
| Investment policy statement (IPS) | May not be applicable to plan assets, but participants may have individual IPS | Applies to plan assets |

### Defined-Benefit Plan Liability Concepts

- Accumulated benefit obligation (ABO): If plan is terminated today, the present value of benefits owed *excluding* expected future wage/salary changes.
- Projected benefit obligation (PBO): If plan is terminated today, the present value of benefits owed *including* expected future wage/salary changes.
- Total future liability: Used internally for setting investment policy, total future liability includes both accumulated and projected future benefits.

IMPORTANT: PBO best represents pension liability for a going concern.

### Funded Status

- Underfunded: asset-to-liability ratios less than 100%
- Fully funded: asset-to-liability ratios equal to or greater than 100%

Plan surplus is the amount over 100%, and acts as a cushion against poor investment results.

IMPORTANT: Duration of future defined-benefit (DB) liabilities will be shorter for plans with a greater proportion of retired lives, or for plans with older active lives.

INST

### Retired and Active Lives

- Retired lives currently receive pension benefits; they are retired.
- Active lives are in the benefit accumulation stage; they are still working.

### Risk Tolerance and Objectives

Underfunded plans tend to be quite willing to assume risk, but have less ability to do so because they have less cushion against poor returns.

Everything else equal, plans have greater ability to assume risk (i.e., higher risk tolerance) when there are the following:

- Plan surplus
- Lower sponsor debt ratios and higher current/expected profitability
- Lower correlation of asset returns with company financial results
- Fewer options such as early retirement or lump-sum distributions
- Greater proportion of active versus retired lives
- Higher proportion of younger workers

Risk objectives may relate to shortfall risk of achieving:

- Funding status of ABO, PBO, or total future liability
- Funding status sufficient to avoid reporting a pension liability
- Funding status above some regulatory threshold

Risk objectives may also attempt to minimize:

- Volatility of future contributions (currently contributing companies)
- Probability of making additional contributions (currently overfunded plans)

### Return Objectives

Plan sponsors wish to achieve a return that will fully fund liabilities on an inflation-adjusted basis, given their funding constraints.

A fully funded plan will have assets equal to the present value of future liabilities and a return at least equal to the discount rate used against the liabilities.

Return on plan assets greater than necessary—usually in a strong market—results in negative pension expense for the plan sponsor.

Retired lives will tend to be a less volatile funding need than active lives, and the two liability types may be separately funded by some plans.

### Liquidity Requirement



Plan sponsors must meet the required benefit payments. Liquidity requirements are higher for plans that have:

- Smaller sponsor contributions relative to disbursements
- Greater retired lives relative to active lives (assuming they are managed together), or retired lives versus active lives

### Time Horizon

The plan's time horizon will be its termination date, or will be infinite if the company is a going concern with no expected plan termination date.

A plan could have a multistage horizon:

- Active lives: average time to normal retirement age
- Retired lives: average beneficiary life expectancy

### Tax Concerns

Investment income and capital gain on private plan assets are usually exempt from taxation.

### Legal and Regulatory Factors

Pension plan trustees have a fiduciary responsibility to beneficiaries, which varies by type of plan and jurisdiction. In the United States, ERISA is the fiduciary standard.

### Unique Circumstances

Plan sponsors may have financial and human resource limitations, making it difficult to perform the complex due diligence required for certain investments (e.g., hedge fund, natural resources, private equity, etc.).

Ethical constraints may exist against:

- Industries and companies with negative ethical or social welfare products or services
- Countries with negative ethical political regimes

> IMPORTANT: Ethical constraints will be a unique circumstance for all types of institutions.

### Defined-Contribution Plan Considerations

Sponsor-directed defined-contibution (DC) plans have investment considerations similar to those of DB plans.

Participant-directed DC plans must consider:

- Diversification: Plan must offer at least three investment options and participant ability to freely switch among them; limitation on sponsor-company stock.
- Investment policy statement (IPS): IPS addresses plan sponsor's selection and evaluation of options offered to participants.
- Education: Plan sponsors provide general education resources, but participants are responsible for allocations based on their individual risk/return profiles.

### Hybrid Plan Considerations

Hybrid plans seek to combine a DC plan's understandability, portability, and easy administration with a DB plan's guarantees and ties to length of service/salary level.

- Cash balance plans: Sponsor contributes a percentage of salary based on age and receives a statement indicating accrued benefit, but there is no separate beneficiary account; may be unfair to older employees in DB plans converted to this.
- Employee stock ownership plan (ESOP): DC plans are sometimes used to liquidate a large block of owner's shares, discourage unfriendly takeovers, or avoid public offerings; ESOPs create correlation of human capital and investment capital if company fails.

## Foundations

### Types

- Independent (private or family): Funded by donor, donor's family, or independent trustees to further educational, religious, or other charitable goals
- Company-sponsored: Same as independent foundation, but a legally independent organization sponsored by a profit-making corporation
- Operating: Funded same as independent foundation, but conducts specific research or provides a special service (e.g., operates a private park or museum)
- Community: Multiple donors or publicly funded to make grants for purposes similar to independent foundation; no spending requirement as with the others

### Risk Objectives

Higher risk tolerance due to noncontractually committed payout.

### Return Objectives

Asset management fees cannot be used toward the spending requirement (although grant-making expenses can count toward that). Foundations seek returns to cover at least inflation-adjusted spending goals and overhead not countable toward the required spending minimum:

$$r = \%\text{ spend} + \%\text{ management} + \%\text{ inflation}$$

or

$$= (1 + \%\text{ spend})(1 + \%\text{ management})(1 + \%\text{ inflation}) - 1$$

### Liquidity Requirement

Foundations must be able to quickly fund spending needs (including noncountable overhead) greater than current contributions.

Private and family foundations must spend percentage of 12-month average in the fiscal year, so they typically have 10% to 20% of assets in reserve to make sure they can make grants equal to at least 5% of assets.

INST

### Time Horizon

Usually the time horizon is infinite, but this depends on the purpose of the foundation. A longer horizon implies greater risk-taking ability.

### Tax Concerns

Excise tax on dividends, interest, and realized capital gains is equal to about 2%, but is reduced to 1% if charitable distributions exceed the minimum percentage of assets required for the year *and* the five-year average payout plus 1% of investment income.

### Legal and Regulatory

The Uniform Prudent Management of Institutional Funds Act (UPMIFA) regulates foundation investment activities in the United States, and the Internal Revenue Code regulates how it conducts foundation activities.

### Unique Circumstances

Foundations with funding primarily via large blocks of stock may, with donor approval, enter swap agreements or other transactions to diversify returns from the stock and avoid single-asset volatility.

## Endowments

Donors establish endowments to make distributions for program purposes yet maintain the principal in perpetuity.

Unlike foundations, endowments have no minimum spending requirement.

Quasi-endowments—also known as funds functioning as endowments (FFEs)—have no spending restrictions and may spend the entire principal over time.

### Risk Objectives

Endowments that moderate impacts of portfolio volatility by adopting spending rules based on smoothed averages of return and previous spending can accept greater risk and potential return than endowments that do not use a smoothing rule.

High debt levels and high donor contributions as a percentage of total spend indicate lower ability to assume risk.

Short-term performance shortfalls reduce willingness to assume risk to protect the endowment value, although endowments generally show high willingness to assume risk via high spending and consequently high return requirements.

IMPORTANT: Desired spending must consider inflation; return objectives must be greater than the inflation-adjusted desired spending rate $S_D/MV$.

INST

### Return Objectives

Endowments calculate return requirements in the same way as foundations do, but support institutions with costs growing faster than the consumer price index (CPI) and gross domestic product (GDP) deflator (e.g., colleges and universities).

Simple spending rate: $$S_t = \frac{S_D}{MV} \times MV_{t-1}$$

Rolling three-year average: $$S_t = \frac{S_D}{MV} \times \frac{1}{3}(MV_{t-1} + MV_{t-2} + MV_{t-3})$$

Geometric smoothing rule: $$S_t = F_s \times S_{t-1}(1 + I_{t-1}) + (1 - F_s) \times \frac{S_D}{MV} \times MV_{t-2}$$

The geometric rule considers the inflation impact on previous period spending. $F_S$ is the smoothing factor or rate, generally between 60% and 80%, indicating greater weight on the most recently completed endowment period: $MV_{t-2}$ = beginning $MV_{t-1}$.

### Liquidity Requirements

Endowments require liquidity for gifts as well as planned capital distributions for construction projects and to allow portfolio rebalancing. Because they face no mandated spending minimums, endowments can hold higher investments in alternative investments and illiquid securities for long-term growth.

Bond maturation, normal security sales, and investment yield provide liquidity.

### Time Horizon

Each period's withdrawal has a specific time horizon because annual spending is based on desired spending rates and yearly market values. However, an infinite horizon results from objectives related to inflation-adjusted desired spending.

### Tax Considerations

Endowments owned by nonprofits effectively pay no tax unless they have unrelated business taxable income (UBTI). Some portion of dividend income from non-U.S. securities may have nonrecoverable tax.

### Legal and Regulatory Factors

Most states have adopted UPMIFA:

- Requires ordinary business care managing investments
- Allows delegation of investment management responsibilities
- Allows spending capital gain returns as well as income
- Requires that the owner's mandates for use of principal be respected
- Prohibits using principal when market value declines below historical book value

Institutions are required under Section 501(c)(3) to ensure that use of endowment funds does not benefit private individuals.



### Unique Circumstances

Types of investments may be constrained by size and ability of staff or board member sophistication. More sophisticated boards will often make significant investment in alternative investments, especially private placements which typically require funds of at least $25 million since they avoid Securities and Exchange Commission (SEC) registration.

## Life Insurance Companies

Insurance companies attempt to achieve premium income and asset growth sufficient to fund potential insurance claims and increases in the *valuation reserve* required by insurance regulators.

The National Association of Insurance Commissioners (NAIC) regulates insurance companies at the state level in the United States. In addition to reserves sufficient to pay policyholder claims as they arise (i.e., policyholder reserves), NAIC has established:

- *Risk-based capital (RBC)* requirements: The net asset position necessary to remain an ongoing concern given company size and risk profile. Greater asset, underwriting, and other risk requires a greater amount of capital relative to liabilities.
- *Asset valuation reserve (AVR)* requirements: The portion of capital reserved for absorbing investment losses.

Firms with poor investment results may have AVR shortfalls requiring write-down of *surplus* (i.e., assets less liabilities, also known as equity or net assets) via a charge to earnings in an amount sufficient to maintain the reserve.

Other influences on life insurers' investment policy include:

- Disintermediation risk: Policy owners withdraw funds to reinvest with other intermediaries in higher-returning assets:
  - Borrowing against cash value
  - Surrendering policies
- Interest-related risk:
  - Assets (e.g., portfolio investments)
  - Liabilities (e.g., annuity contracts)
- Market valuation: Requiring firms to value assets at market value increases earnings volatility.

## Risk Objectives

*Liquidity risk* arises from changes in the firm's investment portfolio that threaten to challenge its reserves.

*Interest rate risk* includes:

- Reinvestment risk: Differences between expected and actual reinvestment income (i.e., reinvesting coupon income at a lower rate than the original yield).
- Valuation risk: Changes in principal value due to changes in expected reinvestment income.

Duration mismatch objectives, part of the *asset–liability management (ALM)* process, help control both liquidity and interest rate risk.

*Credit risk.* Related to issuers failing to make interest payments or repay principal. Insurance companies use credit analysis to minimize credit risk, and have objectives regarding credit risk.

*Cash volatility risk.* Related to timely receipt and reinvestment of cash. Cash receipt and reinvestment assumptions affect required portfolio return.

Threat of *disintermediation* and the need for return requires greater risk, but fiduciary principles limit risk tolerance.

### Return Objectives

The *minimum return requirement* derives from the rate initially specified to fund the contract—that is, accumulation estimated for policyholder reserves held by the company for future disbursement.

Life insurance is competitive; insurers segment by product line to ensure necessary margins. Measuring total return is difficult when assets experience volatility but liabilities do not.

The *net interest spread* is the margin of return received over the minimum return requirement. Positive net interest spread results in a reduction in the liability and an increase in AVR; negative net interest spread results in an increase in the liability and a reduction in AVR.

Return objectives are necessary for public and private equity investments, real estate, and other higher-returning investments used to grow surplus used for expanding lines of business.

### Liquidity Requirement

Insurance companies have limited liquidity needs due to use of derivatives, but may have bank lines of credit to use in emergencies.

### Time Horizon

Different product lines have different time horizons and will be funded by assets matching those time horizons (e.g., 20- to 40-year-maturity bond and mortgage investments for life insurance contracts and 2 to 10 years for group annuities).

### Tax Concerns

Insurance companies focus on after-tax returns to recognize taxes on investment returns.

Changes to certain U.S. laws could affect life insurance companies' competitive position relative to other investment products. For example:

- Only investment income attributable to growth of surplus is taxable; the actuarially assumed share of investment income is not taxable.
- Life insurance and annuity products enjoy tax-free accumulation of investment returns that accrue within the policy.



### Legal and Regulatory Factors

U.S. state regulations:

- Eligible investments: U.S. states generally establish criteria for eligible investments.
- Asset allocation and selection: U.S. states generally apply the prudent investor rule within the universe of eligible investments, establishing modern portfolio theory as the basis for asset allocation. No model law exists across states.

National regulation:

- Valuation methods: U.S. GAAP and EU may allow different valuation methods.
- Anti-money-laundering regulation prevents misuse of investment features of insurance products in illegal activities.

### Unique Circumstances

Reserve and surplus sufficiency will be primary drivers of portfolio policies.

## Non–Life Insurance Companies

Investment policies are similar among non–life insurance companies, but differ from those of life insurance companies:

- Longer claims processing periods (less immediate liquidity required)
- Shorter duration liabilities
- Liability exposures:
    - Some inflation risk on inflation-adjusted payouts
    - Virtually no interest rate risk (i.e., no internal accumulation of value)
- Uncertain timing and value versus life insurance company's value certainty:
    - Long-tail claims reporting (claim may occur long after the incident)
    - Litigated settlement amounts

### Risk Objectives

*Policyholder reserves* use lower-risk assets to satisfy unpredictable operating claims.

*Surplus assets* use higher-risk assets:

- Maintaining surplus during high-volatility markets curtails ability to accept higher risk.
- Self-regulated rather than state-regulated risk constraints exist for surplus assets.

Risk is measured against premiums-to-capital and premiums-to-surplus ratios.

INST

### Return Objectives

Investment earnings on surplus assets must be sufficient to offset periodic operating losses (i.e., claims higher than premium income), and to maintain policyholder reserves.

Insurance companies usually invest in higher-earning common stocks, convertibles, and alternative assets for tax-advantaged dividend exclusion and capital gain.

Larger insurance companies use active management strategies for total return rather than yield or investment income strategies.

Returns vary widely among insurance companies due to differences in:

- Tax liability position
- Insurance regulations

- Surplus and total capital positions
- Preference for capital gain over income returns
- Product mix (i.e., resulting in different liability durations)

### Liquidity Requirement

Liquidity is required primarily to meet policyholder claims; immediate liquidity is obtained in commercial paper or short-term Treasury bills.

Allocation may be made to higher-quality taxable bonds for quick liquidation, if required.

### Time Horizon

Non–life insurance liabilities generally have shorter duration than life insurance liabilities.

Casualty companies with tax-exempt securities allocate to longer maturities to take advantage of the steeper tax-exempt yield curve (in the United States).

Differences between non–life insurance companies may relate to asset–liability mismatch willingness (i.e., for higher return on longer-duration assets).

Emphasis on current earning versus long-term growth has led to lower willingness to invest in less liquid assets with potentially higher returns.

### Tax Concerns

Previously tax-exempt bond income became taxable for U.S. companies in 1986. There may still be advantages to owning the bonds (e.g., capital gain), but companies require complex models that fit their circumstances.

### Legal and Regulatory Factors

Regulatory agencies may specify eligible assets and quality standards up to some percentage, with the remainder eligible to invest in higher-risk/higher-return investments.

Risk-based capital regulations specify minimum capital requirements based on the following, in addition to size:

- Asset risk: Degree of market value fluctuation
- Credit risk: Probability of default
- Underwriting risk: Underpriced current or prospective business (i.e., premiums less than claims)

### Unique Circumstances

Other than liquidity needs and reserve requirements, a non–life insurer must balance taxable income with operating profitability.

## Banks

Liabilities of banks consist primarily of demand and time deposits, but may include publicly traded debt and funds purchased from other banks or the Federal Reserve to satisfy regulatory requirements.

Bank surplus consists of assets less liabilities, the cash portion of which is invested in marketable securities.

Banks use U.S. government securities as collateral to cover the uninsured portion of deposit liabilities (e.g., the pledging requirement).

### Risk Objectives

Banks, due to risk relative to primarily fixed liabilities, have below-average risk tolerance.

A bank's asset–liability risk management committee (ALCO) closely monitors:

- Net interest margin: Net interest income divided by average earning assets
- Interest spread: Average yield on earning assets less average percentage cost of interest-bearing liabilities

*Leverage-adjusted duration gap (LADG)* measures overall interest rate exposure based on duration and market value of assets and liabilities:

$$LADG = D_A - kD_L$$
$$k = V_L / V_A$$

When interest rates rise, banks with positive LADG experience net worth decreases, banks with negative LADG experience net worth increases, and banks with neutral (i.e., immunized) LADG experience no change.

*Value at risk (VaR)* measures position and aggregate portfolio minimum loss over some period at a specified probability.

Banks buy or sell marketable securities to adjust interest rate risk, manage liquidity, offset loan portfolio credit risk, and produce income (up to a quarter or more of revenue).

INST

### Return Objectives

The interest income allocation focuses on positive spread over cost of funds.

The remaining allocation focuses on higher total return.

### Liquidity Requirements

Demand for loans and net outflows drive liquidity needs.

### Time Horizon

A bank's duration spread of assets over liabilities constrains the risk management strategy for its securities portfolio to an intermediate term (i.e., three to seven years).

### Tax Concerns

Securities losses decrease operating income, and gains increase operating income, thus making portfolio returns fully taxable. This can lead to lower quality of earnings as banks sell underperforming securities only when they are otherwise profitable and vice versa (i.e., manage earnings).

### Legal and Regulatory Factors

Banks may hold a large percentage of their portfolios in government securities to pledge against reserves, and regulators restrict allocations to common shares and below-investment-grade bonds.

Regulators may link required capital to risk for both on- and off-balance-sheet assets (i.e., RBC requirements).

### Unique Circumstances

Community needs and historical banking relationships are unique circumstances for banks.

## Investment Companies and Other

Regulated investment companies include open-end and closed-end mutual funds, exchange-traded funds, and unit trusts.

Less regulated investment companies include hedge funds, which sell to institutions and qualified investors (i.e., high net worth individuals meeting certain requirements).

Corporations with large cash holdings may invest *liquid cash* in very short-term money market securities and *core cash* in longer-term money market securities or Treasury bills.

INST

Return and risk considerations for this group depend on their individual investment mandates and other characteristics.

## LINKING PENSION LIABILITIES TO ASSETS
Cross-Reference to CFA Institute Assigned Reading #14

### Contrasting Asset Allocation Assumptions

The *asset-only approach* indicates total return management with no consideration of the underlying liability.

The *liability-relative approach* indicates a portfolio that mimics liabilities exposures.

Plan asset returns can then be compared to returns from a benchmark portfolio comprised of assets that mimic the underlying liabilities exposure.

### Risk

#### Definitions of Risk

Short-term risk concerns the short-term volatility of liabilities to be managed.

Long-term risk addresses the long-term ability of the assets to offset (i.e., *defease*) the liability.

The *market value of a liability* is the discounted value of the expected future benefit, which should consider:

- Expected wage growth (where applicable)
- Expected inflation (where the plan covers it)
- A nominal discount rate that considers inflation

The *risk of a liability* is the variability around the value created by different benefit payment estimates and discount rate assumptions.

### Market-Related Exposures

Assets used to offset pension liability depend on the type of participation and whether payments are fixed or indexed for inflation.

#### Inactive Participants

The pension liability attributable to *inactive participants* includes:

- *Retirees*—Workers who have retired from the firm and are owed a benefit
- *Deferreds*—Vested former employees who are not yet receiving a benefit due

#### Active Participants

The pension liability attributable to active participants includes:

- *Accrued benefits*, which are derived from past service and wages earned and include only the existing workforce.

- *Future benefits*, which are calculated based on future service and wages, and include new entrants to the plan.

The future benefits liability is attributable to:

- Future wages: Estimated future wage increases based on:
    - Real wage growth—Growth in wages that tends to follow economic growth, with equities being the most appropriate matching asset class.
    - Wage inflation, with real rate bonds being the most appropriate matching asset class.
- Future service: Plan sponsors typically do not fund this liability, similar to not paying for salary that has not yet been earned.

### Future Participants

The pension liability attributable to new entrants to the company's workforce is highly uncertain and not usually funded (plans closed to new entrants have zero liability). Otherwise, it would equal the sum of accrued and future benefits for each prospective plan participant.

### Funding

Market-related exposure includes:

- Term structure, including both real interest rate and inflation rate risk inherent in the holding period until the benefit is paid. (Fixed benefits include only this type of exposure.)
- Inflationary wage increase: Current wage payments indexed to future inflation.
- Real wage growth, linked to economic growth.

*Frozen plans* have only an accrued benefits liability; they do not have a future benefits liability for real wage growth or inflation. These plans can be mimicked by nominal bonds.

The inactive and accrued active lives portions have only term structure exposure. These portions can be funded either with nominal bonds if the pension payment does not have a cost of living allowance (COLA) or with real rate bonds if the pension payment does have a COLA.

INST

The future portion of active lives should be funded by:

- Nominal bonds for the term structure component
- Inflation-linked bonds for the inflationary wage increase component
- Equities for the real wage growth component

### Non-Market-Related Exposures (Liability Noise)

For inactive participants:

- Differences between the retirement plan demographic expense and the actuary model, given model certainty; larger plan populations track the actuarial assumptions with less noise.
    - Start-date risk—Risk of deferreds receiving benefits sooner than assumed
    - Longevity risk—Risk of retirees and deferreds living longer than assumed
- Model uncertainty (e.g., unforeseen medical expenses that increase life span)

For active participants, the possibility of disability or withdrawal from a plan contributes to liability noise.

### Portfolio Effectiveness versus Efficiency

A liability-mimicking portfolio has the best chance of tracking the existing liability and should become the appropriate benchmark.

The liability-mimicking portfolio alone is unlikely to offset future cash contributions required for future service benefits and future participants; therefore, plan sponsors desire growth greater than the benchmark.

Plans can hedge the term structure of the liability only by using interest rate futures with the unused assets allocated to long-term bonds, inflation-indexed bonds, and equities in the appropriate amount.

# STUDY SESSION 7: APPLICATIONS OF ECONOMIC ANALYSIS TO PORTFOLIO MANAGEMENT



 

EC

# CAPITAL MARKET EXPECTATIONS
Cross-Reference to CFA Institute Assigned Reading #15

## A Developmental Framework

### Capital Market Expectations

Investors must develop *capital market expectations (CMEs)* (i.e., macro expectations regarding risk and return prospects at the asset class level) to establish a target allocation. This contrasts with *micro expectations* that investors must establish for valuation and asset selection within each asset class.

## Challenges in Developing CMEs

### Data Limitations

- Reporting lag: From economic activity to reporting may take from two weeks in developed countries to two years in less developed countries, which increases uncertainty about current conditions.
- Revision lag.
- Definition/calculation changes.
- Index rebasing: Relevant coincident series using different base years should not be used.

### Measurement Errors/Biases

- Transcription errors may occur.
- Survivorship bias reflects only surviving entities (e.g., only successful hedge funds remain in an index).
- Appraisal (smoothed) data: Data reflecting appraisals rather than market data tend to be less volatile, which makes statistically relating that price to changes in economic data more difficult. Correction to smoothed data may be possible with rescaling to allow visibility of volatility.

EC

### Limitations of Estimates Using Historical Data

Relationships altered during different points in a historical data series (e.g., technology, legal, regulatory, political, etc.) is known as a *regime change*. A regime change results in *nonstationarity* (i.e., different statistical relationships at different points in time).

*Asynchronism* describes using data from nonexplanatory periods when longer explanatory series are not available.

Make sure to check for nonstationarity for long historical data series (e.g., a large covariance matrix that must have more data points than correlation combinations).

### *Ex Post* Risk Bias

While *ex post* (i.e., historical) data can inform, decision makers ideally use only *ex ante* (i.e., forward-looking) risk premiums. Nonrepeating *ex post* situations may influence *ex ante* estimates.

### Methodology Errors

- Data mining: Searching data for a statistically strong relationship although it may have no economic rationale.
- Time-period bias: Applying relationships from data in one time period to data in another period where the relationship does not exist. This may be solved by out-of-sample testing—that is, comparing statistical properties in one subperiod to other subperiods.

Requiring a strong economic rationale helps avoid both types of errors.

### Failure to Use Conditioning Information

Current forecast relationships are conditional on underlying historical relationships. Forecasts should employ relevant *conditioning information* derived from historical relationships.

### Misinterpreting Correlation

Values for *exogenous* (i.e., independent) variables are determined outside of the equations under consideration. *Endogenous* (i.e., dependent) variables are determined by a causative factor. For example, earthquakes are exogenous and property damage claims are endogenous in the relationship.

Two variables, however, could be coincident (i.e., there is no predictive relationship) and both could be predicted by a third variable.

Analysts should exercise care in assuming causation from a correlated pair of variables. Statistical tests (i.e., Granger causality test) can help measure predictive causality of one variable on another.

### Psychological Traps Faced by Professional Forecasters

- Anchoring: Disproportionate weight given to the first piece of information may cause premature conclusions.
- Status quo trap: Believing the future will be like the present. Use rational thinking in a well-defined decision-making process.
- Confirmation bias: Tendency to seek out or overweight information confirming an existing hypothesis.
- Overconfidence: Underestimating potential for incorrect analysis. Use broader consideration of alternative scenarios.
- Prudence: Underestimating variability in forecast outcomes; believing the future will involve only small changes from today. Use broader consideration of alternative scenarios.
- Recallability bias: Overweighting future outcomes based on events that left a strong impression (e.g., unreasonable low equity market values decades after a market crash). Use objective data rather than personal emotions and memories.

### Model Uncertainty

*Model uncertainty* concerns potential model misspecification. This can be reduced by testing several promising models.

Apparent market anomalies could represent an equilibrium of rational beliefs derived from many plausible models.

## Formal Tools

Analysts can produce better forecasts by using sound data and precisely defined, replicable research methods (i.e., *formal tools*).

### Statistical Methods

Statistical models use:

- *Descriptive statistics.* Summarizing data from a large data set (e.g., measures of central tendency and dispersion)
- *Inferential statistics.* Using a smaller group to estimate values for a larger group (e.g., representing a population using sample estimators such as mean, variance, correlations, etc.)

A *sample estimator* from a historical data series can be useful if different time periods exhibit the same statistical properties (i.e., stationarity). An example would be using average historical index return to forecast future return.

EC

In *shrinkage estimation*, analysts improve the forecasting properties of a data series with information from another data series. For example, the *shrinkage estimator* for a covariance matrix involves the weighted average of a historical covariance relationship and covariances calculated by another method, with analysts using subjectively established weights.

A *time-series estimator* involves using lagged values of the same series (and often other data series) in a forecast for the dependent variable—for example, autoregressive conditional heteroskedasticity (ARCH) time-series models; useful in short-term forecasts for economic and financial variables.

A *multifactor model* identifies several factors that directly affect the value of another variable (e.g., using asset factor sensitivities to derive asset returns); useful for estimating covariance:

- Reduces random variation (i.e., noise) in sample-period-specific data.
- Increases consistency within a matrix by using a smaller group of consistent factors.

### Discounted Cash Flow (DCF) Models

An asset's value depends on the present value of its future cash flows:

$$V_0 = \sum_{t=1}^{\infty} \frac{CF_t}{(1+r)^t}$$

DCF models don't address current-period economic conditions; they are more appropriate for long-term analysis.

### Equity DCF Models

The *Gordon growth model*, or *dividend discount model (DDM)*, assumes value growth equal to the dividend growth rate, which equals the earnings growth rate at a constant dividend payout.

Reformulation of the Gordon growth model for expected return on equity is:

$$E(r_i) = \frac{D_0(1+g)}{P_0} + g = \frac{D_1}{P_0} + g$$

Expected gross domestic product (GDP) growth can approximate broad equity index growth; earnings growth for each company equals GDP growth plus its excess over GDP growth, which may be positive or negative.

EC

The *Grinold-Kroner model* restated the Gordon growth model to recognize *repurchase yield* ($\Delta S$), inflation ($I$), and per period percentage change in P/E ratio ($\Delta PE$):

$$E(r_i) = \frac{D_1}{P_0} + g - I - \Delta S + \Delta PE$$

IMPORTANT: Note that the Grinold-Kroner formula recognizes that returns increase when outstanding shares decrease (i.e., a negative *repurchase yield*).

### Fixed-Income DCF Models

The yield to maturity (YTM) for a bond is the single rate discount factor that generates the bond's price.

The YTM rests on an assumption of reinvestment at the same rate. Yield on representative zero-coupon bonds of the same maturity would be a more appropriate reinvestment rate.

Callable bonds generally need downward yield adjustment to recognize the value of the company's call option.

### Risk Premium (Buildup) Approach

The risk premium approach recognizes expected return on risky assets as the risk-free interest rate plus a premium or premiums for compensated risks.

Fixed-income buildup model:

$$E(r_i) = r_F + I + D + L + M + T$$

- The risk-free rate ($r_F$) and inflation ($I$) premiums are together known as the nominal interest rate ($r$).
- Default risk ($D$) increases with issuer default potential.
- Liquidity risk ($L$) increases with potential loss from selling into an illiquid market.
- Maturity risk ($M$) increases with maturity (i.e., term structure).
- Tax ($T$) increases with tax loss on returns.

Analysts can estimate inflation using:

- Default premium over risk-free government bonds
- Yield spread of risk-free government bonds over inflation-protected government bonds

Equity buildup model:

$$E(r_i) = YTM_{F,\,LT} + RP_i$$

- Long-term risk-free rate: 10- to 20-year-maturity government bonds
- Equity risk premium for asset $i$: Expected excess return over long-term government bonds

EC

### Financial Market Equilibrium Models

*Financial market equilibrium models* assume a relationship for return given priced risk in the *global investable market (GIM)* (i.e., the *world market portfolio* representing all investment assets in a market capable of absorbing significant investment amounts).

For perfectly liquid GIM and currency risk premium of zero as expected under purchasing power parity (PPP):

$$E(r_i) = r_F + \beta_i(r_M - r_F)$$

where:

$$\beta_i = \frac{Cov_{i,M}}{\sigma^2_M}$$

Asset beta ($\beta_i$) is sensitivity of asset return to GIM priced return, $r_M - r_F$.

Asset equity risk premium in the GIM:

IMPORTANT: $RP_M/\sigma_M$ is the market Sharpe ratio.

$$RP_i = \sigma_i \rho_{i,M}\left(\frac{RP_M}{\sigma_M}\right)$$

*Integrated markets* have no barriers to cross-border capital mobility. The *Singer-Terhaar* approach adds an illiquidity premium to $r_i$ for imperfect but integrated markets.

*Segmented markets* have meaningful barriers to cross-border mobility; capital must be supplied locally, and the local market is the investable market (i.e., has correlation of 1 with itself). The *Singer-Terhaar* risk premium for segmented markets is:

$$RP_i = \sigma_i\left(\frac{RP_M}{\sigma_M}\right)$$

### Survey and Panel Methods

The *survey method* uses expectations of an expert group to develop CMEs and forecasts, each expert presumably using a disciplined process. The *panel method* surveys the same expert group over time.

Practitioners may have significantly higher expectations than academics because their livelihood largely depends on vibrant markets.

### Inventory Cycle Analysis

The *inventory cycle* results from businesses trying to balance supply with demand, and usually lasts two to four years.

As demand increases, firms' expectations increase, and they increase inventories. As demand decreases, firms' expectations decrease, and they decrease inventories. At some point, demand increases can be met only by a new plant.

Correcting inventory levels usually takes a year or two in each direction.

Analysts often rely on changes in *inventory/sales ratio* trends to assess inflection points.

### Business Cycle Analysis

*Trend analysis* provides information on the direction and strength of a variable series; it is useful in setting equity return expectations and long-run risk premiums.

*Cycle analysis* provides information on inflection points for corporate profits and interest rates, which drive asset class returns within the context of long-run risk/return relationships.

There are longer-term (9- to 11-year) fluctuations of GDP around trend growth.

Generally, changing business and consumer confidence contributes to inflections.

Financial markets react to both expected or perceived current situations, inflections, and central bank actions.

1. Initial recovery—Recovery from low point of recession lasting a few months:
   - Government uses lower interest rates and budget deficits to cure *output gap*.
   - Drawing down inventory or renewed demand strength may initiate recovery.
   - Inflation is still falling; yields are still falling or at bottom.
   - Stock market begins rally; cyclicals outperform.
2. Early upswing—Robust growth without inflation lasting a year to several years:
   - Unemployment begins falling; consumer confidence rises.
   - Strong sales and higher operating levels spur business investment.
   - Lower unit costs drive higher profits.
   - Central bank removes stimulus, driving up short-term interest rates.
   - Bond prices are stable to falling; equity prices are still rising.
3. Late upswing—Output gap closes:
   - Low unemployment with possible labor shortage; high consumer confidence.
   - Rising wages and prices; inflation.
   - Restrictive monetary policy; rising interest rates.
   - Bond prices level off and begin falling; equity prices are stable but volatile.
4. Slowdown—Cresting the hill; lasts a few months to a year:
   - Business confidence wavers; companies begin reducing inventory levels.
   - Inflation accelerates.
   - Interest rates rise, but stabilize at highs.
   - Bond prices stabilize at lows, then rally when interest rates stabilize.
   - Prices on longer maturities rise faster (duration); yield curve may invert.
   - Stock prices crest, then *may* fall; financial services and utilities outperform.

5. Recession—Two consecutive GDP declines (informally); lasts six months to a year:
   - Unemployment rises; consumer confidence falls.
   - Large inventory reduction; profits fall and businesses may lower investment.
   - Lenders become cautious; lending rates rise.
   - After confirmation lag, central bank eases monetary policy.
   - Bond prices rise in anticipation of lower interest rates.
   - Stock prices rise (late stages long before recovery is recognized).

### Monetary Policy during Business Cycles

Central banks use *monetary policy* to expand or contract economic activity with the goal of appropriate growth at stable price levels.

Central bank policy should be:

- Independent: Political influence generally results in accelerating inflation to promote short-term growth.
- Disciplined: Inflation targets are used to inform policy decisions and anchor market expectations.
- Focused: Monetary policy is used to target interest rates.

*Inflation* (i.e., purchasing power of a currency unit decreases) undermines debt because borrowed assets are repaid with currency of lesser value.

*Gold standard.* Cash can be easily converted into gold at a preestablished exchange rate; size of gold reserves constrains money supply.

*Deflation* (i.e., purchasing power of a currency unit increases):

- Undermines debt—Asset value declines can shrink investor margins below the required threshold, resulting in capital calls and foreclosures.
- Undermines central bank credibility—Already low interest rates leave few monetary policy options.
- Historically, deflation may have been caused by reliance on the gold standard.

*Quantitative easing.* The central bank injects money into the financial system via asset purchases.

The *Taylor rule* identifies potential rate inflections:

$$r_{optimal} = r_{neutral} + 0.5[(g_{GDP}^{F} - g_{GDP}^{T}) + (I^{F} - I^{T})]$$

where:
$F$ = forecast
$T$ = trend (GDP)/target (inflation)

The U.S. Federal Reserve targets lower or higher cost of capital to lenders via the *federal funds rate* (i.e., overnight interbank lending rate on reserves).

*Money supply* growth rates also indicate potential inflection points; money supply growth greater than GDP growth indicates potential inflation increases.

| Inflation | Cash | Bonds | Equities | Real Estate/ Other Real |
|---|---|---|---|---|
| Above expected | Pos: ↑$i$ | Neg: ↑YTM, ↓$V$ | Neg: ↑costs; ↓profit[1] | Pos: ↑CF/$r$/$V$ |
| At or below expected | Neutral<br>$i$ +/– to ↓ | Neutral<br>YTM +/– | Positive<br>Bullish | Neutral<br>CF +/– to ↑; $r_{LT}$ |
| Deflation | Neg: ↓ to $r_{ST} = 0$ | Pos: ↓YTM[2] | Neg: ↓ revenues, profits[3] | Neg: CF +/– to ↑; ↓$V$ |

Notes:
[1] May be offset by firms with pricing power.
[2] May be offset by increasing defaults.
[3] Falling commodity prices lower costs for users, but hurt producers.

### Fiscal Policy during Business Cycles

Even without intervention, a budget deficit decreases as economic activity picks up and tax revenues increase while unemployment assistance falls. A budget deficit increases as economic activity and tax revenues fall while unemployment assistance increases.

Tight fiscal policy results as the government deliberately reduces spending, and loose fiscal policy results as the government increases spending. Only deliberate fiscal policy changes result in inflection points as the yield curve, and thus lending, changes:

| | | Fiscal Policy | |
|---|---|---|---|
| | | Loose | Tight |
| Monetary Policy | Loose | Steep upward slope | Moderate upward slope |
| | Tight | Flat | Inverted (downward slope) |

### Economic Growth Trends

A *trend* is a relatively easy-to-forecast general direction of change in an economic series that doesn't change in rate much over time.

GDP growth trends are driven by other trends (i.e., inflation/deflation, population growth and demographics, business productivity and investment, and financial system health).

Higher trend rates tend to reduce the risk of inflation from small growth increases, and allow investors a better return.

The *permanent income hypothesis* attributes relatively minor spending changes during business cycles to longer-term expectations for income.

GDP growth components incude:

- Labor force growth:
    - Population growth
    - Percentage of population in labor force

- Labor productivity:
    - Capital accumulation
    - Technological innovation (usually calculated as a residual after considering other factors)

### Government Economic Policy

*Structural policies* affect investment incentives and the rate and limits of private sector growth.

Pro-growth structural policies generally include:

- Stable fiscal policies: Government should avoid running long-term deficits:
    - Requires foreign capital, which leads to a lower currency exchange rate and ultimately devaluation and higher inflation, or
    - Printing money (if not financed by foreign capital), which leads to higher inflation, or
    - Crowding out private-sector growth.
- Sound tax policies: Taxes distort incentives less and lower societal welfare less by employing:
    - Broad tax base (i.e., includes a large percentage of the population)
    - Simple, stable, and transparent tax rates and policies
    - Low marginal rates
- Minimal private-sector intervention: Enough intervention to provide necessary public goods and prohibit serious externalities (e.g., pollution), but limited labor market intervention because it raises the structural unemployment rate.
- Encouraging competition improves productivity but may limit returns on capital and valuation:
    - Lowering trade barriers
    - Opening markets to foreign investment
- Encouraging human capital/infrastructure development (e.g., education, building health).

### Structural Shocks

*Structural shocks* can interrupt trends, but are unexpected and, while generally unpredictable, may recur.

- Endogenous shocks originate within the financial system (e.g., asset market collapse).
- Exogenous shocks originate outside the financial system (e.g., wars, wholesale change in government policy, technological changes).

Two types of shocks that may recur are:

1. Financial shocks: Endogenous shocks that typically result from excessive risk exposure
2. Oil shocks: Exogenous shocks resulting from supply constriction by oil-producing countries

### International Linkages

*Linkages* imply domestic sensitivity to cross-border events. Diverse economies are less affected than nondiverse economies:

- Macroeconomic: Business cycles in one economy affect a trading partner.
- Interest/exchange rate pegging: Involves setting one currency value relative to another:
    - Exchange rate stability is important for revenue predictability for exports and cost predictability for imports.
    - There is less inflation and, depending on confidence in the peg, possibly lower interest rates.

World capital supply and demand ultimately affect real bond yield, although exchange rate pressures can cause over- or undervaluation on a real basis. Real bond yields, although different across countries, tend to move together.

Inflation and exchange rate outlook affect nominal bond yield.

Countries with undervalued exchange rates that are expected to rise substantially experience lower bond yields as investors purchase bonds denominated in that currency.

### Emerging Markets

*Emerging markets* have low to middle per capita GDP and above average GDP growth rates. This means they also have:

- Higher rates of infrastructure and human capital investment
- Volatile economic and/or political environment:
    - Greater linkages; potential for shocks
    - Inadequate domestic savings; greater foreign borrowing
    - Volatile political environments; unstable policies and protecting vested interests

IMPORTANT: Emerging market analysis is like developed market analysis, but focuses on politics, balance of payments, debt, and liquidity.

Analysts examine:

- Economic freedom (e.g., tax and tariff rates, cost of starting a business, etc.)
- Total debt-to-GDP ratio
- Foreign debt-to-GDP ratio
- Current annual growth
- Current account balance
- Foreign exchange reserves to short-term debt

## Economic Forecasting

### Econometric Analysis

*Econometric analysis* uses economic theory to model relationships between and among variables.

The forecaster supplies estimates for exogenous variables used in one or more equations developed based on parameters generated with least squares regression or other optimization analysis of historical data.

Equations frequently forecast future-period variables based on relationships with lagged independent variables.

**Advantages**

- Provides disciplined approach and quantitative output.
- Includes multiple factors representing reality; robust.
- Quickly generates updated forecasts with new data.

**Disadvantages**

- Most time-consuming and complex to develop.
- Independent variables are difficult to forecast; relationships are unstable.
- Requires careful output review.
- Good upturn forecasts; unreliable for recession forecasts.

### Economic Indicator–Based Analysis

Economic indicator–based analysis uses government or privately generated economic statistics as indicators for future economic activity:

- Leading economic indicators (LEIs) vary consistently with business cycle, but in advance.
- Coincident economic indicators vary consistently and directly with business cycle.
- Lagging economic indicators vary consistently with business cycle, but after the fact.

Coincident and lagging indicators are often used to verify leading indicator–based conclusions. LEI release may not move the market, however, because individual variables may have already been published.

Each type may be individual variables or a composite of useful variables (e.g., *composite index* of LEIs).

A diffusion index identifies the number of relevant variables increasing, decreasing, or remaining relatively unchanged (e.g., 7 of 10 LEIs improving indicates accelerating growth).

**Advantages**

- Simplest approach; limited variables are used.
- Variables and indexes are available via third parties.
- Documented forecasting ability.

**Disadvantages**

- Unstable relationships over time; inconsistent forecasting ability.
- False signals are possible (especially recession warnings).

### Checklist Approach

A checklist approach requires an analyst to evaluate economic variables and either subjectively or objectively—using time-series analysis or other statistical methods—forecast dependent variables (e.g., inflation, short-term interest rates, etc.).

Forecasts can then be evaluated to determine whether they represent cyclical inflection points.

**Advantages**

- Limited complexity
- Flexible; structural changes/shocks easily incorporated

**Disadvantages**

- Subjective
- Manual; time-consuming
- Limited complexity due to manual nature

## Forecasting Asset Class Returns

### Cash and Equivalents

Cash managers earn higher returns by managing maturity and, if allowed, credit risk.

Central bank discount rate forecasts form a baseline for overnight investments; longer maturities will have higher rates based on credit risk even if overnight rates are expected to be stable.

Expected rate increases steepen the yield curve, allowing greater returns for buying longer maturities, and expected rate decreases flatten the yield curve, allowing greater returns for shorting longer maturities.

Cash managers must forecast economic variable inflections *and* central bank reactions.

### Nominal Default-Free Bonds

Nominal default-free bonds are conventional interest-bearing bonds with no default risk, forecasted as:

- Shorter-term instruments: Treasury bill yields reinvested over the same horizon, or
- Longer-term instruments: Yield decomposed into expected real rates (i.e., based on expected demand/supply, real GDP growth, etc.) and inflation.

IMPORTANT: A rise in short-term policy rates expected to slow the economy could cause long-term bond rates to fall (due to expected inflation/rising rates) rather than rise due to potential growth.

The second approach can be useful for shorter terms by focusing on shorter-term rate impacts of business cycles.

If bond markets expect central banks to exactly achieve their monetary policy objectives, longer-maturity bond yields should rise and fall with short-term rates without regard to changes in inflation expectations.

### Defaultable Debt

Most corporate debt carries credit risk (i.e., *defaultable*), which appears as the yield spread over nominal short-term government debt.

Defaultable debt yield for an individual issue responds to that company's specific risk in addition to cyclical risk.



 

When a recession begins, the company's business weakens simultaneously with less available credit through banks and the commercial paper market. Default risk has increased, and bond investors demand higher spreads to supply capital. Fraud risk may also increase.

Spreads narrow as default fears decline during an expansion.

### Emerging Market Bonds

*Emerging market debt* focuses here on sovereign debt of emerging countries. While developed countries can inflate the currency to pay debt and avoid default, emerging countries often borrow in foreign currencies and do not control the money supply.

*Country risk analysis* assesses default risk by analyzing:

- Economic conditions in absolute terms and relative to other countries
- Political willingness to make difficult choices necessary to avoid default

Developed market investors determine emerging market sovereign risk by comparing their domestic bond spread over treasuries to that for comparably rated emerging market corporate bonds.

### Inflation-Indexed Sovereign Bonds

IMPORTANT: Yields fall (i.e., prices rise) on inflation-indexed bonds as inflation becomes more volatile because they provide the demanded protection.

The spread between inflation-indexed bonds (e.g., Treasury inflation-protected securities in the United States and index-linked gilts in the United Kingdom) and similar-maturity conventional sovereigns can reveal the country's expected inflation rate.

The yield on inflation-indexed bonds fluctuates with:

- Short-term rates and economic conditions
- Supply-demand conditions
- Volatility of inflation

Tax effects, particularly in the United States, and low liquidity may also affect realized yields.

### Common Shares

Capital equipment investment levels, along with labor force growth and labor productivity growth, determine the potential GDP growth rate; the GDP growth rate trend ultimately determines the company's earnings growth potential.

Analysts should consider the long-term trend and shorter-term cyclical data for the macroeconomy—including consumer and business sectors—as well as fiscal and monetary policies.

Future earnings multiplied by P/E ratio equals share price:

- Directly correlated with GDP growth and expected earnings
- Higher and more volatile in emerging markets
- Depressed by high inflation rates

## Real Estate

Real estate returns are determined by:

- Consumption expenditures
- Real interest rates
- The term structure of interest rates

Interest rates are important to real estate returns due to:

- Construction financing costs
- Mortgage financing costs

## Currencies

A currency derives its value from the balance of payments:

- Current account activity: Trade, services, and transfers (current account items)
- Capital account activity: Investment capital flows:
  - Direct investment—Productive assets built or purchased; more stable
  - Portfolio investment—Debt and equity capital; more volatile

Increasing GDP growth would suggest offsetting pressures from growing:

- Supply (depreciation): Increased imports coincident with growing GDP
- Demand (appreciation): Increased investment resulting from the growing capital need

Rising interest rates result in increased currency demand and currency *appreciation* as investors convert their currency to invest at the higher rate. However, rising interest rates expected to cause slowing economic growth may cause currency *depreciation*.

Long disequilibrium periods may lead to exchange rate and business instability. Many emerging market countries use a combination of capital controls and currency management (e.g., managed floats, pegs, etc.) to maintain the desired equilibrium exchange rate.

Many investors hedge a portfolio's exchange rate risks rather than forecast and manage currency opportunities.

Approaches to forecasting include:

- Relative purchasing power parity (PPP) (trade flows): Exchange rates settle at competitive equilibrium among countries:
  - Exchange rates offset any inflation rate differences between trading partners.
- Relative economic strength (portfolio investment): Increasing growth increases demand and, as potential returns attract portfolio investment capital, demand for domestic currency increases more than supply of foreign currency:
  - High interest rates decrease speculator willingness to short currency, because appreciation is likely to occur.
  - Very low interest rates encourage borrowing in that currency to finance investment in higher interest rate currencies (e.g., carry trade).
  - Relative economic strength indicates short-term exchange rate response to economic news.

EC

IMPORTANT: PPP and relative economic strength may be combined for better forecasting.

- Capital flows forecasting (direct and long-term portfolio investment): Long-term portfolio investment primarily involves equity securities:
  - Higher relative foreign direct and long-term portfolio investment is expected to cause a country's currency to appreciate.
- Savings–investment imbalances: Increases in government and private-sector current account deficits result in domestic savings deficits. Further deficits must be met with the following:
  - Capital account surplus as foreign investors provide funds to offset domestic savings deficits.
  - By definition, the current account must be in deficit, meaning that imports are higher than exports.
  - The current account deficit can be maintained by a weak/depreciating exchange rate.

# EQUITY MARKET VALUATION

Cross-Reference to CFA Institute Assigned Reading #16

## Top-Down Market Valuation

### Economic Growth

Economic growth ultimately drives corporate earnings growth. Neoclassical growth accounting uses the *Cobb-Douglas production function* to estimate economic growth.

The basic Cobb-Douglas function calculates total economic output ($Y$) as the product of *total factor productivity* ($A$), the elasticity-dependent impact of capital stock ($K^{\alpha}$), and the elasticity-dependent impact of labor ($L^{\beta}$).

Using *constant returns to scale* (rather than diminishing returns) for labor and capital inputs, $\beta = 1 - \alpha$ and the equation for GDP growth becomes:

$$Y = \frac{\Delta A}{A} + \alpha\frac{\Delta K}{K} + (1-\alpha)\frac{\Delta L}{L}$$

The *Solow residual* describes total factor productivity $A$ as the remaining economic growth after contribution from capital and labor—that is, the effectiveness of technology and innovation in economic growth.

*Innovation* includes removing political, social, and other barriers to growth.

The implication of total factor productivity is that the economy can grow faster than the percentage increases in capital and labor.

### Required Return

Required return on equity is the appropriate discount rate for equity cash flows. This may be established empirically with the intertemporal capital asset pricing model (ICAPM) or other models, or subjectively using historical data and analyst judgment.

Analysts can also use justified P/E ratios to determine market-based required return using observed values for market price, earnings, and growth rate.

### Equity Market Valuation

Within the confines of GDP growth rate, a firm's earnings growth rate depends on the dividend payout rate versus the retained earnings rate.

The Gordon growth model is sufficient when a mature company grows in line with a mature economy.

EC

The H-model assumes that earnings and growth decline in a linear fashion from a supernormal short-term rate ($g_S$) for $N$ periods toward a sustainable, perpetual long-term rate ($g_L$):

$$V_0 = \frac{D_0}{r - g_L}[(1 + g_L) + \frac{N}{2}(g_S - g_L)]$$

Economists often prefer to model using real (i.e., inflation-adjusted) variables because inflation is unpredictable. Assume real growth rates unless otherwise indicated.

IMPORTANT: Price is assumed to be equal to value because it is justified from the fundamentals.

### Justified P/E Ratios

The *justified P/E ratio* has been developed based on forecasted fundamentals and may be different than the *prevailing market P/E*.

IMPORTANT: Markets are undervalued when market P/E is less than justified P/E (i.e., market price is less than justified price relative to expected earnings).

$$\frac{P_0}{E_1} = \frac{D_r}{r - g}$$

Use of next-period earnings ($E_1$) against the dividend payout rate ($D_r$) results in next-period dividend. Use of next-period dividend results in the forward-looking *prospective P/E*.

## Top-Down versus Bottom-Up Valuation

### Top-Down Valuation

*Top-down forecasts* begin at the macroeconomic level and work downward through market valuation to individual security valuation.

- Market analysis: Analyze expected returns across global markets:
  - Compare relative value measures (i.e., market-based such as P/E) against historical measures.
  - Analyze trends in those measures.
  - Compare relative value measures across asset classes.
- Industry analysis: Select potentially outperforming industries:
  - Compare selected industry growth rates and profit margins.
  - Select industries based on trends in inflation, interest rates, and exchange rates.
- Company analysis: Identify firms expected to outperform in industries expected to outperform in markets expected to outperform.

Top-down forecasts rely on extrapolating trends in past economic data; they may not predict contemporaneous changes.

### Bottom-Up Valuation

*Bottom-up forecasts* begin at the individual security's microeconomic level (i.e., fundamentals) and work upward.

- Company analysis: Select firms expected to outperform without regard to macroeconomic forecasts:
  - Look for a successful product, service, or technology.
  - Evaluate history, strategy, business model, current management, and growth prospects.
  - Develop value estimates and expected returns using DCF methods.

- Industry analysis: Aggregate results of company analysis by industry level.
- Market analysis: Aggregate expected industry results to market level for every global equity market.

Analysts should take care in using research analyst consensus forecasts, which are based on econometric models and are subject to revision lag. Bottom-up estimates may overestimate returns heading into a recession, and may underestimate returns heading into a recovery.

#### Method Suitability

The end-product requirements indicate the drill-down depth from the macroeconomic level. However, investment policy may require examining the nature of individual components within the final strategic (asset class) or tactical (market composites, segments, or industries) forecast.

### Relative Value Models

*Relative value models* determine firm value relative to prices for earnings, assets, and so on of similar firms. Analysts may then select the asset considered inexpensive relative to similar assets.

#### Fed Model

The *Fed model* suggests that yield on the 10-year Treasury note should equal the S&P 500 earnings yield (i.e., forward earnings divided by price).

Equity prices are too low and undervalued if the S&P earnings yield is greater than 10-year Treasury note yield (a buy signal).

Criticisms of the Fed model and reasons why it has been a poor predictor of future equity returns are that it ignores:

- Equity risk premium
- Earnings growth

Some analysts view "undervalued" as current excess S&P yield relative to historical excess yield; higher current yield is a buy signal.

#### Yardeni Model

Rather than the Fed approach, Yardeni uses:

- Moody's A-rated corporate bond yield ($Y_B$) rather than 10-year Treasury notes.
- Thomson Reuters I/B/E/S five-year long-term earnings growth (LTEG) forecast.
- Market weight of earnings projections ($d$), which has historically been about 0.1 or 10% but can vary greatly.

$$P_0 = \frac{E_1}{r-g} \Rightarrow \frac{E_1}{P_0} = r - g$$

$$\frac{E_1}{P_0} = Y_B - d \bullet LTEG$$

EC

The Yardeni model suggests that justified earnings yield less than market earnings yield indicates undervalued earnings (i.e., market prices too low), a buy signal.

### Cyclically Adjusted P/E Ratio

IMPORTANT: The 2001 CAPE is 2001 real S&P 500 index value divided by average real earnings of the index constituents from 1991 to 2000.

The 10-year moving average (10-YMA) price-earnings ratio, more commonly known as the *cyclically adjusted P/E (CAPE)* ratio, controls for business cycle effects and was suggested by Graham and Dodd.

CAPE value is current-year real S&P 500 index value divided by simple average real earnings over the 10 previous years.

CAPE is mean-reverting; 10-YMA might better smooth index earnings over the 10-year period.

CAPE at some time might be subject to different accounting rules than previous 10-year periods.

### Asset-Based Models

*Tobin's q ratio* is the market value of debt and equity capital divided by replacement cost of assets.

Assuming Tobin's q reverts to 1 (or the historical average reference value):

- Undervalued: q ratio < 1
- At fair value: q ratio = 1
- Overvalued: q ratio >1

Replacement cost of firm assets is difficult to obtain.

Equity q ratio uses market value of equity capitalization (only) divided by net worth if assets are measured at replacement cost. It differs from the ratio of price to book value because equity q uses replacement cost of assets rather than historical book value to estimate equity value (net worth).

EC

### Summary of Relative Value Models

| Method | Method of Prediction for Equities | Advantages | Disadvantages |
|---|---|---|---|
| Fed model | Undervalued when E/P > government securities yield. | Easy to apply; consistent with DCF (i.e., value inverse to discount rate). | Ignores earnings growth.<br>Ignores equity risk premium.<br>Compares current earnings to inflation-discounted bond cash flows. |
| Yardeni model | Undervalued when justified E/P > market E/P. | Improves Fed model by considering earnings growth and debt risk. | Market captures debt default risk rather than equity risk.<br>Forecasted earnings growth may not be accurate or sustainable.<br>Fair value estimate implies constant required return on equity. |
| CAPE ratio | S&P 500 is overvalued when the current CAPE is above its long-term historical average. | Controls for business cycle and inflation by using 10-YMA. | Comparison, if accounting rules change of 10-year period.<br>May have long reversion period.<br>10-YMA earnings may not be best representative of future earnings. |
| Tobin's q, equity q | Equity returns are higher when q ratio is low. | Mean-reverting; uses security values (other than debt in the case of equity q) compared to asset replacement costs.<br>Studies support inverse relationship. | Asset replacement costs are difficult to source.<br>No market.<br>Intangibles valuation is difficult.<br>May have long reversion period. |

EC

# Study Session 8: Asset Allocation and Related Decisions in Portfolio Management (1)

# ASSET ALLOCATION
Cross-Reference to CFA Institute Assigned Reading #17

## Strategic Asset Allocation (SAA)

### Function of SAA in Portfolio Management

- SAA (process): Determining asset class weights in a *policy portfolio* based on capital market expectations and investor preferences and/or constraints.
- SAA (portfolio): A *policy portfolio* optimized for risk and return during the SAA process.

*Systematic risk* identifies the standard deviation of returns from changes in real economic activity and inflation.

Investors can avoid *nonsystematic risk* (i.e., *company-specific risk*) by holding a portfolio of securities.

*Asset classes* are groups of the same type of security (e.g., long-term corporate bonds, small-cap equities, etc.). Asset class returns reflect the individual securities' exposure to systematic risk, and are used to complete the SAA.

IMPORTANT: Strategic asset allocation exposes investors to the desired level of systematic risk over an investment horizon.

Exposures to systematic risk (i.e., asset class returns) account for more than 90% of returns in a diversified portfolio. Timing, style selection, security selection, and other types of return account for the remainder. After additional fees and expenses, however, timing and selection bets do not add value.

### Tactical Asset Allocation (TAA)

*Tactical asset allocation (TAA)* involves short-term adjustment to asset class weights in a policy portfolio based on short-term relative performance predictions.

TAA is an active management strategy that offers:

- Lower terminal wealth potential than security selection for skilled investors
- Lower terminal wealth dispersion (i.e., less risk) than security selection

## Aligning SAA with Risk and Return Performance

### Approaches

*Asset–liability management (ALM)* involves modeling liabilities and then formulating asset allocation in the context of funding liabilities.

The *asset-only (A-O) approach* aligns liability funding needs by adjusting the return requirement; it offers less precision than ALM approaches.

ALM has higher allocation to fixed-income securities than the A-O approach has, and is favored when a user has below-average risk tolerance:

- User has liabilities that are sensitive to interest rates.
- User faces legal and regulatory constraints.
    - Severe penalties for failing to meet liabilities:
        - Very high—banks and insurance
        - High—defined-benefit pensions and foundations/endowments
    - Portfolio risk may limit business risk undertaken.
- Tax laws favor fixed-income investing.

Risk-minimizing ALM approaches:

- Cash flow matching (exact matching) structures bonds to mature when outflows are payable.
- Immunization matches the weighted-average duration (and possibly convexity) of liabilities, and is suitable for highly risk-averse investors.

Static versus dynamic approaches:

- Dynamic: Actual return/liability experience in the current period affects next-period options; more costly and complex than static approach.
- Static: This approach does not consider current-period experience in subsequent-period options.

ALM users prefer dynamic approach.

## Return Objectives

**Types**

- Qualitative: Intuitive wording describing a non-numerical outcome:
    - Individuals provide adequate retirement income.
    - Endowments maintain real purchasing power after distributions.
    - Defined-benefit pension and insurance adequately fund liabilities.
- Quantitative: Numerically specific for asset allocation:
    - Additive—Commonly used in investment policy statement (IPS) to represent qualitative goals.
    - Multiplicative—Preferred by portfolio managers; geometric return.

Approximate conversion to geometric return requirement from arithmetic mean return $E(r)$:

$$r_G = E(r_A) - 0.5\sigma_A^2$$

where returns are in decimal form, and standard deviation of returns applies to $E(R)$.

Funding approach:

- A-O approach: Absolute risk and return of asset portfolio
- ALM approach: Net for risk and return relative to funding liabilities

SAAs should recognize multistage time horizons with differing return requirements. An SAA should also reflect changing investor circumstances.

### Risk Objectives

Quantitative approaches require understanding an investor's utility for an asset allocation $U_m$ based on expected return on the mix $E(R_m)$, variance of the return on the mix $\sigma^2$, and *risk aversion* ($R_A$):

$$U_m = E(R_m) - 0.005 R_A \sigma_m^2$$

with return expressed as a percentage rather than a decimal. Return can be expressed as a decimal by changing 0.005 to 0.5 in the equation.

> IMPORTANT: The implication is a greater reduction in utility for higher levels of risk aversion, everything else being equal. Therefore, $U_m$ can be thought of as the *risk-adjusted return requirement*.

Advisors determine risk aversion based on the investor's responses to a questionnaire.

Other risk quantifiers are:

- Standard deviation of returns.
- Downside risk: risk related to losses or worse than expected gain:
    - Shortfall risk—The risk of falling below a minimum acceptable portfolio value.
    - Shortfall deviation—Portfolio standard deviation is less than 1.65 or 1.28 for 5% and 10% shortfall probability levels, respectively.
    - Semivariance—Average of squared deviations is less than the mean return.
    - Target semivariance—Average of squared deviations is less than the target return.
- Safety-first ratio (Roy's SF): Select the portfolio with the greatest SF Ratio:

$$\text{SF Ratio} = \frac{E(r_P) - r_L}{\sigma_P}$$

> IMPORTANT: Select the risk-free asset if $r_F < r_L$.

### Behavioral Influences

*Prospect theory* refers to investor decisions when faced with various choices among prospects for risk:

- *Loss aversion.* Investors prefer additional risk when faced with the probability of large losses; use downside risk measures to avoid excessive risk.
- *Mental accounting.* Different "buckets" of money, each with a separate risk tolerance, are associated with each goal; may be met with:
    - *Traditional approach*—Funds in all buckets are allocated in one portfolio; unacceptable to client.
    - *Multistrategy approach—Goal-based asset allocation* for each bucket; fails to consider correlations across buckets.

AA

> IMPORTANT: Don't confuse loss aversion with *risk aversion* (i.e., aversion to potential loss).

- Regret avoidance:
  - Promotes diversification.
  - May promote gradual entry into an SAA (e.g., dollar cost averaging).
  - May result in herd mentality to avoid comparisons if there are losses.

## Asset Class Selection

### Asset Class Specification

*Asset classes* are groups of securities with similar properties that support the goals of asset allocation. Appropriately specified asset classes are:

> IMPORTANT: SAA should consider tax aspects of investments; it may not be appropriate for tax-exempt investors.

- Relatively homogeneous: Securities in an asset class have similar risk and return attributes, and similar correlations with other asset classes.
- Mutually exclusive: Investments in different asset classes should not allow overlap.
- Diversifying: There is a relatively low correlation with other asset classes and linear combinations of other asset classes.
- Able to absorb portfolio investments: Reallocation will not cause market disruptions.
- Together inclusive of global investable wealth:
  - Increases potential returns for a given risk level.
  - Expands active investment opportunities.

### Asset Class Evaluation

Investors should theoretically add another asset class to a portfolio when it improves the risk/return profile; that is, when the Sharpe ratio of the new portfolio is greater than the product of the Sharpe ratio for the existing portfolio and correlation of the existing and new portfolios:

> IMPORTANT: Sharpe ratios and correlation are calculated in the investor's home currency.

$$\frac{E(r_{new})-r_F}{\sigma_{new}} > \rho_{new,p}\left[\frac{E(r_p)-r_F}{\sigma_p}\right]$$

The *capital asset line (CAL)* for the new portfolio will have steeper upward slope with a better risk/return ratio.

Lower correlation increases the likelihood that a new asset class should be included.

### Nondomestic Asset Risks and Opportunities

Theoretical: Higher Sharpe ratio adjusted for correlation of international portfolio justifies including nondomestic assets.

Practical:

- Home country bias: Underinvestment in nondomestic markets:
  - Lack of familiarity with language, culture, and business practices; information unavailability
  - High transaction costs, low liquidity, and foreign political risk

- Currency risk: Return volatility in investor currency less return volatility in local currency:
    - Not hedging indicates willingness to bet on currency movement.
    - Foreign currency appreciation during the investment horizon adds to return.
    - Currency returns are less volatile than equity returns.
    - Mitigating factors:
        - Enhanced local business return from lower currency mitigates exchange rate loss.
        - Correlation of asset return and currency return is less than 1.
- Political risk:
    - Irresponsible fiscal and monetary policies
    - Property confiscation without compensation
    - Capital restrictions, including convertibility and repatriation
    - Currency manipulation
    - Unsafe or unstable, resulting in high risk premiums

IMPORTANT: *Low free float* (i.e., founding families, other companies, government, etc. hold large percentage of shares) may also discourage nondomestic investment.

Besides diversification benefits, foreign investment may offer:

- Better valuations
- Better protection than domestic-only portfolios in disaster markets
- Lower intercountry bond correlations than equity correlations

### Emerging Markets

May have positive or negative skewness, as well as leptokurtosis (i.e., extreme positive or negative returns).

Annual capital gains may occur in only a few days, making timing difficult.

Growth may not translate into higher returns:

- Already reflected in stock prices
- Captured by labor as wage increases
- Concentrated in uninvestable assets:
    - Subsidiaries of foreign companies (which could cause overlap with developed nondomestic holdings)
    - Privately held companies
    - Government-owned companies
- Weak corporate governance (i.e., management squanders growth)

IMPORTANT: Investors should broadly diversify across emerging markets.

### Market Integration

*Market integration* can be traced to when the country offers American depositary receipts (ADRs) or closed-end funds begin investment. Degree of market integration can be assessed by percentage of total market capitalization available to foreigners.

Stock markets are becoming more integrated (i.e., more available to foreign investors).

IMPORTANT: Currency risk supports the idea of potential risk reduction from foreign investment despite increased integration.

AA

Expected integration effects include:

- Equity prices increase as investors buy low covariance with global markets.
- Expected return decreases as market price fully incorporates low covariance benefits; industry factors become more important than country factors.
- Return volatility declines as market matures; less "news" movement as information becomes more readily available.
    - Active managers may seek information advantages in less efficient markets.
    - Emerging markets become more correlated with global markets.
- Market efficiency increases due to:
    - Lower trade costs
    - Higher trading volumes
    - Faster execution
- Market transparency increases based on market efficiency and helps reduce volatility.
- Cost of capital declines due to increasing liquidity and less risk.
- Economic growth increases as risk declines and cost of capital decreases, and then ultimately slows to more mature growth rate.

### Conditional Return Correlations

Return correlations can be calculated when markets are normal and when they are stressed to ensure foreign investment correlation does not increase during stressed markets (i.e., *conditional correlations*). Portfolios can then be optimized for normal and stressed market conditions.

### Alternative Investments

Alternative investments include real estate, private equity, and a variety of hedge funds.

In general, alternative assets provide diversification benefits.

Information may be difficult and costly for smaller investors to obtain.

## Asset Allocation Steps

### Risk Tolerance Function

The *risk tolerance function* combines information about an investor's assets, liabilities, net worth, and attitudes toward risk into a mathematical statement.

The risk tolerance function relates the client's beginning-of-period net worth to the risk tolerance for the upcoming period.

Returns and other activity during a period affect the client's next-period beginning balance:

IMPORTANT: The risk tolerance level may change from period to period; the risk tolerance function will not.

- Asset values: Returns affect beginning balance, cash contributions, and withdrawals (i.e., *net additions* or *net new investment*, which may be negative).
- Liabilities: Markets affect values for beginning balance, as well as pay-down of old liabilities and accrual of new liabilities during the period.

## Capital Market Expectations

Forecasts for *capital market expectations (CMEs)* provide asset-class-specific risk, return, and correlation data.

Long-term relationships drive strategic asset allocation; short-term expectations drive tactical asset allocation.

IMPORTANT: Capital market expectations may change from period to period; the forecasting process does not.

## Optimization

An *optimizer* develops an efficient strategic asset allocation (i.e., policy portfolio) based on the investor's risk tolerance function and capital market expectations.

IMPORTANT: The optimization outcome (i.e., SAA recommendation) may change from period to period; the process does not.

The optimizer may range in complexity from a simple rule of thumb to a full-blown computer model, depending on the investor's risk/return parameters and constraints.

Integrated asset allocation implies that all the inputs have been considered (e.g., including liabilities as well as assets) and that all the appropriate steps are performed.

An allocation from any optimization approach should be professionally reviewed.

### Optimization Approaches

#### Mean-Variance Optimization (MVO)

The *efficient frontier* considers the portion of the *minimum variance frontier (MVF)* with optimal risk/return characteristics—that is, the portion of the MVF above the *global minimum variance (GMV) portfolio*. The asset class weights, which is the output of MVO, is highly sensitive to small changes in expected return.

*Unconstrained optimization:*

- Weights must sum to 1.
- Weights may be negative, implying an asset should be shorted.

*Black two-fund theorem:* Asset weights $w_n{}^A$ in any portfolio $n$ with return $r_n{}^P$ are the linear combination of asset weights from two MVF portfolios:

1. Required return for the policy portfolio ($P_P$) equals the weighted average of two MVF portfolios, $P_1$ and $P_2$:

$$r_{P_P} = w_{P_1} r_{P_1} + (1 - w_{P_1}) r_{P_2} = w_{P_1} r_{P_1} + w_{P_2} r_{P_2}.$$

2. Each policy portfolio asset class weight $w^{An}$ depends on the weight of the asset class in each of the two MVF portfolios:

$$w_{P_P}^{A_n} = w_{P_1} w_{P_1}^{A_n} + w_{P_2} w_{P_2}^{A_n}.$$

IMPORTANT:

$\Sigma w_{P_n} = 1$, and

$\Sigma_{P_n}^{A_n} = 1$

Sign-constrained MVF:

- Weights must sum to 1.
- $w^{An} > 0$ (i.e., no short sales).

Signed-constrained optimization also applies to constraints on asset class weights.

*Corner portfolios:*

- Identify the end of sign-constrained MVF segments.
- Mark asset weight change from either 0 to positive or positive to 0.

Portfolios on the MVF between corner portfolios have:

- Identical assets with positive weights or 0
- Constant rate of change in assets moving from one portfolio to another

*Corner portfolio theorem:* The asset weights of any minimum variance portfolio in a sign-constrained optimization are a linear combination of weights for the two nearest corner portfolios.

### Resampled Efficient Frontier

Investors rerun optimization programs many times using a range around point estimates for return, volatility, and correlation forecasts (i.e., sensitivity analysis).

*Simulated efficient portfolios* use asset weights optimized from simulated asset class risk/return measures based on assumed true population parameters.

A *resampled efficient portfolio* indicates a portfolio constructed with average asset class weights for many simulated portfolios at a given return rank.

The *resampled efficient frontier* includes the set of resampled efficient portfolios.

Most if not all asset classes are included in portfolios modeled using this method, if at least one simulation includes the asset class.

There are two advantages of the resampled efficient frontier compared with MVO:

1. Portfolios are more stable over time, which reduces rebalancing costs, such as transaction costs and taxes;
2. Portfolios are less concentrated and better diversified across asset classes. This is particularly relevant for investors with below-average risk tolerance.

Disadvantages include:

- Lack of theoretical backing for the method
- Relevance to current-period asset market values of historical return frequency data

### Black-Litterman Model

The *Black-Litterman model* was developed to overcome unreliable point estimates for returns:

1. Equilibrium asset class market weights and covariance matrix: Develops inputs for equilibrium expected returns.
2. Reverse engineer (back solve) equilibrium expected returns: Neutral starting point for forming return expectations.
3. Investor formulates expectations and strength of "views": Asset class expectations and weights.
4. View-adjusted equilibrium returns: Reflects both market equilibrium and investor view.
5. Mean-variance optimization (MVO): Output is efficient frontier.

This process results in a portfolio on the efficient frontier, with market weights for assets but reverse-engineered returns that are then moderated by investor views.

The *Black-Litterman model (unconstrained)* allows short sales of assets having negative expected returns.

> IMPORTANT: The Black-Litterman model improves on MVO because the small deviation from market portfolio parameters seldom results in counterintuitive and outsized short positions.

### Monte Carlo Simulation

Random scenarios for asset class returns, inflation, and other variables are translated into a range of strategic asset allocations and potential returns.

*Path dependency:* The sequence of cash inflows and outflows, and interaction with returns, affects calculation of final terminal wealth.

Tax impacts of periodic rebalancing become much easier to model.

### Asset–Liability Management (ALM)

Whereas the previous MVO approaches consider only assets, ALM approaches also consider funding liability (e.g., a pension obligation):

- Surplus: Net assets less funding liability:
  - Overfunded plans have surplus (i.e., assets greater than liabilities).
  - Firms can draw down surplus to meet future funding obligations.
- Funding ratio (funded status): Ratio of assets to present value of liabilities.
- Minimum surplus variance (MSV) portfolio: Least risk portfolio from the ALM perspective.
- Surplus efficient frontier: Highest surplus-optimized portfolios.
- Surplus risk: MSV portfolios that result in negative surplus.

AA

> IMPORTANT: Estimation error problems apply to surplus optimization, just as they do to MVO.

The *surplus beta decision* is the difference between expected return for the MSV portfolio and the policy portfolio.

Approaches typically involve:

- Optimization: Determine the MVS portfolio and surplus efficient frontier.
- Monte Carlo simulation: Establish how each proposed allocation might perform given investor's capital market expectations.
- Selection: Choose allocation that satisfies the return requirement at the lowest risk level, or maximizes return at the acceptable risk level.

### Experience-Based Approaches

*Experience-based approaches* involve tradition and rules of thumb in making strategic asset allocation recommendations.

Such approaches inexpensively develop strategies that have worked well for clients:

- A 60% bond/40% bond allocation is a neutral allocation featuring risk reduction (bonds) and capital appreciation (stock).
- Bond allocation increases as risk aversion increases.
- Allocation to equities is calculated as 100 minus investor's age.
- Stock allocation increases as time horizon increases.

## Implementation Approaches

### Methods

- Passive: Replicates returns from a broad index (e.g., S&P 500):
  - Cash market securities, exchange-traded funds, or mutual funds
  - Cash plus long swap representing desired exposure
  - Cash plus long exposure to desired index for an asset
- Active:
  - Cash market portfolio representing investor's skill and insights without reference to index
  - Cash plus long swap representing desired exposure plus market-neutral long–short position representing viewpoint
- Semiactive:
  - Enhanced indexing—Some overweighting/underweighting of asset classes in broad index
  - Derivatives-based asset class position with controlled exposure to active cash position (e.g., controlled duration)
- Combination

## Individual Investor Considerations

### Human Capital

*Financial capital* describes stocks, bonds, and other tradable assets owned by the individual.

*Human capital* ($K_H$) is the present value of all future earnings ($Y_t$) through life expectancy age $n$, and one source of an individual's willingness to bear risk:

$$K_H = \sum_{t=0}^{n} \frac{Y_t}{(1+r)^t}$$

The discount rate for human capital analysis is risk adjusted based on the reliability of the income stream.

Financial capital generally increases over time whereas human capital diminishes as the individual approaches retirement, at which point it becomes 0 (ignoring retirement or social benefits).

- Human capital is greatest at young years because it rests on future earnings potential.
- At some point, increasing financial capital crosses over declining human capital.

Individuals may change their strategic asset allocations due to life cycle and human capital considerations. All else being equal (e.g., risk preference):

- Labor flexibility allows greater risk in investment assets (i.e., can work longer hours or more years to make up any investment losses).
- Lower variability of labor income allows greater risk in investment assets.
- Individuals with labor income correlated to an asset market should reduce their allocation to that asset class (e.g., commission stockbrokers and the equity market).

Relatively stable human capital returns are compared to bonds, thereby allowing nearly all financial capital to be invested in equities. Risky human capital returns require lower allocation to equities in the combined portfolio (i.e., human and financial capital).

### Mortality and Longevity Risks

- Mortality risk—Risk of premature death:
  - Hedged with life insurance.
  - Independent of financial market risk (no SAA applications).
  - Family bears the burden.
- Longevity risk—Risk of outliving capital:
  - Hedged with annuities.
  - Independent of financial market risk (no SAA applications).
  - Individual bears the risk.

IMPORTANT: Although longevity risk is independent of financial market risk, risk-tolerant investors can increase their allocations to financial capital risk as an offset.

Because longevity risk exposure has no potential reward, investors should transfer risk via a life annuity, which pays income over annuitant's life:

- Fixed annuity: Payment amounts are guaranteed for a predetermined premium; insurer bears investment risk.
- Variable annuity: Payment amounts vary based on underlying investment returns; annuitant bears investment risk.
- Equity-indexed annuity: Payment amount is minimum with additional payment for investment returns.

## Institutional Investor Considerations

### Pension Funds

Pension funds generally are not taxable.

Asset allocation strives to provide acceptable:

- Funding shortfall risk
- Pension surplus volatility
- Funding contribution volatility

Asset-only approaches are common, although ALM approaches are preferred.

Constraints include:

- Regulatory: Designed to promote diversification and safety and to limit self-dealing:
    - Use prudent person concept rather than asset class limits.
    - Some countries require minimum domestic asset allocation.
    - There may be "basket" limitations (e.g., percentage maximum allocation to alternative investments).
- Liquidity: Designed to have capital available for planned and potential outflows:
    - Self-limit on illiquid assets (e.g., real estate, private debt, private equity).

### Foundations and Endowments

Goals for both foundations and endowments require high long-term inflation-adjusted returns. Higher allocations are made to equities for growth and to bonds to diversify risk.

Foundations and endowments generally are not taxable.

The primary implementation approach involves passive assets with low implementation and monitoring costs.

Smaller endowments may lack funds for due diligence on alternative investments.

### Insurance Companies

Insurance companies generally are taxable. Non–life insurance companies often purchase municipal bonds (i.e., free from federal tax).

*Portfolio segmentation* (i.e., subportfolios within the general portfolio) allows product-line-specific strategic allocation. Some companies group similar lines based on durations of liabilities:

- Simple allocation method
- Focuses on product line return objectives:
    - More accurate profitability by product line
    - Management of interest rate risk/duration mismatch by product line
- Aids management and regulatory supervision of investment suitability.

Portfolio is still optimized on a company-wide basis.

Insurance companies engage in credit analysis for risky bond holdings, which often comprise a larger allocation than other institutional types have.

Equity investments provide growth of surplus as well as backing for various equity-linked products.

Casualty insurers have a greater liquidity requirement than life insurers due to less payout timing and amount certainty.

### Banks

Banks are taxable *financial intermediaries* (i.e., between investors and investments) with predominantly short- and medium-term liabilities. Primary concerns include:

- Managing interest rate risk (ALM approach)
- Managing liquidity to meet liabilities
- Producing income
- Managing credit risk

Regulatory constraints may involve maximum percentages of certain asset types.

## Tactical Asset Allocation (TAA)

*Tactical asset allocation (TAA)* involves adjusting strategic policy weighting to capture additional gains from short-term capital market expectations.

TAA is considered active management of asset classes:

- Market prices provide objective evidence of potential returns.
- Relative expected returns reflect relative perceived risk.
- Markets are rational and mean reverting.

Trading rules capturing tactical profits, especially from anomalies, may not work forever as other investors stop playing or begin playing on the winning side.

Deviations from expected value could signal different economic relationships:

- Expected inflation changes
- Central bank policy changes
- Underlying risk attributes (including relative risk)
- Business cycle position

Some deviations, then, may not allow reversion to the long-term expectation.

TAA initiates tracking risk relative to the SAA.

TAA must overcome transaction costs to be successful.

# Study Session 9: Asset Allocation and Related Decisions in Portfolio Management (2)

# CURRENCY MANAGEMENT
Cross-Reference to CFA Institute Assigned Reading #18

## Currency Effects on Portfolio Risk and Return

### Notation, Terminology, and Convention

Although *foreign exchange*, *FX*, or *forex* markets identify currency exchange markets, the terms "foreign" and "domestic" are not used except from a trader's perspective.

*Base currency* (B) identifies the subject of the quote in the denominator; *price currency* (P) identifies the currency used against the base in the numerator:

- Quoting format: P/B (i.e., units of price currency per unit of base currency):
  - For example, 0.9800 USD/CHF means 0.9800 U.S. dollars per Swiss franc; alternatively, the price of a Swiss franc is 0.9800 U.S. dollars.
  - Foreign exchange markets may show this as CHF/USD 0.9800, although only the previous description will be used here.
- The exam often indicates currency exchange by completely describing it: "0.98 U.S. dollars per Swiss franc."

Pricing conventions:

- Usually there are four decimals, with the rightmost decimal known as a "pip."
- Forward quotes may have five or six decimals.
- Currencies requiring many units (e.g., JPY) may be carried out to only two decimals.

Dealer quotes:

- *Bid quote:* Price at which the trader will buy and market participant may sell the base currency.
- *Ask quote (offer):* Price at which the trader will sell (offer) and market participant may buy the base currency.
- *Bid–ask spread (bid–offer spread or market width):* The ask less the bid (i.e., *market width*).

IMPORTANT: ABC/XYZ bid–ask spreads can be converted to XYZ/ABC bid–ask spreads via reciprocals, but the positions switch place (i.e., the new ask quote will be the higher of the new reciprocal values).

Ask (offer) prices are almost always higher than bid prices so that the dealer earns a spread.

Forward contracts describe any agreement for settlement past spot closing. Spot closing takes place with T+2 two-day settlement for most and T+1 for U.S./Canadian dollars.

- Points over/under spot: Difference between forward rate quote and spot quote:
  - Scaled to the number of decimal points in the quote
  - Relevant to the maturity (i.e., not annualized)
- Forward premium: Points above spot
- Forward discount: Points below spot

Forward premium/discount for various maturities may be listed as a spot bid–ask in P/B terms, plus/minus the points over/under spot; divide by 10,000 for four-decimal quotes and by 100 for two-digit quotes (JPY).

AA

For example, 1.0168 bid for CHF/USD at –58.94 is converted as:

$$1.0168+\left(\frac{-58.94}{10{,}000}\right)=1.0168-0.005894=1.010906$$

Forward *maturity* describes the time from spot settlement to forward settlement.

Portfolio managers use forwards to hedge currency risk of assets denominated in a foreign currency. To roll over a hedge position, they swap a maturing forward position into a later-maturity forward.

- Matched swaps have equal amount and maturity.
- Swaps with the same maturities are priced using the bid–ask midpoint.

### Return Decomposition

*Decomposition* describes the process of attributing a portfolio outcome (i.e., risk, return, etc.) to the asset classes or securities that make up the portfolio:

- *Foreign currency return, $r_{FC}$*—Return in the asset's home currency
- *Foreign exchange return, $r_{FX}$*—Return attributable to change in value of the P/B relationship
- *Domestic currency return, $r_{DC}$*—Foreign currency return in terms of the investor's home currency

For each asset *i*, weighted based on *domestic* currency asset values:

$$r_{DC,p}=\sum_{i=1}^{n}\omega_i[(1+r_{FC,i})(1+r_{FX,i})-1]$$

Negative weights can represent short positions, but all weights must sum to 100%.

Foreign exchange return must be priced using the investor's reporting (domestic) currency:

$$r_{FX}=\frac{S_{DC/FC,T}}{S_{DC/FC,t}}-1$$

### Volatility Decomposition

IMPORTANT: Reporting generally favors use of standard deviation (i.e., the square root of the variance) to ensure comparability with percentage return.

Domestic return variance $\sigma^2_{DC}$ depends on variances for asset return in domestic currency terms and for foreign exchange return, as well as the correlation of asset return in domestic currency terms and foreign exchange returns:

$$\sigma^2_{DC}=\omega_{FC}\sigma^2_{FC}+\omega_{FX}\sigma^2_{FX}+2\omega_{FC}\sigma_{FC}\omega_{FX}\sigma_{FX}\rho_{FC,FX}$$

With no exchange rate risk, $\sigma^2_{DC} = \sigma^2_{FC}$. Diversification of uncorrelated assets and currencies lowers domestic return risk for the portfolio, as does short selling one of two correlated assets.

Reliability of volatility-related variables may be compromised due to:

- Computational challenges of using multiple assets
- Varying historical volatility relationships
- Dependence on measurement period
- Consensus forecast limitations:
    - Sensitive to sample size and composition
    - Not always available with a consistent starting point
    - Not always immediately reported

Historical volatility may also differ from *implied volatility* (i.e., risk priced into option contracts).

## Strategic Decisions for FX Risk

*Strategic decisions* involve the degree of active management (i.e., exposure to exchange rate risk).

The investment policy statement (IPS) specifies:

- Target percentage of currency exposure passively hedged
- Active management corridor around the target exposure
- Hedge rebalancing frequency
- Benchmark to assess hedging performance
- Permitted hedging instruments (e.g., types of forwards/options)

### Optimization

Portfolios circumvent the calculation problem of simultaneously solving all possible asset/exchange return combinations along with their correlations by:

1. Optimizing the portfolio of fully hedged returns
2. Selecting desired active currency exposures

Portfolio optimization for foreign assets follows the same basic steps as for domestic assets, resulting in a set of efficient portfolios along a risk/return frontier.

### Selecting Currency Exposures

Some studies indicate that FX hedging benefits for global bond and fixed-income portfolios depend on the domestic currency. Other studies indicate that longer-term trends and current market conditions determine hedging benefits.

Reserve currencies (e.g., U.S. dollar) tend to appreciate in a global currency crisis as investors seek safety.

Active viewpoints cite potential alpha from currency exposure:

- Market inefficiencies
- Short-term relationship changes

Hedging costs include:

- Trading costs:
    - Trading infrastructure costs (i.e., *administrative costs* such as technology costs, costs of banking in different currencies, personnel and training costs of front-, middle-, and back-office operations, etc.)
    - Monitoring costs
    - Unrecoverable costs of expired options
    - *Churning* (i.e., paying away the dealer spread, especially to remain fully hedged)
    - Potential losses in rolling forward hedges
- Opportunity costs: Giving up potential FX returns

Hedging viewpoints include:

- Partial hedging: Leave some of the FX risk unhedged.
    - Global equity—Diversification benefits of uncorrelated assets/currencies
    - Fixed income—Less or no hedging:
        - Bonds and FX returns both highly correlated with interest rates
        - Little or no diversification benefit
- Unhedged: Remain unhedged and reduce costs.
    - Purchasing power parity (PPP) and other parity links drive long-term %Δs to 0.
    - There are no long-term benefits to FX hedging.
    - Use an unhedged portfolio benchmark.

Hedge more fully as:

- Risk preference decreases.
- *Ex post* (i.e., lost opportunity) regret decreases.
- Income/liquidity needs increase.
- Time horizon contracts.
- Fixed-income assets in portfolio decrease.
- Cost of hedging decreases.
- Perception of currency exposure benefit decreases.

### Hedging Strategies

From risk averse to risk seeking:

- Passive hedging: Protects portfolio with full hedging; removes manager opinions on FX.
    - Reflects lack of adequate currency return for additional risk.
    - Performance mirrors asset-only return benchmark (i.e., no currency return).
- Discretionary hedging: Manager protects portfolio with hedging; adds alpha.
    - Percentage deviation of actual $MV_{FC}$ from target value in FC terms
    - Performance measured against hedged asset benchmark

- Active currency management: Manager seeks alpha.
    - Mandated risk limits
    - Performance measured against hedged asset benchmark
- Currency overlay portfolio: Separate FX account or separate manager:
    - May be restricted to FX exposure
    - May be FX as an asset class:
        - Not limited to asset portfolio exposures
        - Alpha-seeking active management

IMPORTANT: Currency alpha mandate for FX as an asset class should have minimum correlation with other sources of alpha—especially currency exposures—as well as other asset classes.

## Tactical Decisions

*Tactical decisions* involve manager choices for active currency management.

### Economic Fundamentals

An emphasis on economic fundamentals assumes that exchange rate determination in free markets is based on underlying economic relationships (i.e., purchasing power parity).

Simple model:

- The real exchange rate is determined by the ratio of real purchasing power.
- Short-term variations reflect changes in differential:
    - Inflation
    - Country risk premiums

The base currency in a P/B quote pair appreciates (i.e., more P units are required to purchase each B unit) if there is an increase in:

- B's long-run real purchasing power
- Interest rates (real or nominal), which increases demand for B's currency to lend
- Expected foreign inflation (P and all other countries)
- Foreign risk premiums (P and all other countries)

### Technical Analysis

Underlying assumptions of technical analysis are:

- Underlying economic fundamentals are discounted in favor of supply and demand cues.
- Analysts can forecast future prices using past price data.
- Repetitions in past price data provide opportunities.

IMPORTANT: Technical analysis is less useful in nontrending markets.

A *resistance level* occurs where assets are overbought; a *support level* occurs where assets are oversold. As an asset value approaches a support or resistance level, sell or buy stops are triggered that resist further gain or support the price from further loss.

Momentum carries prices through resistance or support levels.

AA

### Carry Trade

The *carry trade* involves:

- Funding currency: Lower interest rate currencies (borrow)
- Investment currency: Higher interest rate currencies (lend)

$$\%\Delta S_{P/B} \approx i_P - i_B$$

Where base currency is the low interest rate currency in the P/B relationship:

*Uncovered interest rate parity* suggests that positive %Δs should result in future *price* currency depreciation to offset the yield advantage. Currencies may, however, vary from expected value for long periods, creating a return opportunity in forward rates (i.e., *forward rate bias*).

*Covered interest rate parity* suggests that covering the eventual currency repatriation with a forward contract (i.e., buying the *base* currency) should eliminate the forward rate bias (i.e., low interest rate currencies trade at a forward premium to spot):

IMPORTANT: Lower-volatility carry trades have greater opportunity for success.

$$\frac{F_{P/B} - S_{P/B}}{S_{P/B}} = \frac{(i_P - i_B)\left(\frac{t}{360}\right)}{1 + i_B\left(\frac{t}{360}\right)}$$

Carry trade portfolios need not have the same number of funding and investment currencies; managers can weight exposures for $r_{FX}$ and $\sigma_{FX}$ viewpoints.

### Volatility Trading

*Delta hedging* involves using an offsetting spot transaction to completely offset currency risk, or forward contracts in a hedge ratio that completely offsets FX movements.

*Volatility trading* involves hedging all or part of the volatility risk (i.e., sensitivity of option price to changes in price volatility of the underlying) using option *vega*: Note that the currency trader is not long the base currency. Instead, the trader has a strong view about the volatility of the base currency.

- *Straddle:* Offsetting at-the-money put and call; makes money when either put or call goes in-the-money more than option premiums.
- *Strangle:* Offsetting out-of-the-money put and call; makes money when either goes in-the-money more than (less expensive) option premiums.

Managers use delta hedging and volatility trading together to offset price risk while making bets on price volatility (but not direction of price movement).

Volatility will remain low for long periods, but extreme volatility will be brief and result from unexpected market stress. Speculative volatility traders use net-short positions to capture premium from options expiring out-of-the-money.

## Currency Management Tools

Strategic management focuses on long-term benchmark-related decisions, whether passive or in the active management spectrum. Tactical management focuses on shorter-term decisions around the benchmark. Both strategic and tactical approaches use forwards, options, and FX swaps.

### Forward Contracts

Managers use both forward and futures contracts to manage currency exposures. They prefer forwards because:

- Flexible contracts conform more readily to specific portfolio needs; futures are standardized as to amount and maturity date.
- Forwards can be written in any currency pair (i.e., two futures contracts would have to be written to cross-hedge if one of the currency pairs is not readily paired with the other).
- Forwards require no initial margin; futures contracts require initial margin and mark-to-market maintenance.
- Forwards trade in a more liquid market than do futures.

The underlying asset value changes over time, and the hedge ratio may drift from the desired exposure:

- *Static hedge:* No hedge resetting is performed. While less costly, this will increase currency exposure as the underlying drifts.
- *Dynamic hedge:* Size, maturity, and ratio of forwards are adjusted in accordance with the direction/amount of underlying asset change and the degree of active management permitted.

Mismatched swaps (i.e., from changes in the underlying or change in desired exposure) consist of:

- Initiation: Sell foreign currency (equal to initial portfolio value) forward for domestic currency.
- Near leg (i.e., expiring forward):
  - Settle near leg by buying foreign currency for domestic currency in spot market.
  - Receive initial domestic currency value of portfolio.
  - Portfolio profit (or loss) in domestic currency terms results from asset return and FX return; the latter is offset by profit (or loss) in domestic currency terms on the forward.
- Far leg (i.e., new forward):
  - Sell foreign currency (equal to new portfolio value) forward for domestic currency.

*Roll yield* is the spot exchange rate at any given time plus the points for a given maturity (i.e., the implicit cost of the hedge). Roll yield equals the absolute value of the forward premium or discount with a sign corresponding to gain or loss:

$$\left|\frac{F_{P/B} - S_{P/B}}{S_{P/B}}\right|$$

- Positive roll yield (i.e., gain): Trading the *forward rate bias* (i.e., equivalent to a *carry trade*):
    - Buying the base currency at a forward discount
    - Selling the base currency at a forward premium
- Negative roll yield (i.e., loss): Trading against the forward rate bias (i.e., equivalent to a negative carry trade):
    - Selling the base currency at a forward discount
    - Buying the base currency at a forward premium

IMPORTANT: Negative roll yield weighs against using a fully hedged position; trading the forward bias weighs toward complete hedging (or overhedging).

A risk-averse manager will still accept a negative net value hedged position if the risk of a higher FX loss outweighs the certain hedging cost. A risk-neutral manager will *not* implement that hedge.

Risk-averse managers may go unhedged if the negative net value hedged position is so great as to outweigh the unhedged alternative.

IMPORTANT: The advantage of options is avoiding the loss of future currency gains (the same as with forward hedging).

### Currency Options

*Currency options* are European exercise (i.e., exercisable at expiration) instruments that offer the right but not the obligation to buy the underlying currency (calls) or sell the underlying currency (puts) at a preagreed price.

*Protective puts* match put options to a long currency position:

- Depreciation: Manager has the right to exercise the put option for a strike price better than the spot price.
- Appreciation: Manager allows the put to expire unexercised.

Option value drivers include:

- Intrinsic value: Difference between the strike price of the option and the spot exchange rate; at-the money (ATM) options are more expensive than out-of-the-money (OTM) options.
- Time value: Premium for time to expiration:
    - Greater as volatility increases
    - Decays toward expiry

## Hedging Cost-Reduction Strategies

Cost-reduction measures involve:

- Less upside potential
- Less downside protection

### Over-/Underhedging Using Forwards

Less downside protection moves from 100% hedged to more discretionary positions.

- *Overhedged* (expect depreciation): Sell more than 100% of the base position.
- *Fully hedged* (neutral expectation): Sell 100% of the base position.
- *Underhedged* (expect appreciation): Sell less than 100% of the base position.

Dynamic hedging with forwards:

- Base currency depreciates: Increase hedge ratio back to 100% cover.
- Base currency appreciates: Decrease hedge ratio back to 100% cover.

Forwards give upside potential away for lower cost.

### Protective Puts Using OTM Options

Options are used to:

- Limit downside risk while maintaining upside potential.
- Earn option writing premiums.

OTM options are less expensive than ATM options, but introduce downside risk.

IMPORTANT: Short and long positions in risk reversals depend on selling or buying the call, respectively.

Reduce premium on protection with:

- *Short risk reversal* (i.e., collar): Buy OTM put and sell OTM call.
- *Long risk reversal:* Buy OTM call and sell OTM put.

### Put Spread

Put spreads involve buying an OTM put and funding it by writing a deeper OTM put with the same maturity. Cheaper or zero-cost methods are used by altering:

- Notional amounts: Increase in OTM notional:
  - Greater exposure if expiry with price lower than furthest price from ATM
  - More appropriate for expressing manager view than for hedge
- Strike prices: Moving strike prices closer together; decreases hedge protection.

To profit from modest depreciation, fully hedge with forwards and overlay with a put spread as a tactical position.

### Seagull Spread

A *short seagull spread* involves a put spread and a short call; that is, long a protective put to sell the base currency, short a deep OTM put, and short a call. The short positions in a put and a call are the "wings," and the long put closer to the money is the "body."

IMPORTANT: "Long" and "short" spread designations are determined by the option positions in the wings of the spread.

The long position comprising a short seagull spread may allow a more expensive ATM option because the manager sold two options.

A *long seagull spread* involves a short put closer to or at-the-money and long call and long put in the wings. This provides inexpensive downside protection.

### Exotic Options

IMPORTANT: Exotic options allow low-price-risk customization at the expense of less downside protection or upside potential.

*Vanilla options* are simple European put and call options used by corporations and investment funds.

*Exotic options* are more complex options with special features used by currency overlay managers and speculators.

AA

While they are a high-profit-margin item for dealers, exotic options have disadvantages:

- They are difficult to value for regulatory and accounting purposes.
- It is difficult to obtain more favorable hedge treatment for financial reporting.
- There is a lack of familiarity among smaller potential users.

IMPORTANT: Knock-in and knock-out options create less costly, but more restrictive risk protection.

Vanilla options may be modified to exotic with the addition of special features:

- *Knock-in:* A vanilla option is created when the spot price reaches a predetermined price.
- *Knock-out:* The option is extinguished when the spot price reaches a predetermined price.

*Binary options* (also known as *digital options* or *all-or-nothing options*) pay a fixed amount when the spot price reaches a predetermined price. They:

- Leverage bets on FX direction.
- Have a specified extreme payoff if successful.
- Are more expensive.

### Hedging Process

For a price/base (P/B) pair:

- *Price currency:* The portfolio currency, also known as the exposure, transaction, or foreign currency
- *Base currency:* The counter currency, also known as the investor's domestic currency

IMPORTANT: For a portfolio of assets with no gains, losses, or expenses, a complete hedge (i.e., the manager has an uncertain viewpoint or is risk averse) would allow conversion into the same amount of originally invested currency.

Return is calculated in terms of the investor's domestic currency, but includes both an asset return component and a foreign exchange component.

Investors may choose to hedge the value of the portfolio in terms of B (i.e., keep it the same relative to P):

- *Appreciation:* P units increase per unit of B (i.e., B is worth more).
- *Depreciation:* P units decrease per unit of B (i.e., B is worth less).

Considerations in the hedging process, especially with active management, are:

1. Identify currency to hedge (i.e., maintain or increase value of) as the base in the P/B pair.
2. Determine price movement expectation.
3. Active management: Directional bias applied to express market viewpoint:
    - Appreciation—Less hedging (or buy); involves long base currency instrument:
        - Long call option or long forward contract (i.e., buying the base currency forward)
        - Writing options or buying OTM call to reduce costs
        - Bullish exotic strategies that pay off if the base currency appreciates
    - Depreciation—More/complete hedging (or selling) involves:
        - Long put option or short forward contract (i.e., selling the currency forward)
        - Writing options or buying OTM put to reduce costs
        - Bearish exotic strategies that pay off if the base currency depreciates

## Multiple Foreign Currencies

Although the basic tools are the same as for a single currency, hedging multiple foreign currencies requires considering correlations.

### Cross Hedge

A *cross hedge* describes using one asset or derivative to offset risk on another asset. Cross-hedging two assets using negatively correlated currency exposures can avoid the expense of directly hedging the assets.

### Macro Hedge

A macro hedge occurs when risk exposures for the entire portfolio are hedged rather than hedging individual asset risk exposures:

- Gold limits risk from extreme market stress.
- Asset index derivatives.
- Fixed-weight basket of currency derivatives.

### Minimum-Variance Hedge Ratio

A *minimum-variance hedge ratio* describes an optimal cross-hedging ratio ($b$) determined by regression analysis to minimize the error term:

$$\varepsilon = y-(a+bx)$$

IMPORTANT: This is not used for direct hedging via forwards, but is useful for cross-hedging and macro hedges.

Both the percentage change in value of the asset to be hedged ($y$) and the percentage change in value of the hedging instrument ($x$) are measured in terms of the investor's domestic currency.

*Basis risk* occurs due to imperfect correlation between currency price movement and the hedging instrument. This can require reestimating minimum variance hedge ratios.

## Managing Emerging Market Currencies

Emerging market currencies are subject to:

- Normal conditions: Higher transaction costs (i.e., wider bid–ask spreads)
- Extreme conditions: Severe loss of liquidity

Cross-hedging in thinly traded currencies can become expensive. For example, one trade may go through one bank and another trade through another bank, or liquidity for the first leg may be fine but liquidity for the second leg has been impaired by market conditions.

Positions in an illiquid currency asset may be easy to enter gradually, but difficult to exit quickly. This can especially occur with popular carry trades or fad investment regions.

Currencies subject to these extreme illiquidity events have return distributions with fatter tails and negative skewness. This makes comparing Sharpe ratios difficult.

Central banks support a declining currency by increasing the policy interest rate. Hedging costs increase due to negative roll yield as forward prices for the emerging market currency fall in response to the new higher rate and demand for the currency.

Portfolios become more correlated and less diversified when contagion occurs and one country suffers from another country's currency woes. Haven currencies (e.g., USD, GBP, EUR, etc.) become popular, and a large basket of emerging market currencies becomes unpopular.

Extreme market events can occur when pegged currencies break or governments intervene in markets or currencies.

### Nondeliverable Forwards (NDFs)

> IMPORTANT: NDFs will often seek to profit by appreciation of the noncontrolled currency of a pair.

A *nondeliverable forward (NDF)* circumvents currency controls by going long the controlled currency, but cash delivery is made in the noncontrolled currency of a pair (i.e., in the P/B notation, B is cash delivered rather than physical delivery of P).

Forward pricing in NDFs for countries with capital controls may reflect supply-and-demand conditions rather than official pricing of the controlled currency.

# MARKET INDEXES AND BENCHMARKS

Cross-Reference to CFA Institute Assigned Reading #19

## Comparison of Indexes to Benchmarks

A *market index* mathematically reflects performance related to an asset class, market, or market segment.

A *benchmark*, as used in the investment process, mathematically reflects the collection of securities related to the manager's desired risk and return profile. A benchmark also:

- May be the IPS-specified strategic return requirement not mathematically representable by any specific securities.
- Indicates the manager's investment universe (i.e., set of assets the portfolio considers for investment).
- Provides the baseline risk/return profile suitable for judging manager performance and guiding asset selection.

## Benchmarks

### Benchmark Criteria

Valid benchmarks are:

- Investable: Manager can purchase and track performance on the components.
- Unambiguous: Securities or components and their weights are clearly defined in the portfolio.
- Measurable: Easily calculable as necessary for the required purpose.
- Reflective of current investment opinion: Contains investments about which the manager has an opinion.
- Specified in advance: Manager knows the benchmark composition before investing.
- Appropriate: Consistent with manager's objectives and style.
- Owned (or "accountable"): Manager agrees to measure performance against the index.

### Uses

A benchmark for sponsor purposes is useful as a(n):

- Indication of investment strategy and process
- Reference for asset segments established in the IPS
- Indication of risk/return preference and how the funds are to be invested
- More precise tool for identifying actual portfolio exposures
- Indication of manager bets outside the benchmark and success of those bets
- Communication tool for outside parties as to how the manager will be evaluated
- Method of attributing and comparing manager performance
- Method of assessing return on manager contribution

AA

> IMPORTANT: The Global Investment Performance Standards (GIPS) specify that benchmark performance must be included, if available, as part of performance presentation.

In addition, managers use benchmarks to market portfolios and investment management capabilities to investors.

Regulators use benchmarks to assess compliance with standards, regulation, and laws reflecting presentation of performance history and prospective risks and returns, as well as adherence to mandates (e.g., no or limited investment in junk bonds).

Plan sponsors and other parties (e.g., beneficiaries) are responsible for portfolio outcomes and may have benchmarks that reference the liabilities the portfolio has been designed to defease.

### Types

*Asset-based benchmarks* compare manager performance to a portfolio of assets:

- *Absolute return benchmark:* A return target that the manager must beat, stated as an absolute minimum or spread against the benchmark; useful for:
    - Buyout funds and other private equity investment
    - Market-neutral long/short funds
- *Manager universe* (i.e., peer group): Represents managers with similar investment styles and segmented by asset class and investment style; useful for hedge funds and other fund investment styles.
- *Broad market indexes:* Indexes of diversified asset class funds; widely reported in mainstream media because they are easily understood and widely known.
- *Style indexes:* Management of assets, often components of broad market indexes, with characteristics thought to be a determinant of return and risk (e.g., market capitalization, relative P/E, etc.).
- *Factor-model-based benchmarks:* Using models to establish sensitivity to systematic factors thought to be responsible for asset returns.
- *Returns-based benchmarks:* Weighted averages of various style indexes using a factor-model-based process that best tracks portfolio returns.
- *Custom security-based benchmarks* (i.e., *strategy benchmarks*): Exclusively reflect a manager's style based on past exposures and discussions with the manager; appropriate when the manager does not match well to any broad market or style index.

*Liability-based benchmarks* match key characteristic of funding liabilities (e.g., return, volatility, duration, etc.) using nominal bonds, real-return bonds, equities, and so on.

Pension funds and insurance companies use liabilities-based benchmarks to assess funding success.

## Indexes

### Uses

Indexes capture security performance representative of an asset class, market, or market segment:

- *Asset allocation proxies* allow investors to tailor a portfolio with suitable risk/return characteristics based on *ex ante* return, risk, and correlation for the asset class.
- *Policy statements* communicate asset owner expectations to portfolio managers.
- *Performance benchmarks* measure manager's *ex post* performance against an index.

- *Portfolio analysis* involves decomposing return contributions, currency management strategy effectiveness, and so on.
- *Market sentiment gauge* is a convenient summary of how consumers, investors, and the public feel; it may reflect the probability of fiscal/monetary policy changes.
- *Investment vehicles* are the basis for exchange-traded funds (ETFs), index funds, and derivatives.

Enhanced index managers try to limit additional risk while making active bets leading to excess return (i.e., alpha).

### Construction Alternatives

Index construction involves applying existing securities to a set of predefined rules:

- Inclusion criteria: Determining which securities the index will represent:
    - Narrower—A specific subset with definable, representative characteristics
    - Broader—More diversified by industry, size, and other representative characteristics
- Weighting method: How price movements of securities are includable (e.g., price, value, etc.)
- Maintenance method: How securities will be added, or how those in the index will be removed or replaced (e.g., changes resulting from secondary offerings, share buybacks, stock distributions, spin-offs, etc.)

### Construction Trade-Offs

*Completeness* describes the degree to which an index includes all securities. However, not all securities may be investable as the result of low liquidity, private or government ownership, and other factors. Even if investable, some securities may not be desirable based on infrequent trading.

*Reconstitution* refers to making changes in the index constituents. *Rebalancing* involves returning securities to the appropriate allocation within the index. Both require trading expenses on the part of index users. More frequent reconstitution or rebalancing results in higher trading costs but may create a more relevant measurement tool.

IMPORTANT: Some assets migrate from one style to another, although they remain in the same index in the same allocation. This results in the manager who is making style allocations having to vary from the index, with the consequent trading costs, even though the index itself remains unchanged.

Objective and transparent rules allow investors to predict which securities will change at reconstitution. Judgment allows index providers to remain relevant in the face of different circumstances than when the index was developed.

### Market Capitalization Weighting

*Market capitalization weighting* involves the percentage of each company's capitalization value (i.e., shares multiplied by price) compared to total market capitalization value.

- *Macro-consistency* represents performance of portfolios holding all shares of each security; free-float-adjusted indexes represent performance of portfolios holding all shares of each security available to the public (i.e., important in less developed markets).
- Advantages: Broad acceptance; requires less rebalancing because index remains properly weighted after a price change.

- Disadvantages: Overly influenced by overpriced securities; price movements overly concentrated in a few large companies (i.e., reflects less diversification).
- Examples: S&P 500, Russell indexes, MSCI (global), TOPIX (Tokyo stock exchange price index)

### Price Weighting

A price-weighted index weights each security in proportion to its price, resulting in a simple average of prices.

- Represents performance of portfolio holding one share of each security.
- Advantages: Simple; long track record is useful for investment research.
- Disadvantages:
    - Not relevant to most investor strategies.
    - Influenced by highest-priced securities.
    - Must be rebalanced after stock splits or price-appreciated companies become underrepresented.
- Examples: Dow Jones Industrial Average, Nikkei

### Equal Weighting

- Equal weighting: All shares are held in equal weights at rebalancing:
    - Represents performance of portfolio holding an equal dollar value of each security.
    - Advantages: More diversified away from highest-priced companies.
    - Disadvantages: Must be rebalanced as often as quarterly to maintain weighting; smaller company price movements may be overrepresented.
    - Example: Value Line Composite Average

### Fundamental Weighting

Fundamental weighting gives price movements their importance based on fundamental factors such as book value, dividends, cash flow, sales, and so on.

> IMPORTANT: Fundamentals-weighted indexes tend to outperform value-weighted indexes due to bias toward small-capitalization firms. This would not allow investors with large-capitalization mandates to participate effectively.

- Represents performance of portfolio holding securities weighted by their fundamental attribute selected.
- Advantages: Better represents economic importance (i.e., price bubbles don't indicate economic achievement).
- Disadvantages:
    - Rely on creator's subjective judgment (i.e., relative importance of a fundamental factor).
    - Restrictive valuation screens may result in less diversification.
    - Not all investors can hold because smaller companies may have more heavily weighted fundamental factors but fewer shares for investment.
    - Not transparent because valuation weightings are usually proprietary.

## Capitalization-Weighted Index as a Benchmark

Price-weighted and equal-weighted indexes are market indicators rather than reasonable benchmarks.

The proprietary nature of fundamentals-weighted indexes makes them inapplicable as a benchmark for management performance evaluation by investors (i.e., nontransparent).

Capitalization-weighted indexes tell managers how they did versus the broader market of all investable assets and are therefore superior.

- Cap-weighted indexes are the most easily established and tracked.
- They adhere to many criteria for benchmarks, but:
  - They have a large-cap bias.
  - They are not totally transparent (e.g., don't disclose float-adjustment procedures).
  - Float adjustment procedures are not consistent across available indexes.
  - They reflect a market segment rather than manager's style.

IMPORTANT: Consider the cost of establishing and maintaining custom benchmarks before abandoning some allocation to several different benchmarks or a fundamental factors approach; however, those approaches may lead to investing in some inappropriate securities.

# Study Session 10: Fixed-Income Portfolio Management (1)

FI

FI

# FIXED-INCOME PORTFOLIO MANAGEMENT—PART I
Cross-Reference to CFA Institute Assigned Reading #20

## Fixed-Income Portfolio Management Framework

Four activities in the investment management process are:

1. Setting the risk and return objectives and constraints
2. Developing and implementing a portfolio strategy
3. Monitoring the portfolio
4. Adjusting the portfolio



Setting the risk and return objectives and constraints is the first step. Portfolio analysis is done on an after-tax basis and considers the tax-efficiency of fixed-income assets if the client is a taxable investor. For any client, the fixed-income portfolio manager and the client must agree on an appropriate benchmark, based on the needs of the client as expressed in the investment policy statement (IPS).

Two types of investors exist based on investment objectives:

1. *Investors who do not have liability matching as an objective.* A bond mutual fund does not have a set of liabilities, and the fund does not guarantee investors a certain rate of return. A bond market index serves as the benchmark for the portfolio, referred to as benchmark-relative investing.
2. *Investors who have a liability or set of liabilities that needs to be met.* For example, investors may create a liability by leveraging the portfolio, or as a result of legal promises (e.g., defined-benefit pension plan) or quasi-liabilities (e.g., retirement needs). Meeting the liabilities is the investment objective and becomes the benchmark for the portfolio.

## Managing against a Bond Market Index

If the investor has chosen to manage the portfolio's funds against a bond market index, the investor can choose a passive management strategy or an active management strategy.

- **Passive management strategy** assumes that the market's expectations are correct and the investor cannot add value by questioning these expectations. The portfolio's risk is identical to the benchmark index's risk profile. The manager does not make independent forecasts, and the portfolio tracks the index.
- **Active management strategy** relies on the manager's forecasting ability in the belief that the manager possesses superior skills in interest rate forecasting, credit valuation, or other areas. The portfolio's return should increase if the manager's forecasts are more accurate than those reflected in the current prices. The manager can create small mismatches (enhancement) or large mismatches (full-blown active management) relative to the index.

The next step is to select an appropriate investment strategy grouped along a spectrum.

### Classification of Strategies

Five types of strategies range from totally passive to full-blown active management. They are:

1. **Pure bond indexing (or full replication approach).** A portfolio is constructed that is perfectly matched to the index by duplicating all the bonds in the index in the same percentages. Many issues in a bond index are illiquid. Therefore, full replication is rarely attempted because of the difficulty, inefficiency, and high cost of implementation.
2. **Enhanced indexing by matching primary risk factors.** A sampling approach is used to match the primary index risk factors and achieve a higher return than under full replication. Primary risk factors include the level of interest rates, twists in the yield curve, and changes in the spread between Treasuries and non-Treasuries. By investing in a sample of bonds, the manager reduces the cost of the portfolio. The sampling approach will track the index less closely than full replication, but the lower expenses will enhance the return.

   By matching the primary risk factors, the portfolio is affected by broad market-moving events (e.g., changing interest rate levels, twists in the yield curve, spread changes) to the same degree as the index.
3. **Enhanced indexing by small risk factor mismatches.** Duration is matched but the portfolio is tilted in favor of other risk factors. The manager may pursue relative value in certain sectors, quality, and term structure to enhance the portfolio's return and/or risk profile.
4. **Active management by larger risk factor mismatches.** Larger mismatches are created on the primary risk factors to increase return. The manager may overweight credit quality or sectors, or adjust the portfolio's duration away from the index's duration.
5. **Aggressive mismatches** are created on duration, sector weights, and other factors for superior return and risk characteristics, without consideration for the index composition.

### Pure and Enhanced Indexing

Reasons for investing in an indexed portfolio include:

- Indexed portfolios have lower advisory and custodial fees than actively managed accounts. Advisory and custodial fees may be only a few basis points.
- Outperforming an index is difficult when the higher fees and transaction costs of active management are considered.
- Broad-based bond index portfolios provide excellent diversification. Many have over 5,000 issues containing a wide array of maturities, sectors, and qualities. In practice, portfolio managers do not engage in pure indexing because broad-based index portfolios might contain over 5,000 issues, some of which might not be available for trading, resulting in high transaction costs.

### Considerations When Selecting a Benchmark Bond Index

The choice of an index should match the desired characteristics of the portfolio. The choice depends on four factors:

1. **Market value risk.** Given a normal upward-sloping yield curve, as the maturity and duration of a portfolio increase, the market risk increases.
2. **Income risk.** If stability and dependability of income are the primary needs of the investor, then the short-dated portfolio is more risky than the long-dated portfolio.
3. **Credit risk.** The diversification among issuers in the index should be acceptable to the investor.

4. **Liability framework risk.** This risk should be minimized by matching the investment characteristics (e.g., duration). The choice of an appropriate index should reflect the nature of the liabilities. Investors with long-term liabilities should select a long index (i.e., pension).

For the taxable investor, returns and risk need to be evaluated on an after-tax basis. For example, compare the anticipated return on taxable and tax-exempt bond indices on a net-of-taxes basis, or evaluate the different tax rates applied to the income and capital gains components of bond returns. Furthermore, optimization of the asset location decision within a taxable or tax-deferred account is also evaluated.

The bond market can be separated into sectors:

- Issuer sectors: corporate bonds, government bonds, asset-backed securities (ABSs), mortgage-backed securities (MBSs), and so on.
- Credit risk sectors: investment-grade bonds, high-yield bonds, and so on.



Finer sectors could be defined:

- Corporate bonds: industrial, utility, financial sectors, and so on.
- Investment-grade bonds: investment rating (e.g., AAA/Aaa, AA/Aa, A, BBB/Baa), and so on.
- Other key features: maturity, fixed versus floating coupon rates, callable, linked to inflation, and so on.

### Bond Index Investability and Use as a Benchmark

There are several reasons why many bond indices are difficult to track and are not fully investable. The heterogeneity and trading characteristics present in the bond universe are:

- Many decisions are required in constructing the index (i.e., country, credit risk, liquidity, maturity, currency, and sector classification).
- There are many more issuers and types of bonds compared to equities (e.g., government issues, maturities, seniority).
- Secondary markets are less active compared to equities (e.g., stale pricing, estimated values).
- Bond indices can have very different compositions and performance. For example, one corporate bond index could include bonds with sinking fund provisions, whereas another corporate bond index with the same mandate can exclude them.
- Index composition can change frequently. Bond indices are reconstituted or rebalanced regularly, and they continually change as bond maturities change, and as issuers call in and sell new bonds.
- A "bums" problem arises when capitalization-weighted bond indices give more weight to issuers that borrow the most (e.g., the EMBI Global had a 66% exposure to Latin American countries in 1999). An index heavily weighted by bums will have increased risk, and investors tracking such indices may hold a riskier portfolio than they might otherwise desire. Solutions are putting limits to the weights of component securities from particular issuers or investing in equal-weighted indices.
- Investors may not be able to find a bond index with risk characteristics that match their portfolio's exposure (e.g., the index may be dominated by long maturities but the investor may desire shorter durations).

Bond indices are often benchmarks for manager performance analysis, manager selection, and manager retention; however, if a bond index is not investable, it is unrealistic and unfair to expect a manager to match its performance. As such, bond indices often do not serve as valid benchmarks.

Other criteria for valid benchmarks include:

- Unambiguous
- Measurable
- Appropriate (i.e., the index or portfolio should not change composition substantially over time)
- Reflective of current investment opinions (i.e., the index or portfolio contains familiar securities)
- Specified in advance
- Accountable (i.e., a portfolio manager will not agree to the use of a benchmark that contains unfamiliar securities)



For manager performance evaluation, the use of an index as a benchmark can be problematic, especially for active managers who are not as constrained by particular indices. A custom benchmark that is constructed according to the specific characteristics of the manager's portfolio would more likely serve as a valid performance benchmark.

### Risk Profiles

To build an indexed portfolio, the manager begins by selecting an index that will serve as the basis for the portfolio. However, as discussed previously, many indices will not be investable. Therefore, the manager's goal is to then construct a portfolio that mimics (tracks closely) the characteristics of the benchmark index.

The identification and measurement of risk factors play a role both in index selection and in portfolio construction. A portfolio that mimics the index will contain the same risk exposures (risk profile) as the index.

Yield curve risk is a major source of risk for most bonds. Yield curve changes include:

- A parallel shift in the yield curve (90% of the change in value of a bond)
- A twist of the yield curve
- Other curvature changes of the yield curve

Spread risk and various other risks are also evaluated. The portfolio manager may use various techniques to align the portfolio's risk exposures with those of the index.

**Cell-matching (stratified sampling)** categorizes the index into cells that represent various risk factors of the index. The manager then selects sample bonds from each cell for inclusion in the portfolio, making sure that the weight given to each cell in the portfolio matches that cell's weighting in the benchmark index.

A multifactor model makes use of a set of factors that drive bond returns, generally the following seven primary risk factors:

1. **Duration.** An index's effective duration measures the sensitivity of the index's price to a parallel shift in interest rates (i.e., interest rate risk). A convexity adjustment is used to estimate the change in price that is not explained by duration. The indexed

portfolio matches the duration of the index to ensure that the exposure is the same in both. Duration can be inadequate to capture the full effect of changes in interest rates, because a shift that is parallel is rare.

2. **Key rate duration** and **present value distribution of cash flows** capture nonparallel shifts, such as an increase in slope or a twist in the yield curve. Key rate duration measures the effect of shifts in key points along the yield curve. By changing the spot rate for one key maturity while holding constant all other maturities, we are able to measure a portfolio's sensitivity to a change in that maturity. We repeat the process for the other key maturities.

   Present value distribution of cash flows matches the portfolio's present value distribution of cash flows to that of the index by dividing future time into a set of nonoverlapping time periods.
3. **Sector and quality percentage.** The portfolio matches the percentage weight in the various sectors and qualities of the index.
4. **Sector duration contribution.** The goal is to ensure that a change in sector spreads has the same impact on both the portfolio and the index. Therefore, match the amount of the index duration that comes from the various sectors (i.e., the sector duration contribution).
5. **Quality spread duration contribution.** Spread duration measures how a non-Treasury security's price will change as a result of the widening or narrowing of the spread.
6. **Sector/coupon/maturity cell weights.** Some bonds (i.e., MBSs) exhibit negative convexity, making the index's exposure to call risk difficult to replicate. Matching convexity is rarely attempted because staying matched can lead to excessively high transaction costs. A more feasible method of matching the call exposure is to match the sector, coupon, and maturity weights of the callable sectors. As rates change, the changes in call exposure of the portfolio will be matched to the index.
7. **Issuer exposure.** If a manager attempts to replicate the index with too few securities, issuer event risk takes on greater importance.

The degree of success of an indexer in mimicking index returns is measured by **tracking risk**.

### Tracking Risk

**Tracking risk (tracking error)** is defined as the standard deviation of the portfolio's active return, where the active return for each period is defined as:

| Active return = Portfolio's return – Benchmark index's return |
|---|

The smaller the tracking risk, the more closely the portfolio's return matches, or tracks, the benchmark index's return. Tracking risk arises primarily from mismatches between a portfolio's risk profile and the benchmark's risk profile. The seven primary risk factors should be matched closely if the tracking risk is to be kept to a minimum.

### Enhanced Indexing Strategies

A perfectly indexed portfolio will underperform the index by the amount of transaction costs to construct the portfolio. Therefore, an **index enhancement strategy** seeks to recover these costs by enhancing the portfolio's return. The ways in which this may be done include:

- **Lower-cost enhancements.** The manager can increase the portfolio's net return by maintaining tight controls on trading costs and management fees.

- **Issue selection enhancements.** The manager may identify and select securities that are undervalued in the marketplace relative to a valuation model's theoretical value.
- **Yield curve positioning.** The manager may be able to enhance the portfolio's return by overweighting the undervalued areas of the curve and underweighting the overvalued areas.
- **Sector and quality positioning.** This return enhancement technique takes two forms:
  1. Maintaining a yield tilt toward short-duration corporates. The best yield spread per unit of duration risk is usually available in corporate securities with less than five years to maturity.
  2. Periodic over- or underweighting of sectors or qualities. On a small scale, the manager may overweight Treasuries when spreads are expected to widen and underweight them when spreads are expected to narrow.
- **Call exposure positioning.** A decline in yields will lead to underperformance of callable bonds. This underperformance creates an opportunity for the portfolio manager to underweight these issues under these conditions.

### Active Strategies

An active manager is willing to accept a large tracking risk, with a large positive active return. By applying superior analytical skills, the active manager hopes for a portfolio return that is higher than the benchmark return.

### Extra Activities Required for an Active Manager

Active managers select the type of active strategy to pursue. The active manager will:

- **Identify which index mismatches are to be exploited** based on the expertise of the manager. For example, if the manager's strength is interest rate forecasting, deliberate mismatches in duration will be created.
- **Extrapolate the market's expectations from the market data.** Current market prices are the result of all investors applying their judgment to individual bonds. By analyzing these prices and yields, the manager can obtain additional data. For example, forward rates can be calculated from the spot rate yield curve. These forward rates can provide insight into the direction of rates and the level that investors believe rates will be at in the future.
- **Independently forecast the necessary inputs and compare these with the market's expectations.** For example, after calculating the forward rates, the active manager may believe that these rates are too high and that future interest rates will not reach these levels. After comparing his or her forecast of forward rates with those of other investors, the manager may decide to create a duration mismatch.
- **Estimate the relative values of securities in order to identify areas of under- or overvaluation.** Again, the focus is on the skills of the manager. Managers will apply their skills to try to exploit opportunities as they arise.

### Total Return Analysis and Scenario Analysis

Before executing a trade, an active manager analyzes the impact that the trade will have on the portfolio's return. The two primary tools are total return analysis and scenario analysis.

The **total return** on a bond is the rate of return that equates the future value of the bond's cash flows with the full price of the bond. The total return takes into account all three sources of potential return: coupon income, reinvestment income, and change in price. **Total return analysis** assesses the expected effect of a trade on the portfolio's total return given an interest rate forecast.

To compute total return when purchasing a bond with semiannual coupons, the manager needs to specify (1) an investment horizon, (2) an expected reinvestment rate for the coupon payments, and (3) the expected price of the bond at the end of the time horizon given a forecast change in interest rates. The manager may want to start with a prediction of the most likely change in interest rates. The semiannual total return that the manager would expect to earn on the trade is:



$$\text{Semiannual total return} = \left(\frac{\text{Total future dollars}}{\text{Full price of the bond}}\right)^{\frac{1}{n}} - 1$$

where $n$ is the number of periods in the investment horizon.

**Scenario analysis** is performed to evaluate the impact of the trade on expected total return under all reasonable sets of assumptions as opposed to only *one* assumed change in rates.

Scenario analysis is useful in a variety of ways:

- The manager is able to assess the distribution of possible outcomes, in essence conducting a risk analysis on the portfolio's trades.
- The analysis can be reversed, beginning with a range of acceptable outcomes and then calculating the range of interest rate movements (inputs) that would result in a desirable outcome. The manager can then place probabilities on interest rates falling within this acceptable range.
- The contribution of the individual components to the total return may be evaluated. For example, the results of the scenario analysis may show that the effect of a twist in the yield curve is much larger than the manager anticipated.
- The process can be broadened to evaluate the relative merits of entire trading strategies.

### Monitoring/Adjusting the Portfolio and Performance Evaluation

Monitoring and adjusting a fixed-income portfolio, with its related performance evaluation, are the same as for other classes of investments such as equities.

### Managing Funds against Liabilities: Dedication Strategies

Dedication strategies are designed to accommodate specific funding needs of the investor. They are classified as passive, although it is possible to add some active management.

**Immunization** is one type of dedication strategy. Immunization aims to construct a portfolio that, over a specified horizon, will earn a predetermined return regardless of interest rate changes.

FI

**Cash flow matching** is another dedication strategy, which provides the future funding of a liability stream from the coupon and maturing principal payments of the portfolio.

There are four classes of liabilities, shown in the table:

**Classes of Liabilities**

| Amount of Liability | Timing of Liability | Example |
|---|---|---|
| **Known** | Known | A principal repayment |
| **Known** | Unknown | A life insurance payout |
| **Unknown** | Known | A floating-rate annuity payout |
| **Unknown** | Unknown | Postretirement health care benefits |

The more uncertain the liabilities, the more difficult it becomes to use a passive dedication. For this reason, managers often insert elements of active management to increase the upside potential of the portfolio while ensuring that cash flows are adequate for paying anticipated liabilities.

### Immunization Strategies

The purpose of immunization is to identify the portfolio for which the change in price arising from a change in interest rates is exactly equal to the change in reinvestment income at the time horizon. If the manager can construct such a portfolio, an assured rate of return over that horizon is locked in. The immunization strategy depends on the type of liabilities: a single liability, multiple liabilities, or general cash flows (where the cash flows are more arbitrary in their timing).

### Classical Single-Period Immunization

Classical immunization is supported by a fixed-income portfolio that produces an assured return for a specific time horizon, irrespective of any parallel shifts in the yield curve. Characteristics of immunization are:

- Specified time horizon
- Assured rate of return during the holding period to a fixed horizon date
- Insulation from the effects of interest rate changes on the portfolio value at the horizon date

The fundamental mechanism supporting immunization is a portfolio structure that offsets price risk with reinvestment risk. To accomplish this balancing requires the management of duration. Setting the duration of the portfolio equal to the specified portfolio time horizon assures the offsetting.

To immunize a portfolio's target value or target yield against a change in the market yield, a manager must invest in a bond portfolio where:

- Duration is equal to the investment horizon.
- The initial present value of all cash flows equals the present value of the future liability.

### Rebalancing an Immunized Portfolio

Immunization assumes a one-time instantaneous change in the market yield. In actuality, the market yield will fluctuate over the investment horizon. As a result, the duration of the portfolio will change as the market yield changes and because of the passage of time.

Frequent rebalancing increases transaction costs. Less frequent rebalancing causes the duration to wander from the target duration. Both reduce the likelihood of achieving the target return. Thus, the manager faces a trade-off.

### Determining the Target Return

The assured rate of return of immunization, the total return of the portfolio, can be determined by the yield curve prevailing at the beginning of the horizon period and assumes no change in the term structure. This target rate of return will differ from the portfolio's yield to maturity unless the term structure is flat.

For an upward-sloping yield curve, the immunization target rate of return will be less than the yield to maturity because of the lower reinvestment return, and vice versa.

### Time Horizon

The **immunized time horizon** is equal to the portfolio duration. Portfolio duration is equal to a weighted average of the individual security durations where the weights are the relative percentages invested in each.

Securities in the portfolio should be limited to high-quality, liquid instruments, because portfolio rebalancing is required to keep the portfolio duration synchronized with the horizon date.

### Dollar Duration and Controlling Positions

**Dollar duration** is a measure of the change in portfolio value for a 100 bps change in market yields.

$$\text{Dollar duration} = \text{Duration} \times \text{Portfolio value} \times 0.01$$

A portfolio's dollar duration is equal to the sum of the dollar durations of the component securities.

In asset–liability management (ALM), the goal is to reestablish the dollar duration of a portfolio to a desired level. This rebalancing involves the following steps:

1. Move forward in time and include a shift in the yield curve. Using the new market values and durations, calculate the dollar duration of the portfolio at this point in time.
2. Calculate the **rebalancing ratio** by dividing the desired dollar duration by the new dollar duration. This is the percentage amount that each position needs to be changed in order to rebalance the portfolio.
3. Multiply the new market value of the portfolio by the desired percentage change in step 2. This number is the amount of cash needed for rebalancing.

## Spread Duration

Spread duration is a measure of how the market value of a risky bond or portfolio will change with respect to a parallel 100 bps change in its spread above the comparable benchmark security or portfolio (i.e., spread risk).

Bonds with **credit risk** (default or downgrades in credit ratings) have higher yields than comparable risk-free securities. Three major types of spreads are:

1. **Nominal spread:** The spread of a bond or portfolio above the yield of a certain maturity Treasury.
2. **Static spread** or zero-volatility spread: The constant spread above the Treasury spot curve that equates the calculated price of the security to the market price.
3. **Option-adjusted spread (OAS):** The current spread over the benchmark yield minus that component of the spread that is attributable to any embedded optionality.

FI

The **spread duration** of a portfolio is calculated as a market-weighted average of the spread durations of the component securities. For a portfolio of non-Treasury securities, spread duration equals portfolio duration. For a portfolio of Treasury securities, spread duration equals zero. Therefore, a portfolio that includes both Treasury and non-Treasury securities will have a spread duration that is different from the portfolio duration.

A bond index will have an overall spread duration as well as each sector within the index.

## Extensions of Classical Immunization Theory

Classical immunization theory is based on several assumptions:

- Any changes in the yield curve are parallel changes.
- The portfolio is valued at a fixed horizon date, and there are no interim cash inflows or outflows before the horizon date.
- The target value of the investment is defined as the portfolio value at the horizon date if the interest rate structure does not change (i.e., there is no change in forward rates).

If the assumptions of classical theory hold, immunization provides a minimum-risk strategy because an immunized portfolio subjected to parallel shifts in the yield curve will provide at least as great a portfolio value at the horizon date as the assured target value.

An extension of classical immunization theory is in the case of nonparallel shifts in interest rates. The first approach has been to modify the definition of duration so as to allow for nonparallel yield curve shifts, such as key rate duration. The second approach establishes a measure of immunization risk against any arbitrary interest rate change.

A second extension of classical immunization theory applies to overcoming the limitations of a fixed horizon. Under the assumption of parallel interest rate changes, a lower bound exists on the value of an investment portfolio at any particular time, although this lower bound may be below the value realized if interest rates do not change.

Multiple-liability immunization involves an investment strategy that guarantees meeting a specified schedule of future liabilities, regardless of the type of shift in interest rate changes. Moreover, it extends the theory to the general case of arbitrary cash flows (contributions as well as liabilities).

The third extension of classical immunization theory is to analyze the risk-return trade-off for immunized portfolios, called *return maximization*.

The fourth extension of classical immunization theory is to integrate immunization strategies with elements of active bond portfolio management strategies. **Contingent immunization** provides a degree of flexibility in pursuing active strategies while ensuring a certain minimum return in the case of a parallel rate shift. In contingent immunization, immunization serves as a fall-back strategy if the actively managed portfolio does not grow at a certain rate.



Contingent immunization is possible when the prevailing available immunized rate of return is greater than the required rate of return. The manager can actively manage part or all of the portfolio until it reaches the safety net rate of return. If the portfolio return drops to this safety net level, the portfolio is immunized and the active management is dropped. The difference between the minimum acceptable return and the higher possible immunized rate is called the **cushion spread**.

The portfolio strategy can systematically shift the proportion between an active strategy and an immunized strategy in a portfolio to achieve a predetermined minimum return while retaining the potential upside of the active strategy.

### Duration and Convexity of Assets and Liabilities

The **economic surplus** of the portfolio is defined as the market value of assets minus the present value of liabilities. Duration alone will not give a true indication of the total interest rate risk. If liabilities and assets are duration matched but not convexity matched, economic surplus will still be exposed to variation in value from interest rate changes reflecting the convexity mismatch.

The manager must continuously monitor the portfolio. If the duration/convexity is mismatched, the portfolio should be rebalanced to achieve a closer match.

### Types of Risk

As the market environment changes, the portfolio manager faces the risk of not being able to pay liabilities when they come due. Three sources of this risk are:

1. **Interest rate risk.** A rising interest rate environment will adversely affect the value of a portfolio. If assets need to be sold to service liabilities, the manager may encounter a shortfall.
2. **Contingent claims risk.** When a security has a contingent claims provision, explicit or implicit, there is an associated risk, as is the case with mortgage-backed securities.
3. **Cap risk.** An asset that makes floating-rate payments will typically have caps associated with the floating rate. The manager is at risk of the level of market rates rising while the asset returns are capped.

### Risk Minimization for Immunized Portfolios

If a barbell portfolio and a **bullet portfolio** both have durations equal to the horizon length, both portfolios are immune to parallel rate changes. However, when interest rates change in an arbitrary and nonparallel way, the barbell portfolio is riskier than the bullet portfolio because it has more reinvestment risk.

If short-term rates decline while long-term rates go up, both the barbell portfolio and the bullet portfolio would realize a decline of the portfolio value at the end of the investment horizon below the target investment value, because they would experience a capital loss in addition to lower reinvestment rates. However, the decline would be substantially higher for the barbell portfolio because the bullet portfolio has less exposure to changes in the interest rate structure than the barbell portfolio has.

Reinvestment risk determines immunization risk. *The portfolio that has the least reinvestment risk will have the least immunization risk.* When the cash flows are concentrated around the horizon date, as in the bullet portfolio, the portfolio is subject to minimal reinvestment risk. With a zero-coupon bond maturing at the investment horizon, immunization risk is zero because reinvestment risk is absent.

The target value of an immunized portfolio is a lower bound on the terminal value of the portfolio at the investment horizon if yields on all maturities change by the same amount. If yields of different maturities change by different amounts, the target value is not necessarily the lower bound on the investment value.

**Maturity variance** is an immunization risk measure. It measures how much a given immunized portfolio differs from the ideal immunized portfolio consisting of a single pure discount instrument with maturity equal to the time horizon. Given the measure of immunization risk that is to be minimized and the constraint that the duration of the portfolio equals the investment horizon, the optimal immunized portfolio can be found using **linear programming**. Linear programming is appropriate because the risk measure is linear in the portfolio payments.

The immunization risk measure can be used to construct approximate confidence intervals for the target return over the horizon period and the target end-of-period portfolio value. A **confidence interval** represents an uncertainty band around the target return within which the realized return can be expected with a given probability. The expression for the confidence interval is:

Confidence interval = Target return ± ($k$) × (Standard deviation of target return)

where $k$ is the number of standard deviations around the expected target return.

### Multiple-Liability Immunization

Matching the duration of the portfolio to the average duration of the liabilities is not sufficient for immunization in the presence of multiple liabilities. A portfolio is immunized to a liability stream if there are enough funds to pay all the liabilities when due, even if interest rates change by a parallel shift.

Three necessary conditions ensure multiple-liability immunization in the case of parallel shifts:

1. The present value of the assets equals the present value of the liabilities.
2. The duration of the portfolio must equal the duration of the liabilities. The portfolio duration matches the weighted average of the liability durations.
3. The distribution of durations of individual assets must have a wider range than the distribution of the liabilities. This bracketing of shortest- and longest-duration liabilities with even shorter- and longer-duration assets balances changes in portfolio value with changes in reinvestment return.



Classical multiple-period immunization can mask the risks associated with nonparallel yield curve shifts. One portfolio that protects against one type of yield curve shift may expose a portfolio to other types of shifts.

An optimal immunization strategy is to minimize the immunization risk measure. Constructing a minimum-risk immunized portfolio can be done by the use of linear programming as well. Confidence intervals can also be constructed in the case of multiple liabilities.

### Immunization for General Cash Flows

If a given schedule of liabilities to be covered by an immunized investment must be met by investment funds that are not available at the time the portfolio is constructed, then expected cash contributions can be considered the payments on hypothetical securities that are part of the initial holdings. The actual initial investment can then be invested in such a way that the real and hypothetical holdings taken together represent an immunized portfolio.

We can illustrate this using the two-year investment horizon. The initial investment should be constructed with a duration of 3. Half of the funds are in an actual portfolio with a duration of 3, and the other half are in a hypothetical portfolio with a duration of 1. The total stream of cash inflow payments for the portfolio has a duration of 2, matching the horizon length, satisfying a sufficient condition for immunization with respect to a single horizon.

### Return Maximization for Immunized Portfolios

A higher-yielding portfolio may be preferred in spite of its higher risk, if a substantial increase in the expected return can be accomplished with little effect on immunization risk.

The required terminal value, plus a safety margin in money terms, will determine the minimum acceptable return over the horizon period. The difference between the minimum acceptable return and the higher possible immunized rate is the cushion spread. This spread offers an active strategy. The greater the cushion spread, the more active management.

Linear programming can also be used to solve for the optimal portfolio when return maximization is the objective. In addition, parametric linear programming can be employed to determine an efficient frontier for immunized portfolios.

## Cash Flow Matching Strategies

Cash flow matching is an alternative to multiple-liability immunization. Cash flow matching selects only securities matching the timing and amount of liabilities. A bond is selected with a maturity that matches the last liability, and an amount of principal and final coupon payment equal to the amount of the last liability. The remaining elements of the liability stream are then reduced by the coupon payments on this bond, and another bond is chosen for the next-to-last liability, adjusted for any coupon payments received on the first bond selected. Going back in time, this sequence is continued until all liabilities have been matched by payments on the securities selected for the portfolio.



## Cash Flow Matching versus Multiple-Liability Immunization

If all the liability flows were perfectly matched by the asset flows of the portfolio, the resulting portfolio would have no reinvestment risk and therefore no immunization or cash flow matching risk. However, perfect matching is unlikely. Under such conditions, a minimum immunization risk approach would be better than cash flow matching because it would require less money to fund liabilities. There are two reasons:

1. Cash flow matching requires a relatively conservative rate of return assumption for short-term cash, and cash balances may be occasionally substantial.
2. Funds from a cash flow–matched portfolio must be available when each liability is due, because of the difficulty in perfect matching. Because the reinvestment assumption for excess cash for cash flow matching extends many years into the future, a conservative interest rate assumption is appropriate.

Cash flow matching will be inferior to immunization. The ease of use supports its selection in dedication portfolio strategies.

## Extensions of Basic Cash Flow Matching

**Symmetric cash flow matching** allows for the short-term borrowing of funds to satisfy a liability prior to the liability due date. The opportunity to borrow for a short term so that symmetric cash flow matching can be employed results in a reduction in the cost of funding a liability.

**Combination matching** or **horizon matching** creates a portfolio that is duration matched with the added constraint that it be cash flow matched in the first few years. The advantage of combination matching is that liquidity needs are provided for in the initial cash flow–matched period. Cash flow matching the initial portion of the liability stream reduces the risk associated with nonparallel shifts of the yield curve.

## Application Considerations

In applying dedication strategies, the portfolio manager must be concerned with universe selection, optimization, monitoring, and transaction costs.

### Universe Considerations

The lower the quality of the securities considered for construction of a single-period immunized portfolio or a dedicated portfolio, the higher the potential risk and return. Dedication assumes that there will be no defaults. Immunization theory assumes that securities are responsive only to overall changes in interest rates. The lower the quality of securities and the more securities with embedded options, the greater the probability that these assumptions will not be met.

Liquidity is also a consideration for immunized portfolios, because they must be rebalanced periodically.



### Optimization

For an immunized portfolio, optimization typically takes the form of minimizing maturity variance subject to the constraints of matching weighted average duration and having the necessary duration dispersion.

For cash flow matching, optimization takes the form of minimizing the initial portfolio cost subject to the constraint of having sufficient cash at the time a liability arises.

Further considerations such as average quality, minimum and maximum concentration constraints, and issuer constraints may be included.

### Monitoring

Monitoring an immunized or cash flow–matched portfolio requires periodic performance measurement. For a bullet portfolio, performance monitoring may take the form of regular observations of the return to date linked with the current target return and annualized. This return should fluctuate only slightly about the original target return.

The performance of a multiple-liability immunization plan can be monitored easily by comparing the current market value of the assets with the present value of the remaining liabilities. The current internal rate of return on the immunized portfolio should be used to discount the remaining liabilities. This rate is used because it is the expected rate of return necessary to provide sufficient cash flow to fund the liabilities.

### Transaction Costs

Transaction costs are important in meeting the target rate for an immunized portfolio. They must be considered not only when the immunized portfolio is first created but also in the periodic rebalancing.

# RELATIVE-VALUE METHODOLOGIES FOR GLOBAL CREDIT BOND PORTFOLIO MANAGEMENT

Cross-Reference to CFA Institute Assigned Reading #21

FI

## Introduction

Corporate bonds are a subset of the global debt capital markets. The corporate asset class can also be referred to as the credit asset class. It encompasses not only corporate entities but also mortgage-backed securities (MBSs), commercial mortgage-backed securities (CMBSs), asset-backed securities (ABSs), sovereigns, and government-controlled entities with foreign currency debt issues.

Investors buy credit assets because of the presumption of higher returns despite the assumption of credit risk. Except during recessions, credit products usually outperform U.S. Treasury securities and other higher-quality sectors like U.S. agency securities, MBSs, and ABSs.

## Credit Relative-Value Analysis

Bond managers that need to build an optimal credit portfolio begin with an analytical framework (relative-value analysis) and develop a strategic outlook for the global credit markets.

## Relative Value

In the bond market, relative value refers to the ranking of fixed-income investments by sectors, structures, issuers, and issues in terms of their expected performance during some future period of time. Relative-value analysis refers to the methodologies used to generate such rankings of expected returns. On the exam, expect to be asked to choose the best bond out of a pair of two given a set of capital market expectations.

## Classical Relative-Value Analysis

Approaches to global credit bond portfolio management include top-down and bottom-up approaches. The top-down approach focuses on high-level allocations among broadly defined credit asset classes. The goal of top-down research is to form views on large-scale economic and industry developments. These views then drive asset allocation decisions (overweight certain sectors, underweight others).

The bottom-up approach focuses on individual issuers and issues that will outperform their peer groups. Managers follow this approach hoping to outperform their benchmark due to superior security selection, while maintaining neutral weightings to the various sectors in the benchmark.

Classical relative-value analysis is a process combining the best of top-down and bottom-up approaches. This process blends the macro input of a portfolio manager with the micro input of a credit analyst. The goal is to pick the sectors with the most potential upside, populate with the best representative issuers, and select the structures of the designated issuers at the yield curve points that match that for the investor.

### Relative-Value Methodologies

The main methodologies for credit relative-value maximization are:

- Total return analysis
- Primary market analysis
- Liquidity and trading analysis
- Secondary trading rationales and constraints analysis
- Spread analysis
- Structure analysis
- Credit curve analysis
- Credit analysis
- Asset allocation/sector analysis



### Total Return Analysis

The goal for most investors is to optimize the risk-adjusted total return of their credit portfolios. The best place to start is total return analysis. Credit relative-value analysis begins with a detailed analysis of past returns and a projection of expected returns.

If there are macro determinants of the total return of the credit asset class, then credit markets may display regular patterns. For example, the macroeconomic cycle is the major determinant of overall credit spreads. During recessions, default risk widens spreads and reduces credit returns relative to Treasuries, and vice versa.

The development of total return indices for credit debt and analyses of total returns have discovered numerous patterns (i.e., seasonality, election-cycle effects). An understanding of these total-return patterns optimizes portfolio performance.

### Primary Market Analysis

The analysis of primary markets centers on new issue supply and demand. Supply is often misunderstood. New supply tells many to take a defensive stance toward the corporate market and individual issuers. Supply may hurt spreads when applied to an individual issuer, but this does not hold true for the entire credit market. Increases in issuance are associated with market-spread contraction and strong relative returns for credit debt, and vice versa. This counterintuitive effect was noticeable during 1998 when new issuance disappeared in the face of the substantial increases in credit spreads.

Heavy supply narrows spreads and increases relative returns as new primary valuations validate secondary valuations. When primary origination increases, secondary traders gain reinforcement from the primary market and tend to increase their bids, which decreases the spread. For example, 2001 set an all-time record for new credit origination as well as the best relative performance for U.S. credit securities.

### The Effect of Market-Structure Dynamics

Investors often overlook short-term and long-term market-structure dynamics in making portfolio decisions. Market dynamics have less effect on short-term tactical investment decision making than on long-term strategy.

The composition of the global credit bond market has shifted markedly since the early 1980s.

- Medium-term notes (MTNs) dominate issuance in the front end of the credit yield curve.
- Structured notes and swap products entered the mainstream of the credit market.
- The high-yield corporate sector has become an accepted asset class.
- Global origination is more popular for U.S. government agencies, supranationals, and sovereigns.

Globalization of the credit market is the most important development. The development of the Eurobond, the entrance of non-U.S. issuers into the dollar markets, and the creation of the euro have led to the growth of transnational credit portfolios.



These structural changes in the credit asset class arise due to issuers wanting to minimize funding costs, and the needs of both active and asset/liability bond managers to satisfy their risk and return objectives. Portfolio managers adapt their portfolios either in anticipation of or in reaction to these structural changes across the global credit markets.

### The Effect of Product Structure

The global credit market has become more homogeneous. Specifically, bullet and intermediate-maturity structures dominate the credit market. However, in the high-yield market, callables remain popular. With credit-quality improvement, many high-yield issuers expect to refinance at lower rates prior to maturity.

There are three strategic portfolio implications for this structural evolution:

1. Dominance of bullet structures implies that credit securities with embedded options have become rare and therefore demand a premium price, and typically this premium is not captured by option-valuation models.
2. Bonds with maturities beyond 20 years are a small share of outstanding credit debt. This shift of the maturity distribution suggests a rise in the value of long-term credit debt.
3. The growth of credit derivatives leads to new strategies to match desired exposures to credit sectors, issuers, and structures.

### Liquidity and Trading Analysis

Short-term and long-term liquidity needs influence portfolio management decisions. Some investors are reluctant to purchase certain issues such as small-sized issues, private placements, and MTNs because of lower expected liquidity. Other investors gladly exchange a potential liquidity disadvantage for incremental yield.

Liquidity varies with the economic cycle, credit cycle, shape of the yield curve, supply, and season. Shocks such as a wave of defaults reduce liquidity as investors stop purchasing new issues at any spread. In reality, the trend has been more liquidity as fully transparent electronic trading exchanges develop.

## Secondary Trade Rationales

Capital market expectations constantly change (i.e., unexpected recessions, yield curve inversion, credit quality deterioration). In response, portfolio managers adjust their holdings and investors should consider the common rationales of whether to trade.

### Popular Reasons for Trading

The rationales to execute secondary trades in a total return framework include:

- **Yield spread pickup trades.** Yield spread pickup trades are the most common secondary transactions. If five-year, Baal/BBB General Motors paper trades at 150 bps, 10 bps more than five-year, Baal/BBB– Ford Motor paper, some investors will determine the rating differential to be irrelevant and will purchase the General Motors bonds and sell the Ford Motor bonds for a spread gain of 10 bps per annum.
- **Credit-upside trades.** Credit-upside trades take place when the debt asset manager expects an upgrade in an issuer's credit quality that is not already reflected in the current market yield spread. In the illustration of the General Motors and Ford Motor trade, some investors may swap based on their view of potential credit-quality improvement for General Motors. Such trades rely on credit analysis skills because one must be able to identify a potential upgrade before the market does.

  Credit-upside trades are popular in the crossover sector—ratings between Ba2/BB and Baa3/BBB—by two major rating agencies. In this case, the portfolio manager is expressing an expectation that an issue of the highest speculative grade rating (Bal/BB+) has sufficiently positive credit fundamentals to be upgraded to investment grade (i.e., Baa3/BBB–). If this upgrade occurs, not only would the issue's spread narrow based on the credit improvement, but the issue also would benefit from improved liquidity as it becomes investment grade.
- **Credit-defense trades.** Credit-defense trades increase as economic uncertainty increases and induces defensive positioning by investors. Ironically, once a credit is downgraded by a rating agency, internal portfolio guidelines often dictate security liquidation immediately after the loss of single-A or investment-grade status. This is usually the worst possible time to sell a security.
- **New issue swaps.** New issue swaps contribute to secondary turnover. Because of perceived liquidity, many investors prefer to rotate their portfolios into more current and larger-sized on-the-run issues.
- **Sector-rotation trades.** In sector-rotation trades, the manager shifts the portfolio from a sector that is expected to underperform to a sector that is expected to outperform on a total return basis.
- **Curve-adjustment trades.** Yield curve–adjustment trades are taken to reposition a portfolio's duration. If investors could predict yield curve movements, then they would increase their durations in anticipation of a decrease in interest rates. This is also done with respect to anticipated changes in the credit curve. Portfolio managers will shift their portfolios to longer spread duration issues in a sector if they believe credit spreads will tighten while rates remain stable.
- **Structure trades.** Structure trades involve swaps into structures (e.g., callable structures, bullet structures, and putable structures) that are expected to perform better given expected movements in volatility and the shape of the yield curve.
- **Cash flow reinvestment.** Cash flow reinvestment forces investors into the secondary market on a regular basis. Some portfolio cash inflows occur during interludes in the primary market. In these periods, credit portfolio managers must shop the secondary market for investment opportunities to remain fully invested.

### Trading Constraints

Portfolio managers should also review their rationales for not trading. Some of the best investment decisions are not to trade. Conversely, some of the worst investment decisions come from stale views based on dated constraints (e.g., avoid investing in bonds rated below Aa/AA).

### Portfolio Constraints

Collectively, portfolio constraints are the biggest contributors to persistence of market inefficiency across the global credit market. Some examples include:



- The portfolio manager is limited to investment grade and is forced to sell when securities are downgraded to speculative. This selling provides an opportunity for investors with more flexible constraints to buy newly downgraded securities at a discount.
- Some pension funds cannot purchase credit securities with ratings below A3/A–.
- Some pension funds have limitations on their ownership of MTNs and non-U.S. corporate issues.
- Insurance companies have limitations on high-yield corporates.

### Story Disagreement

The proponents of a secondary trade make persuasive arguments, but the portfolio manager may be unwilling to accept the shortfall risk if the investment recommendation does not provide its expected return. For example, Enron was long viewed as a very solid credit risk before its sudden bankruptcy in late 2001. An asset manager convinced of this long-term view might have been reluctant to act on the emergence of less favorable information about Enron in the summer of 2001.

### Buy-and-Hold

Accounting constraints often limit the ability of some investors to trade—for example, not being able to sell positions at a loss compared with book cost. Effectively, these investors remain buy-and-hold investors.

### Seasonality

Secondary trading slows at the conclusion of calendar years. Also, portfolio managers take time to mark their portfolios, prepare reports for their clients, and chart strategy for the next investment period. During these intervals, even compelling secondary offerings can languish.

### Spread Analysis

The global credit market uses nominal spread as the basic unit for both price and relative-value analysis rather than yield.

## Alternative Spread Measures

Many prefer to value credit securities in terms of OAS so they can be more easily compared to MBSs and ABSs.

Interest rate swap spreads have emerged to measure relative value across fixed- and floating-rate note credit structures.

## Swap Spreads

Credit default swap spreads have emerged as the latest valuation tool.

Swap spreads are popular in Europe. The European credit market is homogeneous; most issuances are high quality (Aa3/AA– and above) and intermediate maturity (10 years and less). Consequently, swap spreads are a good proxy for credit spreads in such a uniform market.

The extension of the swap spread framework is less relevant for speculative-grade securities, where default risk becomes more important.

## Spread Tools

Investors should also understand how best to evaluate spread levels in their decision making. Spread valuation includes:

- **Mean-reversion analysis.** Mean-reversion analysis is the most common technique for analyzing spreads. Mean reversion refers to the tendency for the spread between two sectors to revert back to its historical average. Investors would buy a "cheap" sector or issuer because historically the spread has been tighter and it will eventually revert back to that tighter spread, and vice versa.
- **Quality-spread analysis.** Quality-spread analysis examines the spread differentials between low- and high-quality credits. For example, credit portfolio managers can profit from overweighting lower-quality debt at the outset of an upward turn in the economic cycle.
- **Percentage yield spread analysis.** Percentage yield spread analysis is defined as the ratio of credit yields to government yields.

## Structural Analysis

**Structural analysis** is analyzing the performance of different structures. It has become less influential because the global bond markets have moved to the structurally homogeneous European bullet standard, with the exception of the U.S. high-yield and emerging market government (EMG) debt markets.

Structural analysis depends on yield curve forecasts, a key input in making relative-value decisions among structured credit issues, MBSs, and ABSs. Leaving credit aside, yield curve movements will influence structural performance.

### Bullets

The following is how different types of investors use bullet structures with different maturities:

- Front-end bullets (one- to five-year maturities) are useful for investors who pursue a barbell strategy in which both the short and long ends of the barbell are U.S. Treasury securities.
- Intermediate credit bullets (5- to 12-year maturities) have become the most popular segment of the U.S. and European investment-grade and high-yield credit markets.
- The 30-year maturity is the most popular form of long-dated security. These longer-dated securities provide investors with extra positive convexity for an increase in effective duration.

### Callables

The ability to refinance debt in a low-interest-rate environment is valuable to issuers. Conversely, the risk of earlier-than-expected retirement of an above-current market coupon is troublesome to investors.

Call premiums vary through time with capital market conditions. The call option becomes more expensive during low-rate and high-volatility periods. Callables significantly underperform bullets when interest rates decline because of their negative convexity. When the bond market rallies, callable structures do not fully participate given the upper boundary imposed by call prices. Conversely, callable structures outperform bullets in bear bond markets as the probability of early call diminishes.

### Sinking Funds

A sinking fund structure allows an issuer to execute a series of partial calls (annually or semiannually) prior to maturity. Historically, total return investors favored the collection of sinking fund structures at subpar prices. These discounted sinking funds retained price upside during interest rate rallies and, given the issuers' requirement to retire at least annually some portion of the issue at par, the price of these sinking fund structures did not fall as much compared to callables and bullets when interest rates rose.

### Putables

Put bonds typically provide investors with a put option to demand full repayment at par.

Put structures provide investors with a partial defense against sharp increases in interest rates. Put structures triggered by a credit event enable investors to escape from a deteriorating credit. This structure should be favored as an outperformance vehicle only by those investors with a bearish outlook on interest rates.

## Credit Curve Analysis

The rapid growth of credit derivatives has increased interest in techniques to analyze the term structure (maturities) and credit structure (ratings) of credit spread curves.

Credit curves, both term structure and credit structure, are almost always positively sloped. The credit barbell is a strategy to moderate portfolio risk by taking credit risk in short maturities and in long-duration government securities. Accordingly, this strategy diminishes demand for longer-dated credit risk debt instruments. However, insurers and pension plan sponsors often purchase credit debt with maturities beyond 20 years.

Default risk increases nonlinearly as creditworthiness declines. Investors justifiably demand a spread premium for the increased likelihood of potential credit difficulty as rating quality descends through the investment-grade categories.



Credit spreads increase sharply in the high-yield rating categories (Ba1/BB+ through D). Default, especially for weak single-Bs and CCCs, becomes a major possibility. The credit market naturally assigns higher risk spreads as credit risk escalates and credit spread curves change shape over the course of economic cycles. Spread curves steepen when interest rates and credit risk increase.

## Credit Analysis

Superior credit analysis remains the most important determinant of credit bond portfolio relative performance. Genuine credit analysis encompasses actually studying issuers' financial statements, interviewing managements, evaluating industry issues, and reading indentures.

## Asset Allocation/Sector Rotation

In the credit bond market, macro sector rotations among industrials, utilities, financial institutions, sovereigns, and supranationals have a long history.

# Study Session 11: Fixed-Income Portfolio Management (2)

FI

# FIXED-INCOME PORTFOLIO MANAGEMENT—PART II
Cross-Reference to CFA Institute Assigned Reading #22

## Other Fixed-Income Strategies

There are a number of alternatives that fixed-income managers can pursue to enhance performance.

## Combination Strategies

At various phases during an interest rate cycle, a mix of alternative strategies is best for part or all of the cycle.

Strategy combinations have the best expected risk/return trade-off when decision makers face uncertainty. Active/passive and active/immunization are two popular combination strategies.

An **active/passive combination** allocates a core component of the portfolio to a passive strategy (i.e., replicates an index) and the balance to an active component (i.e., a return maximization strategy).

An **active/immunization combination** also consists of two component portfolios. The immunized portfolio provides an assured return over the planning horizon while the second portfolio uses an active high-return/high-risk strategy (i.e., surplus protection strategy).

## Leverage

Leverage helps increase (or decrease) the portfolio's return. If the return on the investment of the borrowed funds is greater than the interest cost, the portfolio's rate of return will be magnified. However, the interest rate sensitivity of the equity in the portfolio increases.

### Effects of Leverage

Two relationships can be seen:

1. The larger the amount of borrowed funds, the greater the variation in potential outcomes.
2. The greater the variability in the return, the greater the variation in potential outcomes.

The expression for the overall return on a leveraged portfolio is:

$$\begin{aligned} Rp &= \text{Portfolio rate of return} \\ &= (\text{Profit on borrowed funds} + \text{Profit on equity})/\text{Amount of equity} \\ &= [B \times (r_F - k) + E \times r_F]/E \\ &= r_F + (B/E) \times (r_F - k) \end{aligned}$$

where:
$E$ = amount of equity
$B$ = amount of borrowed funds
$k$ = cost of borrowing
$r_F$ = return on funds invested

FI

FI

In addition, the duration is higher than the duration of an unlevered bond portfolio, given that the duration of liabilities is low relative to the duration of the assets they are financing.

The expression for the duration of equity reflects the durations of assets and liabilities and their market values.

$$D_E = \frac{D_A A - D_L L}{E}$$

In this expression, *A* and *L* represent the market value of assets and liabilities, respectively.

## Repurchase Agreements

Managers use repurchase agreements (repos) to increase leverage. A **repurchase agreement** is a contract involving the sale of securities such as Treasury instruments coupled with an agreement to repurchase the same securities on a later date. Although a repo is legally a sale and repurchase of securities, the repo transaction functions like a low-cost, collateralized loan. The difference in selling price and purchase price is referred to as the interest on the transaction. The market also enables investors (lenders) to earn a return above the risk-free rate on Treasury securities without sacrificing liquidity.

### Term to Maturity

Repurchase agreements typically have short terms to maturity, usually overnight or a few days, although longer-term repos of several weeks or months may be negotiated. A manager who wants to permanently leverage the portfolio may simply roll over the overnight loans on a permanent basis by entering the repo market daily.

### Transfer of Securities

The buyer of the securities would like to take delivery of the securities. Otherwise, problems may arise if the seller defaults on the repurchase of the securities. Also, if delivery is not insisted on, the potential exists for an unscrupulous seller to sell the same securities to another buyer. Transfer agreements take a variety of forms:

- Physical delivery of the securities is possible; however, the high cost associated with physical delivery makes this method unworkable.
- Securities can be processed by means of credits and debits to the accounts of banks acting as clearing agents for their customers. The banking system's wire transfer system is used to transfer securities electronically from the seller to the buyer and back later. This method is cheaper, but still involves a variety of fees and transfer charges.
- The securities may be delivered to a custodial account at the seller's bank. The bank takes possession and acts as a trustee for both parties.
- In some transactions, the buyer does not insist on delivery if the two parties have a long history and the seller's reputation is excellent.

### Default Risk and Factors That Affect the Repo Rate

If delivery is not taken, the repo is essentially an unsecured loan and its interest rate depends on the respective parties' credit qualities.

A variety of factors will affect the repo rate. Among them are:

- **Quality of the collateral.** The higher the quality, the lower the repo rate.
- **Term of the repo.** The longer the maturity, the higher the rate, reflecting the upward-sloping yield curve.
- **Delivery requirement.** Physical delivery offers the lowest rate because of the lower default risk. The rate increases as we move down to the other options.
- **Availability of collateral.** For securities in short supply and difficult to obtain, the repo rate is lower in order to acquire these securities.
- **Prevailing interest rates in the economy**. The higher the federal funds rate, the higher the repo rate.
- **Seasonal factors.** A seasonal effect on the repo rate exists because some institutions' supply of funds is influenced by seasonal factors.

## Derivatives-Enabled Strategies

Fixed-income portfolios have sensitivities to *factor exposures* such as duration, convexity, liquidity, and credit, and are associated with return and risk characteristics of an investment.

The use of derivatives can create, reduce, or magnify the factor exposures of an investment.

Interest rate risk can be measured and controlled using interest rate futures, interest rate swaps, credit options, credit swaps, and collateralized debt obligations.

## Interest Rate Risk

First-order source of risk for fixed-income portfolios is the duration or sensitivity to interest rate change. The portfolio duration is a weighted average of durations of the individual securities making up the portfolio:

$$\text{Portfolio duration} = \frac{\sum_{i=1}^{n} D_i \times V_i}{V_P}$$

where:
$D_i$ = duration of security $i$
$V_i$ = market value of security $i$
$V_p$ = market value of the portfolio

Dollar duration can be used if the portfolio manager wants to replace one security with another security while keeping portfolio duration constant. Dollar duration is calculated using:

$$\text{Dollar duration} = \frac{D_i \times V_i}{100}$$

where $V_i$ = market value of the portfolio position if held, or the price of one bond if not held.

To maintain the portfolio duration, the dollar durations of the securities being exchanged must be matched. This matching can be accomplished by comparing the dollar durations of each side and thereby determining the necessary par value of the new bond. Specifically,

$$\text{New bond market value} = \frac{DD_0}{D_N} \times 100$$

where:
$DD_O$ = dollar duration of old bond
$D_N$ = duration of new bond

FI

### Other Risk Measures

The risk of a portfolio can be viewed as the uncertainty associated with the portfolio's future returns. Uncertainty implies dispersion of returns.

If we assume that returns have a normal distribution, then standard deviation is a useful measure. The normality assumption may be unrealistic if the portfolio has securities with embedded options. Therefore, alternative measures that focus on the undesirable left-hand side of the distribution have been used. However, each of these alternatives has its own deficiency.

1. **Semivariance** measures the dispersion of the return outcomes that are below the target return.

   *Deficiency:*
   - Semivariance is computationally challenging for large portfolios.
   - Because we estimate downside risk with only half the data, we lose statistical accuracy.
2. **Shortfall risk** refers to the probability of not achieving some specified return target. The focus is on that part of the distribution that represents the downside from the designated return level.

   *Deficiency:* Shortfall risk does not account for the magnitude of losses in money terms.
3. **Value at risk (VaR)** is an estimate of the loss (in money terms) that the portfolio manager expects to be exceeded with a given level of probability over a specified time period.

   *Deficiency:* VaR does not indicate the magnitude of the very worst possible outcomes.

### Bond Variance versus Bond Duration

The variance of a portfolio is determined by the weight of each security in the portfolio, the variance of each security, and the covariance between each pair of securities.

Two major problems associated with using the variance or standard deviation to measure bond portfolio risk are:

1. The number of estimated parameters increases dramatically as the number of bonds considered increases.

2. Accurately estimating the variances and covariances is difficult. The passage of time and embedded options change security characteristics dramatically over time and limit the use of historical estimates.

There are numerous strategies based on derivatives products to manage risk.

### Interest Rate Futures

Interest rate futures contracts are traded on short-term and longer-term instruments, such as Treasury bills and bonds.

The 30-year Treasury bond is an important risk management tool in asset–liability management (ALM).



The underlying instrument for the Treasury bond futures contract is $100,000 par value of a hypothetical 30-year, 6% coupon bond. Although price and yield of the Treasury bond futures contract are quoted in terms of this hypothetical Treasury bond, the seller of the futures contract has the choice of several actual Treasury bonds that are acceptable to deliver.

In the settlement month, the seller of a futures contract (the short) is required to deliver to the buyer (the long) $100,000 par value of a 6%, 30-year Treasury bond. No such bond exists, however, so the seller must choose from other acceptable deliverable bonds that the exchange has specified. The short will select the **cheapest-to-deliver (CTD)** bond and plays a key role in the pricing of this futures contract.

To make delivery equitable to both parties, the Chicago Board of Trade (CBOT; now CME Group) introduced **conversion factors** for determining the invoice price of each acceptable deliverable Treasury issue against the Treasury bond futures contract. The conversion factor is based on the price that a deliverable bond would sell for at the beginning of the delivery month if it were to yield 6%.

### Strategies with Interest Rate Futures

The price of an interest rate futures contract is negatively correlated with the change in interest rates. When interest rates rise, the prices of the deliverable bonds will drop and the futures price will drop; when interest rates drop, the price of the deliverable bonds will rise and the futures price will rise. Therefore, buying a futures contract will increase a portfolio's sensitivity to interest rates, and the portfolio's duration will increase. Conversely, selling a futures contract will lower a portfolio's sensitivity to interest rates, and the portfolio's duration will decrease.

There are a number of advantages to using futures contracts rather than the cash markets for purposes of portfolio duration control.

- Liquidity and cost-effectiveness are advantages to using futures contracts.
- Futures contracts represent a very efficient tool for timely duration management because of the depth of the futures market and low transaction costs.

Various strategies can use interest rate futures contracts and other derivative products, including the following.

## Duration Management

When the current portfolio duration is different from the desired portfolio duration, interest rate futures can be used to maintain its target value (i.e., duration of the benchmark index; interest rate anticipation strategies). A portfolio manager will want to reduce the portfolio's duration when the expectation is that interest rates will rise, and will want to increase duration when the expectation is that interest rates will fall.

To change a portfolio's dollar duration so that it equals a specific' target duration, the portfolio manager needs to estimate the number of futures contracts that must be purchased or sold.

FI

Portfolio's target dollar duration = Current portfolio's dollar duration without futures + Dollar duration of futures contracts

Dollar duration of futures contracts = Dollar duration per futures contract × Number of futures contracts

The number of futures contracts that is needed to achieve the portfolio's target dollar duration can then be estimated by:

$$\text{Approximate number of contracts} = \frac{(D_T - D_I)P_I}{D_{CTD}P_{CTD}} \times \text{Conversion factor for the CTD bond}$$

where:
$D_T$ = target duration for the portfolio
$D_I$ = initial duration for the portfolio
$P_I$ = initial market value of the portfolio
$D_{CTD}$ = duration of the cheapest-to-deliver bond
$P_{CTD}$ = price of the cheapest-to-deliver bond

If the manager wishes to increase the duration, the equation will have a positive sign, and futures contracts will be purchased. The opposite is true if the objective is to shorten the portfolio duration. The calculation is only an approximation.

## Duration Hedging

Futures can be used to hedge interest rate exposure. If the hedge is properly constructed, any loss realized from one position (whether cash or futures) will be offset by a profit on the other position.

In practice, hedging is not that simple for several reasons. Three major sources of hedging error are incorrect duration calculations, inaccurate projected basis values, and inaccurate yield beta estimates.

A good valuation model is critical to ensure the correct calculation of duration, especially for portfolios containing securities with embedded options.

The outcome of a hedge will depend on basis—the difference between the cash price and the futures price when a hedge is placed and when it is lifted. The risk that the basis will change in an unpredictable way is called **basis risk**.

Cross hedging is when the bond to be hedged is not identical to the underlying bond in the futures contract. There is also basis risk in cross hedging. Basis risk exists in the relationship between the cheapest-to-deliver security and the futures contract and in the relationship between the security to be hedged and the cheapest-to-deliver security. Choosing the right **hedge ratio** minimizes risk in a cross hedge. The hedge ratio is chosen with the intention of matching the volatility of the futures contract to the volatility of the asset. Consequently, the hedge ratio is given by:

$$\text{Hedge ratio} = \frac{\text{Factor exposure of the bond (portfolio) to be hedged}}{\text{Factor exposure of hedging instrument}}$$

FI

As the formula shows, if the bond to be hedged has greater factor exposure than the hedging instrument, more of the hedging instrument will be needed.

In the formula for the hedge ratio, we need the exposure not of the cheapest-to-deliver bond, but of the hedging instrument—that is, of the futures contract. Considering only interest rate exposure and assuming a fixed yield spread between the bond to be hedged and the cheapest-to-deliver bond, the hedge ratio is:

$$\text{Hedge ratio} = \frac{D_H P_H}{D_{CTD} P_{CTD}} \times \text{Conversion factor for the CTD bond}$$

Another refinement in the hedging strategy that is necessary for hedging nondeliverable securities is the yield beta. This refinement concerns the assumption about the relative yield spread between the cheapest-to-deliver bond and the bond to be hedged. A hedger can use regression analysis to capture the relationship between yield levels and yield spreads. For hedging purposes, the variables are the yield on the bond to be hedged and the yield on the cheapest-to-deliver bond.

The regression procedure provides an estimate of $b$, called the **yield beta**, which is the expected relative change in the two bonds. The formula for the hedge ratio assumes a constant spread and implicitly assumes that the yield beta in the regression equals 1.0. We would expect a yield beta greater than 1.0 if the portfolio to be hedged contains risky corporate bonds.

The formula for the hedge ratio can be revised to incorporate the impact of the yield beta by including the yield beta as a multiplier.

$$\text{Hedge ratio} = \frac{D_H P_H}{D_{CTD} P_{CTD}} \times \text{Conversion factor for the CTD bond} \times \text{Yield beta}$$

## Interest Rate Swaps

An **interest rate swap** is a contract between two parties (counterparties) to exchange periodic interest payments based on a specified dollar amount of notional principal.

### Dollar Duration of an Interest Rate Swap

The value of a swap will change as interest rates change, and dollar duration is a measure of interest rate sensitivity. From the perspective of the party who pays floating and receives fixed, the interest rate swap position can be viewed as:

> Long a fixed-rate bond + Short a floating-rate bond

FI

This means that the dollar duration of an interest rate swap from the perspective of a floating-rate payer is the difference between the dollar duration of the two bond positions that make up the swap:

> Dollar duration of a swap = Dollar duration of a fixed-rate bond
> − Dollar duration of a floating-rate bond

The dollar duration of the fixed-rate bond determines the dollar duration of the swap because the dollar duration of a floating-rate bond is small.

### Applications of a Swap to Asset–Liability Management

An interest rate swap can be used to change the duration of a portfolio or an entity's surplus.

## Bond and Interest Rate Options

Options can be written on cash instruments or futures. An option on a futures contract gives the buyer the right to buy from or sell to the writer a futures contract at the strike price at any time during the life of the option.

## Bond Options and Duration

The price of a bond option will depend on the price of the underlying instrument, which depends in turn on the interest rate on the underlying instrument. Therefore, the duration of an option can be calculated with the following formula:

> Duration for an option = Delta of option × Duration of underlying
> × (Price of underlying)/(Price of option)

The duration of an option depends on:

- The duration of the underlying instrument.
- The **delta**, the price responsiveness of the option to a change in the underlying instrument.
- The leverage created by a position in an option. The higher the price of the underlying instrument relative to the price of the option, the greater the leverage.

### Hedging with Options

Options can be used to hedge a portfolio against a rise in interest rates. Two strategies, the protective put and the covered call, can be used.



The **protective put** establishes a minimum value for the portfolio but allows it to benefit from a decline in rates. The performance of the portfolio will be reduced by the cost of the put option.

The **covered call** is used when believing that the market will not trade much higher or much lower than its present level. The sale of the calls brings in premium income that can be used to offset declining prices. If rates fall, the portfolio appreciation is limited because the short call position constitutes a liability for the seller. The covered call is best if prices go nowhere; added income would be obtained without sacrificing any gains.

**Interest rate caps**, a series of call options on an interest rate to create a cap (or ceiling) for funding cost, can create a minimum earning rate. Banks that borrow for the short term and lend for the long term are exposed to short-term rate fluctuations and can use caps to effectively place a maximum interest rate on short-term borrowings.

**Interest rate floors**, a series of put options on an interest rate, can create a minimum earning rate. A life insurance company may invest proceeds in a floating-rate instrument. To protect itself from a rate decline while retaining the benefits from an interest rate increase, the insurance company may purchase a floor.

The combination of a cap and a floor creates a **collar**.

### Credit Risk Instruments

Debt securities may face three types of credit risk:

1. **Default risk** is the risk that the issuer may fail to meet its obligations.
2. **Credit spread risk** is the risk that the spread between the rate for a risky bond and the rate for a Treasury may vary after the purchase.
3. **Downgrade risk** is the risk that one of the major rating agencies will lower its rating for an issuer.

Credit risk can be hedged.

FI

### Products That Transfer Credit Risk

**Credit derivatives** exist to transfer the credit risk of a financial instrument to another party.

One type of credit derivative is a credit option.

#### Credit Options

Credit options are structured to offer protection against credit risk. The triggering events can be based on either (1) the value decline of the underlying asset or (2) the spread change over a risk-free rate.

For credit options written on an underlying asset, **binary credit options** provide payoffs contingent on the occurrence of a default of a designated reference entity. The term *binary* means that there are only two possible scenarios: default or no default.

The payoff of a binary credit option can also be based on the credit rating of the underlying asset. Going long a credit put option pays for the difference between the strike price and the market price when a specified credit event occurs. Going long a credit spread call option, the strike price could be a fixed number, or a spread (**strike spread**) could be used to determine the strike price for the payoff when the credit event occurs.

#### Credit Forwards

**Credit forwards** are based on bond values or credit spreads. For the buyer of a credit forward contract, the payoff functions as follows:

$$\text{Payoff} = (\text{Credit spread at the forward contract maturity} - \text{Contracted credit spread}) \times \text{Notional amount} \times \text{Risk factor}$$

The buyer of a credit forward contract benefits from a widening credit spread, and the seller benefits from a narrowing credit spread. The maximum the buyer can lose is limited to the payoff amount in the event that the credit spread becomes zero.

#### Credit Swaps

Credit swaps include credit default swaps, asset swaps, total return swaps, credit-linked notes, synthetic collateralized bond obligations, and basket default swaps.

A **credit default swap** is a contract that shifts credit exposure of an asset from the protection buyer to the protection seller. The protection buyer makes premium payments (default swap spread) to the protection seller. In the case of a credit event, the settlement by the protection buyer can take the form of either physical delivery or a negotiated cash payment.

### International Bond Investing

The motivation for international bond investing includes portfolio risk reduction and return enhancement. The risk reduction benefits from adding foreign-issued bonds to a domestic bond portfolio result from their less-than-perfect correlation with domestic fixed-income assets.

International investing involves exposure to **currency risk**, the risk associated with the uncertainty about the exchange rate at maturity.

### Active versus Passive Management

Opportunities for active management in international investing are created by inefficiencies that may be attributed to differences in tax treatment, local regulations, and coverage by fixed-income analysts. The active manager seeks to add value through the benchmark index.

- **Bond market selection.** Analysis of global economic factors is an important element in selection.
- **Currency selection.** The return on a nondomestic bond holding will depend on the holding's return in local currency terms and the movement of the foreign exchange rate.
- **Duration management/yield curve management**. Duration management can be constrained by the relatively narrow selection of maturities available in many national markets.
- **Sector selection.** The international bond market includes government and corporate bonds issued in local currencies and in U.S. dollars and a wide assortment of coupons, ratings, and maturities.
- **Credit analysis of issuers**. Portfolio managers may attempt to add value through superior credit analysis.
- **Investing in markets outside the benchmark.** The portfolio manager may consider investing in nonsovereign bonds not included in an index to enhance portfolio returns.

The duration measure of a portfolio that includes domestic and foreign bonds must recognize the correlation between the movements in interest rates in the home country and each nondomestic market.

$$\text{Change in value of foreign bond} = \text{Duration} \times \text{Change in foreign yield} \times 100$$

From the perspective of a domestic investor, the concern is the change in value of the foreign bond when domestic rates change. This change in value can be determined by incorporating the relationship between changes in domestic rates and changes in foreign rates as follows:

$$\text{Change in value of foreign bond} = \text{Duration} \times \text{Change in foreign yield given a change in domestic yield} \times 100$$

The relationship between the change in foreign yield and the change in domestic yield can be estimated using monthly data for each country. The following relationship is estimated:

$$\Delta y_{foreign} = \alpha + \beta \Delta y_{domestic}$$

where:

$\Delta y_{foreign}$ = change in a foreign bond's yield in month $t$

$\Delta y_{domestic}$ = change in domestic yield in month time $t$

$\beta = \text{correlation}(\Delta y_{foreign,t}, \Delta y_{domestic,t}) \times \sigma_{foreign}/\sigma_{domestic}$

The parameter β is called the **country beta**. The duration attributed to a foreign bond in the portfolio is found by multiplying the bond's country beta by the bond's duration in local terms.

### Currency Risk

Fluctuations in the exchange rate may decrease or increase the value of foreign investments when converted into the investor's local currency. When a foreign currency depreciates against the investor's home currency, a currency loss occurs; but when it appreciates, a currency gain occurs.



Investors often diversify currency exposures by having exposure to several currencies because currency risks are less than perfectly correlated. A multicurrency portfolio has less currency risk than a portfolio denominated in a single currency.

The currency effect can be split into:

- The expected effect captured by the forward discount or forward premium.
- The unexpected effect, defined as the unexpected movement of the foreign currency relative to its forward rate. Every investor in the foreign markets can either remain exposed to this currency risk or hedge it.

Currency-hedged instruments neutralize the currency exposure while maintaining the exposure to the local bond price.

The forward discount/premium in covered interest rate parity (IRP) is an approach to comparing fully hedged returns across international bond markets.

### Interest Rate Parity

Interest rate parity (IRP) states that the forward foreign exchange rate discount or premium over a fixed period should equal the risk-free interest rate differential between two countries.

The forward discount or premium, *f*, is given by:

$$f = (F - S_0) / S_0$$

where:
$F$ = forward exchange rate (stated as domestic currency/foreign currency)
$S_0$ = spot exchange rate (stated as domestic currency/foreign currency)

The currency quotation convention using direct quotation (domestic currency/foreign currency) means that from the perspective of an investor in a foreign asset an increase in the spot exchange rate is associated with a currency gain from holding the foreign asset. According to IRP,

$$f \approx i_d - i_f$$

where $i_d$ and $i_f$ are the domestic and foreign risk-free interest rates over the time horizon associated with the forward exchange rate.

### Hedging Currency Risk

The decision to hedge is important because currency movements can have a big effect on the investor's return.

The three main methods of currency hedging are:

1. **Forward hedging** involves the use of a forward contract between the bond's currency and the home currency.
2. **Proxy hedging** involves using a forward contract between the home currency and a currency that is highly correlated with the bond's currency.
3. **Cross hedging** refers to hedging using two currencies other than the home currency and is a technique used to convert the currency risk of the bond into a different exposure that has less risk for the investor.



Currency exposures associated with investments with variable cash flows cannot be hedged completely, because forward contracts only cover the expected cash flows. The actual investment payoff may differ from the expected payoff, resulting in an over- or underhedged portfolio.

A foreign bond return stated in terms of the investor's home currency, the **unhedged return** ($R$), is equal to the foreign bond return in local currency terms, $r_l$, plus the currency return, $e$, which is the percentage change in the spot exchange rate stated in terms of home currency per unit of foreign currency (direct quotation):

$$R \approx r_l + e$$

The fully **hedged return**, $HR$, is equal to the sum of $r_l$ plus the forward discount (or premium) $f$, which is the price the investor pays (or receives) to hedge the currency risk of the foreign bond. That is,

$$HR \approx r_l + f$$

If IRP holds, $f$ is approximately equal to the interest rate differential, so that:

$$HR \approx r_l + f \approx r_l + (i_d - i_f) = i_d + (r_l - i_f)$$

In other words, the hedged bond return can be viewed as the sum of the domestic risk-free interest rate ($i_d$) plus the bond's local risk premium of the foreign bond.

If we compare the fully hedged return of international bond issues from different national markets, the expected difference in their fully hedged returns will reflect only the differences in their local risk premiums. This idea provides an easy way to compare the hedged yields of bonds in different markets.

FI

### Breakeven Spread Analysis

Investing in international bonds offers the investor the potential for additional returns from bond and country yield advantages. Although foreign yields look attractive, the investor needs to be aware of the risk that any spread advantage may be lost through spread widening (ignoring any currency impacts). Breakeven spread analysis quantifies the level of widening of the spread that would reduce or eliminate a foreign yield advantage.

$$\text{Change in price} = \text{Duration}_{\textit{Foreign Bond}} \times \Delta\text{Spread}_{\textit{Foreign Bond}}$$

### Emerging Market Debt

Emerging markets are those nations whose economies are considered to be developing. Emerging market debt (EMD) includes sovereign bonds, public companies, and private companies in those countries.

Because of its low correlation with domestic debt portfolios, EMD offers favorable diversification properties to a fixed-income portfolio.

#### Growth and Maturity of the Market

The EMD market has grown rapidly to its current substantial size, estimated in 2006 to be approximately $3.3 trillion.

#### Risk and Return Characteristics

Emerging market debt offers the potential for attractive rates of return. Sovereign emerging market governments possess several advantages over private corporations:

- They can react quickly to negative economic events by cutting spending and raising taxes and interest rates.
- They also have access to lenders on the world stage, such as the International Monetary Fund (IMF) and the World Bank.
- They possess large foreign currency reserves, providing a shock absorber for bumps in their economic roads.

Risks do exist in the sector, however:

- Volatility in the EMD market is high.
- EMD returns are frequently characterized by negative skewness.
- Emerging market countries frequently do not offer the degree of transparency or court-tested laws of developed countries.
- The legal system is less developed than in developed countries.
- Developing countries tend to overborrow. If a default occurs, recovery can be very difficult.
- Little standardization of covenants exists among various emerging market issuers.
- Sovereign debt lacks an enforceable seniority structure, in contrast to private debt.

### Analysis of Emerging Market Debt

An investor in EMD securities must determine the willingness and ability of the issuers to pay their debt obligations.

Analysis begins with a country's fundamentals:

- The source of government revenues
- Fiscal and monetary policies
- Current debt levels
- Willingness of the country's citizens to accept short-term sacrifices in order to strengthen the country's long-term economic situation



Historically, the largest returns have come from countries with strong fundamentals, usually characterized by an export-oriented economy and a high savings rate. In evaluating EMD, the risk of default remains a critical consideration.

Investment in foreign assets carries risk associated with converting the foreign investment cash flows into domestic currency. Additional sources of risk include political risk, changes in liquidity, and taxation.

**Political risk** includes the risk of constraints imposed by foreign government policies, war, government collapse, political instability, expropriation, confiscation, and adverse changes in taxation.

## Selecting a Fixed-Income Manager

When funds are not managed in-house, a search for outside managers must be conducted, often including an active manager.

The due diligence for selection of managers is satisfied primarily by investigating:

- The managers' investment processes
- The types of trades the managers are making
- The managers' organizational strengths and weaknesses

The key to better performance is to find managers who can produce consistent positive style-adjusted alphas. Then, the portfolio can be constructed by optimizing the combination of managers in order to maximize the variety of styles and exposures contributed by each manager.

### Historical Performance as a Predictor of Future Performance

Studies indicate some evidence of persistence of outperformance by some managers relative to their peers over short periods of time. However, over long periods of time (15 years or more) and when fund fees and expenses are factored in, the realized alpha of fixed-income managers has averaged close to zero and little evidence of persistence exists.

### Developing Criteria for Manager Selection

The value of due diligence is found in the details; a fundamental analysis of the manager's strategy must be conducted. Here are some of the factors that should be considered:

- **Style analysis.** Examine the extent to which the portfolio differs from the benchmark's construction, particularly with regard to overweighting of sectors and duration differences.
- **Selection bets.** Seek superior credit or security analysis skills by forecasting changes in relative credit spreads and identifying undervalued securities.
- **The organization's investment process.** What research methods are used by the organization?
- **Correlation of alphas.** The historical correlations of alpha across managers should also be examined.



### Comparison with Selection of Equity Managers

Selecting a fixed-income manager has both similarities with and differences from the selection of an equity manager.

- In both cases, a consultant is frequently used to identify a universe of suitable manager candidates.
- In both sectors, the available evidence indicates that past performance is not a reliable guide to future results.
- The same qualitative factors are common to both analyses: philosophy of the manager and organization, market opportunity, competitive advantages, delegation of responsibility, experience of the professionals, and so forth.
- Management fees and expenses are important in both areas, because they often reduce or eliminate the alpha that managers are able to earn gross of expenses. Fees are more important in the fixed-income area, however, because fixed-income funds have a higher ratio of fees to expected outperformance.

# STUDY SESSION 12: EQUITY PORTFOLIO MANAGEMENT

EQ

# EQUITY PORTFOLIO MANAGEMENT

Cross-Reference to CFA Institute Assigned Reading #23

Equities are a significant part of an investment portfolio in terms of both how to invest and how much of the portfolio to allocate to equities.

## The Role of the Equity Portfolio

Equities are a large source of wealth in the world and are held in both individual and institutional portfolios.

- Equities are considered an inflation hedge. An **inflation hedge** is when the returns to an asset are enough to preserve purchasing power during periods of inflation. The nominal returns to equities are highly correlated with inflation rates because a company's earnings increase with inflation, whereas bond payments are fixed in nominal terms. However, companies face challenges with inflation because individual equities differ in their sensitivities to inflation because of industry and price competition.
- Equities' comparatively high historical long-term real rates of return play a growth role in a portfolio.

## Approaches to Equity Investment

There are three approaches to managing equity portfolios:

1. **Passive management.** Invests in a portfolio that attempts to match the performance of a specified benchmark, typically by **indexing**. Investors do not attempt to reflect their expectations through changes in security holdings. Investors who believe that an equity market is efficient will favor indexing because they think that equity research will not provide a sufficient increment in return to outweigh research and transaction costs.
2. **Active management.** Seeks to outperform a given benchmark portfolio by buying stocks that will outperform the benchmark and avoiding stocks that will underperform the benchmark. Active equity management accounts for the majority of equity assets managed. Active investors believe that the equity market is inefficient and that research will allow them to outperform the market net of costs.
3. **Semiactive management (enhanced indexing).** Seeks to outperform a given benchmark; however, tracking risk is lower than in active management. The performance of the portfolio will have limited volatility around the benchmark's returns. Enhanced indexers believe that they can get information about companies that has not been reflected into stock prices, but with limited tracking risk.

EQ

The expected information ratio of a first quartile manager for each approach is shown in the table.

### Indexing, Enhanced Indexing, and Active Approaches: A Comparison

| | Indexing | Enhanced Indexing | Active |
|---|---|---|---|
| **Expected active return** | 0% | 1%–2% | 2%+ |
| **Tracking risk** | <1% | 1%–2% | 4% + $r$ |
| **Information ratio** | 0 | 0.75 | 0.50 |

### Passive Equity Investing

Studies have found that the active portfolio fails to beat the relevant comparison index after expenses because of the expense disadvantage of active management. A well-run indexed fund is expected to outperform an actively managed fund because of low portfolio turnover and management fees (often 0.1% of assets or less). For tax-sensitive investors, indexing also offers high tax efficiency because turnover is low compared with active investing.

Indexing has advantages in a broad range of equity market segments:

- In large-cap markets, the high informational efficiency of prices favors indexing.
- In small-cap markets, the lower informational efficiency of prices makes the supply of active investment opportunities larger but transaction costs are higher.
- In unfamiliar markets, indexing is a logical choice to gain exposure because of the informational disadvantage in active investing.

### Equity Indices

Performance is important in both active and passive investing.

- Performance is evaluated against an equity benchmark index designed to show how the overall or subsector market has performed.
- Investors find it easier to manage their overall portfolios if an index captures the investment universe of their investment managers (e.g., a S&P 500 manager tracking the S&P 500 index).
- Stock indices are used to measure the returns of a market or market segment, as the basis for creating an index fund, to study factors that influence share price movements, to perform technical analysis, and to calculate a stock's systematic risk (beta).

Four choices determine a stock index's characteristics:

1. *Boundaries of the stock index's universe.* Determines how well the index represents a specific population of stocks. The wider the universe, the better the index will measure broad market performance. The narrower the universe, the better the index will measure a specific group of stocks.
2. *Criteria for inclusion.* Establishes any specific characteristics desired for stocks within the selected universe.
3. *Weighting of the stocks.* The choice to use price weighting, value weighting, or equal weighting.
4. *Computational method.* The choice of price only or total return, which includes the reinvestment of dividends.

### Index Weighting Choices

The greatest differences among indices covering similar universes result from how the index components are weighted. The three basic index weighting methods are:

1. **Price weighted.** Each stock in the index is weighted according to its share price. The index is the sum of the share prices divided by the adjusted number of shares in the index

EQ

(adjusted for stock splits or changes in index components). *The performance of a price-weighted index reflects the performance of a portfolio that bought one share of each.*

2. **Value weighted (market-cap weighted).** Each stock in the index is weighted according to its market cap (share price multiplied by the number of shares outstanding). *The performance of a value-weighted index would reflect the performance of a portfolio that owns all the outstanding shares of each index component.* A value-weighted index self-corrects for stock splits, reverse stock splits, and dividends because such actions are directly reflected in the number of shares outstanding and price per share for the company affected.

   A **free float–adjusted market capitalization index** adjusts for the number of shares outstanding that are actually available to investors, called free float. Float adjustments exclude corporate cross-holdings, large holdings by founding shareholders, and government holdings of shares in partly privatized companies. *The performance of a float-weighted index represents the performance of a portfolio that buys all the shares of each index component that are available for trading.*
3. **Equal weighted.** Each stock in the index is weighted equally. *The performance of an equal-weighted index reflects the performance of a portfolio in which the same amount of money is invested in the shares of each index component.* Equal-weighted indices must be rebalanced periodically to reestablish the equal weighting, because returns will cause stock weights to drift from equal weights.

These different weighting schemes can lead to a number of biases.

- A price-weighted index is biased toward the highest-priced share. Also, the absolute level of a share price is an arbitrary figure. A price-weighted index's main advantages are the simplicity of its construction and that stock price data series are easier to obtain historically than market value series.
- A value-weighted index is biased toward the shares of companies with the largest market capitalizations. An increase for a large-cap company would affect the index more than an equal increase in the share price for a smaller company. The bias toward large-cap issues means that such indices will tend to be biased toward larger, more mature companies, and toward overvalued companies, whose share prices have already risen the most.
- An equal-weighted index is biased toward small companies because such indices include more small companies than large ones. All stocks are treated the same since small companies have the same weight as large companies. The frequent rebalancing to maintain equal weight leads to high transaction costs in a portfolio tracking such an index. In addition, not all components in such an index may have sufficiently liquid markets to absorb the demand of indexers.

An indexer's choice of index to track has important consequences:

- Committee-determined indices have lower turnover than those reconstituted regularly according to an algorithm and therefore have transaction cost and tax advantages.
- Indices that are not reconstituted regularly may drift away from the market segment they are intended to cover.
- Liquidity differences may occur among the component securities of the various indices that cover the same market segment (e.g., S&P SmallCap 600 vs. Russell 2000).
- Investing in less liquid shares may allow the indexer to capture an illiquidity premium.

In choosing the index to replicate, a fund must evaluate the trade-off between differences in transaction costs and differences in return premiums among the indices.

EQ

### Passive Investment Vehicles

Three types of passive investment vehicles are:

1. An investment in an indexed portfolio
2. A long position in cash plus a long position in futures contracts on the underlying index
3. A long position in cash plus a long position in a swap on the index

### Indexed Portfolios

Three categories of indexed portfolios are:

1. Index mutual funds
2. Exchange-traded funds (ETFs), which are based on benchmark index portfolios
3. Separate accounts or pooled accounts, mostly for institutional investors, designed to track a benchmark index

### Differences between Index Mutual Funds and ETFs

| Index Mutual Funds | Exchange-Traded Funds (ETFs) |
|---|---|
| Shareholders in mutual funds buy shares from the fund and sell them back to the fund at a net asset value determined once a day at the market close. | ETF shareholders buy and sell shares in public markets anytime during the trading day. |
| At the fund level, shareholder accounting is a significant cost for mutual funds reflected in the fund's expense ratio. The degree is to the extent that a fund has a large number of small shareholders. | ETFs have no shareholder accounting at the fund level, so their expense ratios are lower than mutual fund expense ratios for funds linked to comparable indices. |
| Mutual funds pay lower index license fees than do ETFs. | ETFs pay higher index license fees than do mutual funds. |
| At the fund level, mutual funds are less tax-efficient than ETFs. Mutual funds experience a tax event from selling portfolio securities when holders of large positions redeem their holdings for cash. | ETFs are more tax-efficient than mutual funds. The redemption mechanism for an ETF is in kind, as it is an exchange of shares. The fund delivers a basket of the fund's portfolio stocks to a redeeming dealer who has turned in shares of the fund for this exchange. In the United States, this transaction is not taxable, and there is no distributable gain on the redemption. |
| Mutual funds can vary greatly in their cost structures and returns because of differences in the funds' expense ratios. | Users of ETFs pay transaction costs, including commissions to trade them, but provide better protection from the cost of providing liquidity to shareholders who are selling fund shares. |
| At the investor level, mutual fund buyers are affected by a fund's cost basis for its positions, which may differ from the positions' current values. As a result, at the time of purchase an investor may buy into a potential tax liability if the positions show a gain. | At the investor level, ETFs are more tax-efficient in that they are less likely than mutual funds to make taxable capital gains distributions. |

A difference between index mutual funds and ETFs as a whole versus indexed institutional portfolios is cost. Indexed institutional portfolios, managed as separate accounts or pooled accounts, are low-cost products with total annual expenses as low as a few basis points because of revenue from lending securities.

An index fund manager will attempt to manage the portfolio by full replication, stratified sampling, or optimization.

**Full replication.** Full replication is used if an index contains fewer than 1,000 stocks and the stocks are liquid. Every issue in the index is represented in the portfolio, and each portfolio position will have the same weight in the fund as in the index. Characteristics of full replication include:

- Minimal tracking risk.
- The advantage of being self-rebalancing for value-weighted indices because the stock weights in the portfolio change as index weights change as a result of changing stock prices. Therefore, trading is needed only for the reinvestment of dividends and to reflect changes in index composition.
- The return on a full replication index fund will be less than the index return because of the cost of managing and administering the fund, the transaction costs of portfolio adjustments to reflect changes in index composition, the transaction costs of investing and disinvesting cash flows, and the drag on performance from any cash positions. Indices do not bear the transaction costs of brokerage commissions, bid–offer spreads, taxes, and the market impact of trades that real portfolios do.



**Stratified sampling (representative sampling).** If the number of issues in the index passes 1,000, an index-tracking portfolio can be built using a subset of stocks in the index. A portfolio manager divides the index, creating multidimensional cells (e.g., market capitalization, industry, value, and growth). Each index stock is placed into the cell that best describes it. Next, the weight of each cell in the index is calculated by totaling the market cap for all stocks in that cell. A portfolio is then built by selecting a random sample of stocks from each cell and ensuring that the sum of the weights of the stocks purchased from each cell is equal to the cell's weight in the index. The advantage of stratified sampling is that it allows the manager to build a portfolio that retains the basic characteristics of the index without having to buy all of the stocks in the index. The greater the number of dimensions, the more closely the portfolio will resemble the index.

**Optimization.** Optimization is a mathematical approach to build a portfolio containing a subset of an index's stocks if the number of issues in the index passes 1,000. Index fund construction involves the use of:

- An objective function that seeks to match the portfolio's risk exposures to those of the index being tracked. Risk exposures can include market cap, beta, industry, and macroeconomic factors such as interest rates.
- An objective function that specifies that securities be held in proportions that minimize expected tracking risk relative to the index.

An advantage of optimization is that it takes into account the covariances among the factors used to explain the return on stocks, whereas the stratified sampling approach assumes the factors are mutually uncorrelated.

Disadvantages of optimization include:

- A risk model that can be misspecified because risk models are based on historical data and risks change over time.
- Periodic trading to keep the risk characteristics of the portfolio lined up with those of the index being tracked.

As a result, the predicted tracking risk of an optimization-based portfolio will typically understate the actual tracking risk.

### Equity Index Futures

Two additional indexing products, closely related with one another, are portfolio trades (basket trades or program trades) and stock index futures. A **portfolio trade** is when a basket of securities, the components of an index, are traded together under standardized terms. A popular trading basket is the S&P 500 basket that increased together with the introduction of S&P 500 index futures contracts. Trading the stock basket for the futures contract on the index, an exchange of futures for physicals (EFP), reduces transaction costs and allows a futures position to be translated into a portfolio position, particularly for risk management purposes.

However, the disadvantages of using futures contracts for risk management purposes include:

- The limited life of a futures contract, which means the futures position must be rolled over periodically to maintain appropriate market exposure
- The difficulty of shorting a basket of stocks because of the uptick rule



Therefore, ETFs have been the instruments of choice for risk management applications because ETFs are exempt from the uptick rule for short sales and they lack an expiration date.

### Equity Total Return Swaps

One type of equity swap is one where one side of the transaction receives the total return of an equity index portfolio and the other side can be either another equity index or an interest payment, such as Libor.

Equity swaps have had other important applications:

- Before changes in U.S. tax law, equity swaps were used by high-tax-bracket investors to achieve diversification, by exchanging the return on an undiversified stock basket for the return on a broad stock market index.
- Today, equity swaps can provide tax-saving opportunities due to differences in tax treatment applied to domestic and international recipients of corporate dividends. Cross-border investors can receive the total return of a nondomestic equity index in return for an interest payment to a counterparty that holds the underlying equities more tax-efficiently.
- In asset allocation transactions, equity swaps can rebalance portfolios to the strategic asset allocation more cheaply than trading the underlying securities.

## Active Equity Investing

Active equity investing is delivering the best possible performance relative to the benchmark's performance while working within the risks and constraints specified in the client's mandate. To add value, an active manager uses investment insights coupled with tools such as valuation models in a way that offers competitive advantage over peers. Active management allows portfolio managers to justify higher expenses compared with passive management. Demand for performance in excess of broad market averages continues to be a feature of the investor landscape.

## Equity Styles

An investment style is a grouping of investment disciplines that has some predictive power in explaining the future dispersion of returns across portfolios. A traditional equity style contrast is between value and growth disciplines. Market oriented is an intermediate grouping that cannot be clearly categorized as value or growth. Market-capitalization segments are also often specified in describing an investor's style.

Style plays roles in both risk management and performance evaluation. A specific style is evaluated relative to a benchmark that reflects that style. An investor can determine whether the manager is skilled or is just earning the return to a style, which might be more inexpensively obtained by indexing.

William F. Sharpe set out to define style to facilitate performance measurement and to reflect the distinct differences in the way active portfolio managers structure their portfolios in terms of their exposures to the four asset classes: large-cap value, large-cap growth, medium cap, and small cap.

EQ

The contrast between value and growth stocks can sometimes be confusing. Almost any stock can be categorized as cheap or expensive depending on one's expectations for the future. For example, Microsoft Corporation was a growth company maintaining 90% market share in personal computer operating software. Microsoft's earnings and cash flows were strong throughout its history. However, in October 2011, a value investor would point to the fact that Microsoft was trading with a price-earnings (P/E) ratio of 9.98, less than half Google's 19.37 and less than Apple's 15.39. For a value investor, Microsoft might be a buy.

## Value Investment Styles

**Value investors** are more concerned about buying a stock whose purchase price is deemed relatively cheap in terms of earnings or assets than about a company's future growth prospects. Arguments for value investing include these:

- A company's earnings have a tendency to revert to their mean value. If the valuation multiple for a stock is depressed because of recent earnings problems, an investor in that stock may benefit from a reversion to the mean in earnings accompanied by expansion in P/E.
- An investment in a stock that is relatively expensive exposes the investor to the risk of contractions in multiples and in earnings. Value investors believe that investors overpay for stocks seen as having good growth prospects while neglecting those with less favorable prospects.
    - Fama and French suggest that stocks that are cheap in terms of assets, a *low* price-to-book (P/B) ratio, have a higher risk of financial distress and thus offer higher expected returns as fair compensation for that risk.

The risks for a value investor include:

- The stock's cheapness may be misinterpretated. The stock may be cheap for good reason that the investor does not appreciate.
- The perceived undervaluation may not be corrected within the investor's investment time horizon.

Value style investing has three substyles:

1. **Low P/E.** Stocks that sell at a low ratio of price to current earnings, typically found in industries categorized as defensive, cyclical, or simply out of favor. The investor buys on the expectation that the P/E will rise as the stock or industry recovers.
2. **Contrarian.** Stocks that have been plagued by problems and are selling at low P/Bs, frequently below 1, typically found in depressed industries that have no current earnings. The investor buys on the expectation of a cyclical rebound that drives up product prices and demand.
3. **High yield.** Stocks that offer high dividend yield, with prospects of maintaining the dividend, knowing that dividend yield has constituted a major portion of the total return on equities.

### Growth Investment Styles



Growth investors are more concerned with earnings. Growth investors pay high market earnings multiples for companies that have high growth rates, typically in technology, health care, and consumer products industries. Growth investors do well in a slowing economy because companies with positive earnings momentum become scarce, commanding higher prices.

Arguments for growth investing include:

- If a company can deliver future growth in earnings per share (EPS), then its share price will appreciate at least at the rate of EPS growth.
- Buying a stock at a premium to the overall market counts on the market to continue paying a premium for the earnings growth that a company may continue to deliver.

The risks facing growth investors include:

- The forecasted EPS growth may not materialize as expected. In that event, P/E multiples may contract at the same time as EPS, amplifying the investor's losses.

Growth style investing has two substyles:

1. **Consistent growth.** Companies with consistent growth have a long history of unit-sales growth, strong profitability, and predictable earnings. They tend to trade at high P/Es and are the leaders in consumer-oriented businesses.
2. **Earnings momentum.** Companies with earnings momentum have high quarterly year-over-year earnings growth. Such companies have higher potential earnings growth rates than consistent growth companies, but the earnings growth is likely to be less sustainable.

### Other Active Management Styles

**Market-oriented (blend or core style) investors** are willing to buy either value or growth stocks, provided they can buy a stock below its perceived intrinsic value using tools such as discounted cash flow models. The drawback is that if the portfolio achieves only market-like returns, then indexing based on a broad equity market index would have been the lower-cost alternative.

The four subcategories of market-oriented investors are:

1. **Market-oriented with a value bias.** Tilting the portfolio toward value, but not so distinctively as to clearly identify it as a value portfolio.
2. **Market-oriented with a growth bias.** Tilting the portfolio toward growth, but not so distinctively as to clearly identify it as a growth portfolio.
3. **Growth at a reasonable price.** Favoring companies with above-average growth prospects that are selling at relatively low valuation levels compared with other growth companies.
4. **Style rotators.** Investing according to the style that will be favored in the marketplace in the near term.

**Market capitalization** is another approach to describing the style of equity investors.

**Small-cap equity investors** focus on the lowest-market-capitalization stocks in the countries in which they invest. The premises of this style include:

- More opportunity exists to find mispriced stocks through research in the small-cap universe than in the more intensely researched large-cap universe.
- Smaller companies tend to have better growth prospects because their product lines tend to be more focused.
- The chance of earning a high rate of return is better if the starting market capitalization is small.

**Mid-cap equity investors** focus on stocks that are between the 200th and 1,000th largest by market cap. Mid-cap investors argue that the companies in this segment are less researched than the largest-cap companies but financially stronger and less volatile than small-cap companies.

**Large-cap equity investors** favor the relative financial stability of large-cap issues and believe that they can add value through superior analysis.

### Techniques for Identifying Investment Styles

Two major approaches to identifying a style are:

1. **Holdings-based style analysis (composition-based style analysis)** relies on an analysis of the characteristics of individual security holdings. Holdings-based style analysis categorizes individual securities by their characteristics, and aggregates results to reach a conclusion about the overall style of the portfolio at a given point in time. For example, the analyst may examine the following variables:
    - Valuation levels
    - Forecasted EPS growth rate
    - Earnings variability
    - Industry sector weightings

2. **Returns-based style analysis** involves regressing portfolio returns (generally monthly returns) on return series of a set of securities indices. It involves a constraint that the betas on the indices are nonnegative and sum to 1. That constraint allows interpreting the betas as the portfolio's proportional exposure to the particular style represented by the index. For example, if a portfolio had a beta of 0.75 on a value index and a beta of 0.25 on a growth index, we would infer that the portfolio was run as a value portfolio.

The indices should be:

- Mutually exclusive
- Exhaustive with respect to the manager's investment universe
- Distinct sources of risk (not highly correlated)

We can also use a returns-based style analysis to calculate a coefficient of determination measuring style fit. The quantity 1 minus the style fit equals security selection, the fraction of return variation unexplained by style. The error term in the style analysis equation, the difference between the portfolio's return and a passive asset mix with the same style as the portfolio, represents selection return.

The advantages and disadvantages of returns-based and holdings-based style analysis include the following:

**Two Approaches to Style Analysis: Advantages and Disadvantages**

| | Advantages | Disadvantages |
|---|---|---|
| **Returns-based style analysis** | • Characterizes entire portfolio.<br>• Facilitates comparisons of portfolios.<br>• Aggregates the effect of the investment process.<br>• Different models usually give broadly similar results and portfolio characterizations.<br>• Provides clear theoretical basis for portfolio categorization.<br>• Requires minimal information.<br>• Can be executed quickly.<br>• Is cost-effective. | • May be ineffective in characterizing current style.<br>• Error in specifying indices in the model may lead to inaccurate conclusions. |
| **Holdings-based style analysis** | • Characterizes each position.<br>• Facilitates comparisons of individual positions.<br>• In looking at present, may capture changes in style more quickly than returns-based analysis. | • Does not reflect the way many portfolio managers approach security selection.<br>• Requires specification of classification attributes for style; different specifications may give different results.<br>• Is more data-intensive than returns-based analysis. |

### Equity Style Indices

Typical elements in classifying the stock universe into growth and value components include price, earnings, book value, dividends, and past and projected growth rates. Attention to the details of style index construction has increased as index publishers compete to serve and capture licensing fees from ETFs and other investment products.

**Buffering** refers to rules for maintaining the style assignment of a stock consistent with a previous assignment when the stock has not clearly moved to a new style. Buffering reduces turnover in style classification and serves to reduce the transaction expenses of funds that track the style index.

### The Style Box

The style box is a popular way of looking at style. Morningstar uses a 3×3 style box to divide a fund portfolio or stock universe by market capitalization and style. The numbers in each box represent the percentage of this fund's portfolio value consisting of stocks that fall in that style box. For example, in the Vanguard Mid-Cap Growth Fund as of 2011, 58% of the portfolio by market value fell in the mid-cap growth box and 27% in the mid-cap blend box. Therefore, most of the value of Vanguard Mid-Cap Growth Fund was centered in mid-cap growth holdings. Morningstar's style box also makes an attempt to define a group of stocks as being a *blend* of growth and value characteristics.

**Morningstar Style Box for Vanguard Mid-Cap Growth Fund**

| | Value | Blend | Growth |
|---|---|---|---|
| **Large-cap** | 0 | 2 | 5 |
| **Mid-cap** | 7 | 27 | 58 |
| **Small-cap** | 1 | 0 | 0 |

*Source*: www.morningstar.com, October 2011.

**Style drift** is the inconsistency in style—for example, a value manager who begins to hold stocks that would be characterized as growth stocks. Style drift is a concern because when a manager begins to stray from the stated style, the investor may no longer be getting exposure to the particular style desired. Also, the manager may now be operating outside his or her area of expertise.

**Socially responsible investing (SRI) (ethical investing)** integrates ethical values and societal concerns with investment decisions. SRI involves the use of negative and positive stock screens involving SRI-related criteria. Negative SRI criteria include:

- Industry classification, reflecting concern for sources of revenue judged to be ethically questionable (tobacco, gaming, alcohol, armaments, etc.)
- Corporate practices (practices relating to environmental pollution, human rights, labor standards, animal welfare, and integrity in corporate governance)

Positive SRI screens include criteria used to identify companies that have ethically desirable characteristics.

EQ

### Long–Short Investing

Long–short investing focuses on a constraint. Many investors face a constraint against short selling of stocks.

In a long-only strategy, the value added by the portfolio manager is **alpha**. In a long–short strategy, the value added can be equal to two alphas, one alpha from the long position and another from the short position. In addition, a market-neutral strategy is constructed to have an overall zero beta and thus show a pattern of returns expected to be uncorrelated with equity market returns. The alpha from such a strategy is **portable**; it can be added to a variety of different systematic (beta) risk exposures.

In a **pairs trade**, an investor is long and short equal currency amounts of two common stocks in a single industry (long a perceived undervalued stock and short a perceived overvalued stock), and the risks are limited almost entirely to the specific company risks.

The risk associated with a long–short strategy involves leveraging. Although leverage magnifies the opportunity to earn alpha, it also magnifies the possibility that a negative short-term price move may force the manager to liquidate the positions prematurely in order to meet margin calls or return borrowed securities.

### Price Inefficiency on the Short Side

EQ

More price inefficiency may be found on the short side of the market than on the long side for several reasons:

- *Restrictions to short selling prevent investor pessimism from being fully expressed.* Many investors are restricted from short selling because a short seller must borrow the shares from someone who already owns them, and the short seller may have to cover the loan by buying back the stock at an inopportune time.
- *Opportunities to short a stock may arise because of management's tendencies to deliberately overstate profits.* Few parallel opportunities exist on the long side because of the underlying assumption that management is honest and that the accounts are accurate.
- *Sell-side analysts issue fewer sell recommendations because of the lower commissions they receive due to a smaller group of users*, those who already own shares or short sellers. In addition, customers who already own a stock are disappointed when an analyst issues a sell recommendation because of the downward pressure on the stock price.
- *Sell-side analysts are reluctant to issue negative opinions on companies' stocks* because the analyst could be cut off from communicating with management and threatened with libel suits.

### Equitizing a Market-Neutral Long–Short Portfolio

A market-neutral long–short portfolio can be **equitized** by holding a stock index futures position giving the total portfolio full stock market exposure. Equitizing a market-neutral long–short portfolio is appropriate when the investor wants to add an equity beta to the skill-based active return the investor hopes to receive from the long–short investment manager.

ETFs may be a more attractive way than futures to equitize a long–short position. The ease of borrowing ETF shares for short-sale transactions and the fund's expense ratio that lowers the expected cost of shorting make shorting ETFs an attractive alternative to rolling over short futures contracts. If the long–short portfolio has been equitized, then it should be treated as equity, with returns benchmarked against the index underlying the equitizing instrument.

### The Long-Only Constraint

Long–short strategies have an efficiency advantage over long-only portfolios. The advantage is the ability to act on negative insights that the investor may have, which can never be fully exploited in a long-only context. In a long-only portfolio, the maximum short position in any given stock is limited by that stock's index weight. If the investor has a strong negative view on a company with a 5% index weight, the best the investor could do is not to hold it at all. On the other hand, if the investor has a favorable view on a company with a 1% index weight, the investor can invest the entire portfolio in that company. As a result, the investor's opportunity set is not symmetrical.

### Short Extension Strategies

**Short extension strategies (partial long–short strategies)** modify equity long-only strategies by specifying the use of a stated level of short selling. Short extension strategies are the partial relaxation of the long-only constraint and allow the portfolio manager to make more efficient use of his or her information. In a long-only portfolio, the manager's maximum response to negative information is to avoid holding the stock. With a short extension strategy, the manager can also go short the stock.

EQ

In contrast to market-neutral long–short strategies, which have a market beta of zero, short extension strategies are designed to have a market beta of 1. For example, in a 130/30 short extension strategy, for every $100 received from the client, the portfolio manager shorts 0.30($100) = $30 worth of securities and invests $100 + $30 = $130 long (the initial $100 plus $30 provided by short sales proceeds).

An advantage of short extension strategies is that they can be established even in the absence of a liquid swap or futures market.

A disadvantage of short extension strategies is that they gain their market return and earn their alpha from the same source. By contrast, an equitized long–short market-neutral portfolio earns the market return from one source and the alpha from another.

### Sell Disciplines/Trading

Two categories of selling disciplines exist with corresponding subcategories:

**Substitution:**

- **Opportunity cost sell discipline** is when the investor looks to replace an existing holding when a better opportunity presents itself. The new stock being added has a higher risk-adjusted return than the stock it is replacing net of transaction costs and taking into account any tax consequences of the replacement.
- **Deteriorating fundamentals sell discipline** is when a company's business prospects deteriorate, initiating a reduction or elimination of the position.

Rule driven:

- **Valuation-level sell discipline** is when a value investor purchases a stock based on a low P/E multiple and sells if the multiple reaches its historical average.
- **Down-from-cost sell discipline** is when the manager decides at the time of purchase to sell any stock in the portfolio once it has declined 15% from its purchase price; this strategy is a similar to a stop-loss measure.
- **Up-from-cost sell discipline** is when the manager specifies at purchase a percentage or absolute gain that will trigger a sale.
- **Target price sell discipline** is when at the time of purchase the manager specifies a target price representing an estimate of intrinsic value, and the stock reaching that price triggers a sale.

Sales generate realized capital gains or losses. Therefore, a sell discipline needs to be evaluated on an after-tax basis for tax-sensitive investors such as private wealth investors and certain institutional investors such as insurance companies.

Value investors have relatively low annual turnover, ranging from 20% to 80%, because they buy cheap stocks hoping to reap a longer-term reward. Growth managers have higher turnover, ranging from 60% to several hundred percent, because they are trying to capitalize on earnings growth and stability.

### Semiactive Equity Investing

EQ

Semiactive strategies (enhanced indexing) are designed for investors who want to outperform their benchmark while carefully managing their portfolio's risk exposures. The portfolio manager creates such a portfolio by making use of investment insights while neutralizing the portfolio's risk characteristics that are inconsistent with those insights. Although tracking risk increases, the enhanced indexer believes that the incremental returns more than compensate for the small increase in risk. Such a portfolio is expected to perform better than the benchmark on a risk-adjusted basis.

Semiactive equity strategies come in two forms:

1. **Derivatives-based semiactive equity strategies** provide exposure to the desired equity market through a derivative and the enhanced return through something other than equity investments. For example, a manager can equitize a cash portfolio and then add value by altering the duration of the underlying cash. In this way, a portfolio manager can attempt to achieve some incremental return over cash from the fixed-income portfolio while obtaining equity exposure through the futures market, thereby creating an enhanced index fund.
2. **Stock-based enhanced indexing strategies** attempt to generate alpha by identifying stocks that will either outperform or underperform the index. Risk control is imposed in order to limit the degree of individual stock underweighting or overweighting and the portfolio's exposure to factor risks and industry concentrations. The resulting portfolio is intended to look like the benchmark in all respects except in those areas on which the manager explicitly wishes to bet. In an enhanced index stock selection strategy, the neutral portfolio is the benchmark. If the manager has no opinion about a given stock, that manager holds the stock at its benchmark weight. Every portfolio position is evaluated relative to the benchmark weight.

Enhanced-index portfolio managers are essentially active managers who build portfolios with a high degree of risk control. Their information ratio can be explained in terms of Grinold and Kahn's Fundamental Law of Active Management. The law states that:

$$IR \approx IC\sqrt{\text{Breadth}}$$

The information ratio (IR) is equal to what you know about a given investment (the information coefficient [IC]) multiplied by the square root of the investment discipline's breadth, which is defined as the number of independent, active investment decisions made each year. Therefore, a lower-breadth strategy necessarily requires more accurate insight about a given investment to produce the same IR as a strategy with higher breadth.

A semiactive stock-selection approach has limitations:

- Any technique that generates positive alpha may become obsolete as other investors try to exploit it.
- Quantitative models derived from analysis of historical returns may be invalid in the future. Markets undergo secular changes, lessening the effectiveness of the past as a guide to the future.

## Managing a Portfolio of Managers

When developing an asset allocation policy, the investor seeks an allocation to a group of equity managers within the equity allocation who maximize active return for a given level of active risk determined by the investor's level of aversion to active risk:

Maximize by choice of managers:

$$U_A = r_A - \lambda_A \sigma_A^2$$

where:
$U_A$ = expected utility of the active return of the manager mix
$r_A$ = expected active return of the manager mix
$\lambda_A$ = the investor's trade-off between active risk and active return; measures risk aversion in active risk terms
$\sigma^2_A$ = variance of the active return

The efficient frontier specified by this objective function is drawn in active risk and active return space. Once active and semiactive managers are in the mix, the investor's trade-off becomes one of active return versus active risk. The amount of active risk an investor wishes to assume determines the mix of specific managers. For example, an investor wishing to assume no active risk at all would hold an index fund. In contrast, investors desiring a high level of active risk and active return may find their mix skewed toward some combination of higher-active-risk managers with little or no exposure to index funds.

### Core–Satellite

A core–satellite portfolio is constructed when applying the optimization to a group of equity managers that includes indexers, enhanced indexers, and active managers, judged by their information ratios. Index and semiactive managers constitute the core holding, and active managers represent the opportunistic ring of satellites around the core, so as to achieve an acceptable level of active return while mitigating some of the active risk. The core should resemble the investor's benchmark for the asset class, while the satellite portfolios may also be benchmarked to the overall asset class benchmark or a style benchmark.

To evaluate such managers, it is useful to divide their total active return into two components:

1. Manager's "true" active return = Manager's return – Manager's normal benchmark
2. Manager's "misfit" active return = Manager's normal benchmark – Investor's benchmark

The **manager's normal benchmark** (normal portfolio) represents the universe of securities from which a manager normally might select securities for the portfolio. The **investor's benchmark** refers to the benchmark the investor uses to evaluate performance of a given portfolio or asset class.

The **manager's "true" active risk** is the standard deviation of true active return. The manager's "misfit" risk is the the standard deviation of "misfit" active return. The **manager's total active risk**, reflecting both true and misfit risk, is:

EQ

$$\text{Manager's total active risk} = \sqrt{(\text{Manager's "true" active risk})^2 + (\text{Manager's "misfit" active risk})^2}$$

The most accurate measure of the manager's risk-adjusted performance is the IR computed as:

$$\text{IR} = \frac{\text{Manager's "true" active return}}{\text{Manager's "true" active risk}}$$

### Completeness Fund

A **completeness fund** establishes an overall portfolio with the same risk exposures as the investor's overall equity benchmark when added to active managers' positions. For example, the completeness fund may be constructed with the objective of making the overall portfolio style neutral with respect to the benchmark while attempting to retain the value added from the active managers' stock selection ability.

One drawback of completeness portfolios is that they seek to eliminate misfit risk. In seeking to eliminate misfit risk through a completeness fund, a fund sponsor is giving up some of the value added from the stock selection of the active managers.

### Other Approaches: Alpha and Beta Separation

**Alpha and beta separation** is an example of **portable alpha** and another method used to build a portfolio of multiple managers. An investor hires an index fund manager to provide beta exposure and pays for alpha by hiring a market-neutral long–short manager. For example, an investor may want beta exposure to an efficient part of the equity market (e.g., the Russell Top 200) but also wants to outperform that part of the market. The investor chooses to hire a Russell Top 200 index fund manager and a manager that seeks to add alpha by managing a long–short portfolio of Canadian equities. The long–short manager could also be a bond manager. The approach allows the investor to understand the fees being paid to capture market (inexpensive) and active (costly) returns.

### Identifying, Selecting, and Contracting with Equity Portfolio Managers

Investors face decisions when deciding what investment managers to engage for the funds they delegate to outside management. The process of developing a universe of suitable manager candidates starts with a general evaluation of the large number of investment managers, and then researching and monitoring those that are worthy of further consideration.

Consultants employ various tools to determine which management firms have talented individuals and truly add value in their investment style. Consultants use both qualitative and quantitative factors in evaluating investment managers. The qualitative factors include the people and organizational structure, the firm's investment philosophy, the decision-making process, and the strength of its equity research. The quantitative factors include performance comparisons with benchmarks and peer groups, as well as the measured style orientation and valuation characteristics of the firm's portfolios.

The best-performing fund manager in any given year is rarely the best performer in the next year. Research shows there is no persistence in risk-adjusted excess returns. However, past performance is still important. A portfolio manager that consistently underperforms its benchmark is unlikely to be considered for active management, because an active manager is expected to generate positive alpha. A good investment record over a long period is more likely to indicate future satisfactory results for the client.

### Fee Structures

Absent management fees, the investor would realize exactly the same alpha that the manager achieves. With management fees, the investor earns a net-of-fees alpha that is smaller than the manager's gross-of-fees alpha.

Fees are set in one of two ways:

1. **Ad valorem fees** are calculated by multiplying a percentage by the value of assets managed (e.g., 0.60% on the first $50 million). Ad valorem fees are also called assets under management (AUM) fees. Ad valorem fees have the advantage of simplicity and predictability.
2. **Performance-based fees** are usually specified by a combination of a base fee plus sharing percentage (e.g., 0.20% on all assets managed plus 20% of any performance in excess of the benchmark return). Performance-based fees, particularly symmetric incentive fees, align the investor's interests with those of the portfolio manager.

A **fee cap** limits the total fee paid regardless of performance and is frequently put in place to limit the portfolio manager's incentive to aim for very high returns by taking a high level of risk. A **high-water mark** is a provision requiring the portfolio manager to have cumulatively generated outperformance since the last performance-based fee was paid.

### The Equity Manager Questionnaire

A typical equity manager questionnaire examines five key areas:

1. **Organization/people**—the investment firm must describe the firm's organization and who will be managing the portfolio.
2. **Philosophy/process** asks questions about how the equity portfolio will be managed.
3. **Resources** looks at the allocation of resources within the organization.
4. **Performance** asks questions about what the equity manager considers to be an appropriate benchmark (and why) and what level of excess return is appropriate.
5. **Fees** looks at what is included in the fee, the type of fee (ad valorem or performance based), and any specific terms and conditions relating to the fees quoted.

The equity manager questionnaire is used to short-list fund managers most suitable for the sponsor's needs and is followed up with face-to-face interviews.

### Structuring Equity Research and Security Selection



Equity research is a necessary component of both active and semiactive investing. The security selection process varies from firm to firm, but some generalities apply.

**Top-down approach** investing focuses on macroeconomic factors. In a top-down global portfolio, the investor wishes to identify:

1. Themes affecting the global economy;
2. The effect of those themes on various economic sectors and industries;
3. Any special country or currency considerations; and
4. Individual stocks within the industries or economic sectors that are likely to benefit most from the global themes.

**Bottom-up approach** investing focuses on company-specific factors such as revenues, earnings, cash flow, or new product development. In a bottom-up global portfolio, the investor approaches the problem by:

1. Identifying factors with which to screen the investment universe (e.g., stocks in the lowest P/E quartile that also have expected above-median earnings growth);
2. Collecting further financial information on companies passing the screen; and
3. Identifying companies from this subset that may be potential investments.

Many investors use some combination of the two approaches.

## Buy-Side versus Sell-Side Research

In reference to the source of equity research, **buy side** refers to those who do research with the intent of assembling a portfolio, such as investment management firms. **Sell side** refers either to independent researchers who sell their work or to investment banks and brokerage firms that use research as a means to generate business for themselves.

Many equity research departments are organized along industry or sector lines. The Global Industry Classification Standard (GICS) is a representative industry classification method that divides stocks into:

- 10 sectors (Consumer Discretionary, Consumer Staples, Energy, Financials, Health Care, Industrials, Information Technology, Materials, Telecommunication, and Utilities)
- 24 industry groups
- 68 industries
- 154 subindustries

# Study Session 13: Alternative Investments for Portfolio Management

AI

# ALTERNATIVE INVESTMENTS PORTFOLIO MANAGEMENT

Cross-Reference to CFA Institute Assigned Reading #24

Institutional and individual investors allocate money to alternative investments to seek risk diversification, apply active management skills, or both.

## Alternative Investments: Definitions, Similarities, and Contrasts

Alternative investments consist of groups of investments with risk and return characteristics that differ from those of traditional stock and bond investments. Common features of alternative investments include:

- Relative illiquidity, associated with a return premium as compensation
- Diversifying potential relative to a portfolio of stocks and bonds
- High due diligence costs
- Difficult performance appraisal because of the complexity of establishing valid benchmarks

Alternative investment markets are considered informationally less efficient than major equity and bond markets, and offer greater scope for adding value through skill and superior information.

**Real estate**, **private equity**, and **commodities** have been viewed as the primary alternatives to traditional stock and bond investments. **Hedge funds** and **managed futures** have been considered modern alternatives not only to traditional investments but also to traditional alternative investments.

Alternative investments can also be placed in three groups by the primary role they play in portfolios:

1. Providing exposure to risk factors not easily accessible through traditional stock and bond investments (e.g., real estate, long-only commodities)
2. Providing exposure to specialized investment strategies that adds value dependent on the skills of the manager (e.g., hedge funds, managed futures)
3. Combining features of the prior two groups (e.g., private equity funds, distressed securities)



## Alternative Investments and Core–Satellite Investing

A traditional core–satellite perspective places competitively priced assets, such as government bonds and large-capitalization stocks, in the core. Because alpha is hard to obtain with such assets, the core may be managed in a passive manner. In the satellite ring, alternative investments designed to add alpha or to diminish portfolio volatility via low correlation with the core are added.

## Real Estate

The reading is focused on *equity investments* in real estate. Investing in instruments such as mortgages, securitizations of mortgages, or hybrid debt/equity interests is not covered.

## The Real Estate Market

Real estate investment is an important part of institutional and individual portfolios for the potential return-enhancement and risk-diversification benefits in a portfolio of stocks, bonds, and other (alternative) investments.

Investors may participate in real estate directly and indirectly. Direct ownership includes investment in residences, business (commercial) real estate, and agricultural land.

Indirect investment includes investing in:

- **Companies** engaged in real estate ownership, development, or management, such as home builders and real estate operating companies
- **Real estate investment trusts (REITs)**, which are publicly traded equities representing pools of money invested in real estate properties and/or real estate debt
- **Commingled real estate funds (CREFs)**, which are professionally managed vehicles for commingled (i.e., pooled) investment in real estate properties
- **Separately managed accounts**
- **Infrastructure funds**, which make private investment in public infrastructure projects in return for rights to revenue streams

Investments in real estate shares and REITs are both made through public stock markets. REITs securitize illiquid real estate assets and permit smaller investors to gain real estate exposure. REITs function as conduits to investors for the cash flows from the underlying real estate holdings. Equity REITs own and manage properties such as office buildings, apartment buildings, and shopping centers where shareholders receive rental income and income from capital appreciation. Mortgage REITs own portfolios in which the assets are mortgages where shareholders receive interest income and capital appreciation income from improvement in the prices of loans. Hybrid REITs operate by buying real estate and by acquiring mortgages on both commercial and residential real estate.

Exchange-traded funds, mutual funds, and traded closed-end investment companies allow investors to obtain a professionally managed diversified portfolio of real estate securities with a relatively small outlay. CREFs include open-end funds and closed-end funds (i.e., funds that are closed to new investment after an initial period). Investors use these private real estate funds to access the real estate expertise of a professional real estate fund manager in selecting, developing, and realizing the value of real estate properties. In contrast to open-end funds, closed-end funds are usually leveraged and have higher return objectives; they operate by opportunistically acquiring, repositioning, and disposing of properties. Individually managed separate accounts are also an important alternative for investors.



In an infrastructure investment, a private company or a consortium of private companies designs, finances, and builds the new project for public use. The consortium maintains the physical infrastructure over a period that often ranges from 25 to 30 years. The public sector (via the government) leases the infrastructure and pays the consortium an annual fee for the use of the completed project over the contracted period.

Estimates have been made that real estate represents one-third to one-half of the world's wealth.

### Benchmarks and Historical Performance

The **NCREIF Property Index** of the National Council of Real Estate Investment Fiduciaries (NCREIF) is the benchmark used to measure the performance of direct real estate investment in the United States.

- The NCREIF Property Index is a value-weighted, quarterly benchmark for real estate covering a sample of commercial properties.
- Property appraisals determine the values in the NCREIF Property Index because ownership changes infrequently. Appraisal-based property values exhibit stale prices because property appraisals are also conducted infrequently (once a year). Therefore, performance tends to underestimate volatility in underlying values. However, methods have been developed to unsmooth or correct for this bias with a transaction-based index called the **NCREIF Index Unsmoothed Index**.

The National Association of Real Estate Investment Trusts (**NAREIT**) is the benchmark used to represent indirect investment in real estate.

- The NAREIT Index is a real-time, market-capitalization-weighted index of all REITs actively traded on the New York Stock Exchange and American Stock Exchange.
- NAREIT computes a monthly index based on month-end share prices of equity REITs. To correct for the stock market noise contained in the NAREIT index, analysts use the **NAREIT Index Hedged Index**.

Historically, direct and indirect real estate investments represented by the major indices have produced better risk-adjusted performance than have stocks and commodities.

The performance of direct and securitized real estate investment differs significantly. REITs exhibit a relatively high return and high standard deviation, whereas appraisal-based real estate returns are low and have low volatility. The low standard deviation of NCREIF Property Index returns is indicative of the smoothing because of stale valuations. After correcting for smoothing, the NCREIF Property Index's volatility more than doubles.

### Real Estate: Investment Characteristics and Roles

Real estate accounts for a major portion of many individuals' wealth. However, most advisors do not include the clients' residences as assets in the strategic asset allocation because residential real estate is the place in which the client lives.

A variety of investment characteristics affect the returns to real estate. The physical real estate market is characterized by:

- Lack of liquidity
- Large lot sizes
- High transaction costs
- Heterogeneity
- Immobility
- Low information transparency

Various market and economic factors affect real estate, including:

- Interest rates
- Gross national product
- Population growth and demographics

**Advantages**

- Mortgage interest and property taxes are tax deductible.
- Mortgage loans permit more financial leverage.
- Real estate investors have direct control over their property and can take action to increase the market value of the property.
- Geographical diversification can be effective in reducing exposure to risks. The values of real estate investments in different locations have low correlations.
- Real estate returns have relatively low volatility.

**Disadvantages**

- Real estate is not easily divisible into smaller pieces.
- It may be a large part of a portfolio.
- There is large idiosyncratic risk.
- The cost of acquiring information is high because each piece of real estate is unique.
- Real estate brokers charge high commissions.
- Real estate has large operating and maintenance costs and requires hands-on management expertise.
- There is risk of neighborhood deterioration beyond the investor's control.
- Income tax deductions are subject to political risk in that they may be discontinued.

### Roles in the Portfolio

Real estate markets follow economic cycles; therefore, forecasting economic cycles results in improved strategies for reallocating among different assets on the basis of expected stages of their respective cycles. Among the variables to focus on as systematic determinants of real estate returns are:

- Growth in consumption
- Real interest rates
- Term structure of interest rates
- Unexpected inflation



#### Role of Real Estate as a Diversifier

In addition to adding value through active management, real estate is an important diversifier. Real estate is not highly correlated with the performance of a stock and bond portfolio. Also, real estate experiences lower volatility because it is less affected by short-term economic conditions. Income-producing real estate is a stable investment because of the income derived from tenants' lease payments.

REITs provide some diversification benefits relative to a stock and/or bond portfolio, but are less effective in that role than are hedge funds and commodities. Direct investment in real estate as represented by the unsmoothed NCREIF returns, however, provides more diversification benefit.

### Diversification within Real Estate Itself

Investors also seek diversification within real estate investing. Investments in different real estate sectors differ in regard to risk and return.

- The property types that have higher levels of embedded risk, such as large office assets, generate lower risk-adjusted returns than other sectors and are likely to have more pronounced market cycles.
- Sectors that offer higher risk-adjusted returns, such as apartments, are less volatile and offer more defensive characteristics.

Overall, investors benefit from including domestic and nondomestic investments in real estate in their portfolios.

Due diligence in active direct real estate investment should cover the checkpoints of market opportunity, investment process, organization, people, terms and structure, service providers, documents, and write-up.

### Private Equity/Venture Capital

Private equity is ownership in a private company (i.e., one that is not publicly traded). The term *private equity* refers to any security by which equity capital is raised via a private placement rather than through a public offering.

**Private equity funds** are pooled investment vehicles through which investors make indirect investments in highly illiquid assets.

These investment activities include:

- **Venture capital (VC):** Equity financing of new or growing private companies.
- **Buyout funds:** Buyouts of established companies, including taking a publicly owned company private, the private purchase of a division of a public corporation, and the buyouts of private companies.

A **private investment in a public entity (PIPE)** is an investment that is usually made at a price less than the current market value. If the share price of a publicly traded company has dropped significantly from its value at the time of going public, the company may seek new sources of capital via a PIPE.

AI

Although public and private equity investments have common elements, private equity investment requires distinct knowledge and experience, as shown in the table.

### (Direct) Private Equity Investment and Investment in Publicly Traded Equities

| Private Equity Investments | Publicly Traded Securities |
|---|---|
| **Structure and Valuation** | |
| Deal structure and price are negotiated between the investor and company management. | Price is set in the context of the market. Deal structure is standardized. |
| **Access to Information for Investment Selection** | |
| Investor can request access to all information, including internal projections. | Analysts can use only publicly available information to assess investment potential. |
| **Postinvestment Activity** | |
| Investors remain involved in the company after the transaction by participating at the board level and through regular contact with management. | Investors typically do not sit on corporate boards; they make ongoing assessments based on publicly available information, and have limited access to management. |

*Source:* Prepared by Andrew Abouchar, CFA, of Tech Capital Partners.

### The Private Equity Market

Characteristics of the private equity marketplace and private equity funds include:

- The original owners often do not have adequate capital for growth or to fund current operations.
- Entrepreneurs frequently lack the professional managerial skills and experience to manage the enterprise they started after it reaches a certain size.
- Venture capital firms are able to supply valuable assistance in the transition to professional management.
- Original owners want to diversify their wealth. For an individual investor, a closely held business represents a significant portion of his or her overall wealth. The liquidity afforded by markets for publicly traded shares allows such investors to diversify their portfolios at lower costs.
- Venture capitalists also can assist in the initial public offering (IPO) of shares, which permits the original owners to eventually realize public market valuations for their holdings.

## The Demand for Venture Capital

### Venture Capital Time Line

| | Formative-Stage Companies | | | Expansion-Stage Companies | | |
|---|---|---|---|---|---|---|
| | Early Stage | | | Later Stage | | Pre-IPO |
| | Seed | Start-Up | First Stage | Second Stage | Third Stage | Mezzanine |
| **Stage characteristics** | Idea, first personnel hired, prototype development | Moving into operation, initial revenues | | Revenue growth | | Preparation for IPO |
| **Stage financing (buyers of private equity)** | Founders, FF&F,[a] angels, venture capital | Angels, venture capital | | Venture capital, strategic partners | | |
| **Purpose of financing** | Supports market research and establishment of business. | Start-up financing supports product development and initial marketing.<br>First-stage financing supports such activities as initial manufacturing and sales. | | Second-stage financing supports the initial expansion of a company already producing and selling a product.<br>Third-stage financing provides capital for major expansion.<br>Mezzanine (bridge) financing provides capital to prepare for the IPO—often a mix of debt and equity. | | |

[a] FF&F = founder's friends and family. The sources of financing are listed in typical order of importance.

### The Supply of Venture Capital

Suppliers of venture capital include the following:

- **Angel investors.** Accredited individuals investing in seed and early-stage companies after the resources of the founder's friends and family have been exhausted.
- **Venture capitalists (VCs).** Specialists managing pools of capital who seek to identify companies that have good business opportunities but need financial, managerial, and strategic support.
- **Large companies.** Companies investing their own money via corporate private equity in promising young companies in the same or a related industry, often referred to as strategic partners.

Most investors participate in private equity through private equity funds. Among these funds, buyout funds constitute a larger segment than VC funds, as measured by assets under management (AUM).

Buyout funds may be separated into two major groups:

- **Mega-cap buyout funds** take public companies private.
- **Middle-market buyout funds** purchase private companies whose revenues and profits are too small to access capital from the public equity markets.

The buyout fund manager seeks to add value by:

- Restructuring operations and improving management
- Purchasing companies at a discount to intrinsic value
- Capturing any gains from the addition or restructuring of debt

To add value, buyout organizations maintain a pool of experienced operating and financial executives who can be inserted into the companies to cut costs, increase revenues, and restructure supply chains and distribution channels. Buyout organizations also have well-developed processes for installing incentive compensation systems.

Buyout funds can realize value gains through:

- Sale of the acquired company,
- IPO, or
- Dividend recapitalization. A dividend recapitalization is the issuance of debt to finance a special dividend to owners to recoup the cash used to acquire a company.

### Types of Private Equity Investment

Characteristics of direct private equity investment include:

- The investment is structured as convertible preferred stock rather than common stock. An event such as a buyout or an acquisition of the common equity at a favorable price will trigger conversion of the convertible preferreds into the common shares of the company.
- The terms of the preferred stock require that the company pay cash before any cash can be paid on the common stock, which is the equity investment of the founders.
- Preferred stock is senior to common stock in its claims on liquidation value, mitigating the risk, and distributing it to the owners/founders. It also provides an incentive to the company to meet the return goals of the outside investors.

Indirect investment is primarily through private equity funds, including VC funds and buyout funds. Characteristics of indirect private equity include:



- Private equity is structured as limited partnerships or limited liability companies (LLCs) for tax purposes with an expected life of 7 to 10 years with an option to extend the life for another 1 to 5 years. The limited partners do not bear any liability beyond the amount of their investments.
- The fund manager's objective is to realize the value of all portfolio investments by the fund's liquidation date. The limited partners commit to a specific investment amount that the general partner draws down over time in a series of capital calls to make specific investments.
- The general partner is the venture capitalist, the party selecting and advising investments. The general partner also commits its own capital, closely aligning the interests of outside investors and the general partner.

- Compensation to the fund manager of a private equity fund consists of a management fee plus an incentive fee. The management fee is usually a percentage of limited partner *commitments* to the fund, often in the 1.5%–2.5% range. The incentive fee, **carried interest**, is the share of the fund's profits that the fund manager is due once the fund has returned the outside investors' capital, usually 20% of the total profits. In some funds, the carried interest is computed on only those profits that represent a return in excess of a hurdle rate, the **preferred return**. Some funds have a **claw-back provision** that specifies that money from the fund manager be returned to investors if at the end of a fund's life investors have not received back their capital contributions and contractual share of profits.

### Benchmarks and Historical Performance

When measuring the performance of a private equity investment, investors typically calculate an internal rate of return (IRR). Similarly, venture capital benchmarks provide IRR estimates for private equity funds that are based on fund cash flows and valuations.

Market price–revealing events such as the raising of new financing, the acquisition of the company by another company, the IPO, or the failure of the business occur infrequently. As a result, infrequent market pricing poses a major challenge to index construction.

Major benchmarks for U.S. and European private equity are those provided by Cambridge Associates and Thomson Venture Economics, which present an overall private equity index representing two major segments: VC funds and buyout funds.

Private equity returns have exhibited a low correlation with publicly traded securities, making them an attractive addition to a portfolio. However, because of a lack of observable market prices for private equity, short-term return and correlation data may be a result of stale prices.

IRR calculations are based on the fund manager's appraisals, not a market price. Appraised values are slow to adjust to new circumstances and be stale data, so the returns may be erroneous. Furthermore, there is no generally accepted standard for appraisals.

Private equity fund investors make comparisons with funds closed in the same year, the **vintage year**, when evaluating past records of returns. This helps ensure that the funds are compared with other funds at a similar stage in their life cycle and the influence that economic conditions have on various funds' probabilities of success is consistent.



### Private Equity: Investment Characteristics and Roles

Private equity plays a growth role in investment portfolios. The private equity investor hopes to control the risk through appropriate due diligence.

The investment characteristics of private equity investments include:

- *Illiquidity*. Private equity fund investors have more restricted opportunities to withdraw investments because the underlying investments are not liquid.
- *Long-term commitments* are required.

- *Higher risk than seasoned public equity investment.* The returns show greater dispersion. The risk of complete loss is higher. The failure rate of new businesses is high.
- *High expected IRR* is required as compensation for the risk and illiquidity of such investments.

For venture capital investments, the following also holds:

- *Limited information.* New ventures break new ground, making projections concerning cash flows limited. As a result, successful ventures have the potential for unusual profits.

Many investments do not work out. For bearing the additional risks, a private equity fund investor targets a substantial premium over expected public equity returns.

The illiquidity of private equity affects the value. Discounts are applied if the owner has a minority interest and if the equity interest does not have a ready market. The **discount for a minority interest** reflects the lack of control that the investor has over the business and distributions, and can range from 20% to 30%. The **discount for lack of marketability** takes into account the lack of liquidity in the investment and reflects both the cost of going public and a further discount if the investor owns a large block of shares.

VC funds and buyout funds have some expected differences in return characteristics, including:

- Buyout funds are highly leveraged.
- The cash flows to buyout fund investors come earlier and more steadily than those to VC fund investors.
- The returns to VC fund investors are subject to greater error in measurement.

Thus, venture capital investing may be expected to involve more frequent losses than buyouts in return for higher upside potential when investments are successful.

### Roles in the Portfolio

AI

Many investors look to private equity investment for long-term return enhancement. However, private equity plays a moderate role as a risk diversifier.

### Other Issues

A major requirement for private equity investing is careful due diligence. Due diligence items for private equity can be placed into one of the following three categories:

1. Evaluation of prospects for market success
2. Operational review, focusing on internal processes, such as sales management, employment contracts, internal financial controls, product engineering and development, and intellectual property management
3. Financial/legal review, including the examination of internal financial statements, audited financial statements, auditor's management letters, prior-year budgets, and so on

## Commodity Investments

A commodity is a tangible asset that is homogeneous in nature (which allows for standardized futures contracts) and can include both direct and indirect investments.

### The Commodity Market

Investors can gain direct exposure to commodities in spot (cash) markets or in markets for deferred delivery, such as futures and forwards markets. Commodity futures markets developed as a response to a need by suppliers and users of various agricultural and nonagricultural goods to transfer or reduce the risk of holding spot inventories. Commodities futures are traded on agricultural products, metals, and energy resources. A commodity futures transaction may be physical delivery or cash-settled. Other types of commodity derivatives include options on commodity futures and swap markets.

### Types of Commodity Investments

There are two broad approaches to investing in commodities:

1. **Direct commodity investment** entails cash market purchase of physical commodities—agricultural products, metals, and crude oil—or exposure to changes in spot market values via derivatives, such as futures. Cash market purchases involve actual possession and storage of the physical commodities and incur carrying costs and storage costs. Thus, investors have generally preferred to use derivatives or indirect commodity investment.
2. **Indirect commodity investment** involves the acquisition of indirect claims on commodities, such as equity in companies specializing in commodity production. Indirect commodity investment does not provide effective exposure to commodity price changes and is dependent on the degree that companies hedge their commodity risk.

### Benchmarks and Historical Performance

The performance of commodity investments can be evaluated by using commodity indices that form the basis for many financial products.

Futures contract returns are often used as a proxy for cash market performance. A variety of indices based on futures prices are used as benchmarks for the performance of futures-based commodity investments. The RJ/CRB, S&P GSCI, DJ-AIGCI, and S&P Commodity Index provide returns comparable to passive long positions in listed futures contracts.

Commodity indices differ widely in composition, weighting scheme, and purpose. For example, the RJ/CRB index and the S&P GSCI include energy, metals, grains, and soft commodities.

For the period 1990–2004, the results for the S&P CI and DJ-AIGCI differ from the results for the S&P GSCI. The differences can be explained by differences in the components of the indices and different approaches to determining the weights of individual commodity futures contracts in each index.

Judged by the Sharpe ratio, commodities have underperformed U.S. and world bonds and equities. In terms of the minimum monthly return, the GSCI registered –14.41%, which is not significantly different from the S&P 500's –14.46%, but is higher than the minimum monthly return of either U.S. or global bonds.

The correlations of commodity indices with the traditional asset classes are close to zero, indicating risk diversifiers.

For the shorter 2000–2004 period, all commodity indices outperformed U.S. and world equities, but not bonds. A consistent feature is correlation. The low correlations among commodities and traditional asset classes are consistent with the evidence for the longer time period.

### Commodity Index Return Components

The return on a commodity futures contract is not the same as the return on the underlying spot commodity. The returns have three components:

1. **Spot return (price return)** is the change in the spot price of the underlying. The spot return measures the change in commodity futures prices that result from changes in the underlying spot prices, according to the cost of carry model.
2. **Collateral return (collateral yield)** comes from the assumption that the full value of the underlying futures contract is invested to earn the risk-free interest rate. An investor long a futures contract posts 100% margin in the form of Treasury bills (fully collateralized). The implied yield is the collateral return.
3. **Roll return (roll yield)** arises from rolling long futures positions forward through time. A monthly roll return is computed as the change in the futures contract price over the month minus the change in the spot price over the month. When the futures markets are in **backwardation**, a positive return will be earned from a simple buy-and-hold strategy. The positive return is earned because as the futures contract gets closer to maturity, its price must converge to that of the spot price of the commodity. In backwardation the spot price is greater than the futures price; therefore, the futures price must increase in value. The opposite is true with an upward-sloping term structure of futures prices, or **contango**.



Over the 1990–2004 period, there was an overall positive relationship between the mean monthly roll return and intramonth spot price volatility in the GSCI. The effect is more pronounced for nonperishable, storable commodities, whose convenience yield rises in periods of increased volatility because of demand-and-supply shocks. The total return on a commodity index = Collateral return + Roll return + Spot return. Thus, for 2000, the total return on the GSCI = 8.6% + 14.2% + 26.9% = 49.7%.

### Commodities: Investment Characteristics and Roles

Direct investment in commodities for most investors will be via the futures markets. For investors seeking passive exposure to commodities, the liquidity of the market for futures contracts on a given commodity index is a major consideration.

Commodities have low correlations with equities and bonds. In periods of financial distress, commodity prices tend to rise, providing valuable diversification. Long-term growth in world demand for certain commodities in limited supply, such as petroleum-related commodities, is a factor in their long-term trend growth. Nevertheless, commodities are sensitive to business cycles. The reason commodities behave differently under different economic conditions is a result of their sources of returns. The determinants of commodity returns include the following:

- **Business cycle–related supply and demand.** Commodity prices are determined by the supply and demand of the underlying commodities. Commodity prices are sensitive to the business cycle but have negative correlation with stocks and bonds. There are three reasons commodity returns are weakly correlated with stock and bond returns:

    1. Commodities correlate positively with inflation, whereas stocks and bonds are negatively correlated with inflation.
    2. Commodity prices and stock/bond prices react differently in different phases of the business cycle. Commodity future prices are more affected by short-term expectations, whereas stock and bond prices are affected by long-term expectations.
    3. Commodity prices decline during times of a weak economy.

- **Convenience yield.** The theory of storage splits the difference between the futures price and the spot price into three components: the forgone interest from purchasing and storing the commodity, storage costs, and the commodity's convenience yield. The convenience yield reflects an embedded consumption-timing option in holding a storable commodity. The theory predicts an inverse relationship between the level of inventories and convenience yield: At low inventory levels, convenience yields are high, and vice versa.
- **Real options under uncertainty.** Oil futures markets are often backwardated; in these markets, futures prices are often below the current spot price. This may be caused by the existence of real options under uncertainty. A **real option** is an option involving decisions related to tangible assets or processes. In other words, producers are holding valuable real options—options to produce or not to produce—and will not exercise them unless the spot prices start to climb up. Production occurs only if discounted futures prices are below spot prices, and backwardation results if the risk of future prices is sufficiently high. A major consequence of a downward-sloping term structure of futures prices is the opportunity to capture a positive roll return as investment in expiring contracts is moved to cheaper new outstanding contracts.



Among the reasons for including commodities in a portfolio are these:

- Natural sources of return over the long term, as discussed earlier, and
- Protection for a portfolio against unexpected inflation. Certain commodities, such as gold, have been held as stores of value by investors during inflationary times.

For the period between 1990 and 2004, stocks and bonds exhibited a negative correlation with unexpected inflation (–0.23 and –0.06, respectively), as did some commodity classes (e.g., agriculture, livestock, and nonenergy). However, storable commodities directly related to the intensity of economic activity exhibit positive correlation with unexpected inflation (0.15 for precious metals and 0.46 for energy). These results suggest that direct investment in energy and, to a lesser degree, precious metals provides a significant inflation hedge.

The roles for commodities in the portfolio are as:

- Portfolio risk diversifiers
- An inflation hedge, offsetting losses to assets such as bonds, which lose value during periods of unexpected inflation

Long-term investors with liabilities indexed to inflation, such as defined benefit plans, are able to improve their risk/return trade-off by including commodities in the portfolio. For university endowments, which support the inflation-sensitive costs of operating a university, commodities have a role as good risk diversifiers in a portfolio that needs inflation protection.

During the period 1990–2004, commodities underperformed U.S. and world bond and equity markets. However, the low or negative correlations of GSCI returns with returns to the S&P 500 (–0.08), Lehman Government/Corporate Bond Index (0.03), HFCI (0.09), MSCI World Index (–0.06), and Lehman Global Bond Index (0.06) suggest diversification benefits and the potential for improvement in the Sharpe ratio by including commodities.

Commodities also offer potential for active management that may involve short as well as long positions. Active programs may be executed within a separately managed account or a private commodity pool.

### Hedge Funds

There is no universally accepted definition of a hedge fund, and hedge funds can take many forms. Originally, hedge funds were private partnerships that took long and short equity positions to reduce net market exposure in exchange for accepting a lower rate of investment return. Today, the organizational and structural characteristics of the portfolio define it as a hedge fund. Their private pool structures permit them to be loosely regulated, avoid certain reporting, and take aggressive, leveraged, long or short positions.



Hedge funds are constructed to take advantage of certain market opportunities. They are classified according to their investment style, which is wide ranging in risk attributes and investment opportunities.

### Types of Hedge Fund Investments

Many style classifications of hedge funds exist:

- *Equity market neutral*. This strategy attempts to identify overvalued and undervalued equity securities while neutralizing the portfolio's exposure to market risk by combining long and short positions. The market opportunity comes from their flexibility to take positions without regard to the securities' weights in a benchmark and the existence of inefficiencies in equity markets, particularly overvalued securities because many investors face constraints relative to shorting stocks.

- *Convertible arbitrage*. This strategy attempts to exploit anomalies in the prices of corporate convertible securities. The simplest example is buying convertible bonds and hedging the equity component of the bonds' risk by shorting the associated stock. The cash proceeds from the short sale remain with the hedge fund's prime broker but earn interest, and the hedge fund may earn an extra margin through leverage when the bonds' current yield exceeds the borrowing rate of money from the prime broker.
- *Fixed-income arbitrage*. This strategy attempts to identify overvalued and undervalued fixed-income securities on the basis of expectations of changes in the term structure of interest rates or the credit quality of various related issues. Fixed-income portfolios neutralize against directional market movements because the portfolios combine long and short positions.
- *Distressed securities*. This strategy invests in both the debt and the equity of companies that are in or near bankruptcy.
- *Merger arbitrage*. This strategy seeks to capture the price spread between current market prices of corporate securities and their value upon successful completion of a takeover, merger, spin-off, or similar transaction involving more than one company. In merger arbitrage, the opportunity typically involves buying the stock of a target company after a merger announcement and shorting an appropriate amount of the acquiring company's stock.
- *Hedged equity*. Hedged equity strategies attempt to identify overvalued and undervalued equity securities; they are not necessarily market neutral, and may be highly concentrated. The portfolio may have a net long or a net short exposure to the equity market.
- *Global macro*. This strategy attempts to take advantage of systematic moves in markets through trading in currencies, futures, and option contracts, and traditional equity and bond markets.
- *Emerging markets*. This strategy focuses on the emerging and less mature markets.
- *Fund of funds (FOF)*. An FOF invests in a number of underlying hedge funds.

Hedge fund strategies can be classified into the following five broad groups:

1. *Relative value*, which seeks to exploit valuation discrepancies through long and short positions (i.e., equity market neutral, convertible arbitrage, and hedged equity).
2. *Event driven*, which focuses on opportunities created by corporate transactions (e.g., merger arbitrage, distressed securities).
3. *Equity hedge*, which invests in long and short equity positions with varying degrees of equity market exposure and leverage.
4. *Global asset allocators*, which are opportunistically long and short a variety of financial and/or nonfinancial assets.
5. *Short selling*, in which the manager shorts equities in the expectation of a market decline.

The compensation structure of hedge funds consists of a management fee plus an incentive fee. The management fee is a percentage of net asset value (NAV), or AUM fee, ranging from 1% to 2%. The incentive fee is a percentage of profits, typically around 20%.

Many funds have:

- **High-water mark (HWM)**, which specifies the NAV level that a fund must exceed before performance fees are paid to the hedge fund manager. The purpose of a HWM provision is to ensure that the hedge fund manager earns an incentive fee only once for the same gain.
- **Hurdle rate**, which specifies that no incentive fee is earned until a specified minimum rate of return is earned.
- **Lockup period**, typically one to three years, in order to insulate from unwinding positions unfavorably. FOFs usually do not impose lockup periods; however, the FOF manager must hold a cash buffer that may reduce expected returns.

### Benchmarks and Historical Performance

The Center for International Securities and Derivatives Markets (CISDM), Hedge Fund Research (HFR), Dow Jones, Standard & Poor's, and Morgan Stanley provide monthly or daily indices that track the performance of active manager-based benchmarks of hedge fund performance.

Defining the hedge fund universe is difficult because there is no general agreement among institutional investors regarding which investment strategies are considered hedge fund strategies and what weights should be given to each strategy. There are many differences in the construction of the major manager-based hedge fund indices. Principal differences include:

- *Selection criteria.* Decision rules determine which hedge funds are included in the index.
- *Style classification.* Indices have various approaches to how each hedge fund is assigned to a style-specific index.
- *Weighting scheme.* Indices have different schemes to determine how much weight a particular fund's return is given in the index. A common weighting scheme is equally weighted.
- *Rebalancing scheme.* Rebalancing rules determine when assets are reallocated among the funds in an equally weighted index.
- *Investability.* An index may be directly or only indirectly investable.



Performance appraisal is an issue in the hedge fund industry because hedge funds are promoted as absolute-return vehicles; however, absolute-return vehicles have no direct benchmark portfolios. Estimates of alpha must be made relative to a benchmark portfolio. A problem in alpha determination is the differences in the selected benchmark, resulting in large differences in reported alpha.

The lack of a clear hedge fund benchmark, however, is not indicative of an inability to determine comparable returns for a hedge fund strategy. Hedge fund strategies within a particular style often trade similar assets with similar methodologies and are sensitive to similar market factors. Two principal means of establishing comparable portfolios are (1) using a single-factor or multifactor methodology and (2) using optimization to create tracking portfolios with similar risk and return characteristics.

Over the 1990–2004 period, the HFCI had superior return performance relative to other traditional asset classes. During the sharp decline of the S&P 500 between mid 2000 and late 2002, the HFCI had a small but positive trend. The HFCI had a higher Sharpe ratio than any of the other reported assets. The HFCI's correlation of 0.59 with the S&P 500 is consistent with the potential for risk-diversification benefits.

There was considerable variation in the risk and return characteristics among styles. As expected, those hedge fund groups whose strategies call for eliminating market risk (e.g., equity market neutral) have low correlations with stock or bond indices. Those hedge fund strategies with equity exposure (e.g., event driven and hedged equity) have moderate correlations with the S&P 500.

The actual performance of hedge fund strategies depends on the market conditions affecting that strategy. Equity-based hedge fund strategies are correlated with several equity and bond market factors. Credit-sensitive strategies (e.g., distressed securities) are correlated with similar factors as credit-sensitive bond instruments. Relative-value strategies (e.g., equity market neutral) are sensitive to different return factors from those to which hedged equity strategies are sensitive; therefore, they have low correlations with the S&P 500 and are considered risk diversifiers. Diversification among hedge fund strategies therefore would reduce the volatility of hedge fund–based investment portfolios.

Comparable hedge fund indices are sensitive to the same set of risk factors. Therefore, the return differences among indices reflect the differences in weights of different strategy groups. Value weighting may result in a particular index taking on the return characteristics of the best-performing hedge funds in a particular time period, creating a momentum effect in returns. Equal-weighted indices may reflect potential diversification of hedge funds better than value-weighted indices; however, the costs of rebalancing a fund to index weights make it difficult to create an investable form. Many hedge fund investors use custom benchmarks. Many indices use multifactor models in identifying market factors that describe the sources of hedge fund returns. However, the sensitivity of various hedge fund indices to these economic factors may change over time.

The usefulness of historical hedge fund data is problematic. **Survivorship bias** results when managers with poor track records exit the business and are dropped from the database whereas managers with good records remain. If the survivorship bias is large, then the historical return record of the average surviving manager is higher than the average return of all managers over the test period, resulting in overestimation of historical returns by an estimated 1.5% to 3% per year.



The problem of survivorship bias may be reduced by conducting superior due diligence. Also, an FOF may be able to avoid managers destined to fail, mitigating the survivorship bias problem, in exchange for an additional layer of management fees.

**Backfill bias** results when missing past return data for a component of an index are provided at the discretion of the hedge fund when it joins the index. Backfill bias overestimates results because only hedge funds with good past results will be motivated to supply them.

### Hedge Funds: Investment Characteristics and Roles

Hedge funds are skill-based investment strategies, obtaining returns from the firm's competitive advantages in information or its interpretation. Therefore, a hedge fund's returns derived from a manager's skill will be uncorrelated with the returns of stock and bond markets.

For hedge funds, a common set of return drivers based on trading strategy factors (e.g., option-like payoffs) and location factors (e.g., payoffs from a buy-and-hold policy) helps to explain returns of each strategy.

The returns for long-bias equity-based and fixed-income–based hedge fund strategies are affected by changes of the underlying stock and bond markets. Therefore, they are less portfolio return diversifiers and more portfolio return enhancers. Equity market neutral and bond arbitrage are regarded more as diversifiers than enhancers.

The diversification benefits of adding hedge funds in different style groups can be distinct. A randomly selected equal-weighted portfolio of five to seven hedge funds has a standard deviation similar to that of the population from which it is drawn.

The allocations produced by mean-variance optimization (MVO) are sensitive to errors in return estimates. Therefore, basing allocations on historical hedge fund index returns in MVO may be unreliable.

For the 1990–2004 period, when the HFCI is added to U.S. stocks, bonds, or a portfolio of U.S. stocks and bonds, the risk-adjusted return improves. The Sharpe ratio of a balanced portfolio with U.S. stocks and bonds increases to 0.87 from 0.67 when hedge funds are added. Similarly, when hedge funds are added to a balanced portfolio of world equities and bonds, the Sharpe ratio increases significantly from 0.43 to 0.65. The correlation between the HFCI and the U.S. stock/bond portfolio is 0.59 and between the HFCI and the world stock/bond portfolio is 0.51.

Hedge funds achieved historically high returns in the first half of the 1990s. However, for the period 2000–2004, the annualized return of hedge funds was 6.84%, lower than for the 1990–2004 period of 13.46%, but the benefits that hedge funds add to the portfolios are similar to those for the period that includes the early 1990s. Including hedge funds also leads to lower skewness and higher kurtosis, which are exactly opposite to the attributes of positive skewness and moderate kurtosis that investors want.



In addition to market factors, individual fund factors affect expected performance. Results from research support the following three conclusions:

1. *Young funds outperform old funds on a total-return basis.* The impact of lockup periods affects hedge fund performance. Periods of severe drawdown (e.g., 1998) influence funds to dissolve rather than face the prospect of not earning the incentive fees because of HWM provisions.
2. *Large funds underperform small funds on average.* The large fund may be able to attract and retain more talented people than a small fund and receive more attention from, for example, its prime broker.
3. *FOFs may provide closer approximation to return estimation than indices do.* FOF returns may differ from overall hedge fund performance because of various issues, including a less direct impact of survivorship bias on FOFs because hedge funds that dissolve are included in the returns of the FOFs.

Hedge funds are loosely regulated entities without the disclosure requirements of other investment vehicles. Although hedge funds typically provide an annual performance, they rarely disclose their portfolio positions. Because hedge funds are opaque, reducing risk in hedge fund investing starts with due diligence. The framework for due diligence includes covering market opportunity, investment process, organization, people, terms and structure, service providers, documents, and write-ups.

### Performance Evaluation Concerns

Hedge funds typically report data to hedge fund data providers monthly, and the default compounding frequency for hedge fund performance evaluation and reporting is monthly. The rate of return reported by hedge funds is the nominal monthly-holding-period return computed as follows:

$$\text{Rate of return} = (\text{Ending value of portfolio} - \text{Beginning value of portfolio}) / \text{Beginning value of portfolio}$$

These returns are typically compounded over 12 monthly periods to obtain the annualized rate of return.

Investors sometimes examine the rolling returns to a hedge fund. The **rolling return**, *RR*, is the moving average of the holding-period returns for a specified period (e.g., a calendar year) that matches the investor's time horizon. For example, if the investor's time horizon is 12 months, the rolling return would be calculated using:

$$RRn,t = [Rt + Rt - 1 + Rt - 2 + \ldots + Rt - (n-1)] / n$$

so

$$RR12,t = (Rt + Rt - 1 + Rt - 2 + \ldots + Rt - 11) / 12$$

Rolling returns provide some insight into the characteristics and qualities of returns. In particular, they show how consistent the returns are over the investment period and identify any cyclicality in the returns.

### Volatility and Downside Volatility

**Standard deviation** is a common measure of risk in hedge fund performance. However, hedge funds have more instances of extremely high and extremely low returns than would be expected with a normal distribution (i.e., positive excess kurtosis) and some funds also display skewness. When those conditions hold, standard deviation incorrectly represents the actual risk of a hedge fund's strategies.

**Downside deviation (semideviation)** is an alternative risk measure that mitigates one critique of standard deviation, namely, that it penalizes high positive returns. Downside deviation computes deviation from a specified threshold (i.e., below a specified return, $r^*$); only the negative deviations are included in the calculation. Another popular risk measure is drawdown. **Maximum drawdown** is the largest difference between a high-water point and a subsequent low.

### Performance Appraisal Measures

The **Sharpe ratio**, the average amount of return in excess of the risk-free rate per unit of standard deviation of return, is extensively used. However, the Sharpe ratio has a number of limitations:

- The Sharpe ratio is not an appropriate measure when the investment has an asymmetrical return distribution, with either negative or positive skewness.
- Illiquid holdings bias the Sharpe ratio upward.
- Sharpe ratios are overestimated when investment returns are serially correlated (i.e., returns trend), which causes a lower estimate of the standard deviation.
- The Sharpe ratio is for stand-alone investments and does not take into consideration the correlations with other assets in a portfolio.
- The Sharpe ratio has not been found to have predictive ability for hedge funds in general.
- The Sharpe ratio can be gamed. The reported Sharpe ratio can be increased without the investment really delivering higher risk-adjusted returns by five methods:
  1. Lengthening the measurement interval.
  2. Compounding the monthly returns but calculating the standard deviation from the monthly returns (not compounded).
  3. Writing out-of-the-money puts and calls on a portfolio.
  4. Smoothing returns. Using certain derivative structures, infrequent marking to market of illiquid assets, and pricing models that understate monthly gains or losses can reduce reported volatility.
  5. Removing extreme returns that increase the standard deviation.

The **Sortino ratio** replaces standard deviation in the Sharpe ratio with downside deviation. Instead of using the mean rate of return to calculate the downside deviation, the investor's minimum acceptable return or the risk-free rate is typically used.

Sortino ratio = (Annualized rate of return − Annualized risk-free rate)/Downside deviation

The **gain-to-loss ratio** measures the ratio of positive returns to negative returns over a specified period of time. The higher the gain-to-loss ratio (in absolute value), the better:

Gain-to-loss ratio = (Number months with positive returns / Number months with negative returns) × (Average up-month return / Average down-month return)

AI

### Managed Futures

Managed futures are private pooled investment vehicles that can invest in cash, spot, and derivative markets and have the ability to use leverage in a wide variety of trading strategies similar to hedge funds, with which they are often grouped. The distinguishing difference between hedge funds and managed futures is that managed futures trade exclusively in derivatives markets whereas hedge funds tend to be more active in spot markets while using futures markets for hedging.

## Managed Futures Market

Managed futures programs are an industry consisting of specialist professional money managers. In the United States, such programs are run by general partners known as commodity pool operators (CPOs), who are, or have hired, professional commodity trading advisors (CTAs) to manage money in the pool. In the United States, both CPOs and CTAs are registered with the U.S. Commodity Futures Trading Commission and National Futures Association (a self-regulatory body).

## Types of Managed Futures Investments

Managed futures are skill-based investment strategies like hedge funds and can been described as absolute-return strategies. Managed futures funds share the compensation structure of hedge funds consisting of a management fee plus incentive fee, typically a 2 plus 20 arrangement. Managed futures are classified according to investment style. The trading strategies of managed futures include the following:

- *Systematic trading strategies* trade according to a rules-based trading model usually based on past prices.
- *Discretionary trading strategies* trade financial, currency, and commodity futures and options.

By the markets emphasized in trading, managed futures may be classified as:

- *Financial* (trading financial futures/options, currency futures/options, and forward contracts).
- *Currency* (trading currency futures/options and forward contracts).
- *Diversified* (trading financial futures/options, currency futures/options, and forward contracts, as well as physical commodity futures/options).

A market classification can also be used to distinguish subcategories of systematic and discretionary trading strategies.

## Benchmarks and Historical Performance

The benchmarks for managed futures are similar to those for hedge funds, in that indices represent the performance of a group of managers who use a similar trading strategy or style. The CISDM CTA trading strategy benchmark is an example of a benchmark based on peer groups of CTAs.

For the 1990–2004 period, the volatility of the CTA$ Index (9.96%) was less than that of either the S&P 500 (14.65%) or the MSCI World Index (14.62%) but greater than that of U.S. or global bonds (4.46% and 5.23%, respectively). The Sharpe ratio for the CTA$ was better than those of equities but not those of bonds.

In general, the correlations among CTA strategies appear to be influenced by the degree to which the strategies are trend-following or discretionary. The overall dollar-weighted and equal-weighted indices are highly correlated with diversified, financial, and trend-following strategies and less correlated with currency and discretionary strategies.

In evaluating historical managed futures return data, the investor should be aware of the upward bias that survivorship can impart, in the order of 3.5% between the surviving CTAs and the full sample that includes defunct CTAs.

### Managed Futures: Investment Characteristics and Roles

Similar to hedge funds, managed futures are active skill-based strategies that investors can examine for the potential to improve a portfolio's risk and return characteristics.

Derivative markets are zero-sum games. As a result, the long-term return to a passively managed, unlevered futures position is the risk-free return less management fees and transaction costs. Therefore, for derivative-based investment strategies like managed futures to produce excess returns, there must be a sufficient number of hedgers. Hedgers pay a risk premium to liquidity providers for the insurance they obtain. If that condition is met, managed futures are able to earn positive excess returns (i.e., be the winning side in the zero-sum transactions). CTAs also attempt to conduct arbitrage when relationships are out of equilibrium.

Managed futures are useful in diversifying risk even in a diversified portfolio of stocks, bonds, and hedge funds. Managed futures frequently use derivatives and leverage in their strategies; therefore, investors should conduct the same due diligence as hedge funds.

## Distressed Securities

Distressed securities are the securities of companies that are in financial distress or near bankruptcy. Investing in distressed securities involves purchasing the claims of companies that have already filed for Chapter 11 (protection for reorganization) or are in immediate danger of doing so.



Investment strategies using distressed securities exploit the fact that many investors are unable to hold below-investment-grade securities because of regulatory or investment policy restrictions. Furthermore, relatively few analysts cover distressed securities markets and bankruptcies, resulting in unresearched investment opportunities for knowledgeable investors.

### Types of Distressed Securities Investments

Investors can access distressed securities investing through two structures:

1. Hedge fund structure
2. Private equity fund structure

Distressed securities managers trade in many types of assets, including the following:

- The publicly traded debt and equity securities of the distressed company
- Newly issued equity of a company emerging from reorganization that appears to be undervalued (**orphan equity**)
- Bank debt and trade claims
- "Lender of last resort" notes
- A variety of derivative instruments for hedging the market risk of a position

### Benchmarks and Historical Performance

Hedge fund industry data is the chief source for evaluating modern distressed securities investing. In the context of hedge funds, distressed securities investing is often classed as a substyle of event-driven strategies. The EACM, CISDM, and HFR indices all have distressed securities subindices.

For the period 1990–2004, the return distribution for distressed securities was non-normal, reflecting significant downside risk with a negative skewness. For the same period, distressed securities outperformed all stock and bond investments. The Sharpe ratio for the HRF Distressed Securities Index was 1.59, which was greater than the ratio for all the other assets. Because returns of distressed securities display negative skewness and high kurtosis, however, risk represented by standard deviation is probably understated.

In terms of performance, the strategy depends on the business cycle and how well the economy is doing. When the economy is not doing well, bankruptcies increase and this strategy does well.

### Distressed Securities: Investment Characteristics and Roles

Investors look to distressed securities investing primarily for the possibility of high returns from security selection (exploiting mispricing), activism, and other factors. Although certain types of distressed securities investing can be considered for risk-diversification potential, the risks are not well captured by such measures as correlation and standard deviation.

The market opportunity that distressed securities investing offers to some investors arises from the problems that corporate distress poses to other investors. Many investors are barred either by regulations or by their investment policy statements from holding below-investment-grade debt. These investors must sell any debt in their portfolios that has crossed the threshold from investment grade to high yield (**fallen angels**). In addition, banks and trade creditors prefer to convert their claims to cash rather than participate as creditors in a possibly long reorganization process. Failed leveraged buyouts also have been a source of distressed securities opportunities. The impetus of these investors to off-load distressed debt creates opportunities for bargain hunters.

AI

### Long-Only Value Investing

The simplest approach to distressed debt investing involves investing in perceived undervalued distressed securities in the expectation that they will rise in value as other investors see the distressed company's prospects improve. When the distressed securities are public debt, this approach is **high-yield investing**. When the securities are orphan equities, this approach is **orphan equities investing**.

### Distressed Debt Arbitrage

**Distressed debt arbitrage (distressed arbitrage)** involves purchasing the traded bonds of bankrupt companies and selling the common equity short. The hedge fund manager attempts to buy the debt at deep discounts. If the company's prospects worsen, the value of the company's debt and equity should decline, but the hedge fund manager hopes that the equity, in which the fund has a short position, will decline to a greater degree. As a residual claim, the value of equity may be wiped out. If the company's prospects improve, the portfolio manager hopes that debt will appreciate at a higher rate than the equity because the initial benefits to a credit improvement accrue to bonds as the senior claim. Typically, the company will have already suspended any dividends, but debtholders will receive accrued interest.

### Private Equity

Private equity investing is an active approach because it involves corporate activism. The investor first becomes a major creditor of the target company to obtain influence on the board of directors or on the creditor committee. The investor buys the debt at deep discounts, and then assists in the recovery or reorganization process. The objective is to increase the value of the troubled company by deploying the company's assets more efficiently than in the past. If the investor obtains new shares in the company as part of the reorganization, the investor hopes to sell them subsequently at a profit.

Distressed securities investors following an active approach are aggressive in protecting and increasing the value of their claims; they are often referred to as "vulture" investors, and their funds as "vulture capital." If the company is turned around, other parties benefit, and the vultures are bearing risk that other investors wish to transfer to them.

The risks of a distressed securities strategy include:

- Event risk
- Market liquidity risk
- Market risk
- J-factor risk, which relates to the past precedents set by the judge that will oversee the bankruptcy proceedings in court.

# Study Session 14: Risk Management

RM

# RISK MANAGEMENT
Cross-Reference to CFA Institute Assigned Reading #25

## Risk Management Process

The process of risk management involves the following four steps:

1. *Identify risks.* Risks include financial risks and nonfinancial risks.
2. *Define risk tolerance.* Level of risk tolerance depends on clients and management.
3. *Measure risk.* Provide quantitative measures of risk, such as beta, standard deviation, and duration.
4. *Execute revisions and adjustments* when risk measures are out of line.

Risk management involves more than risk reduction or hedging. Risk management is a general practice that involves risk modification.

## Risk Governance

Risk governance is an element of corporate governance. Risk governance can be achieved by using enterprise risk management (ERM) in six steps.

1. Identify each risk factor to which the company is exposed.
2. Quantify each risk factor's size in monetary terms.
3. Map these inputs into a risk estimation calculation.
4. Identify overall risk exposure as well as the contribution to overall risk deriving from each risk factor.
5. Set up a process to report on these risks periodically to senior management.
6. Monitor compliance with policies and risk limits.

## Risk Identification

Financial risks are all risk factors derived from the external financial markets; nonfinancial risks are all other forms of risk. Financial risk factors are directly related to investments in security markets. Most of these risk factors can be hedged using derivative contracts. Financial risk includes six types of risk:

1. Market risk
2. Credit risk
3. Liquidity risk
4. Asset price risk
5. Exchange rate risk
6. Interest rate risk

RM

Nonfinancial risk factors are often difficult to hedge, yet they can be significant and we need to be fully aware of them and manage them. Nonfinancial risk includes the following eight types of risk, among others:

1. Operational risk
2. Model risk
3. Settlement risk (also known as Herstaat risk)
4. Regulatory risk
5. Legal/contract risk
6. Tax risk
7. Accounting risk
8. Sovereign and political risk

### Measuring Market Risk

Market risk can be measured in five ways:

1. Asset/portfolio return (not price) volatility, computed as the annualized return standard deviation ($\sigma$), measures the asset's or portfolio's overall return uncertainty.
2. Active risk, tracking risk, tracking error, or tracking error volatility is the volatility of the deviations of a portfolio's returns in excess of a stated benchmark portfolio's returns.
3. Beta ($\beta$) measures the amount of systematic risk in an asset's or a portfolio's returns.
4. Duration measures the sensitivity of a bond or bond portfolio to a small parallel shift in the yield curve.
5. Delta for options measures an option's sensitivity to a small change in the value of its underlying asset.

### Value at Risk (VaR)

Value at risk (VaR) has become an industry standard of risk measure. It is the minimum amount of money we expect to lose in a given reporting period with a given level of probability.

- VaR has a probability dimension and a time dimension (e.g., 5% VaR vs. 1% VaR, and monthly VaR vs. annual VaR).
- The true loss, based on the same given level of probability, is expected to be larger than the VaR amount because the VaR amount is the minimum level of loss.
- If the VaR is $X at a probability of 5% for a given time period, then the VaR is larger in magnitude when we reduce the probability to 1%. Know this property. It helps the candidate to understand VaR.

The analytical or variance-covariance method assumes normality in asset return distributions. Based on correlations between asset returns, using portfolio theory, we compute an analytical solution of the portfolio's mean and standard deviation in order to compute a VaR value.

The historical method is a nonparametric method. VaR estimates are based on historical realizations of past returns. From the historical return distributions, we compute, say, the 5th percentile and use the returns based on the 5th percentile to estimate a 5% VaR of a portfolio.

The Monte Carlo simulation method uses a probability distribution for each variable of interest to randomly generate outcomes according to each distribution. Based on a large pool of generated outcomes, we compute the VaR for a given probability of lowest outcome. It is used when an analytical solution is not available. Monte Carlo simulation uses computers to generate a large number of potential realizations of portfolio returns and to compute the VaR based on the simulated portfolio returns.

Surplus at risk is calculated when the VaR method is applied to pension fund portfolios. The goal is to estimate the probability and magnitude when a pension fund surplus goes negative.

Limitations of VaR: Even though VaR has been an industry standard for measuring risk exposures in recent years, the VaR measure and its methods have their limitations, including these three:

1. VaR can be difficult to estimate, and different methods may yield different VaR values.
2. VaR considers only the downside risk and fails to incorporate upside benefits.
3. VaR calculation is often based on distributional assumptions, which may not be valid.

### Stress Testing

In addition to VaR analysis, stress testing is also performed in risk management. The goal of stress testing is to identify unusual conditions that would lead to losses in excess of a threshold.

Scenario analysis examines the value of a portfolio under different extreme conditions called stylized scenarios. These extreme conditions may be based on historical actual extreme events or on hypothetical events. For example:

- Stock index experiences a large (10%) increase or decrease.
- Stock market volatility (VIX) doubles or triples over a short period of time.
- Major exchange rates change by a large percentage.
- There is a sudden decrease of market liquidity in one asset class or in multiple asset classes.

Stressing models are another way to perform stress tests.

- The challenge in the stressing model is that the risk manager needs to build a mathematical model to value the portfolio of securities. Then the risk manager performs something called factor push, which is a process of pushing the risk factor(s) in the model to produce the worst-case scenario of the value of the portfolio.
- Stress testing provides a complementary dimension to VaR measures and helps portfolio managers to be more effective in portfolio risk management.

There are two other methods:

1. Maximum loss optimization—optimize mathematically the risk variables that will produce the maximum loss.
2. Worst-case scenario analysis—examine the worst case that we expect to occur.

### Measuring Credit Risk

Credit losses have two dimensions: the likelihood of loss and the associated amount of loss in case a loss occurs. Credit risk exposure is partitioned into two components: current credit risk and potential credit risk.

- Current credit risk is also known as jump-to-default risk. It is the risk of ongoing default or a pending default that will occur in the immediate future.
- Potential credit risk is risk of possible default in the future.
- Another type of credit risk can be viewed as a hybrid of current credit risk and potential credit risk. It is the risk to a portfolio manager that a counterparty defaults on a current debt obligation to a third-party creditor. A cross-default provision triggers default of the counterparty.

Credit VaR (default VaR) reports the minimum expected loss due to a negative credit event with a given probability during a period of time.

Credit risk exposure exists in a corporate setting. Stocks of a levered firm can be viewed as a call option on the firm's assets. Bonds of a levered firm can be viewed as a portfolio of a long default-free bond and a short put option on the firm's assets.

### The Credit Risk of Forward Contracts

Because there is no marking to market in a forward contract, gains and losses in a forward contract accumulate over time. The counterparty that holds a positive value (an asset) in the forward contract carries the credit risk of its counterparty (who holds a liability in the forward contract). Note that the counterparty holding a liability does not carry (current) credit risk of the party who holds a positive value in the forward contract. The exposure of the credit risk is the value of the forward contract.

### The Credit Risk of Swaps

The statements about credit risk in a forward contract apply to a swap contract. A swap contract involves multiple transactions. The counterparties should be aware of both current credit risk and potential credit risk.

The amount of credit risk varies significantly over the life of a swap contract. For an interest rate swap and an equity swap, potential credit risk is highest during the middle period of the swap's life. For a currency swap, potential credit risk is highest between the middle period and the end of the swap's life because notional principals are exchanged at the tenor of a currency swap.

### The Credit Risk of Options

Because of the nature of an option contract, credit risk applies to only option buyers. Option buyers cannot default, and they do not produce credit risk to their counterparties (option writers).

Option buyers carry the credit risk of option writers. When an option writer fails to fulfill the exercise of an option, the option writer defaults on the option contract and the option buyer suffers from the credit/default risk of the option writer. The magnitude of the credit risk exposure to an option buyer is the value of the option premium.

### Liquidity Risk

Liquidity risk is a key risk factor facing all traders and portfolio managers. Wide bid–ask spreads, high price impact, low trading volume, and low turnover ratio are all associated with illiquid markets. To best incorporate liquidity risk, we can use liquidity-adjusted VaR instead of traditional VaR measures.

### Managing Risk

Risk should be managed in four ways:

1. Apply an effective risk governance model.
2. Use the enterprise risk management (ERM) system.
3. Use risk budgeting that is relevant in both an organizational and a portfolio management context.
   - Performance stop-outs
   - Working capital allocations
   - VaR limits
   - Scenario analysis limits
   - Risk factor limits
   - Position concentration limits
   - Leverage limits
   - Liquidity limits
4. Reduce or transfer credit risk:
   - Reduce credit risk by limiting exposure.
   - Reduce credit risk by marking to market.
   - Reduce credit risk by requiring collateral.
   - Reduce credit risk by netting.
   - Reduce credit risk with minimum credit standards and enhanced derivative product companies.
   - Transfer credit risk with credit derivatives.

### Performance Evaluation

1. The Sharpe ratio is one of the most popular performance measures. It has become the industry standard of risk-adjusted performance benchmark. It measures the reward-to-risk ratio, and it measures excess return (over the risk-free rate) per unit of standard deviation of the returns. The higher the Sharpe ratio, the better the performance on a risk-adjusted basis.

$$\text{Sharpe ratio} = \frac{\text{Mean portfolio return} - \text{Risk-free rate}}{\text{Standard deviation of portfolio returns}}$$

2. Risk-adjusted return on capital (RAROC): Its general form of definition is the ratio of expected return on an investment and a measure of the investment's risk. A project or an investment is considered a good one if the RAROC is higher than a certain preset benchmark.
3. Return over maximum drawdown (RoMAD): Maximum drawdown is the maximum difference between a fund's previous high-water mark and its subsequent level. Return over the maximum drawdown is the rate of return of a fund over its drawdown level.



 

4. Sortino ratio measures the excess portfolio return over a minimum acceptable return (MAR) divided by the downside deviation. The Sortino ratio is similar to the Sharpe ratio. The benchmark rate is set to be a MAR instead of the risk-free rate, and the risk measure is set to be downside deviation instead of the standard deviation of the portfolio returns.

$$\text{Sortino ratio} = \frac{\text{Mean portfolio return} - \text{MAR}}{\text{Downside deviation of portfolio returns}}$$

## Capital Allocation

Capital allocation is a key step in risk management. There are five aspects:

1. Nominal, notional, or monetary position limits
2. VaR-based position limits
3. Maximum loss limits
4. Internal capital requirements
5. Regulatory capital requirements

# Study Session 15: Risk Management Applications of Derivatives

DE

# RISK MANAGEMENT APPLICATIONS OF FORWARD AND FUTURES STRATEGIES

Cross-Reference to CFA Institute Assigned Reading #26

The goal of this reading is to understand how to use forward and futures contracts to achieve a particular level of risk exposure of an underlying risk factor. Risk factors include market risk, sector risk, interest rate risk, currency risk, and others. We may either reduce our existing risk exposure (hedging) or increase our existing risk exposure (speculation).

## Managing Equity Market Risk

Market risk is measured by beta, so our risk management of an equity portfolio is all around beta measures. The current stock portfolio has a beta $\beta_S$, the stock index futures have a beta $\beta_f$, and the target beta of the stock portfolio is $\beta_T$. We have the following relation:

$$\beta_T S = \beta_S S + N_f \beta_f f$$

We solve for the number of futures contracts needed to reach the target beta:

$$N_f = \left(\frac{\beta_T - \beta_S}{\beta_f}\right)\left(\frac{S}{f}\right)$$

Clearly, if the target beta $\beta_T$ is zero, $N_f$ will be negative, which means we need to sell stock index futures contracts to neutralize our existing long equity position. If the target beta $\beta_T$ is smaller (or greater) than the current beta $\beta_S$, $N_f$ will be negative (or positive), which means we need to sell (or buy) stock index futures contracts to reduce (or increase) our existing equity exposure.

## Creating Equity out of Cash

This section focuses on the following two pieces of logic:

$$\text{Long risk-free bond} + \text{Long futures} = \text{Long stock index}$$

$$\text{Long stock index} + \text{Short futures} = \text{Long risk-free bond}$$

The first equation demonstrates how to synthetically create a stock index fund: holding cash (a long risk-free bond) and buying stock index futures. The second equation demonstrates how to create cash out of equity: holding a stock index and selling stock index futures.

DE

The number of stock index futures contracts needed to achieve the goals is given by the following expression:

$$N_f^* = \text{Round}\left[\frac{V(1+r)^T}{fq}\right]$$

where $V$ is the amount of money to be invested, $r$ is the risk-free rate, $T$ is the investment horizon, $q$ is the futures contract price multiplier, $f$ is the stock index futures price, and $N_f^*$ is an integer representing the number of long stock index futures contracts to convert a cash position to an equity position or the number of short stock index futures contracts to convert an existing equity position into a cash position.

### Asset Allocation with Futures

Futures contracts can be used to adjust asset allocation among asset classes. The idea is simple. For a given existing portfolio, use stock index futures contracts to adjust the beta of the portfolio to its target beta level and use bond futures contracts to adjust the modified duration of the portfolio to its target modified duration. Stock index futures and bond futures allow us to synthetically lever up/down equity beta as well as bond modified duration. The technique is not new. It is a combination of what we covered in the previous two sections, where we independently handle the equity component and fixed-income component.

$$N_{Sf} = \left(\frac{\beta_T - \beta_S}{\beta_f}\right)\left(\frac{S}{f_S}\right)$$

$$N_{Bf} = \left(\frac{MDUR_T - MDUR_S}{MDUR_f}\right)\frac{B}{f_B}\beta_y$$

The first expression is the number of stock index futures contracts used to lever up (if $N_{Sf}$ is positive) or lever down (if $N_{Sf}$ is negative) the portfolio's existing equity market risk to achieve a synthetic target equity allocation. The second expression is the number of Treasury bond futures contracts used to lever up (if $N_{Bf}$ is positive) or lever down (if $N_{Bf}$ is negative) the portfolio's existing interest rate risk to achieve a synthetic target bond allocation.

Similarly, we can use futures contracts to adjust allocations between one bond class and another (e.g., long-term bonds and short-term bonds), or to adjust allocations between one equity class and another (e.g., large-cap and small-cap stocks, the S&P 500 Index, and the Nasdaq-100 Index).

Using futures contracts, we can also gain exposure to an asset class in advance of actually committing funds to that asset class. Essentially we buy futures contracts on that asset class today. When funds become available in the future, we close out futures contracts and commit funds to that asset class. Gains and/or losses from futures contracts would represent gains and/or losses in the underlying asset class as if we were to participate in that market today. The sequence of transactions can be best summarized by the following equation:

$$\text{Long risk-free bond} + \text{Long futures} = \text{Long stock index}$$

## Managing Foreign Currency Risk

If we expect to receive foreign currency in the future, we can sell currency futures or forward contracts today to lock in an exchange rate. If we expect to pay foreign currency in the future, we can buy currency futures or forward contracts today to lock in an exchange rate.

When we hold a foreign market portfolio, we are subject to both the equity risk in the foreign stock portfolio and currency exchange rate risk. Should we hedge both risk factors?

If we hedge the foreign equity risk by selling futures contracts on a foreign stock index, we get a foreign risk-free bond. At this point, we carry only exchange rate risk.

If we further hedge the exchange rate risk, we get a domestic risk-free bond.

## Forward Contracts versus Futures Contracts

Forward contracts and futures contracts can be compared in the following five ways:

1. Futures contracts are standardized. Forward contracts are customized.
2. Futures contracts are guaranteed by the clearinghouse against default. Forward contracts subject each party to the possibility of default by the other party.
3. Futures contracts require margin deposits and daily settlement of gains and losses. Forward contracts pay off the full value at the contracts' expiration.
4. Futures contracts are regulated. Forward contracts are essentially unregulated.
5. Futures contracts are conducted in a futures exchange. Forward contracts are negotiated privately.

DE

# RISK MANAGEMENT APPLICATIONS OF OPTION STRATEGIES

Cross-Reference to CFA Institute Assigned Reading #27

The goal of this reading is to help understand how to use call and put options to hedge or speculate equity, interest rate, and currency risks and how to use option and underlying asset combinations. Additionally, we need to understand how to use interest rate options to hedge future borrowing or lending transactions. Option Greeks are also covered in this reading.

## Option Strategies for Equity Portfolios

There are eight equity positions with or without options:

1. Long stock
2. Short stock
3. Long call
4. Short call
5. Long put
6. Short put
7. Covered call = long stock and short call
8. Protective put = long stock and long put

There are nine option combinations:

1. Bull spread = Buy an option and sell an otherwise identical option with a higher exercise price.
2. Bear spread (a short position in a bull spread) = Buy an option and sell an otherwise identical option with a lower exercise price.
3. Butterfly spread = Buy an option with a low exercise price; buy an otherwise identical option with a high exercise price; sell two otherwise identical options with an exercise price that is equal to the average exercise price of the first two options.
4. Collar = Buy stock, buy a put, and sell a call. If the call option premium and put option premium are the same, they would exactly offset each other because we have a long put and a short call. In the case where the call option premium is the same as the put option premium, the collar is called a zero-cost collar.
5. Straddle = Buy a call and buy an otherwise identical put.
6. Strap = Buy two calls and buy an otherwise identical put.
7. Strip = Buy a call and buy two otherwise identical puts.
8. Strangle = Buy a call and buy an otherwise identical put with a different exercise price.
9. Box spread = Buy a bull spread using call options and buy a bear spread using put options.

For each strategy, candidates should know the following six factors:

1. Value of the strategy at initiation
2. Value of the strategy at option expiration
3. Profits of the strategy at option expiration
4. Maximum profit
5. Maximum loss
6. Breakeven point(s)

### Interest Rate Option Strategies

The payoff of an interest rate call option is:

$$\text{Interest rate call option payoff} = \text{Notional principal} \times \max(\text{Underlying rate at expiration} - \text{Exercise rate}, 0) \times \frac{\text{Days in underlying rate}}{360}$$

The payoff of an interest rate put option is:

$$\text{Interest rate put option payoff} = \text{Notional principal} \times \max(\text{Exercise rate} - \text{Underlying rate at expiration}, 0) \times \frac{\text{Days in underlying rate}}{360}$$

### Using Interest Rate Calls with Borrowing

When we have a scheduled borrowing transaction in the future, we are at the risk of interest rate increases, which in turn increases our cost of debt. To reduce this risk while keeping the benefit of potential rate decreases in the future, we may purchase an interest rate call option. A five-step sequence of transactions is as follows:

1. Today we purchase an interest rate call option. The call option's expiration should match the timing of a future borrowing event. The duration of the underlying interest rate of the call option should match the term of the loan. For example, in January, we decide to borrow funds in March for six months. To implement the strategy, we should buy an interest rate call option on the six-month LIBOR rate in January that matures in March.
2. At the loan initiation, we go ahead to borrow at the spot rate in the bond market. If the borrowing rate is lower than the interest rate call option's exercise rate, the call option expires worthless and we enjoy low cost of debt. If the borrowing rate is higher than the interest rate call option's exercise rate, the call option generates a payoff that will be delivered at the end of the loan repayment date. Note that the payoff of an interest rate option is *not* delivered at the option expiration; rather, it is delivered one time period after option expiration. Using the previous example, in March, if the interest rate call option finishes in-the-money, the call option payoff is paid in September (and not in March at option expiration).
3. We need to consider both the call option premium as well as the time value (opportunity cost/financing cost) of the call option premium. We should reduce from the amount we receive on the day of borrowing by the future value of the call option premium. The future value reflects both the call option premium and any and all interest on the call premium accrued between the option purchase and loan initiation (option expiration). The net amount is the funds we receive after considering hedging costs. Using the previous example, in March, we should reduce the call option premium and financing cost (interest accrued) between January and March from the funds we receive in March.
4. At the loan expiration, we need to pay off the loan, but if the call option was previously finished in-the-money, the call option payoff is harvested at the loan expiration. So the net cash flow, the future value of the loan (a cash outflow from

the borrowing firm's perspective) less the call option payoff (a cash inflow from the borrowing firm's perspective), if any, is the total cost of the loan after considering hedging benefits. Using the previous example, in September, we should subtract the call option payoff (if any) from the future value of the loan to reach the net cash flow after considering hedging benefits.

5. The yield implied by the net cash flow in step 3 (present value [PV]) and the net cash flow in step 4 (future value [FV]) is the effective cost of the borrowing after using an interest rate call.

### Using Interest Rate Puts with Lending

When we have a scheduled lending (investing) transaction in the future, we are at the risk of interest rate declines, which in turn reduces our investment rate of return. To reduce this risk while keeping the benefit of potential rate increases in the future, we may purchase an interest rate put option. A five-step sequence of transactions is as follows:

1. Today we purchase an interest rate put option. The put option's expiration should match the future lending/investment horizon. The duration of the underlying interest rate of the put option should match the term of the lending/investment. For example, in January, we decide to invest funds in March for six months. To implement the strategy, we should buy an interest rate put option on the six-month LIBOR rate in January that matures in March.
2. On the day of lending/investment, we go ahead to invest the funds at the spot rate. If the investment rate is higher than the interest rate put option's exercise rate, the put option expires worthless and we enjoy a high rate of return on our investment. If the investment rate is lower than the interest rate put option's exercise rate, the put option generates a payoff that will be delivered at the end of the investment horizon. Note that the payoff of an interest rate option is *not* delivered at the option expiration; rather, it is delivered one time period after option expiration. Using the previous example, in March, if the interest rate put option finishes in-the-money, the put option payoff is paid in September (and not in March at option expiration).
3. We need to consider both the put option premium as well as the time value (opportunity cost/financing cost) of the put option premium. We should increase the amount we invest by the future value of the put option premium. The future value reflects both the put option premium and any and all interest on the put premium accrued between the option purchase and start of the investment (option expiration). The total amount is the funds we committed after considering hedging costs. Using the previous example, in March, we should add the put option premium and financing cost (interest accrued) between January and March to the funds we invest in March.
4. At the end of the investment horizon, we need to harvest our investment, but if the put option was previously finished in-the-money, the put option payoff is also captured at the end of the investment horizon. So the total cash flow, the future value of the investment (a cash inflow from the investment firm's prospective) plus the put option payoff (a cash inflow from the investment firm's prospective), if any, is the total benefit of the investment after considering hedging activities. Using the previous example, in September, we should add the put option payoff (if any) to the future value of the investment to reach the total cash inflow after considering hedging benefits.
5. The yield implied by the total cash flow in step 3 (PV) and the total cash flow in step 4 (FV) is the effective rate of return of the investment after using the interest rate put.

### Using an Interest Rate Cap or Floor with a Floating-Rate Loan

A floating-rate loan may extend over multiple years. During the life of the floater, the underlying floating rate may change dramatically. High floating rates bring benefits to holders and harm to issuers of floaters, whereas low floating rates bring benefits to issuers and harm to holders of floaters. Interest rate caps and interest rate floors are perfect derivative instruments to hedge or speculate interest rate risks in floating-rate bonds.

An interest rate cap is a portfolio of individual interest rate call options called caplets. Each caplet has a unique expiration. The collection of all maturities of caplets covers the maturities of the interest rate cap. Similarly, an interest rate floor is a portfolio of individual interest rate put options called floorlets. Each floorlet has a unique expiration. The collection of all maturities of floorlets covers the maturities of the interest rate floor.

The issuer of a floater may buy an interest rate cap so that when the underlying interest rate is high, the payoff from the interest rate cap offsets any excess interest costs beyond the interest rate cap's exercise rate, so that the floater becomes a rate-capped floater. Mathematically:

$$-\text{Floater} + \text{Interest rate cap} = -\text{Rate-capped floater}$$

Similarly, a holder of a floater who does not expect interest rates to increase significantly may choose to sell an interest rate cap for its income. In this case, the holder synthetically holds a rate-capped floater.

$$\text{Floater} - \text{Interest rate cap} = \text{Rate-capped floater}$$

The holder of a floater may buy an interest rate floor so that when the underlying interest rate is low, the payoff from the interest rate floor makes up the difference between the interest rate floor's exercise rate and the spot rate, so that the floater becomes a rate-floored floater. Mathematically:

$$\text{Floater} + \text{Interest rate floor} = \text{Rate-floored floater}$$

Similarly, the issuer of a floater who does not expect interest rates to fall significantly may choose to sell an interest rate floor for its income. In this case, the issuer synthetically holds a rate-floored floater.

$$-\text{Floater} - \text{Interest rate floor} = -\text{Rate-floored floater}$$

### Using an Interest Rate Collar with a Floating-Rate Loan

Extending our previous discussion on interest rate caps and floors, if a holder of a floater sells an interest cap and buys an interest rate floor, this makes up an interest rate collar position. In this case the holder synthetically holds a rate-capped and rate-floored floater. The floating rate is always bounded above by the cap rate and bounded below by the floor rate.

$$\text{Floater} - \text{Interest rate cap} + \text{Interest rate floor} = \text{Rate-capped and rate-floored floater}$$

DE

## Option Greeks and Risk Management Strategies

Options are risky positions. An option trader does not hold an option positon without hedging it. To hedge an option, we need the hedge ratio, also known as option delta.

$$\text{Option delta} = \frac{\text{Change in option price}}{\text{Change in underlying stock price}} = \frac{\Delta c}{\Delta S}$$

To hedge $N_c$ number of options, we need $N_S$ number of stocks.

$$\Delta V = 0 = N_S \Delta S + N_c \Delta c$$

$$N_S = -N_c \frac{\Delta c}{\Delta S}$$

Because delta is a function of the underlying asset value, as the value changes, delta changes with it. Consequently, a previously constructed delta-hedged portfolio is no longer hedged after the underlying asset value changes. It is a problem because it requires a portfolio manager to monitor and rebalance a hedged portfolio frequently. Option gamma measures the sensitivity of option delta with respect to changes in the underlying stock price.

$$\text{Option gamma} = \frac{\text{Change in option delta}}{\text{Change in underlying stock price}}$$

As an option moves toward its expiration, the delta of an in-the-money call option moves toward 1; the delta of an in-the-money put option moves toward –1; the delta of an out-of-the-money option movies toward zero.

Gamma approaches zero as an option moves toward expiration, because delta moves toward a constant. However, gamma is greatest for options that are at-the-money and close to expiration because of the uncertainty of whether the option will be exercised or not.

Option value is also particularly sensitive to the volatility of the underlying asset returns. Option vega captures the sensitivity of option price changes with respect to changes in the stock return volatility, measured by annualized stock return standard deviation.

$$\text{Option vega} = \frac{\text{Change in option price}}{\text{Change in stock return volatility}}$$

# RISK MANAGEMENT APPLICATIONS OF SWAP STRATEGIES

Cross-Reference to CFA Institute Assigned Reading #28

A swap is a financial contract in which two counterparties agree to exchange a sequence of cash flows. This reading covers applications of interest rate swaps, currency swaps, equity swaps, and swaptions.

## Using Interest Rate Swaps to Convert a Floating-Rate Loan to a Fixed-Rate Loan (and Vice Versa)

A pay fixed, receive floating interest rate swap can be viewed as a portfolio of a long floating-rate bond and a short fixed-rate bond. Similarly, a pay floating, receive fixed interest rate swap can be viewed as a portfolio of a long fixed-rate bond and a short floating-rate bond. Based on this insight, we have the following:

| Floating-rate bond = Fixed-rate bond + [Pay fixed, receive floating interest rate swap] |
|---|

| Fixed-rate bond = Floating-rate bond + [Pay floating, receive fixed interest rate swap] |
|---|

These two equations are the recipe for converting a floater to a fixed-rate bond or converting a fixed-rate bond to a floater.

## Using Swaps to Adjust the Duration of a Fixed-Income Portfolio

An interest rate swap can be viewed as a portfolio of a long floating/fixed-rate bond and a short fixed/floating-rate bond. The value of an interest rate swap is sensitive to interest rate changes. Consequently, an interest rate swap has duration, just like a bond does.

Now we need to make two assumptions:

1. The duration of a fixed-rate bond is 75% of its maturity in years (e.g., a 10-year fixed-rate bond has a duration of 7.5).
2. The duration of a floating-rate bond is 50% of coupon resetting period in years (e.g., a 7-year floating-rate bond with semiannual coupon payment has a duration of 0.25).

The duration of an interest rate swap is the difference between the long bond's duration and the short bond's duration.

| Duration [Pay fixed and receive floating interest rate swap] = Duration(Floating-rate bond)<br>– Duration (Fixed-rate bond) |
|---|

| Duration [pay floating and receive fixed interest rate swap] = Duration (Fixed-rate bond)<br>– Duration (Floating-rate bond) |
|---|

DE

With these properties in mind, we are ready to use interest rate swaps to lever up or lever down duration of an existing bond portfolio to a target duration. To achieve a target portfolio duration, we may use an interest rate swap based on the following relation:

$$V_P(MDUR_P) + NP(MDUR_S) = V_P(MDUR_T)$$

or:

$$NP = V_P\left(\frac{MDUR_T - MDUR_P}{MDUR_S}\right)$$

where $MDUR_S$ is the modified duration of an interest rate swap, and $NP$ is the required notional principal to change the duration of the existing portfolio duration $MDUR_P$ to the target duration of $MDUR_T$.

### Using Swaps to Create and Manage the Risk of Structured Notes

Interest rate swaps can be used to create and manage leveraged floating-rate notes (leveraged floaters) and inverse floaters.

Leveraged floaters: A firm intends to issue a leveraged floater with a notional principal of *FP* and a floating rate of *kL*, where *k* is the leverage factor (e.g., 2.5) and *L* is the LIBOR rate. There are three steps to the process.

1. To achieve the goal, the firm enters into an interest rate swap with a notional principal of *k*(*FP*). The firm chooses to be the fixed rate (*FS*) payer and floating rate receiver. The firm pays (*FS*)*k*(*FP*) and receives (*L*)*k*(*FP*), where *FS* is the fixed rate in the interest rate swap to make the interest rate swap have a zero value at swap initiation. *FS* is the price of the swap.
2. The firm now passes through the cash inflow from the interest rate swap (*L*)*k*(*FP*) as interest payments of the leveraged floater with a notional principal of *FP* and a floating rate of *kL*.
3. Now the issuer may sell a leveraged floater with a notional principal of *FP* and a floating rate of *kL* and use the funds to buy a fixed-rate bond to (partly) offset the fixed-rate payments in the interest rate swap (*FS*)*k*(*FP*). The leveraged floater is successfully engineered.

Inverse floaters: A firm intends to issue an inverse floater with a notional principal of *FP* and a floating rate of (*b* – *L*), where *b* is a constant rate (e.g., 8%) and *L* is the LIBOR rate. There are three steps to the process.

1. To achieve the goal, the firm enters into an interest rate swap with a notional principal of *FP*. The firm chooses to be the fixed rate (*FS*) receiver and floating rate payer. The issuer pays *L*(*FP*) and receives (*FS*)(*FP*), where *FS* is the fixed rate in the interest rate swap to make the interest rate swap have a zero value at swap initiation. *FS* is the price of the swap.
2. The firm now issues an inverse floater with a notional principal of *FP* and a floating rate of (*b* – *L*). Interest payment is (*b* – *L*)*FP*. Cash inflow from the interest rate swap

is $(FS)(FP)$. Cash outflow from the interest rate swap is $L(FP)$. Consequently, the total cash flow to the firm is:

$$-(b-L)FP+(FS)(FP)-L(FP)=(FS-b)(FP)$$

3. The inverse floater is successfully engineered.

If the constant rate $b$ is chosen to be $FS$, the net cash flow to the firm is zero. Otherwise, the firm has a net positive or negative fixed-rate cash flow, depending on the sign of $(FS-b)$ being positive or negative.

### Strategies and Applications for Managing Exchange Rate Risk

The cost of raising capital in a foreign country can be substantially high. To reduce a firm's cost of foreign debt, the firm may choose to (1) issue domestic debt and (2) use a currency swap to synthetically convert the domestic debt into a foreign debt. The goal is to avoid the high cost of directly issuing debt in a foreign country.

A currency swap can be viewed as a portfolio of a long bond in one currency and a short bond in another currency. For example, a pay dollars and receive euros currency swap can be viewed as a portfolio of a long bond in euros and a short bond in U.S. dollars.

$$\text{Currency swap} = \text{Bond}_{€} - \text{Bond}_{\$}$$

### Converting a Loan in One Currency into a Loan in Another Currency

A portfolio manager who holds a bond denominated in U.S. dollars may use a currency swap to synthetically convert the bond into a bond denominated in a foreign currency, say, euros.

$$\text{Bond}_{\$} + \text{Currency swap} = \text{Bond}_{\$} + (\text{Bond}_{€} - \text{Bond}_{\$}) = \text{Synthetic bond}_{€}$$

Similarly, a U.S. corporation that intends to issue a bond denominated in Japanese yen may find it more cost efficient to issue a bond at home and use a currency swap to synthetically convert the U.S. dollar bond into a Japanese yen bond.

$$-\text{Bond}_{\$} + \text{Currency swap} = -\text{Bond}_{\$} + (\text{Bond}_{\$} - \text{Bond}_{¥}) = -\text{Synthetic bond}_{¥}$$

### Converting Foreign Cash Receipts into Domestic Currency

Another use of currency swaps is to convert a sequence of foreign cash receipts into domestic cash receipts. Here we negotiate a currency swap, where we do not exchange the notional principals either at the beginning or at the end of the currency swap. All we exchange are the "coupon" payments of the domestic and foreign bonds. The transformation of cash flows is similar to the conversion of bonds denominated in one currency to bonds denominated in a different currency using currency swaps. The mathematics is expressed as follows:

$$\text{Cash flow}_{\$} + \text{Currency swap} = \text{Cash flow}_{\$} + (\text{Cash flow}_{€} - \text{Cash flow}_{\$})\ \text{Synthetic cash flow}_{€}$$

### Using Currency Swaps to Create and Manage the Risk of a Dual-Currency Bond

A dual-currency bond is a bond on which the interest is paid in a foreign currency and the principal is paid in the home currency. It can be useful to a firm with periodic foreign cash receipts or foreign cash payments. A firm may hedge the risk of interest payments in a foreign currency by using currency swaps, similarly to the preceding example.

$$\begin{aligned}\text{Interest payments}_{€} + \text{Currency swap} &= \text{Interest payments}_{€} + (\text{Interest payments}_{\$} \\ &\quad - \text{Interest payments}_{€}) \\ &= \text{Synthetic interest payments}_{\$}\end{aligned}$$

### Strategies and Applications for Managing Equity Market Risk

In an equity swap, one party pays returns on a stock index and receives returns on (1) another stock or a different stock index, (2) a bond portfolio, or (3) another security.

### Diversifying a Concentrated Portfolio

An equity swap can synthetically diversify a concentrated portfolio. Holders of a concentrated portfolio may enter into an equity swap where the holder pays the returns on the concentrated portfolio and receives the returns on a diversified stock index.

$$\begin{aligned}\text{Return on a concentrated portfolio} + \text{Equity swap} &= \text{Return on a concentrated portfolio} \\ &\quad + (\text{Return on a diversified stock index} \\ &\quad - \text{Return on a concentrated portfolio}) \\ &= \text{Synthetic return on a diversified stock index}\end{aligned}$$

### Achieving International Diversification

An equity swap can synthetically diversify a domestic portfolio. Holders of a domestic portfolio may enter into an equity swap where the holder pays the returns on the domestic portfolio and receives the returns on an international stock index.

$$\begin{aligned}\text{Return on a domestic portfolio} + \text{Equity swap} &= \text{Return on a domestic portfolio} \\ &\quad + (\text{Return on an international stock index} \\ &\quad - \text{Return on a domestic portfolio}) \\ &= \text{Synthetic return on an international stock index}\end{aligned}$$

### Changing an Asset Allocation between Stocks and Bonds

An equity swap can synthetically change asset allocation between stocks and bonds by adjusting the portfolio weights between the two asset classes. Consider a simple and naive case where a portfolio has only a stock index component and a bond fund component. Let the current portfolio weight of the stock component be $w_{cs}$ and let the target portfolio weight of the stock component be $w_{ts}$. We need to synthetically convert the $(w_{ts} - w_{cs})$ proportion of the existing portfolio from a stock index to a bond fund.

Return on a stock index + Equity swap = Return on a stock index
+ (Return on a bond fund − Return on a stock index)
= Synthetic return on a bond fund

### Strategies and Applications Using Swaptions

An American-style payer swaption holder has the right to enter an interest rate swap at any time during the life of the swaption as the fixed-rate payer paying the exercise rate specified in the swaption contract. It can be viewed as a put option on a bond because the payer swaption is in-the-money when interest rates go up.

An American-style receiver swaption holder has the right to enter an interest rate swap at any time during the life of the swaption as the fixed-rate receiver receiving the exercise rate specified in the swaption contract. It can be viewed as a call option on a bond because the receiver swaption is in-the-money when interest rates go down.

### Using an Interest Rate Swaption in Anticipation of a Future Borrowing

Consider a firm that intends to borrow funds in the future. The firm is at risk of increases of interest rates between now and a future issuing day because increases in interest rates make the firm's cost of debt higher. The firm may purchase a payer swaption to mitigate the risk of high interest rates in the future. Here is how, in three steps:

1. The firm buys a payer swaption today. The maturity of the swaption is the expected future borrowing day. The tenor of the underlying swap matches the remaining term of the loan after the borrowing day. The notional principal of the swap matches the size of loan.
2. On the borrowing day, the firm issues a bond at the spot market interest rate (say LIBOR). If LIBOR is lower than the exercise rate (call it *FS*) of the payer swaption, clearly, the payer swaption finishes out-of-the-money and expires worthless. The firm enjoys low rates of borrowing funds. However, if LIBOR is higher than the exercise rate (*FS*) of the payer swaption, the payer swaption finishes in-the-money. The firm exercises the payer swaption and enters into a pay fixed rate (*FS*) and receive LIBOR interest rate swap. The net cost of borrowing after considering the impact of the payer swaption is:

$$-\text{LIBOR} + \text{Payer swaption} = -\text{LIBOR} + (\text{LIBOR} - FS) = -FS$$

3. The payer swaption has effectively eliminated the borrowing firm's risk of facing high interest rates and kept the borrowing firm's potential benefits of enjoying low interest rates.

DE

### Using an Interest Rate Swaption to Terminate a Swap

Another use of a swaption is to terminate an existing swap. Here is how to terminate a pay fixed and receive floating interest rate swap, in five steps.

1. Consider a firm that holds an existing pay fixed ($X\%$) and receive floating (LIBOR) interest rate swap that has five years to maturity. The firm is concerned that in two years interest rates may decrease, making the swap a liability to the firm.
2. The firm buys a receiver swaption with an exercise rate of $Y\%$. The swaption expires in two years on a three-year swap.
3. In two years, when the swaption expires, let the fixed rate in a three-year interest rate swap be $Z\%$.
4. If $Z\%$ is higher than $Y\%$, the receiver swaption expires worthless. The LIBOR rates must be high and the firm's existing swap is an asset to the firm. The firm may either keep the existing swap alive or enter into a new pay floating (LIBOR) and receive fixed ($Z\%$) interest rate swap. With the new swap, the annualized net cash flow to the firm would be:

$$(-X\% + \text{LIBOR}) + (Z\% - \text{LIBOR}) = Z\% - X\%$$

   The firm has synthetically terminated the existing swap.
5. If $Z\%$ is lower than $Y\%$, the receiver swaption expires in-the-money. The LIBOR rates must be low and the firm's existing swap is a liability to the firm. The firm exercises the swaption and enters into a new pay floating (LIBOR) and receive fixed ($Y\%$) interest rate swap. With the new swap, the annualized net cash flow to the firm would be:

$$(-X\% + \text{LIBOR}) + (Y\% - \text{LIBOR}) = Y\% - X\%$$

   The firm has synthetically terminated the existing swap.

Here is how to terminate a receive fixed and pay floating interest rate swap, in five steps.

1. Consider a firm that holds an existing receive fixed ($X\%$) and pay floating (LIBOR) interest rate swap that has five years to maturity. The firm is concerned that in two years interest rates may increase, making the swap a liability to the firm.
2. The firm buys a payer swaption with an exercise rate of $Y\%$. The swaption expires in two years on a three-year swap.
3. In two years, when the swaption expires, let the fixed rate in a three-year interest rate swap be $Z\%$.
4. If $Z\%$ is lower than $Y\%$, the payer swaption expires worthless. The LIBOR rates must be low and the firm's existing swap is an asset to the firm. The firm may either keep the existing swap alive or enter into a new receive floating (LIBOR) and pay fixed ($Z\%$) interest rate swap. With the new swap, the annualized net cash flow to the firm would be:

$$(X\% - \text{LIBOR}) + (\text{LIBOR} - Z\%) = X\% - Z\%$$

   The firm has synthetically terminated the existing swap.

5. If $Z\%$ is higher than $Y\%$, the payer swaption expires in-the-money. The LIBOR rates must be high and the firm's existing swap is a liability to the firm. The firm exercises the swaption and enters into a new receive floating (LIBOR) and pay fixed ($Y\%$) interest rate swap. With the new swap, the annualized net cash flow to the firm would be:

$$(X\% - \text{LIBOR}) + (\text{LIBOR} - Y\%) = X\% - Y\%$$

The firm has synthetically terminated the existing swap.

### Synthetically Removing a Call Feature from Callable Debt or Adding It to Noncallable Debt

This part of swaptions is very interesting. To make this challenging topic simple, we need to revisit the first two statements we made at the beginning of the swaption section of this reading:

> An American-style payer swaption holder has the right to enter an interest rate swap at any time during the life of the swaption as the fixed-rate payer paying the exercise rate specified in the swaption contract. It can be viewed as a put option on a bond because the payer swaption is in-the-money when interest rates go up.
>
> An American-style receiver swaption holder has the right to enter an interest rate swap at any time during the life of the swaption as the fixed-rate receiver receiving the exercise rate specified in the swaption contract. It can be viewed as a call option on a bond because the receiver swaption is in-the-money when interest rates go down.

The key insight is that a payer swaption is a put option on a bond and that a receive swaption is a call option on a bond.

$$\text{Payer swaption} = \text{Put option on a bond}$$

$$\text{Receiver swaption} = \text{Call option on a bond}$$

Additionally, we establish the nature of callable and putable bonds:

$$\text{Callable bond} = \text{Straight bond} - \text{Call option on a bond}$$

$$\text{Putable bond} = \text{Straight bond} + \text{Put option on a bond}$$

Combining these properties, we can achieve any transformation between callable, putable, and straight bonds with great ease:

To add a call feature to a straight bond:

$$\begin{aligned}\text{Straight bond} - \text{Receiver swaption} &= \text{Straight bond} - \text{Call option on a bond} \\ &= \text{Callable bond}\end{aligned}$$

To remove a call feature from a callable bond:

Callable bond + Receiver swaption = Callable bond + Call option on a bond
= Straight bond

To add a put feature to a straight bond:

Straight bond + Payer swaption = Straight bond + Put option on a bond
= Putable bond

To remove a put feature from a putable bond:

Putable bond – Payer swaption = Putable bond – Put option on a bond
= Straight bond

# STUDY SESSION 16: TRADING, MONITORING, AND REBALANCING

TMR

# EXECUTION OF PORTFOLIO DECISIONS
## Cross-Reference to CFA Institute Assigned Reading #29

The investment process is supported by securities research, portfolio management, and securities trading. In this reading, we focus on securities trading. Keep in mind that a portfolio decision is not complete until security transaction orders are fully executed.

A portfolio manager plays three roles to:

1. Communicate effectively with professional traders.
2. Evaluate the quality of the execution services being provided for the firm's clients.
3. Take responsibility for achieving best execution on behalf of clients in the portfolio manager's role as a fiduciary.

TMR

### Types of Orders

There are seven main types of orders:

1. Market order: An instruction to execute an order promptly in the public markets at the best price available.
2. Limit order: An instruction to trade at the best price available but only if the price is at least as good as the limit price specified in the order. Limit orders carry execution uncertainty.
3. Market-not-held order: The order gives the agent greater discretion than a traditional market order to execute the trade. "Not held" means that the broker is not required to trade at any specific price or in any specific time interval, as would be required with a simple market order.
4. Participate (do not initiate) order: A variant of the market-not-held order. The broker is to be deliberately low-key and wait for and respond to initiatives of more active traders.
5. Best efforts order: The order gives the trader's agent even more discretion to work the order only when the agent judges market conditions to be favorable.
6. Market-on-open order: A market order to be executed at the opening of the market.
7. Market-on-close order: A market order to be executed at the close of the market.

Two types of trades are:

1. Principal trade: A trade with a broker in which the broker commits capital to facilitate the prompt execution of the trader's order to buy or sell.
2. Portfolio trade (or program trade or basket trade): A trade that involves an order that requires the execution of purchases (or sales) in a specified basket (list) of securities at as close to the same time as possible.

### Types of Markets

There are four types of markets:

1. Quote-driven markets are also called dealer markets. They rely on dealers to establish firm prices at which securities can be bought and sold. A dealer is also called a market maker, who provides liquidity to the market by posting bid and ask prices to buy and sell securities to satisfy market demand and supply. The bid price is the price at which a dealer is willing to buy a security, and the ask price is the price at which a dealer is willing to sell a security. The ask price is higher than the bid price. The highest bid among all dealers is the market bid price, and the lowest ask price among all dealers is the market ask price. The difference between the ask price and the bid price is called the bid–ask spread. The effective spread is two times the deviation of the actual execution price from the midpoint of the market bid–ask quote. The number of shares (quantity) associated with the bid price is called the bid size, and the quantity associated with the ask price is called the ask size. The quoted spread is the simplest measure of round-trip transaction costs for an average-size order. The effective spread is a better representation of the true cost of a round-trip transaction because it captures both price improvement and market impact.
2. Order-driven markets are markets in which transaction prices are established by public limit orders to buy or sell a security at specified prices.
    - Electronic crossing networks (ECNs) are markets in which buy and sell orders are batched (accumulated) and crossed at a specific point in time.
    - Auction markets are markets in which the orders of multiple buyers compete for execution.
3. Brokered markets are markets in which transactions are largely performed through a search-brokerage mechanism away from public markets.
4. Hybrid markets are combinations of the aforementioned markets.

TMR

### Roles of Brokers and Dealers

Brokers have six roles:

1. Representing the order
2. Finding the opposite side of a trade
3. Supplying market information
4. Providing discretion and secrecy
5. Providing other supporting investment services
6. Supporting the market mechanism

Dealers have two roles:

1. Dealers face adverse selection risk.
2. Dealers provide liquidity to market participants.

### Evaluating Market Quality

A liquid market has the following three characteristics:

1. The market has relatively low bid–ask spreads.
2. The market is deep, meaning it has high quoted depth.
3. The market is resilient.

Market liquidity is affected by the following four factors:

1. Many buyers and sellers
2. Diversity of opinion, information, and investment needs among market participants
3. Convenience
4. Market integrity.

### Costs of Trading

There are four components of transaction costs:

1. The bid–ask spread
2. Market impact
3. Missed trade opportunity costs
4. Delay costs



### Volume-Weighted Average Price (VWAP)

Volume-weighted average price (VWAP) is the average price at which the security traded during the day, where each trade price is weighted by the fraction of the day's volume associated with the trade. The VWAP is an appealing price benchmark because it considers both transaction prices and transaction volume during the day.

Three advantages are:

1. The VWAP is easy to compute and easy to understand.
2. It can be computed quickly to assist traders during the execution.
3. It works best for comparing smaller trades in nontrending markets.

Four disadvantages are:

1. The VWAP does not account for costs of trades that are delayed or canceled.
2. It becomes misleading when a trade is a substantial proportion of trading volume.
3. It is not sensitive to trade size or market conditions.
4. It can be gamed by delaying trades.

### Implementation Shortfall

Implementation shortfall is the return difference between the return on a notional portfolio in which positions are established at the decision price, also known as the arrival price or the strike price, and the actual portfolio's return. It has four components:

1. Explicit costs, including commissions, taxes, and fees.
2. Realized profit or loss, reflecting the price movement from the decision price to the execution price for the part of the trade executed on the day it is placed.
3. Delay costs, also called slippage, reflecting the change in price (close-to-close price movement) over the day an order is placed when the order is not executed that day; the calculation is based on the amount of the order actually filled subsequently.
4. Missed trade opportunity cost (unrealized profit/loss), reflecting the price difference between the trade cancellation price and the original benchmark price based on the amount of the order that was not filled.

The implementation shortfall method correctly captures all elements of transaction costs. The method takes into account not only explicit trading costs, but also the implicit costs, which are often significant for large orders.

Five advantages are:

1. Links trading to portfolio manager activity; can relate cost to the value of investment ideas.
2. Recognizes the trade-off between immediacy and price.
3. Allows attribution of costs.
4. Can be built into portfolio optimizers to reduce turnover and increase realized performance.
5. Cannot be gamed.

TMR

Two disadvantages are:

1. Requires extensive data collection and interpretation.
2. Imposes an unfamiliar evaluation framework on traders.

### Pretrade Analysis

Market microstructure theory suggests that trading costs are systematically related to the following four factors:

1. Stock liquidity characteristics (e.g., market capitalization, price level, trading frequency, volume, index membership, bid–ask spread)
2. Risk (e.g., the volatility of the stock's returns)
3. Trade size relative to available liquidity (e.g., order size divided by average daily volume)
4. Momentum (e.g., it is more costly to buy in an up market than in a down market)

### Types of Traders

There are four types of traders:

1. Information-motivated traders seek timely trades.
2. Value-motivated traders use limit orders and seek to trade at the best prices.
3. Liquidity-motivated traders seek timely trades.
4. Passive traders seek low-cost trading.

### Trade Execution Decisions and Tactics

Three considerations in trading are:

1. Small, liquidity-motivated trades can be executed via direct market access and algorithmic trading.
2. Large, information-driven trades demand immediate skilled attention to manage the trade-off between price impact and delay costs.
3. Traders need to be aware of client trading restrictions, cash balances, and brokerage allocations.

### Objectives in Trading and Trading Tactics

There are five trading focuses:

1. Liquidity-at-any-cost trading focus
2. Costs-are-not-important trading focus
3. Need-trustworthy-agent trading focus
4. Advertise-to-draw-liquidity trading focus
5. Low-cost-whatever-the-liquidity trading focus

### Automated Trading



Automated or algorithmic trading refers to automated electronic trading subject to quantitative rules and user-specified benchmarks and constraints. The four strategies are:

1. Simple logical participation strategies:
   - Volume-weighted average price (VWAP) strategy
   - Time-weighted average price (TWAP) strategy
2. Implementation shortfall strategies, which seek to minimize the implementation shortfall by executing trades immediately provided there is enough liquidity to do so
3. Opportunistic participation strategies
4. Specialized strategies

### Serving the Client's Interests

The CFA Institute Trade Management Guidelines define best execution as "the trading process firms apply that seeks to maximize the value of a client's portfolio within the client's stated investment objectives and constraints." The Trade Management Guidelines are divided into three areas:

1. Processes
2. Disclosures
3. Record keeping

# MONITORING AND REBALANCING

Cross-Reference to CFA Institute Assigned Reading #30

Portfolio managers have to monitor and rebalance clients' portfolios based on investment policy statements (ISPs) to ensure that asset allocations do not deviate significantly from their preset target levels.

## Monitoring

TMR

Fiduciaries pay particular attention to adequate monitoring in fulfilling their ethical and legal responsibilities to clients. Portfolio managers monitor the following three areas:

1. Investor circumstances, including wealth and constraints:
    - Changes in investor circumstances and wealth
    - Changes in liquidity requirements
    - Changes in time horizons
    - Changes in tax circumstances
    - Changes in laws and regulations
    - Changes in unique circumstances
2. Market and economic changes:
    - Changes in asset risk attributes
    - Changes in market cycles
    - Changes in central bank policy
    - Changes in yield curve and inflation
3. The portfolio itself:
    - Tactical asset allocation
    - Style and sector exposures
    - Individual security exposures

## Costs and Benefits of Rebalancing

Portfolio rebalancing involves a trade-off between the costs and the benefits portfolio rebalancing.

Two costs are:

1. Transaction costs
2. Tax costs

Two benefits are:

1. Keep a portfolio's asset allocation at or near its target level to best reflect the client's preference and the mandate from the investment policy statement (ISP).
2. Control the risk of the overall portfolio within a range to fit the risk tolerance of the client.

## Rebalancing Disciplines

Five rebalancing disciplines are the following:

1. Calendar rebalancing is rebalancing on a periodic basis.
2. Percentage-of-portfolio rebalancing: Also known as percent-range or interval rebalancing, this is rebalancing when a preset rebalancing threshold or trigger point is reached.
3. Calendar-and-percentage-of-portfolio rebalancing is a hybrid of the first two methods.
4. Equal probability rebalancing: The manager specifies a corridor for each asset class as a common multiple of the standard deviation of the asset class's returns. Rebalancing to the target proportions occurs when any asset class weight moves outside its corridor.
5. Tactical rebalancing is a variation of calendar rebalancing that specifies less frequent rebalancing when markets appear to be trending and more frequent rebalancing when they are characterized by reversals.



## Factors That Affect Rebalancing Frequencies

Five factors affect rebalancing costs:

1. Transaction costs
2. Risk tolerance concerning tracking risk versus the strategic asset allocation
3. Correlation with other asset classes
4. Volatility
5. Volatilities of other asset classes

## The Perold–Sharpe Analysis of Rebalancing Strategies

Perold–Sharpe analysis deals with four types of rebalancing strategies:

1. Buy-and-hold strategies
2. Constant-mix strategies
3. Constant-proportion strategy and constant proportion portfolio insurance (CPPI)
4. Linear, concave, and convex investment strategies

## Execution Choices in Rebalancing

The following are execution choices to be made in rebalancing:

1. Cash market trades
2. Derivative market trades:
   - Lower transaction costs
   - More rapid implementation
   - Leaving active managers' strategies undisturbed

# Study Session 17: Performance Evaluation

PERF

# EVALUATING PORTFOLIO PERFORMANCE

Cross-Reference to CFA Institute Assigned Reading #31

*Ex post* performance evaluation is a crucial part of the investment management process. We focus on the following three elements from the perspective of fund sponsor and investment manager.

1. How a manager's portfolio performed relative to expectations: performance measurement
2. The sources of under- and outperformance: performance attribution
3. What the performance tells us about a manager's skills: performance appraisal

## Performance Measurement without Intraperiod Cash Flows

The holding period return without dividends or income and without additional cash inflows or outflows is given as:

$$r_t = \frac{MV_1 - MV_0}{MV_0}$$

If there are additional cash inflows or outflows, the holding period return should reflect the impact of these cash flows:

$$r_t = \frac{MV_1 - (MV_0 \pm CF_0)}{MV_0 \pm CF_0}$$

or:

$$r_t = \frac{(MV_1 \pm CF_1) - MV_0}{MV_0}$$

or:

$$r_t = \frac{(MV_1 \pm CF_1) - (MV_0 \pm CF_0)}{MV_0 \pm CF_0}$$

where $MV$ is the market value of the asset.

PERF

### Time-Weighted Rate of Return

The time-weighted rate of return (TWR) is the compound rate of return over a holding period. Its calculation requires that the account return be measured every time an external cash flow occurs.

$$r_{twr} = (1+r_{t1})\times(1+r_{t2})\times\ldots\times(1+r_{tn})-1$$

where each holding period return $r_{tk}$ considers both income yield and capital gains yield.

### Money-Weighted Rate of Return

The money-weighted rate of return (MWR) is the compound rate of return of an investment account over a holding period. It incorporates all additional cash investments and withdrawals to the account, which (partially) reflects market timing of the investor. The MWR is the internal rate of return (IRR) for a given sequence of cash flows to/from a portfolio.

$$MV_t = MV_0(1+r_{mwr})^t + CF_{t1}(1+r_{mwr})^{t-t1} + CF_{t2}(1+r_{mwr})^{t-t2} + \ldots + CF_{tn}(1+r_{mwr})^{t-tn}$$

where $r_{mwr}$ is the IRR of the set of cash flows.

PERF

Linked internal rate of return (LIRR) is the compounded money-weighted rate of return that measures the performance over multiple reporting periods.

Holding period returns and LIRRs might not be measured over a one-year period. Consequently, they might not be annualized returns. They measure the performance of a portfolio or a manager over a reporting period, which may differ from a year. Annualized holding period returns are holding period returns annualized over a one-year period, and they can be used to compare across different investments and across different managers.

### Characteristics of a Valid Benchmark

To be considered valid, benchmarks must have seven characteristics:

1. *Unambiguous:* A benchmark is well-defined.
2. *Investable:* The benchmark is a passive alternative to active management.
3. *Measurable:* The return performance of a benchmark is readily available.
4. *Appropriate:* A benchmark is consistent with the portfolio manager's style.
5. *Reflective of current investment opinions:* The manager has current investment knowledge (positive, negative, or neutral) of the securities or factor exposures within the benchmark.
6. *Specified in advance:* A benchmark is clearly specified before the beginning of an evaluation period.
7. *Acknowledged:* Both the sponsor and the manager recognize the benchmark as a fair basis of comparison.

### Alternative Benchmark Candidates

There are seven alternative benchmark candidates:

1. Absolute return
2. Manager universe
3. Board market index
4. Investment style index
5. Factor-model-based
6. Return-based
7. Custom security-based

### Steps to Construct a Custom Security-Based Benchmark

A custom security-based benchmark is constructed in five steps:

1. Identify prominent aspects of the manager's investment process.
2. Select securities consistent with that investment process.
3. Devise a weighting scheme for the benchmark securities, including a cash position.
4. Review the preliminary benchmark and make modifications.
5. Rebalance the benchmark portfolio on a predetermined schedule.

Fund sponsors often use the median account in a particular peer group as a return benchmark. It's measurable, but it has many weaknesses, such as these five:

1. It cannot be specified in advance.
2. It's not investable.
3. It's not unambiguous.
4. It's not appropriate.
5. It suffers from survivorship bias.

Benchmark quality tests have the following six considerations:

1. Systematic bias
2. Tracking error
3. Risk characteristics
4. Coverage
5. Turnover
6. Positive active positions

## Hedge Funds and Hedge Fund Benchmarks

$$r_v = r_P - r_B$$

$$r_v = \sum_{i=1}^{n}(w_{vi} \times r_i) = \sum_{i=1}^{n}[(w_{Pi} - w_{Bi}) \times r_i] = \sum_{i=1}^{n}(w_{Pi} \times r_i) - \sum_{i=1}^{n}(w_{Bi} \times r_i) = r_P - r_B$$

where:
$r_v$ = value-added return
$r_P$ = portfolio return
$r_B$ = benchmark return

## Performance Attribution

$$P = M + (B - M) + (P - B) = M + S + A$$

where:
$P$ = return performance of a portfolio under management
$M$ = return on market portfolio
$B$ = return on a market sector index that matches the portfolio's investment style
$A$ = portfolio manager's active return; $A = P - B$
$S$ = return contribution due to style selection; $S = B - M$

PERF

## Macro Attribution

Macro attribution is often performed at the fund sponsor level. It requires three sets of inputs:

1. Policy allocations
2. Benchmark portfolio returns
3. Fund returns, valuations, and external cash flows

Macro attribution analyzes the following six components of investment policy decision making:

1. Net contributions
2. Risk-free asset
3. Asset categories
4. Benchmarks
5. Investment managers
6. Allocation effect

## Micro Attribution

Micro attribution is often performed at the investment manager level. It focuses on value-added return:

$$r_v = r_P - r_B = \sum_{i=1}^{S}[(w_{Pi} - w_{Bi}) \times (r_{Bi} - r_B)] + \sum_{i=1}^{S}[(w_{Pi} - w_{Bi}) \times (r_{Pi} - r_{Bi})] + \sum_{i=1}^{S}[w_{Bi} \times (r_{Pi} - r_{Bi})]$$

$$\text{Pure selection allocation} = \sum_{i=1}^{S}[(w_{Pi} - w_{Bi}) \times (r_{Bi} - r_B)]$$

$$\text{Allocation / selection interaction effect} = \sum_{i=1}^{S}[(w_{Pi} - w_{Bi}) \times (r_{Pi} - r_{Bi})]$$

$$\text{Selection effect} = \sum_{i=1}^{S}[w_{Bi} \times (r_{Pi} - r_{Bi})]$$

## Fundamental Factor Models

Fundamental factor model micro attribution is performed to analyze active returns in the context of a factor model. The analysis identifies the portfolio exposure to these risk factors above and beyond the exposure of normal benchmark exposures. The incremental exposure in each risk factor is a strategic decision of the investment manager as a result of active management.

## Fixed-Income Micro Attribution

The total return of a fixed-income portfolio is made up of the following two groups of components:

1. Effect of the external interest environment:
   - Return on the default-free benchmark, assuming no change in forward rates
   - Return due to changes in forward rates
2. Contribution of the investment manager:
   - Return from interest rate management
   - Return from sector/quality management
   - Return from selection of specific securities
   - Return from trading activities

Fixed-income attribution analysis focuses on the manager's performance in addressing four factors within the manager's control:

1. Interest rate management effect
2. Sector/quality effect
3. Security selection effect
4. Trading activity

PERF

## Risk-Adjusted Performance Measures

The following are five risk-adjusted performance measures:

1. *Ex post* alpha

$$R_t - r_{ft} = \alpha + \beta(R_{Mt} - r_{ft}) + \varepsilon_t$$

2. Treynor measure

$$T_A = \frac{\overline{R}_A - \overline{r}_f}{\hat{\beta}_A}$$

3. Sharpe ratio

$$Sharpe\ ratio_A = \frac{\overline{R}_A - \overline{r}_f}{\hat{\sigma}_A}$$

4. $M^2$

$$M^2 = \overline{r}_f + \left(\frac{\overline{R}_A - \overline{r}_f}{\hat{\sigma}_A}\right)\hat{\sigma}_M$$

5. Information ratio

$$IR_A = \frac{\overline{R}_A - \overline{R}_B}{\hat{\sigma}_{A-B}}$$

PERF

Note that the *Ex post* alpha and Treynor measure provide the same conclusion about manager rankings because they are based on systematic risk. The Sharpe ratio and $M^2$ also provide the same conclusion about manager rankings because they are based on total risk.

## Performance Evaluation

Quality control charts are one effective and visual means of presenting the performance of an investment manager over time. It uses statistical methods to systematically evaluate performance data and assist in making retention or removal decisions.

Manager continuation policies (MCPs):

- Retain managers with investment skills.
- Remove managers without investment skills, and do so before they produce negative results.
- Minimize manager turnover.
- Include relevant nonperformance information in the manager review process.

Reduce the following two errors:

- Type I error: keeping (or hiring) managers who do not have investment skills.
- Type II error: firing (or not hiring) managers who do have investment skills.

# Study Session 18: Global Investment Performance Standards

GIPS

# OVERVIEW: GLOBAL INVESTMENT PERFORMANCE STANDARDS

Cross-Reference to CFA Institute Assigned Reading #32

## Purpose and Objectives of GIPS

### Goals and Objectives

Goals of the Global Investment Performance Standards (GIPS) Executive Committee:

- Establish industry-wide best practices for calculating and presenting performance information.
- Obtain worldwide acceptance of a common performance measurement and presentation standard based on principles of *fair representation* and *full disclosure*.
- Promote use of accurate and consistent performance information.
- Encourage fair, global competition for all markets without creating barriers to entry for new firms.
- Foster industry self-regulation on a global basis.

Objectives:

- Establish best practices for calculating and presenting performance information.
- Promote confidence that performance information has been prepared using globally common valuation principles and methods.
- Promote asset manager quality assessment by discussing how historical results were achieved.

### Key Characteristics and Scope

Key characteristics:

- Voluntary ethical standards.
- Intended to ensure fair representation and full disclosure; firms may have responsibility to include information not required by GIPS.

Scope:

- Apply to investment management firms and not to individuals.
- All actual fee-paying discretionary portfolio composites are defined by investment mandate, objective, or strategy.

IMPORTANT: Where GIPS conflicts with local law, firms should follow local law and make appropriate disclosures.

GIPS has *requirements* that must be followed, and *recommendations* that lead to best practices. Firms do not violate GIPS standards by following requirements but not recommendations.

## Provisions of the GIPS Standards

### Fundamentals of Compliance

GIPS standards apply on a firm-wide basis rather than only for a specific composite, asset class, strategy, or other.

Firms must comply with *all* requirements of the GIPS standards as well as provide any additional information required for fair representation and full disclosure.

- No compliance "except for"
- No partial compliance
- No characterizing as being "in accordance with," "in compliance with," or "consistent with the GIPS standards"

In addition to GIPS standards, firms must also comply with requirements and clarifications presented in:

- Guidance statements
- Interpretations
- Question-and-answer publications
- Clarifications published by GIPS Executive Committee and CFA Institute

IMPORTANT: Only an investment management firm may claim compliance; software providers and third-party performance measurement[1] vendors cannot.

Firms must establish, maintain, and consistently apply policies and procedures related to GIPS standards.

The firm may not refer to an individual account as having been calculated in compliance with the GIPS standards, except when presenting to the individual client.

Firms must not present false or misleading information.

IMPORTANT: Even if not organizationally separate, functional separation may qualify a unit as a distinct business entity.

GIPS

Firms are defined for GIPS compliance as an investment management firm, subsidiary, or division presented as a distinct business entity. A *distinct business entity* has:

- Organizational and functional segregation from other business entities
- Autonomy over the investment decision-making process
- Discretion over assets under management

*Total firm assets:* Fair value of *all* firm assets under investment management responsibility (even if not discretionary or fee-paying). Firms with discretion over subadvisors must include those results in firm composites. (Market value of all firm assets was used prior to January 1, 2011.)

Changes in firm definition must not alter composite performance history. In joint marketing, compliant performance must be segregated from noncompliant performance, and the compliant firm must be easily distinguished from other participating firms.

Recommendations:

- Comply with recommendations.
- Compliant performance should undergo third-party verification.
- Adopt the broadest, most meaningful definition of the firm.
- Annually provide a compliant presentation to each client.

### Input Data

Firms must capture and maintain all information required to produce compliant presentations:

- Use fair value data (i.e., not market value) beginning January 1, 2011:
  - Use market value (not cost or book value) prior to January 1, 2011.
  - Only use cost or book value for calculations requiring after-tax performance.
- Use trade data (rather than settlement date) accounting beginning January 1, 2005.
- Use accrual accounting for assets earning interest income:
  - It is recommended to accrue dividends as of ex-dividend date.

*External cash flows* describe capital that enters or leaves a portfolio. After January 1, 2010, portfolios must be revalued at each *large external cash flow* and end of each calendar month-end or last business day.

- Beginning January 1, 2001—at least monthly
- Prior to January 1, 2001—at least quarterly

GIPS standards do not specify "large" with respect to cash flows; firms must individually define it.

IMPORTANT: Firms must not opportunistically value portfolios at other times (i.e., to improve reported returns).

Firms must use the same beginning and ending annual dates (calendar or last business day) unless the composite reports on a non-calendar fiscal year.

Recommendations:

- Perform valuation at all (rather than just large) external cash flows.
- Obtain valuation from qualified independent third party; no source shopping to secure highest valuation.
- Accrue investment management fees for net-of-fee performance presentation.

GIPS

### Portfolio Return Calculations

Total return provides the best measure of portfolio return because it considers income and unrealized gain. In the case of no external cash flows:

$$r_t = \frac{V_t - V_0}{V_0}$$

If there are external cash flows, the inter-flow returns should be geometrically linked through the reporting period:

$$r_{twr} = (1+r_1)\times(1+r_2)\times\ldots\times(1+r_t)-1$$

GIPS standards require such time-weighted return linking at large external cash flows (although such linking at all cash flows is recommended).

Prior to January 1, 2005, GIPS allows midpoint return calculations (Dietz method) based on net external cash flow ($CF$):

$$r_{Dietz} = \frac{V_1 - V_0 - CF}{V_0 + 0.5CF}$$

Beginning January 1, 2005, GIPS requires daily weighted cash flows (modified Dietz method):

$$r_{Mod\ Dietz} = \frac{V_1 - V_0 - CF}{V_0 + \sum_{i=1}^{n} w_i CF_i}$$

The proportion of days the cash flow is in the portfolio is calendar days ($CD$) less the number of calendar days *before* the cash flow occurs ($D_i$):

$$w_i = \frac{CD - D_i}{CD}$$

If cash flows are assumed to occur at the beginning of the day, add 1 to the numerator.

The *modified IRR method* calculates the internal rate of return (IRR) for the period adjusted for cash flows:

GIPS

$$V_1 = \sum_{i=1}^{n}\left[CF_1(1+r)^{w_i}\right] + V_0(1+r)$$

The equation is solved for the value of $r$ that equates the weighted cash flows equal to the ending value. Because this is weighted by $w_i$, it qualifies as time-weighted. The original IRR would be money-weighted.

IMPORTANT: When calculating gross-of-fee returns where fees are bundled, the portion with the trading expense must be deducted, or, if not separable, the entire bundled fee must be deducted.

The portfolio manager's return must be included in portfolio composite returns even if a different manager earned the cash return.

Actual, not estimated, *trading expenses* (e.g., brokerage commissions, spreads from internal or external brokers, exchange fees and taxes) must be considered in the return calculation. *Custody fees* are not considered for return calculations.

Recommendations:

- Accrue withholding taxes subject to reclamation.
- Deduct non-reclaimable taxes when calculating return.

## Composite Return Calculations

A *composite* involves proportion-aggregated returns from portfolios similar in investment mandate, objective, or strategy. The composite return is the sum of individual portfolio returns weighted by the proportion of beginning portfolio assets in the composite:

$$r_C = \sum_{i=1}^{n} \left[ r_i \times \frac{V_{0,i}}{\sum_{i=1}^{n} V_{0,i}} \right]$$

The method involving weighted external cash flows is:

$$V_P = V_0 + \sum_{i=1}^{n} (CF_i \times w_i)$$

Each $V_P$ across $i$ portfolios can be substituted into the equation for composite return:

$$r_C = \sum_{i=1}^{n} \left[ r_{P,i} \times \frac{V_{P,i}}{\sum_{i=1}^{n} V_{P,i}} \right]$$

IMPORTANT: The GIPS standards require weighting at least monthly beginning January 1, 2010. Weighting less frequently reduces the composite's ability to reflect aggregate portfolio performance.

Another method considers all the portfolio values and external cash flows during the period as one portfolio, and uses the modified Dietz method for the return calculation.

## Inclusion in Composites

IMPORTANT: The GIPS standards recommend that firms disclose when proprietary assets—which are usually non-fee-paying—are included in a composite.

All actual, fee-paying, discretionary accounts must be included in at least one portfolio.

- Firms must not link simulated or model portfolio performance with actual performance; such performance can be shown as *supplemental information*.
- Non-fee-paying discretionary portfolios may be included with appropriate disclosure.
- Nondiscretionary portfolios may not be included; they do not reflect management skill at managing to the mandate, objective, or strategy.

A *discretionary portfolio* is one for which the investment manager has discretion necessary to implement the intended strategy:

- Investment policy statement (IPS)–mandated restrictions do not necessarily render a portfolio nondiscretionary.
- Frequent withdrawals may be sufficient to make strategy implementation impossible.

### Defining Investment Strategies

Firms are not allowed to include portfolios managed to different mandates, objectives, or strategies in the same composite.

The hierarchy for composite definition includes:

- Investment mandate: Summary or product description (e.g., large-cap global equities).
- Asset classes: Firms may further define by country or region (e.g., equity, European equity).
- Style or strategy (e.g., growth, value, active, indexed, telecommunications).
- Benchmark: Often used where the benchmark describes the investment universe (e.g., S&P 500 Index, BM&FBovespa).
- Risk/return characteristics: Based on targeted excess return, tracking error from index, or benchmark.

### Entering and Exiting Composites

New portfolios should ideally be included in the first full month after the firm receives control over the funds. However, delays investing the funds may result from asset redeployment, purchase of relatively illiquid assets, and so on.

GIPS allows flexibility in investing the funds, but firms must define a policy for each composite.

Firms must keep portfolios in a composite through the last full period in which the firm managed the funds or maintained discretion over the portfolio.

IMPORTANT: The portfolio's performance must remain with the original composite.

Portfolios should not change composite unless:

- The composite definition changes and the portfolio no longer fits.
- The portfolio's mandate, objectives, or strategy changes and the composite no longer fits.

Firms should use *temporary new accounts* to accommodate significant external cash flows rather than remove entire portfolios from a composite.

- A large cash inflow would be held in a temporary new account until it could be deployed in the client's strategy.
- Cash and securities to fund a large cash outflow would be held in a temporary new account until liquidation.



Firms must not include new portfolios with less than the minimum asset level set for a composite, and must establish standards when portfolios already in a composite fall below minimum asset levels.

Guidance recommends establishing a corridor (e.g., +/– 5%) around the minimum asset threshold. If the portfolio falls below the corridor value for two consecutive periods, it would be excluded from the composite. Conversely, the portfolio must remain above the corridor for two months before it would be included.

IMPORTANT: A minimum asset level can be changed prospectively, but not retroactively.

GIPS recommends that firms do not present to a client materials about a composite that does not meet the minimum requirements.

## Carve-Out Segments

A *carve-out segment* identifies a group of portfolios within a composite that could represent a stand-alone composite (e.g., an investment mandate, asset class, etc.):

- Prior to January 1, 2010: Identify and disclose the policy used to allocate cash to the carve-out.
- Between January 1, 2006, and prior to January 1, 2011: Include percentage of composite represented by carve-out portfolios.

IMPORTANT: A carve-out must not be included in a composite unless it is managed separately with its own cash balance.

## Claim of Compliance

A firm may claim compliance only with respect to the entire firm; it does not claim compliance "except for" anything. Claims used in advertising appear later.

Firms verified by third-party verification may use the following statement:

> [Insert name of firm] claims compliance with the Global Investment Performance Standards (GIPS®) and has prepared and presented this report in compliance with the GIPS standards. [Insert name of firm] has been independently verified for the periods [insert dates]. The verification report(s) is/are available upon request.
>
> Verification assesses whether (1) the firm has complied with all the composite construction requirements of the GIPS standards on a firm-wide basis, and (2) the firm's policies and procedures are designed to calculate and present performance in compliance with the GIPS standards. Verification does not ensure the accuracy of any specific composite presentation.

Unverified firms must use the following statement:

> [Insert name of firm] claims compliance with the Global Investment Performance Standards (GIPS®) and has prepared and presented this report in compliance with the GIPS standards. [Insert name of firm] has not been independently verified.

In addition, firms may obtain third-party verification for a specific composite, which is called an examination:

> [Insert name of firm] claims compliance with the Global Investment Performance Standards (GIPS®) and has prepared and presented this report in compliance with the GIPS standards. [Insert name of firm] has been independently verified for the periods [insert dates].
>
> Verification assesses whether (1) the firm has complied with all the composite construction requirements of the GIPS standards on a firm-wide basis, and (2) the firm's processes and procedures are designed to calculate and present performance in compliance with the GIPS standards. The [insert name of composite] composite has been examined for the periods [insert dates]. The verification and examination reports are available upon request.

## Disclosures

Disclosures are required unless noted as recommended:

- Definition of the firm:
  - Redefinition requires disclosure of redefinition, date, and reason.
  - List other firms within same parent company (recommended).
- Management events that would help clients interpret presentation:
  - Results achieved by portfolio manager or research group no longer with the firm
  - Any past results achieved by other firms or affiliations
  - Use and dates for subadvisors (after January 1, 2006; recommended for prior periods)
- Valuation events:
  - Policies for portfolio valuation, return calculation, and compliant performance presentation are available on request.
  - Portfolios not valued as of last business day or calendar month end (prior to January 1, 2010)
  - Use of subjective unobservable inputs that materially affect valuation (after January 1, 2011)
  - Material differences in GIPS valuation hierarchy
  - Recommended:
    - Key valuation principles and dates, description, and reason for any changes
    - Use of subjective unobservable inputs that materially affect valuation (prior to January 1, 2011)
    - Disclosure of material changes to calculation methods
- List of firm composites available on request; includes those discontinued within prior five years:
  - Description sufficient to understand investment mandate, objective, or strategy
  - *Composite creation date*—Date when accounts were first grouped into the composite
  - Composite redefinition date, description, and reason
  - Minimum asset levels and any changes to minimums
  - Policy used to allocate cash to carve-outs (periods prior to January 1, 2010)
  - Definition of significant cash flows and applicable periods for definition
  - If composite contains proprietary asset portfolio(s) (recommended)
- Currency used to present performance:
  - Differences in exchange rates and valuation resources between portfolios
  - Differences in exchange rates and valuation resources between composites and the benchmark (after January 1, 2011)
- Treatment of withholding tax on dividends, interest, and capital gains, and whether benchmark is net of withholding tax
- Benchmark description:
  - If a custom benchmark, state the components, weights, and rebalancing process.
  - If no applicable benchmark, disclose why.
  - If benchmark changes, describe date, change, and reason.
  - Describe differences between the composite and the benchmark (recommended).

- Treatment of fees:
    - Gross-of-fee returns are investment returns less trading expenses.
    - Disclose any fees deducted in addition to trading expenses.
    - Net-of-fee returns are gross-of-fee returns reduced for management fees (including performance-based fees and carried interest):
        - Disclose any fees deducted in addition to trading expenses and investment management fee.
        - Disclose whether fees are model or actual investment management fees.
        - Disclose deduction of performance-based fees.
- Disclose fee schedule appropriate to compliant performance presentation:
    - Bundled fees: Types of fees included
    - Management fees
- Internal dispersion measure used/presented
- Derivatives: Description of material use, presence, and extent sufficient to understand risk
- Local laws/regulations/GIPS standards: If the performance presentation conforms and, if not, type and reason for nonconformance:
    - List periods of GIPS noncompliance prior to January 1, 2000
    - Only compliant periods may be shown after January 1, 2000
- Annualized three-year *ex post* standard deviation for monthly composite returns and benchmark returns:
    - Firms must disclose if that measure is unavailable.
    - Firms must disclose if an alternative method is used:
        - Describe why standard measure is not appropriate or relevant.
        - Describe alternative method and why selected.

IMPORTANT: Distinguish between *carried interest*, an allocation of an investment vehicle's profits, and *performance-based fees*, which are a percentage applied after exceeding a minimum return.

### Presentation and Reporting

GIPS-compliant performance presentations embody the ideals of full disclosure and fair representation. The core elements of a GIPS-compliant presentation for all periods include:

- Composite and benchmark annual performance for all years
- The number of portfolios in the composite (if greater than five)
- Assets represented in the composite for all years:
    - Dollar value
    - Percentage of total firm assets represented by the composite *or* total firm assets
- Measure of *internal dispersion* if composite includes more than five portfolios (i.e., dispersion of returns for portfolios included in the composite)

IMPORTANT: Excessive internal dispersion indicates overly broad composite definition.

GIPS

Each GIPS-compliant composite performance presentation requires:

- Annual performance:
    - Since inception or a minimum of five years
    - Building to 10 years of performance
- Nonannualized partial period returns (if 10-year period includes inception/termination dates on or after January 1, 2011):
    - Composite inception through initial annual period end
    - Annual period start through composite termination
- Benchmark total return for each annual period presented

IMPORTANT: While composite return can be used for calculating variance in an *equal-weighted standard deviation*, use asset-weighted return as the proxy for composite return when calculating *asset-weighted standard deviation*. Assets should be weighted using beginning-of-period values:

$$S_{aw} = \sqrt{\sum_{i=1}^{n} w_i (r_i - \bar{r}_{proxy})^2}$$

$$\bar{r}_{proxy} = \sum_{i=1}^{n} w_i r_i$$

$$w_i = \frac{V_{i,0}}{V_{total,0}}$$

- Method of dispersion including but not limited to:
    - High-low values
    - Range
    - Interquartile range (i.e., the middle 50% of observations; excludes outliers)
    - Standard deviation:
        - Equal-weighted standard deviation
        - Asset-weighted standard deviation
- For both composite and benchmark (identical periodicity of measures):
    - Three-year annualized *ex post* standard deviation using monthly returns (for periods beginning January 1, 2011)
    - Additional *ex post* measure, with appropriate disclosures, if standard deviation is inappropriate (e.g., asymmetric returns distribution)
- Carve-outs: Percentage of total composite assets represented in the composite (periods beginning January 1, 2006, and before January 1, 2011); no requirement to disclose outside that period
- Non-fee-paying portfolios: Percentage of non-fee-paying portfolios represented in the composite (end of annual period)
- Past-performance linking (composite-specific basis):
    - New firm employs substantially all the previous investment decision makers.
    - Decision-making process remains independent and substantially intact within the new firm.
    - Reported performance can be supported and documented.

Additional recommendations for firms to present:

- Gross-of-fee returns (i.e., best representation of attaining strategy indicated by the benchmark)
- Returns without deduction for administrative expenses (i.e., they are outside manager control)
- Cumulative benchmark and composite returns over the presentation period
- Equal-weighted mean and median returns (in addition to required asset-weighted returns)
- Quarterly performance presentation updating, including monthly or quarterly returns
- Annualized composite and benchmark returns for periods longer than one year (e.g., 10-year cumulative return geometrically decomposed into annual return)
- Annualized three-year standard deviation of returns (and other measures) for periods prior to January 1, 2011:
    - Corresponding benchmark and composite returns presented for same periods
    - Additional relevant *ex post* dispersion measures
    - Any other additional quantitative information that clients will find useful for evaluating strategy risk
- Compliant reporting for all historical periods (rather than noncompliant performance presentation as allowed prior to January 1, 2000)
- More than 10 years of compliant performance

## Real Estate

*Real estate* as an asset class includes:

- Partially or wholly owned properties
- Insurance company separate accounts, commingled funds, and property unit trusts
- Private placement securities of real estate investment trusts (REITs) and real estate operating companies (REOCs)
- Participating mortgage loans or other instruments that participate in operating results

Certain real estate–related instruments are excluded from the special real estate provisions:

- REITs and other publicly traded real estate securities
- Mortgage-backed securities
- Commercial and residential loans and other private debt investments having no participation in property performance

> IMPORTANT: Firms must not link periods of noncompliant performance with compliant performance. Noncompliant performance prior to January 1, 2006, must be disclosed. No noncompliant performance may be presented after January 1, 2006.

Requirements and recommendations are considered effective for periods beginning January 1, 2011, unless otherwise noted.

- Valuation:
  - Principles:
    - Fair value beginning January 1, 2011
    - Market value prior to January 1, 2011 (2005 GIPS market value conventions)
  - Internal frequency (i.e., may be performed by in-house valuators):
    - End-of-quarter beginning January 1, 2010
    - Quarterly beginning January 1, 2008
    - Every 12 months prior to January 1, 2008
  - External frequency (i.e., must be performed by unrelated third-party valuators):
    - Every 36 months prior to January 1, 2012
    - Every 12 months beginning January 1, 2012, unless client agreements specify otherwise; then, at least every 36 months unless client agreement specifies more frequently (e.g., 24 months)
  - Third-party valuators must be:
    - External, independently licensed, certified, professionally designated appraisers/valuators
    - If credentials are unavailable, must be well-qualified with experience in type of property being valued
  - Firms must present the percentage of assets receiving external valuation as of each reporting period end.
- Return calculations after transaction costs (i.e., gross-of-fee returns) must be made at least quarterly beginning January 1, 2006.
- Includes trading expenses (i.e., commissions, closing costs, etc.) and advisory, legal, financial, and investment banking costs incident to buying, selling, restructuring, or recapitalizing.
- Annual component returns (i.e., capital returns and income returns) must be calculated separately using geometrically linked time-weighted rates of return beginning January 1, 2011.
- Quarterly component and composite returns must be calculated by asset-weighting individual portfolio returns.

IMPORTANT: Core real estate strategies focus on income returns, opportunistic strategies focus on capital returns, and total return strategies attempt both income and capital returns.

- Component return presentations must clearly identify whether composite and component returns are gross of fee or net of fee:
  - Should present gross-of-fee component returns if only gross-of-fee composite return is presented.
  - Should present net-of-fee component returns if only net-of-fee composite return is presented.
  - Should present at least gross-of-fee component returns if both gross- and net-of-fee composites are presented.
  - Firms using monthly component return calculation may use a quarterly aggregation method that fairly and accurately reports results across all portfolios in a composite (i.e., they are not limited to geometrically link monthly results that will not properly cumulate).
- Disclosures:
  - Definition of discretion
  - Valuation method(s), including method of comparables, income capitalization, and so on
  - Changes to valuation methods beginning January 1, 2011
  - Valuation frequency
  - Linked noncompliant periods prior to 2006
  - Dispersion method (high and low annual time-weighted return

Recommendations include:

- Annual period-end independent valuation for all assets prior to January 1, 2012 (i.e., not just beginning on that date)
- Both gross-of-fee and net-of-fee composite and composite component returns
- Disclosure of:
  - Accounting principles (i.e., U.S. GAAP, IFRS, etc.)
  - Differences between performance reporting and financial reporting at the end of each annual period
  - Material changes to valuation policies for periods prior to January 1, 2011
  - Non–real estate percentage in composites at the annual period end

GIPS standards specify additional requirements for closed-end real estate funds:

- Since-inception internal rate of return (SI-IRR) items:
  - Net-of-fees SI-IRR (i.e., since-inception IRR) presented in addition to time-weighted return
  - Nonannualized partial period net-of-fees SI-IRR (if 10-year period includes inception/termination dates on or after January 1, 2011):
    - Composite inception through initial annual period end
    - Annual period start through final liquidation date
  - If gross-of-fees SI-IRR is presented, must be for same periods as net-of-fees SI-IRR
  - SI-IRR for benchmark as of each annual period end
- Composite definition based on *vintage year* as well as investment mandate, strategy, or objective:
  - Year of first drawdown or capital call from investors, or
  - Year first committed capital from outside investors is closed and legally binding

- Financial history and status must include:
    - Committed capital: Amount of capital that has been promised
    - Since-inception paid-in capital: Amount of capital that has been drawn down
    - Since-inception distributions
- Ratios:
    - PIC multiple: Paid-in capital to committed capital
    - TVPI (*investment multiple*): Total value to since-inception paid-in capital
    - DPI (realization multiple): Since-inception distribution to since-inception paid-in capital
    - RVPI (unrealized multiple): Residual value to since-inception paid-in capital

IMPORTANT: The financial history and ratios are the same for real estate and private equity presentation.

## Private Equity

*Private equity* includes fixed-life, fixed-commitment vehicles (i.e., not open for subscriptions or redemptions):

- *Primary fund vehicles* make direct investments in companies.
- *Funds of funds* invest in other closed-end primary funds but may make direct investments.
- *Secondary funds* invest in other funds of funds.

*General partners* screen early stage business plans, select potential candidates, conduct due diligence on those potential candidates, structure deals, place capital calls against capital committed by limited partners, and manage the ongoing relationship with the investment. As the investment matures, the general partners take companies public and pay out the limited partners.

*Limited partners* provide funding, and their loss is limited to their investment.

- Input data: Fair value determination at least annually beginning January 1, 2011
- Return calculations: Must use SI-IRR in addition to return specified by GIPS:
    - Daily or monthly cash flows prior to January 1, 2011.
    - Daily-only cash flows beginning January 1, 2011.
    - Distribution of stock must be valued at distribution and considered a cash flow.
- Presentation:
    - Gross-of-fee returns must be presented using actual transaction costs.
    - Net-of-fee returns must be presented after deduction of actual investment management fees and carried interest.
    - All fund-of-funds returns must be net of underlying fund/partnership fees and expenses, including carried interest.
- Composites:
    - Primary fund vehicles must be included in at least one composite by vintage year *and* investment mandate, objectives, or strategy.
    - Funds of funds must be included in at least one composite by vintage year for the fund of funds and/or investment mandate, objectives, or strategy.
- Disclosure:
    - Vintage year and how determined, and *final liquidation date*
    - Valuation methods, and material changes during periods beginning January 1, 2011
    - Any valuation methods in addition to GIPS
    - Periodicity of cash flows if not daily for periods prior to January 1, 2011

    - Periods of noncompliance prior to January 1, 2006
    - Gross-of-fee returns—any expenses other than transaction costs deducted
    - Net-of-fee returns—any expenses other than transaction costs and management fees
    - Benchmark calculation method—method used for calculating public market equivalent (PME) benchmarks
- Presentation:
    - Composite SI-IRR gross-of-fees and net-of-fees returns must be clearly presented.
    - Partial years (inception/termination) must not be annualized.
    - SI-IRR of composite and benchmark as of each year end.
    - Benchmark same vintage year and investment mandate, objectives, or strategy as composite for all periods.
    - No noncompliant performance for periods after January 1, 2006.
    - Percentage of primary fund assets in fund-of-funds vehicles (beginning January 1, 2011).
    - Fund-of-funds composites defined only by investment mandate, objective, or strategy:
        - Must aggregate underlying investments by vintage year and present SI-IRR gross of management fees for those.
        - The benchmark, if presented, must reflect the same vintage year and underlying mandate, objectives, or strategy.
        - Percentage of direct investments included in fund-of-funds composites (beginning January 1, 2011).
- Financial history and status must include:
    - Committed capital: Amount of capital that has been promised
    - Since-inception paid-in capital: Amount of capital that has been drawn down
    - Since-inception distributions
- Ratios:
    - PIC multiple: Paid-in capital to committed capital
    - TVPI (*investment multiple*): Total value to since-inception paid-in capital
    - DPI (realization multiple): Since-inception distribution to since-inception paid-in capital
    - RVPI (unrealized multiple): Residual value to since-inception paid-in capital

IMPORTANT: The financial history and ratios are the same for real estate and private equity presentation.

GIPS

Recommendations:

- Value investments at least quarterly.
- SI-IRR calculations use daily cash flows for periods prior to January 1, 2011.
- Material differences between performance and financial reporting should be disclosed and explained.

## Separately Managed Accounts (SMAs)

IMPORTANT: Combining both wrap-fee SMAs with non-wrap-fee SMAs in the same composite may result in a competitive disadvantage for the non-wrap-fee accounts.

Account sponsors often hire subaccount managers, each of which has expenses and fees. The account sponsor then presents them to clients with the sponsor's own fee "wrapped" around the subaccount manager fees. A sponsor may also have separately managed accounts (SMAs) with no wrap fee imposed.

GIPS standards regarding wrap-fee SMAs exist in addition to core GIPS, especially with respect to bundled fees.

Disclosures:

- A composite containing a wrap-fee SMA must disclose each period that the composite does not contain the wrap-fee SMA.
- Periods of noncompliance prior to January 1, 2006, must be disclosed.
- Firms may not link noncompliant periods on or after January 1, 2006, to compliant periods.
- Style-defined composites that include wrap-fee accounts must include all appropriate accounts.
- Performance must be presented net of the entire wrap fee.
- Firms providing SMA services to a sponsor under a wrap-fee arrangement must disclose the sponsor if presenting results specific to a sponsor.
- Firms may present performance gross of the wrap fee to gain business, but must include disclosure that the presentation is only for use by the prospective sponsor.

## GIPS Valuation Principles

Performance reporting should focus on:

- *Fair representation:* Accurate asset values obtained through appropriate policies and procedures
- *Full disclosure:* Providing valuation-related information required by GIPS, as well as documentation of policies and procedures appropriate for valuation

GIPS standards require firms to apply *fair value* (rather than *market value*) beginning January 1, 2011.

IMPORTANT: Fair value must include accrued income.

Fair value transactions result from knowledgeable and prudent negotiations between unrelated parties acting in their own best interests (i.e., at arm's length). This value must be established by using an objective, observable, unaltered market price from active markets on the valuation date, if available.

### Valuation Hierarchy

Where objective, observable, unaltered market prices are unavailable, firms should use market prices for similar investments in active markets.

If market valuations for similar investments are not available, use (in order):

- Quoted prices for identical or similar investments in inactive markets
- Observable market-based inputs other than quoted price
- Subjective, unobservable inputs (assumptions about assumptions other market participants would use)

Inactive markets are characterized by:

- Thinly traded assets (i.e., few transactions)
- Noncurrent prices
- Substantial price variations from market makers

Real estate valuation:

- Must not use valuation where valuator's compensation depends on value
- Use only single value (rather than range of values)
- Rotate appraisal firms every three to five years (recommended)

Private equity valuation:

- Valuation method selected must be most appropriate for investment characteristics.
- Selection of valuation method should be based on:
    - Data quality and reliability
    - Data comparability for other transactions and/or firms
    - Business development stage
    - Considerations unique to the investment

### Advertising Guidelines

*Advertisement* includes any type of communication addressed to or intended for more than one prospective client.

One-on-one presentations, including presentations to the investment committee or board of a plan sponsor or other prospective single client, are not considered advertising.

Firms that choose to claim GIPS compliance in advertising may:

- Include a compliant presentation in the advertisement, or
- Follow the GIPS Advertising Guidelines.

#### Advertisement Requirements

All advertisements are required to disclose:

- Definition of the firm
- How to obtain composite descriptions and performance presentations
- Compliance statement for advertisements:
- [Insert name of firm] claims compliance with the Global Investment Performance Standards (GIPS®).



Advertisements that provide performance data are required to derive it from a compliant presentation:

- Noncompliance for periods prior to January 1, 2001
- Composite and benchmark description (same as compliant presentation)
- Currency in which return is presented
- Gross-of-fees, net-of-fees, or both types of performance
- One of the following types of returns:
    - Annualized one-, three-, and five-year composite returns through the most recent period
    - Period-to-date one-, three-, and five-year composite returns through the most recent period (through same period corresponding to the compliant presentation)

    - Period-to-date composite returns in addition to five years of annual composite returns (through same period corresponding to the compliant presentation)
- Presence, frequency of use, characteristics of, and extent of derivatives and short positions sufficient to identify risks

IMPORTANT: Firms may include other information as long as it is not given more prominence than the required information.

## Verification

Verification describes the process of an independent verifier assessing whether the firm has:

- Complied with the GIPS standards on a firm-wide basis
- Implemented policies and procedures designed to calculate and present GIPS-compliant performance

The minimum initial period for verification is since inception or one year. GIPS standards recommend verification for all periods claimed by the firm as being compliant.

### Purpose

Verification supports fair representation and full disclosure principles.

Third-party verification provides greater assurance that GIPS standards were adhered to in presenting performance, but does not guarantee the accuracy of any composite performance presentation.

### Scope

Verification applies on a firm-wide basis. The output product from verification is a single report assessing compliance on a firm-wide basis.

A verified firm may request further verification of a specific composite or composites.

A principal verifier may accept the work of another independent verifier if it is reasonably sure the other verifier is qualified. The principal verifier must document the basis for such acceptance.

Sampling is allowed, with sample size based on:

- Number of composites at the firm
- Number of portfolios in each composite
- Types of composites
- Assets under management
- Internal control procedures
- Years under examination
- Computer applications used to construct and/or maintain composites and calculate performance
- Use of external firms to measure performance

IMPORTANT: A large sample size or additional procedures are warranted should the verifier encounter errors or record-keeping deficiencies.

### Pre-Verification Procedures

GIPS verifiers must make themselves familiar with:

- GIPS
- Relevant laws and regulations
- Corporate structure and operating methods of the firm
- Firm's GIPS-related policies and procedures
- Firm's methods for calculating portfolio value and investment performance

### Verification

Verifiers must be able to determine appropriate:

- Firm definition
- Calculation and disclosure of firm assets
- Composite descriptions, membership, and relevant benchmark
- Application of discretion
- Procedures for assuring existence and ownership of client assets
- Inclusion of all actual, fee-paying, discretionary accounts in at least one portfolio
- Treatment of:
    - Income, interest, and dividend accruals
    - Taxes, tax accruals, and tax reclaims
    - Purchase, sale, open/close of positions
    - Investment accounting and valuation

Verifiers must confirm:

- Firms are using a GIPS-compliant return formula:
    - Recalculate and compare return presented for selected portfolios and composites.
- Accuracy of calculations for composites and benchmarks (from sample):
    - Consistency with compliant presentation
- Portfolios are correctly classified as discretionary or nondiscretionary.
- Portfolios are included in the correct composite:
    - Trace selected composites from management agreement to composite.
    - Check that movements among composites are appropriate.
- Firm disclosures are consistent with internal policies and verifier findings.

Verifiers must maintain documentation justifying their recommendation. This includes a letter from the firm undergoing verification that it has followed all its policies and procedures and that they are compliant with GIPS standards for the period under verification, and must contain any specific representations to the verifier.

## After-Tax Return Calculations

Effective January 1, 2011, all after-tax information is supplemental information and subject to the GIPS Guidance Statement on the Use of Supplemental Information.

Substantial additional information must be captured and maintained when after-tax return calculations have to be made.

- Custom benchmarks are better suited to after-tax portfolio performance comparison, but will not generally be suited to composite performance comparison.
- *Shadow portfolios* using mutual funds or exchange-traded funds can simulate purchases and sales in client portfolios.
- After-tax benchmarks become problematic because the client's individual asset values and tax situation would drive the tax issues addressed by the benchmark.

The following cases do not necessarily consider the portfolio manager's ability to optimize tax liability via well-timed purchases and sales within the portfolio.

### Pre-Liquidation Method

The *pre-liquidation method* reduces pre-tax income and price-appreciation return by the amount of applicable taxes. The method disregards unrealized gains and losses and may underestimate taxes embedded in the unrealized amount.

### Mark-to-Liquidation Method

The *mark-to-liquidation method* assumes all investments are sold at the end of the period and taxes become immediately due. This method overstates tax liability by disregarding time value of money effects on future tax liability.

### Nondiscretionary Tax Consequences

Performance measurement allows comparison of manager skill; firms may wish to eliminate the tax effects of nondiscretionary portfolio flows. The adjustment should assume that all securities are proportionately liquidated in order to avoid management selecting highly appreciated securities for the hypothetical adjustment.

### Tax-Loss Harvesting

Firms should disclose the percentage return benefit created for a composite by tax-loss harvesting if realized losses exceed realized gains during the period.